Making It Happen

Interaction in the Second
Language Classroom

From Theory to Practice

Second Edition

Patricia A. Richard-Amato

Making It Happen, Second Edition

Longman, 10 Bank Street, White Plains, NY 10606

Text credits: Credits appear on pages xiv-xv.

Editorial director: Joanne Dressner
Acquisitions editior: Allen Ascher
Assistant editor: Jessica Miller
Production editor: Christine Cervoni
Text design adaptation: Curt Belshe
Cover design: Curt Belshe
Cover art: Wassily Kandinsky, "Improvisation No. 23," 1911. Munson-Williams-Proctor
Institute, Museum of Art, Utica, New York. (Background of cover: detail of same)

Library of Congress Cataloging-in-Publication Data

Richard-Amato, Patricia A.
Making it happen: interaction in the second language classroom: from theory to practice/
Patricia A. Richard-Amato.—2nd ed. p. cm.
Includes bibliographical references and index.
ISBN 0-201-42018-X
1. Language and languages—Study and teaching. 2. Second language acquisiton. 3. English
language—Study and teaching—Foreign speakers.

P53.R49 1995
418'.007—dc20
95-15297
CIP

ISBN: 0-201-42018-X

8 9 10–MA–00 99

For my father,
Wallace Marvin Abbott

Contents

Preface

These times are very exciting for us as language teachers. We have gone through a reassessment of how to approach the language teaching process and have witnessed a rather dramatic shift, at least theoretically, from grammar-based approaches to communicative approaches. We are moving toward longitudinal research that should add a great deal to our knowledge about how languages are learned in classrooms. No longer do we have to depend solely upon a discovery process as our only source of knowledge. Nor do we have to depend upon a single method or way to teach. Although our own experiences as learners and as teachers are important to our development, we must take full advantage of what others have to offer. We can then incorporate what makes sense to us into our already existing frameworks so that we can respond to our students' needs in more creative and insightful ways. If we ignore the theoretical concepts under current consideration and if we turn our backs on relevant research, we will be stifling our capacity for growth and change. We owe it to ourselves and to our students to keep abreast of what is happening in our own field and in closely related fields so that we do not stagnate.

This book is an attempt to bring to you some of the important theoretical concepts and research supporting *interaction* in the classroom and ways of making it happen there. By "interaction" I am not referring to the mechanistic definition given to it in many scientific paradigms in which the entities that come together remain unchanged as a result of their contact. Rather, interaction as I define it incorporates elements of a *transactional* nature. In other words, *the entities doing the interacting are affected and often changed by the contact and by the total social situation surrounding it.* This definition of the interactional process has important implications for what goes on in classrooms and why interaction, as I have defined it, doesn't occur there as often as we might like it to. More often than not, students play only passive or superficial roles in the events of the classroom.

What needs to develop, it seems to me, is a *classroom community* in order for transactional elements to be fully realized. In a classroom community, teaching goes far beyond organizing a syllabus, deciding upon an overall pedagogical strategy, and executing a program. It means facilitating learning and seeking learner input into the decision-making process. It means forming a more dialectical relationship with students in which they are considered to be important sources of knowledge, in addition to the teacher. It means involving parents, native or near-native peers, and others in the school environment and the outside community in the learning/teaching process. And it means flowing with the needs of students as these needs are perceived. The classroom is not just preparation for the "the real world" as many would have us believe. It *is* the real world for millions of students around the globe who spend much of their young lives there.

This book is an attempt, however limited, to bridge the gap between the theoretical and the practical. The information presented here is not intended to be the final word on second-language teaching. Each teacher in each classroom needs to develop his or her own philosophical foundation and ways of doing things. This book is simply a resource from which to draw.

Patricia Abbott Richard-Amato
California State University, Los Angeles

Acknowledgments

First, I am indebted to my former ESL students at Alameda High School and Alameda Junior High School in Lakewood, Colorado and to my students at Pueblo High School in Tucson, Arizona. Many of the activities presented in this book could not have been developed had it not been for them.

My graduate students at three universities (California State University, Los Angeles; the University of Nevada, Reno; and the University of New Mexico,) in addition to my students at several TESOL Institutes and at the Mediterranean Institute in Barcelona, Spain, have been especially instrumental in helping me work out several of the ideas and see them in practice. Many a fleeting notion has become fleshed out through lengthy class discussions.

Appreciation goes to Holbrook Mahn, whose relevant questions helped me shape the two new chapters on literacy and revise the chapter on the natural approach; to Diane Larsen-Freeman, whose knowledge of the language acquisition process and its relationship to instructed grammar was critical to my revisions of the first three chapters; to Kathleen Bailey, whose insightful comments and suggestions on language assessment were instrumental in my development of that new chapter; to Barbara Kroll, whose expertise on the writing process provided much help in my completing the chapters on literacy; to José Galván, whose insights based on his own use of the book were invaluable, particularly in the book's reorganization; and to Linda Sasser, whose vast experience and knowledge helped me revise the exploration of methods and activities. However, please note that I take full responsibility for the conclusions arrived at throughout the book.

I am grateful to Kathy Weed, who shared with me many of her ideas and those of her graduate students at the Coachella Valley Campus of California State University, San Bernardino who had used the first edition of the book; to Mary Ann Christison, Barbara Penman, Ann Snow, and Fred Tarpley, who shared with me their experiences using the book and gave me wonderful feedback and suggestions for improving it overall; to Armando Baltra and Fred Carrillo, who gave me several useful ideas in phone conversations with them; and to Pam McCollum, Catherine Doughty, and others who reviewed the book in current journals.

And, of course, I cannot forget the people who contributed so much to the first edition: John Oller, Jr. (whose idea it was that I write this book in the first place), Ruth Larimer, Mary McGroarty, Carolyn Madden, Leslie Jo Adams, Marty Furch, Alan Crawford, James Wiebe, Robert White, Rod Young, Steve Strauss, Bess Altwerger, Wendy Hansen, Jennifer Claire Johnson, Pamela Branch, Ramon Díaz, Sue Gould, and Rey Baca.

I also owe a debt of gratitude to Allen Ascher, my editor for the second edition, and to Joanne Dresner, who first published my work and has encouraged me all along. In addition, I want to thank the many other editors at Addison-Wesley/Longman who have been so supportive including Jessica Miller, development editor, and Christine Cervoni, production editor.

I am grateful also to the following publishing companies and individuals for permission to reprint or adapt materials for which they own copyrights:

Bonne, Rose. Excerpt from "There Was an Old Woman Who Swallowed a Fly," illustrated by Pam Adams. Copyright Michael Twinn, Child's Play Ltd. Reprinted by permission of Michael Twinn, Child's Play (International) Ltd. An excerpt only—taken from last page in book.

Christison, Mary Ann. Illustration by Kathleen Peterson, *English Through Poetry*, p. 29, 1982. Reprinted by permission of Alemany Press/Janus Book Publishers, Inc., Haywood, California.

Cummins, James. "Language Proficiency, Bilingualism, and Academic Achievement" from *Bilingualism and Special Education: Issues in Assessment and Pedagogy*, pp. 136–151. San Diego, California: College-Hill. Copyright © 1984 by James Cummins. Reprinted by permission of College-Hill, San Diego, California.

Ellis, Rod. "Theories of Second Language Acquisition" from *Understanding Second Language Acquisition*, pp. 248–276. Copyright © 1986. Reprinted by permission of Oxford University Press.

Evans, Joy and Moore, Jo Ellen. Adaptation of illustration, p. 57, from *Art Moves the Basics Along: Units About Children*; 1982. Reprinted by permission of Evan-Moor, Carmel, California.

Evans, Joy and Moore, Jo Ellen. Adaptation of illustration, p. 80, from *Art Moves the Basics Along: Animal Units*, Copyright © 1979. Reprinted by permission of Evan-Moor, Carmel, California.

Gliedman, John. "Interview (with Noam Chomsky)," *Omni*, edited by Patrice Aderet, 6 (2): November, 1983. Copyright © 1983 by John Gliedman and reprinted with permission of Omni Publications International, Ltd.

Krashen, Stephen. Figure 2, "The Relationship between Affective Factors and Language Acquisition," p. 110 in *Second Language Acquisition and Second Language Learning*; Copyright © 1981 by Stephen Krashen. Reprinted by permission of Oxford: Pergamon.

Krashen, Stephen. Figure from "Immersion: Why it Works and What it Taught Us," in *Language and Society 12* (Winter 1984), p. 63. Copyright © 1981 by Stephen Krashen. Reprinted by permission of the Office of Official Language, Ontario, Canada and the Minister of Supply and Services, Canada.

Krashen, Stephen. Figure 2.1 from *Principles and Practice in Second Language Acquisition;* Copyright © 1982 by Stephen Krashen. Reprinted by permission of Oxford: Pergamon.

Krashen, Stephen and Terrell, T. From *The Natural Approach,* pp. 67–70. Copyright © 1983. Reprinted by permission of Alemany Press/Janus Book Publishers, Inc. Haywood, California.

Palmer, Hap. "Put Your Hands Up in the Air," from *Songbook: Learning Basic Skills Through Music I.* Copyright © 1971. Reprinted by permission of Educational Activities, Inc., Baldwin, New York.

Prelutsky, Jack. "The Creature in the Classroom," from *The Random House Book of Poetry for Children,* selected and introduced by Jack Prelutsky. Copyright © 1983 by Random House, Inc. Reprinted by permission of the Publisher.

Silverstein, Shel. "Gooloo" from *A Light in the Attic.* Copyright © 1981 by Snake Eye Music, Inc. Reprinted by permission of Harper and Row Publishers, Inc. and Edite Kroll Literary Agency.

Vygotsky, L. S. pp. 79–91 of *Mind in Society: Development of Higher Psychological Processes.* Edited by M. Cole. Cambridge, Massachusetts: Harvard University Press. Copyright © 1978 by the President and Fellows of Harvard College. Reprinted by permission of the publishers.

Whitecloud, Thomas. Adaptation of "Blue Winds Dancing" is reprinted with the permission of Scribner, an imprint of Simon and Schuster, Inc., from *Scribner's Magazine.* Copyright © 1938 Charles Scribner's Sons; copyright renewed.

Thanks are also in order to the following individuals for allowing me to summarize their programs: Sally Cummings and Carolyn Duffy (Saint Michael's College, Colchester, Vermont); Blanca Arazi (Instituto Cultural Argentina Norteamericano, Buenos Aires); Ann Snow and Janet Tricamo (California State University, Los Angeles); Linda Sasser (Alhambra School District, Alhambra, California); Pamela Branch and Christina Rivera (ABC Unified School District, Cerritos, California); Sandra Brown (North Hollywood Adult Learning Center, North Hollywood, California); Brandon Zaslow, Eva Wegrzecka-Monkiewicz and Beverly McNeilly (Los Angeles Unified School District; Los Angeles, California); Lorenzo Trujillo (Jefferson County Public Schools, Lakewood, Colorado), and Ken Cressman (Lakehead Board of Education, Thunder Bay, Ontario, Canada).

And last to my husband, Jay (yes, we are still married). He stuck with me in spite of the fact that, as before, many weekends were lost to "the book." I will always be grateful to him for his patience, love, and encouragement.

Introduction

Since the first edition of *Making it Happen* came out in 1988, a very significant change has taken place in the way second-language teacher education is viewed.[1] This change has had to do with the movement away from teacher education as *training process*, during which the teacher is indoctrinated with "how to" prescriptions (sometimes represented by a dogmatic methods approach to teaching), to teacher education as a *developmental process*, during which the teacher not only explores methods and activities, but through experience makes decisions, poses questions, reflects, modifies strategies, and so forth.

Out of this fundamental change and/or parallel to it have sprung three myths about teacher education that, if allowed to persist, could damage the movement itself and keep teachers from reaching their full potential in the classroom.

Myth 1 **A study of linguistic and cognitive theory about how languages are learned and its supporting research is no longer relevant and may even "taint" the thinking of teachers in preparation.**

Teachers generally need and want to know the contributions of linguistic and cognitive theorists and researchers in order to go about forming *their own* principles of second-language teaching. They cannot be spoon-fed someone else's set of principles; nor can they simply be left to "discover" for themselves the theories and research that have taken the last thirty years to develop. To deprive teachers in preparation of this knowledge would be unconscionable and foolhardy. From the interaction between what they are learning and experiencing and what they already know about language teaching and second-language

---

[1] See especially Richards, 1989, 1991; Prabhu, 1990; Richards and Nunan, 1990; Freeman, 1991, 1992; Fanselow, 1992; Freeman and Richards, 1993; Kumarvadivelu, 1994.

acquisition, a set of principles begins to take shape within each teacher, which then can then evolve throughout his or her entire teaching career.

Myth 2 A study of methods has no place in today's language teacher education programs.

Methods are defined generally as sets of strategies and techniques accompanied by an articulated underlying theory. They are nothing to be afraid of. A few of them have made significant contributions to the field as a whole and do not deserve to be trivialized.

Methods are not inherently authoritative, prepackaged programs, although it is true that many of them have been made that way by entrepreneurs and others claiming miracles. But we must be careful not to confuse what sometimes happens with a Method (with a capital *M*) and the concept *method* (with a small *m*). Most teachers in preparation need and want to know about already developed methods, prepackaged for consumption or not. This is not because they plan to slavishly adhere to their tenets and practices, but because they can be interesting sources from which to draw, in developing their own methodologies. For some they are a starting place. Methods (with a small *m*) should be considered dynamic, not static; their selected components must be allowed to grow and change within each individual teacher in each classroom situation.

Myth 3 All "training" aspects of teacher education should be abandoned in favor of developmental aspects such as reflection, questioning, and decision making.

It is important to look at the relationship between these elements, not as being dichotomous (only one can be selected), but as part of the same entity. Sometimes the focus will be more on one than the other, depending upon the program and upon the individuals within the program. But to completely abandon either one in favor of the other would be a dangerous proposition indeed. While it is important that programs not be prescriptive and authoritative in their approach to the preparation process, it is not a bad idea to expose students to various methods, activities, and sets of strategies, give demonstrations using these strategies, let the students try them out in hypothetical situations to see what they can learn from them, discuss them, reflect upon their use, and eventually draw from them whatever seems efficacious and appropriate at the time. All the while, teachers are developing and making their own decisions about what they will use, how they will use it, when they will use it, and with whom, as they move from simulated experience in supportive environments to actual experience with learners in real classrooms.

AN INTERACTIVE CONCEPTUALIZATION FOR SECOND-LANGUAGE TEACHER EDUCATION

I first presented a version of this rudimentary conceptualization at the TESOL Convention in New York in 1991. Since that time, it has evolved and is still evolving, thanks to the helpful input I have received, not only at that convention, but from the many teacher educators who have been in my seminars at the various institutes. The conceptualization consists of three basic components: The AFFECTIVE BASE, The KNOWLEDGE BASE, and The EXPERIENCE BASE (see Figure I.1).

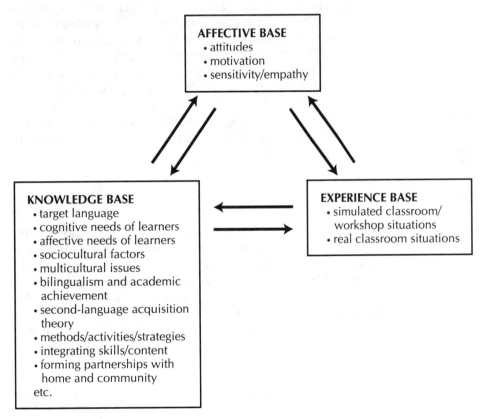

Figure I.1. An Interactive Conceptualization for Second-Language Teacher Education

Each component in this conceptualization consists of at least the items enumerated within the boxes above. Related factors include the personal qualities of the individual: creativity, flexibility, intelligence, the ability to make decisions, and so forth. The conceptualization is interactive in that the influence that each component has on any other is two-way (notice the arrows). Each component informs and validates the others. Another feature is that the conceptualization is *independent* of any specific methods or methodology.

In an effort to consider all three components in the model, *Making It Happen* intends to provide a rich knowledge base (not a watered-down one) from which second- and foreign-language[2] teachers in preparation, can derive their own principles and methodology for second-language teaching. Such teachers are encouraged throughout the book to take a critical look at what is there and to integrate what they accept with what it they already know and believe about second-language learning and teaching. The text also provides for simulated experience in a supportive environment, during which teachers in preparation can try out various methods, activities, and strategies in hypothetical situations, often using a target language that is basically unfamiliar to the group with which they are working. During this experience, teachers in preparation are asked to reflect upon what happens and, after receiving peer feedback, form their own conclusions about that with which they are experimenting. Moreover, they are asked to be *learners* (especially in the case in which the language being taught is unfamiliar) and are asked to respond to each other from a *learner's point-of-view*. Too often this component is completely absent in teacher education programs.

OVERVIEW

In this second edition of *Making It Happen*, I have attempted to respond to the feedback and suggestions of many of the teacher educators and students who have used the book in the past or are currently using it. In addition to updating the supporting research throughout, I have added two new chapters on literacy development and a third on language assessment. Many topics within several other chapters have been expanded, such as the comparison between first- and second-language acquisition and the use and preparation of peer teachers and lay assistants. Several new sections have been added to already existing chapters, i.e., universal grammar, interlanguage development, instructed grammar, learning strategies, and many more. A few topics have been moved out of the chapters to which they were originally assigned to other chapters (e.g., the Episode Hypothesis has been moved to Chapter 15). New

---

[2] Second-language teaching usually refers to a target language that is being taught in the country where it is a dominant language. Foreign-language teaching, on the other hand, usually refers to a target language that is being taught in a country where it is not a dominant language. See pages 255–256 for a description of the teaching implications related to each type of language teaching. It is important to note that sometimes the terms are used interchangeably, particularly when contrasting the terms "first-language acquisition" and "second-language acquisition." In this case "second" usually refers to any language that is not the first one learned.

program descriptions have been added to replace some of those originally discussed in Part IV. And the related reading section, out of necessity, has been reduced to four "vintage" selections.

This edition, like the first, concentrates on ways of providing opportunities for meaningful interaction in second-language classroom settings. **Part I** presents a theoretical orientation to the remaining chapters. It begins with a brief overview of the grammar-focused methods of the past and goes on to highlight some of the seminal ideas of Chomsky, Wilkins, Widdowson, Breen, Candlin, and others (Chapter 1). Then it presents evidence supporting the notion that acquisition can and does take place in the classroom under certain conditions (Chapter 2). Next, it attempts to develop an interactional approach drawing from the insights of Vygotsky, Krashen, Bruner, John-Steiner, Seliger, Schumann, Carroll, and many others (Chapter 3). It then explores literacy development and skills integration by looking at a natural language framework (Chapter 4). It continues by examining the important role played by the affective domain in second-language acquisition in the classroom (Chapter 5). Finally, it discusses language assessment and ways of making evaluation an integral part of the classroom environment (Chapter 6).

Part II examines several methods and activities that are for the most part compatible with an interactional approach: the total physical response and the audio-motor unit (Chapter 7); the natural approach and how it has evolved (Chapter 8); Jazz chants, music, and poetry (Chapter 9); storytelling, role play, and drama (Chapter 10); games (Chapter 11); ways to promote literacy development (Chapter 12); and affective activities (Chapter 13).

Several considerations to be taken into account when one is developing and implementing programs are discussed in **Part III**. They include classroom management (Chapter 14); the selection of tools of the trade, including textbooks, computer programs, and videos (Chapter 15); and teaching through the content areas (Chapter 16).

Part IV presents programs in action. Chapter 17 (ESL Programs) discusses a college center for international programs at Saint Michael's College in Colchester, Vermont; a university support program at California State University, Los Angeles; a life-skills adult basic education program at the North Hollywood Adult Learning Center in North Hollywood, California; a secondary sheltered English model at Artesia High School in Artesia, California; a high school academic program at Thomas Jefferson High School in Los Angeles; an elementary district-wide program in the Alhambra School District in Alhambra, California; and a kindergarten ESL program within a Spanish bilingual school at Loma Vista Elementary in Maywood, California. Chapter 18 (Foreign-Language Programs) describes A bicultural institute for children, adolescents, and adults at the Instituto Cultural Argentine Norteamericano (ICANA) in Buenos Aires, Argentina; a French immersion model for elementary students in Thunder Bay, Ontario, Canada; a middle school Spanish-language program at Millikan

Junior High School in Los Angeles; a high school Spanish program at Artesia High School in Artesia, California; and Jefferson County's approach to foreign language teaching in Lakewood, Colorado. All these programs were selected because of the quality of some of their more salient features. However, they are not meant to be representative of all the programs available.

The Conclusion reiterates many of the main points of the book and provides a retrospective look at its major themes.

Part V, the Related Readings section, presents edited readings from four people who have contributed, either directly or indirectly, to the development of second-language pedagogy: Chomsky, Ellis, Vygotsky, and Cummins. While the section is intended for anyone desiring supplemental materials, it will probably be most useful to the teaching of graduate-level theory and/or methods courses, since it offers additional areas for thought, classroom discussion, and research.

PART I

A Theoretical Foundation: Developing Your Own Language Teaching Principles

Presented here are selected theories and hypotheses intended to serve as an undergirding for the methods, activities, and ideas presented in the remainder of the book. No attempt has been made to include all of the people involved in furthering the development of an interactional approach. It is hoped that those included will, in some sense, represent many whose contributions may have been just as important.

Because second-language acquisition is so complex, no two learners will get there by exactly the same route. However, in spite of the variations, it is possible to describe some of the processes that seem to be common to large numbers of people struggling with a new language and, in many cases, a new culture. Most people agree that simple exposure to the new language and/or culture is not enough. By understanding more about those processes that language learners seem to share, we can be in a better position to develop our own language teaching principles and to plan classroom experiences that are conducive to second-language acquisition. Thus we can continue to develop means by which both language and culture are made more accessible to second-language students.

CHAPTER 1

From Grammatical to Communicative Approaches

Not to let a word get in the way
of its sentence
Nor to let a sentence get in the way
of its intention,
But to send your mind out to meet the
intention
as a guest;
That is understanding.

Chinese proverb,
Fourth Century B.C.
(in Wells, 1981)

QUESTIONS TO THINK ABOUT

1. How do you think humans learn language? Do you think we are born with something that helps us learn language?

2. With what grammar-based approaches to second- or foreign-language teaching are you already familiar? Do you know of any other approaches to second- or foreign-language teaching?

3. What do you think an effective communicative approach might be? How might it be different from the other approaches with which you are familiar?

Because grammar has traditionally been the focus of second- and foreign-language teaching for the past two thousand years or more (see Rutherford, 1987), it isn't surprising that today many language teachers still cling to the notion that grammar should take center stage in language programs. Even though Canale and Swain (1980) derogated its role considerably when they laid out the basic components of communicative competence,[1] grammar nevertheless has remained the approach of choice until recently.

GRAMMAR-BASED APPROACHES

Many language teachers have felt that language teaching is facilitated by stressing grammar as content and/or by exposing the student to input in the target language that concentrates on one aspect of the grammar system at a time—present tense before past, comparative before superlative, first-person singular before third-person singular, and so forth. The approaches used have included grammar-translation, audiolingualism, cognitive-code approaches, and the direct method. The most characteristic features of these approaches are presented below. Many variations exist, however, that are not noted in this brief analysis.

Grammar-Translation

Grammar-translation, also known as the "Prussian Method," was the most popular method of foreign-language teaching in Europe and America from about the mid-nineteenth to the mid-twentieth century. Versions of it still exist today in many countries around the world. Its goal was to produce students who could read and write in the target language by teaching them rules and applications.

A typical grammar-translation lesson began with a reading (to be translated into the first language) followed by the rule it illustrated. Often several strings of unrelated sentences were given to demonstrate how the rule worked. New words were presented in a list along with definitions in the first language. These new words were also included in the reading, which, more often than not, was syntactically and semantically far above the students' levels of proficiency. The topics may have involved a trip to the library, a brief historical sketch of an area, a shopping expedition, a trip by train, or the like. Lessons were grammatically sequenced and students were expected to produce errorless translations from the

---

[1] In addition to linguistic competence (grammatical knowledge, mainly at the subconscious level), the components of communicative competence include discourse competence (how things get done with language, using logical sequence, etc.), sociolinguistic competence (using language appropriately), and strategic competence (compensation strategies such as requests for repetition or clarification, rephrasing, etc.).

beginning. Little attempt was made to communicate orally in the target language. Directions and explanations were always given in the first language.

Audiolingualism

Audiolingualism (ALM) was the new "scientific" oral method that was based on behaviorism (Skinner, 1957). It adheres to the theory that language is acquired through the process of habit formation and the stimulus/response association. Learning a second language is a matter of fighting off the habits of the first.

Audiolingualism was developed to replace or enhance grammar-translation. It was introduced as a component of the "Army Method" used during World War II (a version of it had been developed earlier by Bloomfield for linguists to use when studying languages). It was recognized as the "audiolingual method" when it began to gain favor in teaching English as a foreign language and English as a second language in the 1950s. In America it was closely related to structural linguistics and contrastive analysis[2] (see Fries, 1945; Lado, 1977).

Through the use of this method, structures of the target language were carefully ordered and dialogues were repeated in an attempt to develop correct habits of speaking. Sentences in the substitution, mim-mem (mimic and memorize), and other drills were often related only syntactically ("I go to the store," "You go to the store," "He goes to the store"), and they usually had nothing to do with anything actually happening. Sometimes, however, they did resemble real communication in that the situational scenarios to be memorized included greetings and idiomatic expressions. Rules were presented but often not formally explained, and activities such as minimal pairs (seat—sit, yellow—Jell-O, etc.) were commonly used in an effort to overcome the negative transfer (interference) of first-language (L1) sounds. Listening and speaking skills took precedence over reading and writing skills. However, in most of the applications, there was very little use of creative language,[3] and a great deal of attention was paid to correct pronunciation. Often practice sessions took place in fully equipped language laboratories.

---

[2] *Structural linguistics* is a grammatical system whereby the elements and rules of a language are listed and described. Phonemes, morphemes and/or words, phrases, and sentences are ordered linearly and are learned orally as a set of habits. *Contrastive analysis*, emphasizing the differences between the student's first language and the target language, was relied upon in an effort to create exercises contrasting the two. The first language was thought of chiefly as an interference, hindering the successful mastery of the second.

[3] One exception was Fries's own language program at the University of Michigan. According to Morley, Robinett, Selinker, and Woods (1984), Fries utilized a two-part approach: one part focused on the structural points being drilled and the second part on automatic use through meaning. The "personalized" elements that were considered vital to the program somehow became lost in most of its adaptations.

Cognitive-Code Approaches

Cognitive-code approaches, most evident since the 1960s, are referred to rather vaguely in the literature. According to Richards and Rodgers, the term *cognitive-code* is ". . . sometimes invoked to refer to any conscious attempt to organize materials around a grammatical syllabus while allowing for meaningful practice and use of language" (1986, p. 60). Subskills in listening, speaking, reading, and writing such as sound discrimination, pronunciation of specific elements, distinguishing between letters that are similar in appearance, and so on, needed to be mastered before the student could participate in real communication activities. Generally speaking, it was felt that phonemes needed to be learned before words, words before phrases and sentences, simple sentences before more complicated ones, and so forth.

Lessons were usually highly structured through a deductive process, and the "rule of the day" was practiced. Although creative language was used at higher levels during the practice, students generally had to produce correctly right from the first. A great deal of time was devoted to temporally related but often unmotivated (contextually unjustified) discourse (see Chapter 15).

The Direct Method

Also known today as "Berlitz," this approach was derived from an earlier version called the "Natural Method," which was developed by Sauveur in the mid-nineteenth century and later applied by de Sauzé. The direct method was natural in the sense that it made an effort to "immerse" students in the target language. Teacher monologues, formal questions and answers, and direct repetitions in the input were frequent. Although the discourse, used today in Berlitz schools, is often structured temporally, the topic for discussion is often the grammar itself. The students inductively discover the rules of the language. Books based on the Direct Method often move students so quickly through new syntactic structures, that their internalization becomes difficult, if not impossible.

Although these methods varied from one another, they all generally adhered to the same principle: Grammar is the foundation upon which language should be taught.

Even as early as 1904, Otto Jespersen saw the artificiality inherent in this principle. He criticized the French texts of his era by saying,

> The reader often gets the impression that Frenchmen must be strictly systematical beings who one day speak merely in futures, another day in *passé définis* and who say the most disconnected things only for the sake of being able to use all the persons in the tense which for the time being happens to be the subject for conversation while they carefully postpone the use of the subjunctive until next year (1904, p. 17; also in Oller and Obrecht, 1969, p. 119).

Those advocating cognitive-code approaches are of particular interest with respect to their interpretation of Chomsky, who developed what is commonly known to linguists as *transformational grammar.* Transformational grammar claims that sentences are "transformed" within the brain to other sentences by the application of what are called *phrase structure rules.* For example, a phrase structure rule known as *extraposition* can be applied to the sentence "That summer follows spring is a known fact" transforming it into "It is a known fact that summer follows spring." The first sentence is what is called the "deep structure" (also referred to as a kernel sentence by some cognitive-code advocates). The sentence that it is transformed into is called the "surface form." Some applications of cognitive-code approaches began instruction with the translation of kernel sentences. It was thought that kernel sentences of different languages would be very similar and that positive transfer would then occur. At later stages transformations could be applied.

Second-language (L2) teachers who used cognitive-code approaches often taught sentences that were neither temporally sequenced nor logically motivated. Rather their main reason for existence seemed to be to demonstrate the use of some grammatical structure or other in an effort to aid the development of linguistic competence. These teachers were disappointed to find that Chomsky himself did not advocate such a method nor any specific method for that matter. In his address to the 1965 Northeast Conference on the Teaching of Foreign Languages, Chomsky stated that neither the linguist nor the psychologist had enough knowledge about the process of language acquisition to serve as a basis for methodology.

> I am, frankly, rather skeptical about the significance, for the teaching of languages, of such insights and understanding as have been attained in linguistics and psychology. . . . I should like to make it clear from the outset that I am participating in this conference not as an expert on any aspect of the teaching of languages, but rather as someone whose primary concern is with the structure of language and, more generally, the nature of cognitive processes (in Allen and Van Buren, 1971, p. 152).

He cautioned teachers against passively accepting theory on grounds of authority, real or presumed.

CHOMSKY'S CONTRIBUTIONS

Inferences drawn from Chomsky's innatist theory are perhaps more important to second-language teaching than any of the applications of transformational grammar, which appear for the most part to be misguided. His theory embraces the idea that language development is too complicated a phenomenon to be explained on the basis of behaviorism alone. That children seem to have a mastery over the structure of their first language by the age of five or earlier, points to the idea that there must be a great deal about language that is innate.

Bruner gives Chomsky credit for "freeing us from the paralyzing dogma of the association-imitation-reinforcement paradigm" (1978b, p. 245). Chomsky opposed the idea that the mind is simply a *tabula rasa*. He refused to believe that grammar is simply an "output" on the basis of a record of data. However, he did not deny that the mind is capable of the abilities attributed to it by behaviorism. He reminded us that language is not "made" by us but rather develops as a result of the way we are constituted, when we are placed in the "appropriate external environment" (1980, p. 11). He felt that it remains to be seen just how much of language is actually shaped by experience and how much is intrinsically determined.

Support for the idea that certain aspects of language are innate first came from early psycholinguistic research. Roger Brown (1973) discovered much about universal trends in language acquisition by recording the speech of several children in natural situations over a period of years. Slobin (1971) and others added to this body of research. They have found that children across languages use similar linguistic structures in their language development and that they make the same kinds of errors. In addition, they found that the linguistic structures are learned in the same order.

These findings have led many researchers to agree that the brain is more than simply a blank slate upon which humans store impressions. It contains highly complex structures that seem to come into operation through an interactional process. To house these complex structures of the brain, Chomsky proposed the notion of a "language organ" which is called the *Language Acquisition Device* (LAD).

The Language Acquisition Device

This device, with which Chomsky feels we are born, is associated with all that is universal in human languages. Its structures (or networking of structures) become activated when we are exposed to natural language. To help clarify what happens during the process of activation, Chomsky compares the LAD to a computer (see Related Reading 1).

According to his view, this computer contains a series of preprogrammed subsystems responsible for meaning, syntax, relationships between various types of words, and their functions. Within each subsystem, the individual through experience makes subconscious choices from a linguistic menu. To simplify for the purpose of illustration, let's say that the menu contains choices about word order when using an object. Perhaps the choices consist of something like this: Subject-Verb-Object (SVO), Verb-Subject-Object (VSO), Subject-Object-Verb (SOV), and Object-Subject-Verb (OSV). Children born into Spanish, Chinese, and English environments, for example, subconsciously select SVO; a child born into an Arabic environment subconsciously selects VSO; one born into a Korean environment SOV, and so forth. Other choices might be available for varying degrees of inflection, the dropping of pronouns under certain conditions, and so on. Depending on the language environment in which it finds itself, the brain selects items appropriate to the specific language to which it is exposed. All humanly possible options are included in this computer within the brain.

Another perspective also brought to us by Chomsky as well as other linguists is the formal notion *Universal Grammar* (UG).

Universal Grammar

Universal Grammar, according to Chomsky, is the embodiment of the basic principles shared by all languages. Because all humans are born with this set of principles, it is possible for them to acquire something as complex as the structure of their first language at a very early age.

The shared principles can vary along certain parameters. Each parameter is theorized by some linguists to have a setting with which the child is born called the *unmarked* setting (that which is most common and most restrictive to all languages). As the child is exposed to the language of the environment, some of the initial settings within the brain are reset to *marked* forms to reflect the more uncommon features of a particular language.

To return to our example using word order, let's say that the parameter for using an object is first set to SVO (assuming that SVO is the unmarked setting). The brain of a child born into an Arabic environment would then reset this parameter to VSO, since that is the order to which the child is exposed through the input from the community. Some rules of language are thought to be so marked that they can only be acquired by experience because they are not parameterized (Larsen-Freeman and Long, 1991, p. 231).

Implications for Second-Language Acquisition

It has been proposed that, in the case of second-language acquisition, the brain resets the parameters when the language to which it is exposed deviates from the way the parameters were set for the first language (White, 1989; Flynn, 1987, 1990; Hulk, 1991). However, there is considerable controversy concerning whether the brain can reset parameters as easily as it did originally, considering that second-language learners are usually older when exposed to their second language. It is possible that there may be what is called a *critical period* (an optimal time) for the resetting of parameters (see especially Schachter, 1990 and Johnson, 1992). However, Felix (1988), Tomaselli and Schwartz (1990) in addition to White, Flynn, and Hulk, mentioned earlier, insist that the brain is indeed capable of resetting parameters for a second language.

Although some innatists may feel that exposure is enough to trigger the appropriate settings, at least for children learning a first language, there are many who take an interactionist point of view and insist that for normal development to occur, the individual must receive input tailored to his or her developing proficiency. In other words, the child must receive *motherese* or *caretaker* speech, if not from parents then from siblings or others in the environment willing to give it. Motherese or caretaker speech often consists generally of shorter utterances, the use of high frequency vocabulary, a slower rate, some exaggeration in expression, redundancy, frequent explanations, repetitions, and the like. In addition, the topics are usually about the *here* and *now* rather than about something removed in time and space from the immediate environment. Interestingly, the speech addressed to second-language learners by fluent speakers of the target language often contains many of the same modifications in the input (see Chapter 3).

While the theories of Universal Grammar based on Chomskyan thought are highly abstract, they are worth thinking about in that they may give us clues as to what might actually be happening in the brain when we acquire language, be it first or second.

WILKINS AND BEYOND

Chomsky was criticized rather severely (and perhaps deservedly) by those who pointed out that his basic linguistic model[4] was too restrictive in failing to include the societal aspects of language (Hymes, 1970; Halliday, 1979; and many others). Most (other than Halliday) agreed with the competence/performance distinction but felt that competence should include not only grammatical sectors but psycholinguistic, sociocultural, and *de facto* sectors as well, to use Hymes's terms. Halliday rejected the distinction between competence and performance altogether by calling it misleading or irrelevant. Halliday felt that the more we are able to relate the grammar system to meaning in social contexts and behavioral settings, the more insight we will have into the language system. It was this basic idea that Wilkins used in constructing his notional-functional syllabus as a structure for input in the classroom.

The Notional-Functional Syllabus

Wilkins was concerned with helping the student meet specific communication needs through the input. Such input for the student, according to a notional-functional framework, was to be organized into a set of notional categories for

---

[4] Chomsky's basic linguistic model distinguished two aspects of language: competence (the underlying knowledge of the grammatical system) and performance (the use of that knowledge to communicate).

the purpose of a syllabus design. For example, a category may have included various ways to express probability: I am *certain* this project will be finished by Friday. *Maybe* it will be finished by Friday. I *doubt* if it will be finished by Friday, and so forth. Syllabi based on a notional approach often included such topics as accepting/rejecting invitations, requesting information, and expressing needs or emotions of various kinds.

Although Wilkins felt that a notional syllabus (which included categories of function) was superior to a grammatical one, he was not yet ready actually to replace grammatically focused systems for teaching with functionally focused ones. He did, however, see a notional approach as providing another dimension to existing systems. It "can provide a way of developing communicatively what is already known, while at the same time enabling the teacher to fill the gaps in the learners' knowledge of the language" (1979b, p. 92). Widdowson warned us, however, that although some linguists might boast of ensuring communicative competence through the use of a notional syllabus, such an approach did not necessarily mean such competence would be the result. For one thing, a notional syllabus isolated for study the components of communication. He stated:

> There is one rather crucial fact that such an inventory [typically included in a notional syllabus] does not, and cannot of its nature, take into account, which is that communication does not take place through the linguistic exponence of concepts and functions as self-contained units of meaning. It takes place as discourse, whereby meanings are negotiated through interaction (1979a, p. 253).

Perhaps it is because a notional approach utilized an artificial breakdown of communication into discrete functions, that most of its applications lost their potential as providers of effective input. As the reader will see, activities based on a notional approach did not always involve real communication situations any more than repetitive dialogues or "structures for the day" did.

Consider the following excerpt from a textbook utilizing a notional approach (Jones and von Baeyer, 1983):

> Here are some useful ways of requesting. They are marked with stars [in this case asterisks] according to how polite they are.
>   * Hey, I need some change. I'm all out of change.
>   ** You don't have a quarter, do you? Have you got a quarter, by any chance? Could I borrow a quarter?
>   *** You couldn't lend me a dollar, could you? Do you think you could lend me a dollar? I wonder if you could lend me a dollar.
> **** Would you mind lending me five dollars? If you could lend me five dollars, I'd be very grateful.
> ***** Could you possibly lend me your typewriter? Do you think you could possibly lend me your typewriter? I wonder if you could possibly lend me your typewriter.

****** I hope you don't mind my asking, but I wonder if it might be at all pos-
    sible for you to lend me your car.
Decide with your teacher when you would use these request forms. Can you
add any more forms to the list?

Not only would such an analysis be superficial but the subtleties involved
would be very difficult for an ESL student even at an advanced level. Native
speakers also might have trouble in determining many of the differences. For
example, is "Would you mind lending me five dollars?" more or less polite than
"Do you think you could lend me a dollar?" In addition to the activity's syntactic problems, semantic and situational differences are not at all clear. Asking
someone for a car is certainly different from asking someone for a quarter.
Important variables are missing, such as the positions, ages, and other characteristics of the interlocutors and their relationships to one another. Thus the
activity lacks not only meaning but comprehensibility.

What kinds of activities then would be meaningful and comprehensible?
Although some organizing principles might lend themselves to effective communicative approaches more than others, it is not so much the organizational
principle that makes the difference. Nor is it the content itself. For example,
even grammar may be considered a stimulating topic for communication by
some students and their teachers (see especially Fotis and Ellis, 1991).

An Effective Communicative Approach

Breen and Candlin (1979) characterize an effective communicative approach as
being one in which a shared knowledge is explored and modified as a result. It
implies a negotiation of "potential meanings in a new language" and it implies
a socialization process. Breen and Candlin reject systems in which the learner
is separated from that which is to be learned as though the target language
could be objectively broken down into isolated components. They argue further that:

> In a communicative methodology, content ceases to become some external
> control over learning-teaching procedures. Choosing directions becomes a
> part of the curriculum itself, and involves negotiation between learners and
> learners, learners and teachers, and learners and text.

Thus they feel that a *negotiation for meaning* is crucial to a successfully
applied communicative methodology.[5] This idea seems to suggest the need for
greater interdependence and a greater flexibility on the parts of teachers and
students to allow the syllabus and its content to develop in ways that make
acquisition of the target language most likely.

---

[5] That is not to say, however, that all attempts to negotiate meaning result in comprehensive language. It is the intention to understand and to be understood that is most important here.

SUMMARY

Although methods, like models of cars, have varied over the years, the content of language teaching has remained basically the same until recently. An analysis of language has been in the driver's seat while meaningful interaction about content of interest has had to find room where it can if it is to be included at all.

Chomsky's transformational grammar has been mistakenly used to justify and perpetuate a focus on structure in language teaching while his real contributions to the field in general have remained largely ignored. His exposure of the cognitive paralysis brought about by behaviorism, while having an impact on theory, is just beginning to be felt in the classroom. Although we are not sure where it will lead us, his concepts of a possible language acquisition device and Universal Grammar may have profound consequences for classroom practice once we have more understanding of the content, structure(s), and networking involved.

Hymes, Halliday, Wilkins, Widdowson, Breen and Candlin, and many others have added to our knowledge of the sociocultural aspects in defining a language system. In addition, their ideas have been influential in the development of approaches that involve students in meaningful experiences in the new language.

READINGS, REFLECTION, AND DISCUSSION

Suggested Readings and Reference Materials

Austin, J. (1962). *How to do things with words.* Oxford: Clarendon. A seminal work consisting of several lectures given in 1955 at Harvard. Through them we gain insight into the author's ideas concerning speech act theory, which places an emphasis on function as opposed to form.

Brumfit, C. J., and Johnson, K., eds. (1979). *The communicative approach to language teaching.* Oxford: Oxford University. An in-depth analysis of the fundamental arguments underlying communicative approaches. Included are key writings of Hymes, Halliday, Wilkins, Widdowson, and many others who have led the way to a new look at language teaching processes.

Canale, M., and Swain, M. (1980). Theoretical bases of communicative approaches to second-language teaching and testing. *Applied Linguistics, 1* (1), 1–47. This important article defines communicative competence and identifies and describes its basic components.

Chomsky, N. (1975). *Reflections on language.* New York: Pantheon. In this book, Chomsky attempts to clarify his stand on many issues. For example, he stresses the fact that he did not intend for his term "deep structure" in language to represent in any way that which is really deep. He continues his fierce battle with empiricism and all of its ramifications, but here he fights with more literary finesse than before.

Chomsky, N. (1980). *Rules and representations.* New York: Columbia University. Here Chomsky further develops his theme that genetically based structure is an *a priori* basis for higher mental functions which come into being when humans come into contact with external environmental factors. In this book he addresses performance models which, he asserts, must include theories of both grammatical and pragmatic competence. Performance and competence models are mutually supportive, he feels.

Diller, K. (1978). *The language teaching controversy.* Rowley, Mass.: Newbury House. This book presents a comprehensive overview of several linguistic theories and their contributions over the years to language teaching.

Questions for Reflection and Discussion

1. Many have speculated about what the language acquisition device might contain and how it might work. Both the computer analogy (see also Related Reading 1) and the notion of parameter setting have been posited as possibilities. Discuss the feasibility of each of these hypotheses. Do you have any hypotheses of your own about what such a device might contain and how it might work?

2. The nature versus nurture controversy is still with us today in the area of language acquisition. Can you think of some evidence showing the importance of nature or what we are born with? How about nurture or our experience with the environment? Which do you think is most important, nature or nuture?

3. Widdowson (1978) argues that "we do not progress very far in our pedagogy by simply replacing abstract isolates of a linguistic kind by those of a cognitive or behavioral kind." Explain what you think he means. Can you think of abstract isolates, other than those mentioned in this chapter, on which programs might attempt to focus?

4. Take a close look at several language textbooks with which you are already familiar or to which you have access. Which activities appear to focus on an analysis of language? Which on communication?

CHAPTER 2

The Classroom as an Environment for Language Acquistion

This would not necessarily mean changing or disguising the classroom in the hope that it will momentarily serve as some kind of "communicative situation" resembling situations in the outside world. The classroom itself has a unique social environment with its own human activities and its own conventions governing these activities.

M. Breen and C. Candlin, 1979

QUESTIONS TO THINK ABOUT

1. Have you attempted to learn another language in a classroom setting? Maybe you've tried to learn more than one. Think about the experiences you've had in language classrooms. How successful were you as a result of these experiences? Did you ever become fluent in the second language you studied? If so, at what point did you feel fluent? What kinds of experiences seemed necessary to your fluency?

2. How do you think learning a second or foreign language might be like learning a first? How do you think it might be different?

3. Do you think it is possible to become fluent in a second or foreign language in a classroom? If so, how do you think it can happen?

The positions taken in the remainder of this book are based on the following two assumptions: (1) *Although important differences must be taken into account, there are a sufficient number of similarities between first- and second-language acquisition to support a common theory;* (2) *the classroom can indeed be an appropriate environment for language acquisition.*

A COMPARISON BETWEEN FIRST- AND SECOND-LANGUAGE ACQUISITION

Similarities

Ervin-Tripp, as early as 1974, directly challenges the widely held idea that it is not logical to attempt to develop a common theory for first- and second-language acquisition. According to her, the idea that first-language (L1) and second-language (L2) acquisition have little in common theoretically has been based on two common misconceptions: (1) The foundation for L2 is built largely from a transfer of the rules of L1, and (2) only L2 is constructed from prior conceptual knowledge within the learner.

Concerning the first misconception, Newmark (1979) states that students who have a need to perform before they are ready will revert to L1 syntactic rules. According to Newmark this is more a result of ignorance than interference. The dependence on L1 seems to occur predominantly in the beginning stages, when there is an intense desire to communicate. Sometimes the student at this stage will use not only L1 structures with L2 words but L1 words as well. While the L1 is heavily depended upon during initial stages of second-language acquisition, the need for it dies out as the student gains proficiency in the L2.

Regarding the second misconception, it must be noted that L1, like L2, is constructed from prior conceptual knowledge. Bruner, referring to L1, observed that "language emerges as a procedural acquisition to deal with events that the child already understands conceptually and to achieve communicative objectives that the child, at least partially, can realize by other means" (1978b, p. 247).

Ervin-Tripp feels that if the human brain is equipped to handle language, then certainly this ability is not meant only for L1. To show that the brain uses similar strategies for L2 acquisition, she points to her study of American children learning French in Geneva. The children utilized three sources for acquiring French: peers (interaction in and out of the classroom), school (content-area subject matter was taught in French), and home (exposure to parents who often spoke French, to servants, and to the mass media). Generally speaking, "the conclusion is tenable that first- and second-language learning is similar in natural situations . . . the first hypothesis we might have is that in all second-language learning we will find the same processes: overgeneralizations, production simplification, loss of sentence medial items, and so on" (1974, p. 205).[1]

---

[1] See Slobin (1973) for the "Operating Principles" associated with the acquisition of L1.

B. Taylor, like Ervin-Tripp, found evidence giving credibility to the notion that second-language learners use similar strategies to those learning their first language. He looked at the use of overgeneralization and transfer made by elementary and intermediate students of ESL. By examining errors, he found that "reliance on overgeneralization is directly proportional to proficiency in the target language, and reliance on transfer is inversely proportional" (1980, p. 146). In other words, during initial stages of acquisition the learner will depend quite heavily on first-language knowledge to communicate in the target language, but once the student is able to form hypotheses about the new language, he or she will begin to work within the framework of that language. The student then will make errors mainly due to overgeneralization of the newly acquired structures. For example a student of English who has just hypothesized that past tense verbs end with "ed" may put "ed" on everything that happens in the past. Thus, "sat" may become "sitted" or maybe even "satted." Taylor points out that overgeneralization (and transfer too, for that matter) is the result of a necessity to reduce language to the simplest possible system. He points to Jain's (1969) observation that this phenomenon represents an effort to lessen the cognitive burden involved in trying to master something as complex as language. The second-language learner, like the first, attempts to "regularize, analogize, and simplify" in an effort to communicate.

Both first and second languages develop in predictable stages. In reference to the natural order hypothesis, Krashen (1982) points to some rather striking similarities between L1 and L2 acquisition orders. If valid, these similarities may add credence to the argument that there are many parallels in cognitive strategies. He bases his conclusions on the following morpheme studies: (1) Dulay and Burt (1974), who found in their research done on Spanish and Chinese children learning English what may be a universal order in L2 morpheme acquisition; (2) Bailey, Madden, and Krashen (1974), who found that adults and children followed a similar order in learning a second language; and (3) R. Brown (1973) and DeVilliers and DeVilliers (1973), who reached similar conclusions in their well-known findings on L1 morpheme acquisition order. Krashen states, "In general, the bound morphemes have the same relative order for first- and second-language acquisition (*ing, plural, ir past, reg past, third person singular,* and *possessive*) while the auxiliary and copula tend to be acquired relatively later in first-language acquisition than in second-language acquisition" (1982, p. 13). It is interesting to note that Larsen-Freeman (1978) found in her study that morpheme orders seem to reflect the frequency of certain morphemes in the input. She stresses the importance of carefully examining the input when investigating such orders.

Caution must be used, however, in interpreting the morpheme studies. Although the evidence appears impressive, equating accuracy order with acquisition order (as was done in the cross-sectional studies)[2] is a questionable procedure at best. Structures are known to fluctuate within given speakers. Because the student uses "sat" at one point in time does not mean that it has been acquired, as we learned earlier.

More convincing evidence supporting a common theory comes from Cazden (1972) and others who based their conclusions on longitudinal studies.[3] To illustrate, Ellis (1986) points out that the L1 orders Cazden noted in the acquisition of the transitional forms of negatives and interrogatives are very similar to those of L2 acquisition. For example, negatives begin with the "no" attachment (no can walk here) followed by "no" moving to an internal position (Juan no can walk here). Finally, "no" is part of the verb (Juan can't walk here). Concerning question formation, rising intonation is used to mark questions before the incorporation of *wh-* structures, and word order inversion does not occur until later.

Similarity between speech addressed to children in their first language (motherese) and speech addressed to foreigners (foreigner talk) is evidence that others at least perceive the strategies of L1 and L2 acquisition to be similar in many ways. Shorter sentences, high-frequency vocabulary, "here and now" items (but to a lesser extent), indirect correction, frequent gesture, and lack of overt attention to form, are among the many similarities observed in situations in which the interlocutors are involved in real communication (Henzl, 1973; Freed, 1978; Hatch, Shapira, and Gough, 1978; Arthur, Weiner, Culver, Young, and Thomas, 1980; Long, 1981; Wesche and Ready, 1985; Richard-Amato, 1984).

Additional support for a common theory comes from Asher, who states that "a reasonable hypothesis is that the brain and nervous system are biologically programmed to acquire language, either the first or second, in a particular sequence and in a particular mode." He stresses that both require a *silent period*, i.e., time to simply comprehend language without having to orally produce it. He states, "If you want to learn a second language gracefully and with a minimum of stress, then invent a learning strategy that is in harmony with the biological system" (1972, p. 134).

We already know that children learning their first language require a fairly extensive silent period before they begin to produce utterances that are meaningful. It is interesting to note that Postovsky (1977) showed the benefits of a silent period for second-language learners in a study of adult American students of Russian at the Defense Language Institute in Monterey, California. The students in the experimental group were asked to *write* their responses to input rather than *speak;* in contrast, the control group had to produce orally right from the beginning. The first group did better than the second not only in syntactic control of the language but in accuracy of pronunciation.

---

[2]Cross-sectional studies measure what students can do at a specified point in time.

[3]Longitudinal studies measure long-term effects and stages of development over a period of time.

Gary's (1975) research also gives strength to arguments for a silent period. The study involved fifty American children learning Spanish. Half the students were allowed a silent period during which they could respond with nods, pointing, and other gestures. The other half had to respond orally using an audiolingual format. The experimental group outperformed the control group in both listening comprehension and speaking performance.

Differences

Because learners are usually older when learning their second language than they were when learning their first,[4] they are more developed cognitively than first-language learners. They have distinct advantages in several areas: they have a greater knowledge of the world in general, they have more control over the input they receive (e.g., they are able to ask for repetitions, renegotiate meaning, change the topic, and so forth more readily), they are able to learn and apply rules that may aid in facilitating the acquisition process (unless they are still very young children), they have a first language (and perhaps one or more second languages) from which they can transfer strategies and linguistic knowledge, and they have one or more cultures that give them advanced information about expectations, discourse in general, and how to get things done with language. Of course, there will be many differences between the first language and culture and the second with which the learners will eventually become familiar.

But being older is not always advantageous in learning a second language. Older learners may have increased inhibitions and anxiety and may find themselves afraid to make errors. The latter may be, in part, the result of an undue emphasis on form in their earlier experiences with language learning. In addition, they may have poor attitudes and lack motivation, depending upon their feelings and the conditions under which they are learning the second language (see also Chapter 5). Perhaps they are studying the language only because it is required in a program in which they happen to have enrolled. Perhaps they find themselves in a country with a language and culture in which they have little interest. Another disadvantage is that, although the influence of the first language is usually positive in learning the second, there may be some interference later on, particularly for items that are similar, either structurally or semantically (Newmark, 1979). It is probable, too, that students may avoid using certain structures in their utterances altogether because they are not part of their first-language repertoire (see Schachter, 1974 and Kleinmann, 1977).

---

[4] An exception would be the compound bilingual, one who learns the second language at the same time as the first. Depending upon the situation, one might argue that the individual has two first languages. However, usually one of the languages will take precedence over the other and will be considered the first language.

In Figure 2.1 is a chart summarizing some of the relevant characteristics we have mentioned so far belonging to first- and second-language learners.[5] There will, no doubt, be other characteristics you will want to add to the summary as you read further.

Important differences between first- and second-language development appear to lie in the areas of level of cognitive development and affect. The similarities appear to lie mainly in the process itself.

THE PROCESS OF LEARNING A SECOND LANGUAGE

It seems appropriate at this point to discuss the process that second-language learners go through in becoming fluent. But first it might aid our discussion to look at the differences between *contrastive analysis* and *error analysis* (proposed by Corder in 1967), in order to get perspective on the process of learning a second language in general.

Contrastive analysis is based on behaviorism. It considers L1 to be mainly an interference to the mastery of L2. In order to become proficient in L2, the habits of L1 need to be "beaten down," so to speak, before the habits of L2 can become firmly established. Thus audiolingualism, its most well-known manifestation (see Chapter 1), presented us with mim-mem drills and practice with minimal pairs such as *ch*ew and *sh*oe (for Spanish speakers), *g*lass and *g*rass (for Japanese speakers), and dialogues to be memorized so that we could avoid errors in the new language and take on its proper forms.

One problem with this philosophy is that contrastive analysis is not a very good predictor of errors in L2. The fact is that most of the errors students make in L2 cannot be traced to the differences between L1 and L2. In addition, regardless of the features of the students' first languages, they appear to go through basically the same stages in the second language anyway. For example, those students whose first languages use inversion to form questions (as does English) still go through the same process as other students for interrogatives. They usually will use intonation initially to mark a question (He is going?) before they use inversion (Is he going?) during the second-language learning process.

Error analysis, on the other hand, is based on developmentalism (learning develops in stages as learners interact with the environment). It looks at the errors made by learners while they are learning and asks questions about them. Why are these errors being made? What do they have to say about the hypotheses being tested (generally subconsciously) by learners? Do they mean that the learners are doing something wrong? Or do they mean that the learners have acquired a rule

---

[5] The assumption is made here that second-language learners are usually older than first-language learners except in the case of compound bilinguals. Thus qualifiers such as "generally" and "in most cases" are used.

Characteristics	L1 Learner	L2 Learner
constructs language from prior conceptual knowledge	✓	✓
is an active learner who tests and revises hypotheses	✓	✓
requires an interactional process	✓	✓
uses cognitive strategies (oversimplification, etc.)	✓	✓
is aided by modified input	✓	✓
develops language in predictable stages	✓	✓
makes developmental errors	✓	✓
requires a silent period	✓	
benefits from a silent period		✓
is usually cognitively more highly developed		✓
generally has a greater knowledge of the world		✓
in most cases, can learn and apply rules more readily		✓
usually has more control over the input		✓
has an L1 as a resource		✓
may have other second languages from which to draw		✓
is familiar with one or more other cultures		✓
may have a problem with attitude and/or motivation		✓
is more likely to be inhibited, anxious, and/or afraid of making errors		✓

Figure 2.1

and are, in reality, progressing in the language? Take, for example, the student mentioned earlier who may change "sat" to "sitted" or "satted" because the past tense "ed" has just been internalized. Error analysis looks at errors such as this one positively and considers such errors as necessary to the development of language, be it first or second.

Overall, error analysis considers L1 to be mainly of benefit to the development of L2, as we learned earlier from Newmark (1979). At first, students rely heavily on L1 structures and sometimes even vocabulary to get meaning across. As the L2 becomes internalized, the L1 is relied upon less and less as the students move toward more nativelike proficiency.

The interim language that develops is neither L1 or L2. It has, not only some features of each, it has its own features that are not found in either language. It is called *interlanguage* (Selinker, 1972).

The term *interlanguage* is used to refer to the progression taking place within each language learner. This progression has to do with the systematic development of the syntax, semantics, and pragmatics of the second language and is very similar to that developed in first-language learners. During the process, hypothesis testing occurs usually at the subconscious level and predictable errors are made along the way, regardless of what first language the students speak (see Fuller and Gundel, 1987; Butterworth and Hatch, 1978; Ravem, 1978, and many others).

It is important to note here that the progression toward nativelike competence is not linear. Students move forward and back, and forward and back again, all the while stretching to increasingly more advanced levels. Although students regress frequently, the general movement is forward, toward the goal. We need considerably more research to find out more about this progression. We do have evidence (mentioned earlier) about how students progress, particularly in the formation of negatives and interrogatives. In addition, the formation of relative clauses has been studied. For example, Schumann (1980) looked at the speech of five Spanish speakers learning English and found that clauses first are used to modify objects (Roberto has a book is about electricity). Notice that the relative pronoun is missing. This will come later to form "Roberto has a book *that* is about electricity." As time goes on, we will gain more and more knowledge about the interlanguage process. We have only just begun.

Although the movement of progression is generally forward, there may be times when students seem to reach a plateau in the process, beyond which they seem unable to move. We say that at this point or for that particular structure (sometimes called a "pidginized form") the students' interlanguage has *fossilized*. When pidginized forms become obligatory in the students' production, we say that fossilization has occurred.

We know relatively little about what causes fossilization and what can be done to reverse its effects. We do know that there are many related factors:

increased anxiety about the learning situation, lack of good linguistic models, not enough flexibility within the learner, insufficient motivation, to name a few. Of these, lack of motivation seems to be key. Often the learner whose language is said to be fossilized has reached certain communicative goals and no longer feels the need to become more nativelike.

We know, too, that once the students' interlanguage has fossilized, it seems very difficult, if not impossible to remedy the situation. Some teachers have tried rule-based exercises, reteaching certain forms, and other similar cures, but often to little or no avail. It is important to remember here that the language of many adults will fossilize at some point in the interlanguage process, particularly in the area of pronunciation (see especially Mendes Figueiredo, 1991).

However, there is convincing evidence to support the idea that, although the language of many adults does fossilize, fossilization is not a necessary condition; adults can indeed acquire *all* aspects of a second language under the right conditions. Sorenson (1967) studied the Tukano tribes of South America who must, according to their culture, marry someone outside of their first-language group. He found that, as adults, they do indeed learn second languages with nativelike proficiency. (Incidentally, they are permitted a very long silent period.) Ioup, Boustagui, El Tigi, and Moselle (1994) found that their subject, Julie from the United Kingdom, gained nativelike proficiency with Egyptian Arabic (she was married to an Egyptian). In the cases referred to, the motivation seemed extremely high. While we obviously cannot heighten motivation to this extent in our classrooms, we can, it seems to me, do a great deal to prevent fossilization from occurring prematurely and, maybe even keep it from happening at all.

Perhaps by bringing our students into increased contact with fluent speakers of the language, especially peers, we can greatly increase motivation. Setting up peer–teacher situations (see Chapter 14), inviting fluent speakers of the target language to the classroom (including administrators, counselors, teachers, adults from the community, as well as peers), organizing pen-pal relationships between students and peers who are more advanced in the language, arranging field trips and planning celebrations that involve more advanced speakers of the language, and so forth can sometimes provide just enough motivation to prevent fossilization or, in some cases, get students moving again in the language development process. In addition, by providing appropriate written materials that the students *want* to read, we can heighten the motivation to become as proficient as possible.

Although error analysis is an important tool in studying interlanguage, we must move beyond that to include discourse and performance analyses as well as ethnography. We have much to learn about the total situations of the learners, the details of the interactional events, the feelings, attitudes, and motivational factors relevant to the process of learning another language in the classroom.

LANGUAGE ACQUISITION IN THE CLASSROOM

The second assumption mentioned at the beginning of this chapter is that the classroom can be an appropriate environment for language acquisition. The view has been expressed that discussions of psycholinguistic research concerning the acquisition process are not relevant, for the most part, to the second-language classroom (see Strevens, 1978). Before an attempt is made to refute this view, we need to look at acquisition theory itself.

Several (mostly compatible) second-language acquisition models and hypotheses have been described by Ellis (see Related Reading 2). Although many of them are referred to in this and other chapters, the two that seem most appropriate to the present discussion are the Monitor Model proposed by Krashen and the Variable Competence Model proposed by Ellis. The Monitor Model is probably the most well known of the models and, at the same time, the most controversial.

As part of the rationalization for this model, Krashen distinguishes between two different linguistic systems: acquisition and learning (Krashen, 1981b, 1982). It is his view that acquisition is subconscious and learning is conscious. Below are adaptations of the acquisition and performance models that he has used to help clarify the entire process.

The items that are *acquired* (Figure 2.2) are those that were able to pass through the affective filter, which consists of inhibitions, motivation, personality factors, and so on, and move into the subconscious to become intake, a term proposed by Corder in 1967 to describe what is actually internalized. On the other hand, the items that are *learned* (i.e., the formal rules of the target language) become part of the monitor (see Figure 2.3) and are used in production only if they are relatively simple, if the speaker is focused on form, and if there is time to apply them. Ordinarily, in the flow of normal discourse, the speaker does not have the opportunity to monitor the output to any great extent unless he or she is what some linguists refer to as a "super monitor user," in other words, one who is adept at applying rules and communicating simultaneously (some language teachers fit into this category). Now and then a language learner appears not to monitor at all; see, for example, Schmidt's (1984) subject W (Chapter 5). He would be referred to in Krashen's terminology as an "underuser." However,

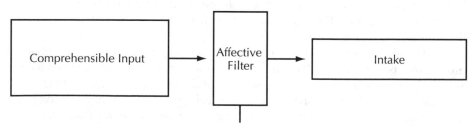

Figure 2.2. The Acquisition Process (Krashen, 1981b)

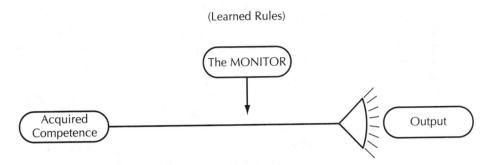

Figure 2.3. Performance Model (Krashen, 1982)

Krashen (1981b) also identifies the "optimal user," one who applies the monitor appropriately. There are situations in which the monitor can be maximally effective: when the language learner is taking grammar tests, writing papers, or preparing planned speeches. Although items in the learning store as such do not directly become part of the acquisition store, according to Krashen, the rules of the target language do become acquired, but only by exposure to language that students can understand.

He cites supportive evidence from the descriptive studies of Stafford and Covitt (1978) and Krashen and Pon (1975). Stafford and Covitt's subject V demonstrated a high level of proficiency with spoken English, but in an interview with him, they discovered that he showed no conscious knowledge of the rules. Conversely, Krashen and Pon's subject P proved to be an optimal monitor user when writing English but did not apply the well-learned, well-practiced rules to her speech production. Instead she made many errors. However, McLaughlin, Rossman, and McLeod (1984) point out that the brain often has difficulty in handling two competitive cognitive demands at once—carrying on a conversation and being accurate grammatically. It is possible that once the cognitive burden is lessened, the learner might be able to apply some of the rules.

Another complication is what Stevick (1980) refers to as the *Eureka* phenomenon, which can occur when the student is made consciously aware of the acquired rule through teaching. This awareness might lead the student into thinking that the learned rule, because it has been learned, goes directly into the acquisition store, when it may actually have been acquired through exposure to the language itself. However, it is highly probable that the subconscious/conscious dichotomy has been too simplistically drawn in the first place. Who is to say that things learned cannot go into the acquisition store? Many have questioned the dichotomy by arguing that it is possible for rules that have been consciously applied over and over in a variety of situations to become automatic and thus internalized (Bialystok and Fröhlich, 1977; McLaughlin, 1978; Stevick, 1980; Sharwood-Smith, 1981; Gregg, 1984; Ellis, 1986).

In addition, we seem continually to "monitor" subconsciously and we become aware of doing so only when there has been a mismatch between our acquired hypotheses and what we hear and/or produce (see also Morrison and Low, 1983). Thus the issues involved here appear to go much deeper and are obviously much more complicated than we have been led to believe.

McLaughlin, Rossman, and McLeod (1984) are also critical of the distinction Krashen has drawn between learning and acquisition. They prefer to speak of controlled and automatic information processing. Either one can be the focus of attention (usually true of controlled processes) or on the periphery of attention (usually true of automatic processes). What differentiates these concepts from Krashen's is that controlled and automatic processes do not fall unequivocally into a conscious/subconscious dichotomy. They see both processes as falling somewhere on a continuum between conscious and subconscious functioning. They emphasize that individual learning styles are an additional factor to be considered. They do concede, however, that when input is comprehensible, implicit learning might be most successful. However, they point out that some adults prefer working from the rules, whereas others prefer working from the output.

While it appears that some headway is being made in discovering the nature of language processing systems, we are particularly unsure about how the various processes occur and how they relate to one another. We may hypothesize that acquisition serves as an undergirding for those things learned, producing the Eureka effect. However, we cannot ignore indications that in some circumstances the opposite may occur. Consider, for example, students who have spent years in grammar-translation or cognitive-code programs, then go to a country where the target language is spoken and become fluent in a very short time. In those cases, the learning system appears to have in some sense predisposed the learner to a more rapid acquisition of the language. However, one might wonder how soon the students would have become fluent had they been exposed to meaningful, comprehensible communication in the target language right from the beginning.

Although the Monitor Model may be flawed as a theory, Krashen has highlighted an extremely important issue. He has brought the point home to many language teachers that the classroom does not have to confine itself to formal instruction in the target language. It can instead provide the kind of input that he feels will best facilitate the second-language acquisition process, that is, input that is comprehensible, interesting, and/or relevant, that is not grammatically sequenced, and that is present in sufficient quantity.

While Krashen emphasizes the importance of providing comprehensible input, Ellis (1984a, 1986) in his Variable Competence Model focuses on interaction. He believes it is not enough to be concerned with input. A key factor in the second-language acquisition process is "the opportunity afforded the learner to *negotiate* meaning with an interlocutor, preferably one who has more linguistic resources than the learner and who is adept at 'foreigner/teacher talk'" (1984a, p. 184). (See Chapter 3 for the development of a similar idea.) In his model of second-language acquisition, Ellis recognizes a single knowledge store in which variable transitional rules are contained. Some rules tend to be more automatic, others more analyzed. The second-language learner demonstrates variation in the production of interlanguage forms (see also Larsen-Freeman, 1991). Sometimes the learner will appear to have mastered a particular structure and other times he or she will regress to earlier forms. The variation, according to Ellis, is often the result of whether the process is a primary one (using automatic rules) in unplanned discourse or a secondary one (using analyzed rules) in planned discourse. (See Figure 3 and its description in Related Reading 2.) Primary processes are those that utilize and facilitate the *automatic system*, and secondary processes utilize and facilitate the *analytic system*. Both systems represent a continuum rather than a dichotomy. The rate of acquisition depends upon the quantity and quality of the interaction in which the learner is involved. Ellis claims that "rapid development along the 'natural' route occurs when the learner has the chance to negotiate meaning in unplanned discourse" (1984a, p. 186). However, he reminds us that this process is influenced by such affective factors as motivation and personality (see Chapter 5).

Although relatively little research has been done on the language acquisition process in second-language classrooms, progress has been made in accessing the product. Many of the studies, for example, indicate that the French immersion programs in Canada[6] have been among the most successful (Lambert and Tucker, 1972, Tucker and d'Anglejan, 1972, Selinker, Swain, and Dumas, 1975; Swain 1975; Swain, Lapkin, and Barik, 1976) as has the Spanish immersion program in Culver City, California (Cathcart, 1972; Cohen, 1974; Plann, 1977). What these programs have in common is that the emphasis is placed on the content to be learned rather than on language itself. At later levels, formal instruction is also included in varying degrees. All immersion students are at similar levels in the target language to begin with (unlike submersion programs, in which they are the minority among native speakers) and all the content-area subjects are taught in the target language until English is gradually added at later levels (see Chapter 16).

It is interesting to note, however, that Selinker, Swain, and Dumas found that although the students in French immersion gained proficiency, their speech contained pidginized forms which may have been due to their lack of sufficient interaction with peers and others who were native speakers of French. Plann discovered the same tendency toward the development of pidginized forms in the Spanish immersion program. In fact, he found that the students appeared to have developed their own classroom dialect. It is likely that in both situations the students did not have sufficient opportunities for interaction with native or near-native speaking linguistic models (see page 270, for discussion of fossilization as related to cooperative learning; see also

---

[6] The Thunder Bay Program described on pages 360–365 is an example of immersion.

Swain's explanation on pages 51–52). Sanaoui and Lapkin (1992) found that through computer networking with native French-speaking peers, Anglophone students of French in Toronto were able to improve their language use.

Other studies also indicate that our knowledge of the second-language acquisition process is relevant to the classroom and that acquisition, in fact, does occur there. This is especially true when the methods themselves are consonant with our cognitive systems to the extent that they provide input that can be understood in communicative situations (Asher, 1972; Asher, Kusudo, and de la Torre, 1974; Swaffer and Woodruff, 1978; Voge, 1981; Edwards, Wesche, Krashen, Clement, and Krudenier, 1984; Lafayette and Buscaglia, 1985; Hammond, 1988). Asher as well as Asher, Kusudo, and de la Torre compared the total physical response with traditional methods (see Chapter 7); Swaffer and Woodruff looked at a college-level reading program in which total physical response, yoga breathing, and gymnastics were used in combination to acquire language through meaningful reading; Voge compared the natural approach (see Chapter 8) to the direct method; Edwards et al. looked at sheltered psychology classes at the University of Ottawa; Lafayette and Buscaglia compared second-language classroom environments in which history was being taught; and Hammond examined Spanish courses (first semester) at two universities and found that those students in the natural approach experimental groups scored consistently higher on department-administered exams than did the control groups exposed to modified grammar-translation methodology, utilizing deductive grammar instruction.

In addition, Wagner-Gough and Hatch (1975) argue that, on the basis of their observations, the classroom is more than just one more environment in which acquisition occurs. It can be a place that is especially conducive to acquisition. They feel that for beginners up to the intermediate-level, the classroom can potentially be more effective than the outside world for acquiring a second language. They remind us that it is often difficult for students to get comprehensible input from a world that is not aware of their need for it.

SUMMARY

Two assumptions concerning second-language acquisition are supported: (1) although important differences must be taken into account, there are a sufficient number of similarities between first- and second-language acquisition to support a common theory, and (2) the classroom can be an appropriate environment for acquisition.

Related to the two assumptions are Krashen's Monitor Model and Ellis's Variable Competence Model. The first, although it may be flawed as a theory, emphasizes the importance of comprehensible input; the second emphasizes interaction and negotiated meaning in a variety of situations.

Although the natural environment might, in fact, be ideal for some, others might find it difficult to receive comprehensible input and to find the opportunity to participate in quality interaction. For them the classroom may be the best environment available.

READINGS, REFLECTION, AND DISCUSSION

Suggested Readings and Reference Materials

Brown, R. (1973). *A first language: The early stages.* Cambridge, Mass.: Harvard University. A classic in the study of first-language acquisition. The proponents of interactional approaches in second-language learning often refer to its insights, particularly to the role the caretaker plays in facilitating the interaction.

Ellis, R. (1986). *Understanding second language acquisition.* Oxford: Oxford University. In this book, Ellis gives perspective to much of the early relevant research on second-language acquisition and its relationship to the theories that have been developed.

Hatch, E. (1978). *Second language acquisition: A book of readings.* Rowley, Mass.: Newbury House. Still relevant, this book includes representative selections in second-language acquisition including papers by Wagner-Gough; Ervin-Tripp; Ravem; Schumann; Dulay and Burt; Bailey, Madden, Krashen; Larsen-Freeman; and many others. An additional section contains abstracts on acquisition research.

Krashen, S. (1982). *Principles and practice in second language acquisition.* Oxford: Pergamon. This book examines the relationship between theory and practice, the processes involved in second-language acquisition, the roles of comprehensible input and grammar, and various teaching approaches.

Larsen-Freeman, D., and Long, M. (1991). *An introduction to second language acquisition research.* London: Longman. A comprehensive analysis of the important research accomplished in second-language acquisition. Its topics include interlanguage studies, types of data analysis, theories in second-language acquisition, and many others.

Lightbrown, P. and Spada, N. (1993). *How languages are learned.* Oxford: Oxford University. A very readable discussion of the process by which languages are learned. Highlighted are the following topics: first- and second-language learning, affective factors, interlanguage (they refer to it as *learner language*) development, instructed and natural environments, and common myths about language learning.

Richards, J. (1978). *Understanding second and foreign language learning: Issues and approaches.* Rowley, Mass.: Newbury House. A now classic collection of readings on strategies for learning and teaching L2. Among the selections are contributions from Hatch, Corder, Schumann, Strevens, Tucker, d'Anglejan, and Swain.

Questions for Reflection and Discussion

1. Classroom acquisition research has recently come under fire because of what some see as a failure on the part of many researchers to consider carefully both *product* and *process.* Long states, "Product evaluations cannot distinguish among the many possible explanations for the results they obtain, because they focus on the product of a program while ignoring the process by which that product came about" (1984, p. 413). What kinds of factors might be overlooked if one focuses on the product alone? What implications does this have for our interpretations of the studies themselves and the conclusions based upon them?

2. In spite of the many similarities between first- and second-language learning, the important differences must be considered in curriculum development. What implications might they have, particularly for planning the content of language programs?

3. A few people (for example, see Strevens, mentioned earlier) feel that the acquisition process is not relevant to the classroom. On what do you think they based this conclusion? In your opinion, is there any justification for this point of view?

4. Speculate about the role a learner's first language has in the acquisition of the second. Take into account your own experience in language learning. Has its role been given too much or too little importance in the formulation of second-language theory? Discuss.

CHAPTER 3

Toward an Interactional Approach

How can we help the child learn a language?

Believe that your child can understand more than he or she can say, and seek, above all, to communicate. To understand and to be understood. To keep your minds fixed on the same target. In doing that, you will, without thinking about it, make one hundred or one thousand alterations in your speech and action. Do not try to practice them as such. There is no set of rules of how to talk to a child that can even approach what you unconsciously know. If you concentrate on communicating, everything else will follow.

R. Brown, 1977

QUESTIONS TO THINK ABOUT

1. Think about learning in general. Is learning a process that people do best by themselves? To what extent do people need other people and/or books or media to help them learn?

2. Do you think learning a language is different from learning other things? In what ways might it be different? In what ways might it be the same?

3. How do you think errors should be treated during the language learning process? Do you remember any of your own experiences with receiving error correction? Do you think the treatment of errors should be different for first- and second-language learners? If so, in what ways?

4. What about formal instruction in grammar? How important do you think rule-learning is to becoming fluent in a second or foreign language?

The Zone of Proximal Development (Vygotsky, 1962, 1978) and the $i + 1$ (Krashen, 1981b, 1982) are both hypotheses that seek to explain, at least in part, the cognitive operations involved in language acquisition. Underlying the surface complexity of these concepts are fundamentals that have remained largely ignored by language teachers until recently.

Although neither one can account for the whole process of language acquisition, they can teach us much about the role of input in the interaction, particularly in full two-way communication.[1] Of course, second-language acquisition can take place without full two-way communication. Gass and Varonis (1985) found, for example, that in one-way communication, when there is sufficient shared knowledge on the part of participants, there may be less need for interaction. However, research seems to indicate that interaction involving two-way communication is the best way to negotiated meaning and ultimately to acquisition of the target language (Long, 1983b, 1983c; Pica and Doughty, 1985; Swain, 1985).

Even though the role of input will be the focus of this chapter, the role of output cannot be underestimated in an informed theory of language acquisition. It will be considered later as an independent variable.

THE ZONE OF PROXIMAL DEVELOPMENT AND THE IMPORTANCE OF SOCIAL INTERACTION

Although Vygotsky (1978), like Chomsky, did not speak directly to second-language pedagogy, he did formulate ideas concerning learning and development in children that have important implications for second-language teaching and the providing of optimal input (see Related Reading 3). Before we proceed, it may be advantageous to compare Vygotsky's view of the relationship of learning and development to Piaget's in order more fully to understand the former.

To Piaget (1979) the processes of learning and mental development are independent of each other. Learning utilizes development but does not shape its course. He believed that maturation precedes learning. Educators who adhere to this idea emphasize the "readiness" principle. A student must be exposed primarily to input that can be handled without difficulty. In other words, the input must be at the student's actual level of development.

Vygotsky differed in that he saw the individual as having two developmental levels that have interacted with learning since the time of birth. In his theory learning precedes maturation. The individual through interaction progresses from what he called an *actual developmental level* to a *potential developmental level*.

---

[1] Burt and Dulay (1983) identify three communication phases: one-way (the learner receives input but gives no overt response); partial two-way (the learner responds orally in L1 or by simple gestures); and full two-way (the learner gives messages and responds in the target language to messages of others).

Between the two levels is the "Zone of Proximal Development," which he defined as "the distance between the actual developmental level as determined by independent problem solving and the level of potential development as determined through problem solving under adult guidance of and in a collaboration with more capable peers" (page 422 in Related Reading 3). The potential developmental level becomes the next actual developmental level through learning that "presupposes a specific social nature and a process by which children grow into the intellectual life of those around them." Learning then should always be one step ahead of development.

Whereas Piaget stressed *biology* as the determiner in universal stages of development, Vygotsky stressed *society* as the determiner of development, although the resulting stages are similar. However, Vygotsky felt that these stages are not universal in nature because each person's history is different; each person's opportunity of interaction is different. He emphasized a dialectical unity or an "interlacement" (a John-Steiner and Souberman term, 1978) between biological foundations and dynamic social conditions. He was convinced that higher psychological functions entail new psychological systems; they are not simply superimposed over the more elementary processes as Piaget believed.

In addition, Vygotsky placed a great deal of stress on play, which he saw as being rule governed. Children don't usually jump around aimlessly. If they do, it is usually for a very brief time. In order for this kind of activity to be fun, they have to have rules. Even being a "mother" requires rules. Play, like school, should create a Zone of Proximal Development. Through it the "child always behaves beyond his average age, above his daily behavior; in play it is as though he were a head taller than himself" (1978, p. 102).

Although learning and development are directly related, they do not increase in equal amounts or in parallel ways. "Development in children never follows school learning the way a shadow follows the object that casts it" (page 428 in Related Reading 3). The relationship between the two is extremely complex and uneven and cannot be reduced to a simple formula. Vygotsky was convinced that *learning itself is a dynamic social process through which the teacher in a dialogue with a student can focus on emerging skills and abilities.*

Freire (1970) enlarges on this concept in *Pedagogy of the Oppressed* in which he distinguishes between two kinds of education: banking and libertarian. Banking education involves the act of depositing. The student is an empty depository and the teacher is the depositor. The students "receive, memorize, and repeat." There is no real communication. The role of the student is a passive one, a sort of "disengaged brain." On the other hand, in libertarian education the teacher and students are partners. Meaning is inherent in the communication. Through it students are involved in acts of cognition and are not simply empty heads waiting to be filled with information. The process is a dialectical one. Sometimes the teacher is a student and the students are teachers in a dialogue through which all individuals can benefit.

This cooperative relationship is particularly important to second-language teaching, for it leads to meaningful interaction about some content of interest. Through such interaction the teacher is naturally attuned to the students' emerging skills and abilities. Otherwise, meaningful communication could not take place. If we consider the "development" to include the students' actual levels with the target language and the students' potential levels, then Vygotsky's theory makes sense for students learning a second language at any age, whether cognitive structures are already highly developed or not.

Meaningful interaction seems to be the key.

One example of the importance of interaction comes from John-Steiner (1985), who refers to the study done with Finnish immigrant children entering Swedish schools. She reports that they experienced "severe difficulties in their academic and linguistic development" because they were at first placed in very structured classrooms where there was little chance for meaningful interaction. The teacher did most of the talking and the activities were written.

John-Steiner, in the same paper, cites Wong-Fillmore's (1976) study of five new arrivals to the United States from Mexico. These children were paired with Anglo peers and their communication was taped over the period of a school year. The children stretched their knowledge of the target language remarkably. Sometimes these extensions were inadequate in getting across intentions but the peers were able to fill in the gaps.

Additional evidence of the importance of meaningful interaction in second-language teaching is found in a study by Seliger (1977). He first became interested in social interaction as a phenomenon when he observed his own two-year-old child. She would:

> . . . often push her father's newspaper aside to get his attention and then direct a stream of gibberish at him mixed with a few hardly understood words. He, in turn, could discuss the weather, the stock market, her siblings, or American foreign policy with her. It didn't seem to matter what was said as long as some interaction was taking place. As long as the child was answered, she would continue the same for quite some time.

The question Seliger poses is why a child would participate in and prolong an activity without having much understanding of what was being said to her. He concluded that this phenomenon is actually rather typical behavior and that the strategy being used may be important to the acquisition process itself.

In his study, he proposes that a similar strategy is used by adults who are successfully learning a second language. Although his study is not without critics (see Day, 1984),[2] it is an important one. It attempts to measure not only a public willingness to interact in the classroom but a willingness to participate in

---

[2] One of Day's findings in his study of ESL students in Honolulu was that there appeared to be no significant relationship between a measure of public exchanges (involving both responses to general solicits by the teacher and student self-initiated turns) and scores given on an oral interview and on a cloze test.

private classroom interaction as well. His subjects had studied English as a foreign language and were currently enrolled in an upper-intermediate level class in the English Language Institute at Queens College, C.U.N.Y. Each student fell into one of two groups: the "high input generator" group at one end of an interaction continuum, or "the low input generator" group at the other end. The members of the high input generator group interacted intensively, not only with the teacher but with each other. In addition, they initiated much of the interaction. The low input generator group, on the other hand, either avoided interaction altogether or remained fairly passive in situations in which they could have interacted. They seemed more dependent upon formal instruction.

Even though (as Day reminds us) Seliger's subjects are few in number (only three in each category), the study, nevertheless, has interesting implications. It was concluded from the scores on pretests and posttests that by receiving more focused input through interaction, the high input generators were able to "test more hypotheses about the shape and use of L2 thus accounting for increased success." Low input generators, on the other hand, were particularly dependent upon the classroom environment to force interaction because they did not tend to initiate or allow themselves to become involved in it on their own.[3]

More evidence comes from the Heidelberg Project (cited in Schumann, 1978b) to support the notion that social interaction is important to second-language acquisition. In this study of Italian and Spanish guest workers acquiring German in Germany, the correlations were extremely high between German proficiency and leisure social contact (.64), and between German proficiency and social contact at work (.53).

Carroll (1967) comes to a similar conclusion based on his study of university students majoring in French, German, Italian, Russian, and Spanish. Even a brief time spent abroad, where they had social interaction, had a substantial effect on proficiency.[4]

---

[3] At the end of the semester Seliger gave a discrete point test of English structure (Lado-Fries) and an integrative test of aural comprehension (The Queens College English Language Institute Test of Aural Comprehension) in addition to a cloze test. It was found that the scores on the pretests were not good predictors of scores on the posttests. However, measures of social interaction were. The amount of interaction accounted for 85 percent of the variance in the posttest scores on the discrete point test and for 69 percent of the variance in the posttest scores on the Aural Comprehension test.

[4] MLA Foreign Language Proficiency Tests for Teachers and Advanced Students were administered in 1965 to 2,782 seniors majoring in foreign languages at 203 institutions. The correlations between time spent abroad and test scores were .47,[a] .60,[a] .24,[b] and .27[b] for French, German, Russian, and Spanish respectively. (Italian was probably not included because there was not a sufficient number of cases.)
Note: [a]significance at the .01 level or better.
     [b]significance at the .05 level or better.

Bruner, who believes strongly in the social nature of language acquisition, chastises those who are committed philosophically to the idea that language learning is reducible to a concatenation of simple forms, which thereby become complex forms. Of course, here he is referring to methods advocated by the behaviorists and later by the cognitive-code theorists. Bruner emphasizes the fact that these people "failed to take into account the inherently social nature of what is learned when one learns language and, by the same token, to consider the essentially social way in which the acquisition of knowledge of language must occur" (1978b, p. 244).

THE $i + 1$ AND THE NATURE OF SOCIAL INTERACTION

Krashen concentrates on input and the role it plays in the language acquisition process in his formulation of the $i + 1$ concept. Like the Zone of Proximal Development, it refers to the distance between actual language development (represented by i) and potential language development (represented by $i + 1$).

This distance is perhaps realized most fully in motherese, that special language used by caretakers who wish to communicate with their children. "Children," according to Macnamara, "learn their mother tongue by first determining, independent of language, the meaning which a speaker intends to convey to them and then working out the relationship between the meaning and the expression they heard" (1983, p. 250).

Brown (1973) also stresses this concern with content rather than form in motherese. The child forms his or her own hypotheses about the rules and the relationship between meaning and form. Brown states that meaningful communication on one level always serves as the "launching platform" for attempts at a higher level. It is not so much a mechanism to teach language as it is a way to continue or extend the rapport within a conversation for as long as possible.

Motherese involves the simplification of speech in an intense desire on the part of the caretaker to be understood by the child. According to Corder (1978) this simplification is done chiefly in terms of choosing the kinds of topics and range of speech functions, the utterance length, the rate of speech as well as the amount of repetition, rephrasing, and redundancy in the message. In addition it is specifically related to situational context.

It is interesting to note that in motherese there is seldom a direct correction of ungrammatical forms in the output. Krashen (1982) supports Brown's conclusion that the caretaker seems to be more interested in the truth value of the utterance. As an example of this, he points to Brown, Cazden, and Bellugi (1973), who report that "Her curl my hair" was not corrected in their study because the statement was true, whereas "Walt Disney comes on Tuesday" was corrected because in reality Walt Disney comes (on television) on Wednesday. Thus content, not form, is the emphasis.

It is interesting also that parents are usually thrilled by any effort at all that the child makes in forming utterances. For example, when the child says "Daddy home" for the first time, no one labels this a mistake or calls it substandard or even considers it an error at all. Instead it is thought of as being ingenious and cute and the child is hugged or rewarded verbally. The utterance is considered evidence that the child is indeed acquiring the language.

What if in the classroom the language teacher treated "errors" as being evidence that the language was being acquired and that generalizations (often overgeneralizations) were being formed by the student? How would that facilitate the acquisition of the language? It is probable that in such an environment, the learner would be more willing to take the risk of being wrong and would be freer and more uninhibited in developing an interlanguage. The forms would thus become acquired, as they are in L1, mainly through extensive use of modified language in meaningful situations (Wagner-Gough and Hatch, 1975; Chaudron, 1985; Ellis, 1985).

What happens in the classroom in which the teacher is concerned both with the accuracy and fluency of the output, as most of us are? Sutherland feels that both of these goals "cannot realistically be achieved in the early stages of learning. Fortunately, and perhaps more importantly, they do not need to be achieved simultaneously in order to ultimately produce effective speakers" (1979, p. 25). He further says that learners in classrooms in which accuracy is first tend to develop very little proficiency in the target language. In such classrooms the teachers often look upon themselves as "Guardians of the Linguistic Norm" and feel that their main reason for being there is to ensure correctness. They often think that if students are allowed to make mistakes at beginning levels, they are doomed to a lifetime of linguistic errors (it's a matter of habit formation, they say). However, Sutherland points out that "since errors persist in learners anyway—no matter what method is employed—we certainly cannot look to methods to explain this phenomenon" (1979, p. 27).

Considerable research done in the area of error correction seems to support the idea that increased direct error correction does not lead to greater accuracy in the target language (Hendrickson, 1976; Dvorak, 1977; Semke, 1984; and many more). However, more recent studies have indicated possible advantages in providing correction in context sometimes coupled with some sort of explanation or focus on a rule (see especially White, Spada, Lightbrown, and Ranta, 1991; and Carroll and Swain, 1993). Caution must be used, however, in interpreting such studies. Although researchers may label various teachers' corrective behaviors, they often do not provide adequate documentation or even descriptions of these behaviors, including how many times these behaviors were used, the learners' follow-up questions or practice, the pattern of behaviors, and so forth (see especially Chaudron, 1991).[5] And, more important, most

---

[5] The Carrol and Swain study is an exception in that the teacher correction behaviors were very controlled.

of the research seems to involve short-term, experimental studies using pretest and posttest data rather than longitudinal data. It is almost impossible to learn what effect a treatment has had on the interlanguage process unless it is looked at over a long period of time. In addition, critical factors about learners seem not to be taken into account in many studies. Factors such as motivation, attitude, anxiety levels, willingness to take risks, age, cultural expectations concerning the language learning situation, and many more should not be ignored.

As discussed in Chapter 2, most errors found in the interlanguage of learners are developmental (at least after the very beginning stages during which transfer from L1 seems to be a viable strategy). Yorio (1980) suggests that we keep careful note of the errors our students make to determine whether the errors are systematic (appear with regularity) or random (caused by memory lapse, inattention, not having acquired the rule, or overgeneralization). It is the systematic errors with which we should be concerned. Are the errors increasing? (The student is regressing.) Are the errors decreasing? (The student is learning.) Are they stationary? (The students' language is fossilizing.) Of course, if the student appears to be regressing, something must be done before the forms have had a chance to fossilize. However, Yorio warns that it is important not to inundate the students' papers with red ink, but to discuss errors in a meaningful way. Perhaps sessions can be held with several students at once who seem to be making the same kinds of errors. He suggests also that students be given a chance to find their own errors and correct them. With oral errors, he recommends we focus on meaning as opposed to form. Modeling or repeating what the learner has said, but in correct form, is one way to correct indirectly. However, he notes that adults often want to know the nature of the errors they are making. They may ask for explanations, which indicates that they probably are motivated to learn that particular rule and that they may be ready to incorporate it into their linguistic systems. However, if the goal of the student is to understand and to be understood in social and/or academic situations, then methods must focus primarily on real communication in those kinds of situations.

The student, like the child learning a first language, acquires language best through meaningful input addressed directly to him or her, similar to the input of motherese. "It makes rules become more salient and helps (the student) to perceive more easily the relationship between meaning and form" (d'Anglejan, 1978, p. 225).

What kind of input, then, is most conducive to forming generalizations about the language, thereby making acquisition possible? Krashen suggests that in addition to being relevant and/or interesting (see Chapter 2), the input must approximate the student's $i + 1$. It must be comprehensible in that it is near the student's actual level of development (i), but then it must stretch beyond that to include concepts and structures that the student has not yet acquired $(i + 1)$. Free conversation with native speakers does not generally produce input that can be comprehended unless the native speakers are talking directly to the student and are aware of the student's approximate $i + 1$. Neither does TV or radio ordinarily produce such input. The student ideally must be in a situation in which all the interlocutors desire to understand and be understood. It is often through gestures, the context itself, and linguistic modifications that the new concepts become internalized. In other words, the student needs to receive foreigner talk.

The term "foreigner talk" was coined by Ferguson (1975), who defined it as a simplified register or style of speech used when addressing people who are nonnative speakers.[6] Foreigner talk in the classroom is generally well formed and includes, but often to a greater degree, many of the same strategies used in regular teacher talk: exaggeration of pronunciation and facial expression; decreasing speech rate and increasing volume; frequent use of pause, gestures, graphic illustrations, questions, and dramatization; sentence expansion, rephrasing, and simplification; prompting; and completing utterances made by the student (Henzl, 1973; Gaies, 1977; Kleifgen, 1985; Wesche and Ready, 1985; Richard-Amato, 1984). The input is automatically adjusted in the attempt to ensure understanding. See the example below:

Two teachers are talking to a group of foreign students in the Intensive English Center at the University of New Mexico.

		Strategy Used
TEACHER 1:	Who's the man with the hood on his face? (points	question
	to the word "executioner" on the chalkboard)	gesture
		graphic aid
TEACHER 2:	Yeh. You've seen the pictures . . . they have black	decreased rate
	hoods (She pantomimes as she crouches and omi-	increased volume
	nously pulls a pretend hood over her head.) . . .	pausing
	with the eyes. (She uses her fingers to encircle her	expansion
	eyes to appear as though she is looking through a	dramatization
	mask. Teacher 1 does the same, and they both scan	simplification
	the group as if to frighten them.) . . . You know . . .	expansion
	really creepy looking . . . scary . . . oh . . . what is	question
	it called?	

(Richard-Amato and Lucero, 1980, p. 6)

It is important to point out that comprehensible input is a relative concept determined by the total interaction and cannot be defined simply by a list of

---

[6] An important question here is how does foreigner talk differ from regular teacher talk in the classroom? Studies have been done in an attempt to at least partially answer this question (see Kleifgen, 1985; Wesche and Ready, 1985; Richard-Amato, 1984).

features (Tarone, 1981; Ellis, 1985). As Ellis concludes on the basis of his nine-month study of an ESL teacher's interactions with two pupils,

> Different features may aid development at different times. For instance, in his study of T-P [teacher-pupil] interactions, teacher self-repetitions were more frequent at an early stage of development, and teacher expansions at a later stage. Also the context of activity in which interaction takes place is characterized by a dynamic, utterance-by-utterance adjustment by both partners in the conversation. Both the learner and the native speaker adjust their behavior in the light of the continuous feedback about the success of the discourse with which they provide each other (1985, p. 82).

Accommodation is often motivated by the students themselves. In the Western world, in particular, beginners in the target language are often asked to perform beyond their levels of proficiency by the teacher. Then the teacher helps ensure success by offering the necessary accommodation during the performance. (Poole, 1992; Ochs and Schiefflin, R., 1984).

In addition, Pica (1988) found in her study of negotiation for meaning that nonnative speakers often shape their utterances toward target norms when they realize that they are not being understood. They are frequently assisted by the native speakers with whom they are interacting who tend to modify their interlanguage for them by saying things such as, "Is this what you mean?" followed by a restatement.

The following sample dialogue illustrates the negotiation of meaning in a one-to-one communication situation. In this kind of collaboration between student and teacher or student and a more advanced peer, the "stretching" to higher levels of development becomes more obvious.

STUDENT: I throw it—box. (He points to a box on the floor.)
TEACHER: You threw the box.
STUDENT: No, I threw *in* the box.
TEACHER: What did you throw in the box?
STUDENT: My . . . I paint . . .
TEACHER: Your painting?
STUDENT: Painting?
TEACHER: You know . . . painting. (The teacher makes painting movements on an imaginary paper.)
STUDENT: Yes, painting.
TEACHER: You threw your painting in the box.
STUDENT: Yes, I threw my painting in box.

The teacher is speaking near the student's $i + 1$ and is providing scaffolds upon which the student can build. The conversation is about the immediate environment. The vocabulary is simple. Repetitions are frequent. Acting out is used. All in response to the feedback. The focus is on the meaning as opposed to the form. Correct forms are being acquired not by the process of direct correction, but through the content and the process of indirect correction or modeling. Notice that *throw* in the student's speech becomes *threw, in* is incorporated into the prepositional phrase, and the article *the* is picked up before *box* but then lost again. It will probably take a lot more comprehensible input containing these forms before they become firmly established in the student's acquisition store.

Thus the grammar is being acquired through the natural process of communication. A conscious use of grammatical sequencing does not appear to be necessary. Similar conclusions are borne out by many others (Long, Adams, McLean, and Castanos, 1976; d'Angeljan, 1978; Krashen, 1982; Hatch, 1983; B. Taylor, 1983; Hammond, 1988; Ioup, Boustagui, El Tigi, and Moselle, 1994).

There are those who insist that in order to acquire acceptable forms of the target language, learners must focus first on instructed grammar rules and only second on communication (see especially Higgs and Clifford, 1982).

In their frequently cited article, Higgs and Clifford claim that students in communicative foreign language courses in which grammar is expected to be acquired inductively through interactive processes become victims of early fossilization from which they are unlikely to recover. However, upon closer examination, their report presents no evidence that sufficiently supports this conclusion. In addition, the courses upon which their study is based are only vaguely referred to and not described. Even more troublesome is that it is not clear how *fossilization* is being defined. We do know that in order for their language to fossilize, students need to be moving through an interlanguage process to begin with which requires interaction. If they reach a plateau and stay there, we say their language has fossilized (see also pages 28–29). In order to determine whether fossilization has indeed occurred requires longitudinal studies that cover several years. Errors by themselves do not tell us much. It is the pattern of errors over time that is revealing.

Similar problems often can be found in second-language acquisition research; lack of adequate definition of one or more key concepts; the use of cross-sectional designs, measuring what students can do at a specified point in time, instead of longitudinal ones which reveal long-term effects and stages of development; and a paucity of description and documentation of the instruction, communicative events, and/or the discourse upon which the studies are based. Moreover, many of the studies which compare an instructed-grammar environment with a naturalistic environment equate the first with classroom learning and the second with street learning. Of course, the classroom will usually come out best considering that it is often very difficult to receive comprehensible input in the street, and the linguistic models there may not be speakers of a standard variety. The common failure of street learning is often used to derogate classrooms which are associated with "communication first." A giant leap indeed.

What we need to do, it seems to me, is compare instructed classrooms with natural classrooms if we want to find out what is going on in each. But even this would be a bit simplistic in that no one classroom would be or could be completely one or the other.

Moreover, individual learners draw from a variety of sources of which neither the teacher nor the researcher may be aware. For example, a communicative event might be consciously analyzed by the learner for its grammatical qualities; an instructed grammar event might be of value to a specific individual only in that it presents comprehensible input. It may be of greater benefit for us to refine our studies by looking at various types of grammar instruction, the timing of the instruction, learner strategies, and so forth, in relation to their effects on the interlanguage process. Studies of this type, although highly complex, would be far more valuable to informed decisions about using instructed grammar in the second- and foreign-language classroom.

WHEN INSTRUCTED GRAMMAR MIGHT HELP

While instructed grammar is not considered generally to be the most important contributor to interlanguage development and while the order of the stages of development appears not to be affected to any great extent by instructed grammar (Van Patten, 1986; Lightbrown, 1983; Pienemann, 1984), there is some evidence that a judicious use of it may be helpful in the following ways: (1) students, by knowing certain rules, may be more likely to "notice the gap" between their own output and the input they receive (Schmidt, 1990), (2) students may benefit, at least for the short term, from simple rules such as plural *s* and third-person singular *s* (Pica, 1983; Pienemann, 1984), (3) in general, learned rules seem to feed into something similar to what Krashen refers to as the monitor which can then be used when planning output (either written or oral) and while taking grammar tests (Kadia, 1988; Zobl, 1985).

There may be other benefits as well of a judicious use of instructed grammar. Rutherford and Sharwood-Smith (1988) theorize that instructed grammar can result in *consciousness raising* which they define as " . . . a deliberate attempt to draw the learner's attention specifically to the formal properties of the target language" (page 107). By noticing not only the gap between what they say and what they hear, but also *how* things are said, learners can (when time allows it) consciously plan their utterances. Fotis and Ellis (1991) hypothesized that these utterances can then serve as input upon which learners can internalize grammar rules. In addition, Fotis and Ellis feel that knowing about a structure may make it more salient to begin with and therefore easier to internalize. However, they suggest that, at the present time, the main goal of instructed grammar be to increase *explicit* knowledge rather than to increase *implicit* knowledge where its role is not clearly understood.

Some researchers feel that instructed grammar increases the rate of acquisition for some structures (Doughty, 1991; Pienemann, 1984; Weslander and Stephany, 1983; Gass, 1982) and that there may be long-term benefits for acquisition in general (Long, 1988). To support the latter, Long points to Pavesi (1984) who found that instructed learners seemed to reach higher levels of attainment in their second language than did the uninstructed learners. However, this finding was weakened by Pavesi's own conclusion that the results may have been due to the fact that the instructed learners had received more elaborated and richer input than did the uninstructed learners.

Cultural expectations are often mentioned too in discussions about instructed grammar. For example, Celce-Murcia (1991) reminds us that students may ". . .demand some grammar because of cultural expectations regarding what constitutes language instruction" (p. 463). She goes on to say that even though they may not benefit linguistically from such instruction, because their cultural expectations have been satisfied to some extent, they may be more accepting of other kinds of activities.

Concerning foreign-language teaching in particular, Terrell (1991) proposed some areas (most have already been mentioned) in which instructed grammar might be beneficial. He hypothesized that instructed grammar may hasten parts of the interlanguage process for those who are only exposed to the target language for very short periods of time each day (which is typical of foreign-language teaching with the exception of immersion situations). However, it is possible that exposing students to even less interactional opportunity and more instructed grammar may be counterproductive, considering that time spent in class may be very limited. On the other hand, if the instruction in grammar is well-timed and based on individual needs (see Pienemann's hypothesis below), it may, in reality, further interlanguage development rather than hinder it.

Perhaps some of the most exciting research in the area of instructed grammar that holds great possibilities for future study comes from Pienemann, who developed the Learnability/Teachability Hypothesis. This hypothesis states that instructed grammar may help the learner progress but *only* if the learner is developmentally ready to incorporate the structure(s) taught. He does not believe that we "squirrel away" rules only to pull them out and apply them later.

He found evidence supporting this hypothesis in his 1984 study of five Italian children learning German as a second language. The children were instructed in the use of inversion. The two learners who had reached the stage prior to inversion in their interlanguage did, in fact, learn it; the three who had not yet reached that stage did not. Then, in 1988 he replicated the study with twelve university students of German as a second language and found similar results: Those who were ready learned the structure. In addition, data gathered from the spontaneous language samples of three informants over the period of one year indicated that their interlanguage development did not coincide with the structures they were being taught in the German course they were taking (Pienemann, 1983). It was concluded that because they were not developmentally ready for structures when they were taught, they did not incorporate them into their repertoire of language.

Deciding *when* the time is right for instruction concerning a specific form or rule seems to be critical if it is to be attempted at all. A knowledge of the process involved in acquiring particular structures is certain to be of value to teachers making decisions about what the student may or may not be ready for. Although we already know something about the process involved with negation, question formation, and relative clause formation (see pages 24 and 28), we have much to learn about what happens during interlanguage development and the structures about which we can verbalize rules.

It is possible that someday we will have computer programs into which we can feed data for analysis. These programs, if properly designed, may be able to help us determine which structures our students are struggling with (or perhaps avoiding) and which they may be ready for. Such programs may even be able to suggest possible courses of action in each case. Even if we can eventually use computer programs to assist us in determining when the time is right, in the final analysis, it is the teacher who needs to decide. It should be remembered, too, that such analysis will never be an exact science. There are too many factors involved, many of which have to do with affect: motivation, attitude, level of anxiety, and so on (see Chapter 5).

One strategy that presently holds promise in identifying structures for which the students may be ready is teacher-generated error analysis (see pages 26 and 28). What structures are the students trying to use in their output, both oral and written? Are the mistakes variable? Sometimes work with specific structures will be valuable to learners who might use them following appropriate instruction or after considerable exposure to input containing them.

Of course, the structures for which the students are deemed ready are going to be different for different learners. Once some of these structures are determined and considered teachable, small groups could be formed of students for whom work with a particular rule might help. Other rules could be worked on by individuals. What all of this means, is that we, as teachers, can no longer rely on a single grammatical syllabus for everyone. There will have to be as many grammatical syllabi as there are students. What I am proposing here is an *individual grammatical syllabus* for each student which must change as the student changes. Some may not need grammatical instruction at all; others may need and will be able to benefit from considerable work with rule application as new forms begin to emerge. It is important, however, that students spend enough of their time in interactive activities within a rich environment in order to develop an interlanguage to begin with. Without that, the rules, no matter how well they are taught, will not be relevant to the language acquisition process.

It is important also to remember that most of language cannot be reduced to teachable rules. Consider for example the uses of what appear to be very simple concepts in English: *in* and *on*. We say *in* the car. When we say *on* the car, we mean *on top of* the car. But yet we say *on* the boat which means *in* the boat, if it has a roof. To get even more complex, we say *on* the ceiling. Using logic, one would think we mean *on top of* the ceiling. However, what we mean is *under* the ceiling and *attached to* it. Although there are rules governing these differences, they are for the most part subconscious. When we try to verbalize them, we generally get into trouble. *The rules governing much of language can only be internalized through a complex interactional process.*

It is obvious that a great deal more research needs to be done before we can make informed decisions in the area of instructed grammar and its role in the language classroom. But perhaps we are at least beginning to ask the right questions concerning to whom, what, when, and how grammar should be taught. Perhaps the most critical question of all is what long-term effects does grammar instruction have on the language acquisition process? Only through longitudinal research will we ever even come close to gaining insights into this question.

THE ROLE OF OUTPUT IN THE ACQUISITION PROCESS

Just as the role of instructed grammar is controversial as it relates to the second-language acquisition process, so is the role of output, but to a lesser degree. Krashen (1985) minimizes the role of output. He reminds us that language can be acquired simply by comprehending input. He argues particularly against those who believe that output is used for hypothesis testing, a process by which the learner tries out new structures in discourse and acquires a specific rule, provided enough positive responses are received. He feels that second-language learners test hypotheses, not through the use of output, but by subconsciously matching forms in the input to their own notions about the language. Of course, he does admit that full two-way communication, because it necessitates more negotiation of meaning, results in more comprehensible input.

Swain (1985) prefers to take a stronger stand for the importance of the role of output in the acquisition process. In fact, she argues that among other functions, output *is* a significant way to test out hypotheses about the target language (also see Corder, 1967 and Seliger, discussed earlier in this chapter). She concludes, on the basis of her study of English-speaking children in a French immersion program:

> Comprehensible output . . . is a necessary mechanism of acquisition independent of the role of comprehensible input. Its role is, at minimum, to provide opportunities for contextualized, meaningful use, to test out hypotheses about the target language, and to move the learner from a purely semantic analysis of language to a syntactic analysis of it (1985, p. 252).

She found that although immersion students comprehended what their teachers said and focused on meaning, they were still not fully acquiring the syntactic system of French. She agrees with those who suggest that "it is not input *per se* that is important to second-language acquisition but input that occurs in interaction where meaning is negotiated" (1985, p. 246). Simply knowing that one will eventually be expected to produce may be the "trigger that forces the learner to pay attention to the means of expressions needed in order to successfully convey his or her own intended meaning" (1985, p. 249). Obviously, there is less chance to give output in subject-matter classes in which the teachers do most of the talking and the students do the listening. She feels that the grammatical development of immersion students will suffer because of their relatively limited opportunity to interact. Output has a much greater role than simply to provide more comprehensible input. She is convinced that when the second-language student receives negative input in the form of confirmation checks and other repairs, he or she is given impetus to seek alternative ways to get the meaning across.

Once the meaning has been negotiated, it becomes possible for the student during similar future exchanges to "move from semantic processing to syntactic processing" (1985, p. 249). In other words, once the meaning is understood, the learner is free to focus on form within the interactional situation. Swain laments the fact that in addition to their opportunities for output being limited, immersion students appear to be satisfied with their strategies for getting meaning across, since they are readily understood by those around them. In her words, "There appears to be little social or cognitive pressure to produce language that reflects more appropriately or precisely their intended meaning; there is no push to be more comprehensible than they already are" (1985, p. 249).

If Swain is right, then output is more than just a means for receiving more comprehensible input. It is important to the acquisition process itself.

LEARNING STRATEGIES

Critical also to the language acquisition process are learning strategies.[7] Usually learning strategies are applied spontaneously and they often (but not always) come to us naturally as the situation demands. However, there are times when such strategies are applied methodically after having been learned from others (the teacher, a book, other language learners) or through deliberate trial-and-error procedures. These strategies, if used often enough, may eventually become spontaneous.

---

[7] In the literature on learning strategies, some researchers distinguish between strategies and tactics (see especially Seliger, 1991; Oxford and Cohen, 1992). Strategies are the more general category under which tactics (specific behaviors or devices) fall. For the purpose of this discussion, the word *strategies* will refer to both general and specific behaviors.

The strategies our students choose to use will generally be consonant with their learning styles,[8] personalities, and cultural backgrounds. For example, students who are high-risk takers and for whom being assertive is acceptable culturally will be more willing to use overt strategies such as seeking out people (even strangers) with whom they can interact, purposely steering the discourse in ways that are beneficial; asking questions, even though some sort of disapproval might result; and so forth.

Steve Wilke, a Californian who moved to Indonesia with his family, demonstrates characteristics of a high-risk taker. Upon the recommendations of a "how to" book he had read prior to leaving, he took very deliberate steps to be exposed to the kind of language he felt he needed in order to learn Indonesian. First he found an Indonesian family with whom he and his own family could live. Then he employed a language helper with whom he could communicate and who would help him in his quest for comprehensible input. Closely following the advice of the book, he first memorized short chunks of dialogue and forced himself to use these chunks with neighbors whom he had not yet met. He would begin with something like, "Good morning (in Indonesian it translates into 'safe morning') My name is Steve. What's your name?" Later, he sought the input of shop owners and even total strangers on the street. Often he would tape his interactions with them and afterwards he would meet with his language helper to have a debriefing session, and make observations about the structures he had learned and the hypotheses he had tested. He then recorded language items he wanted to remember (lexical items, structures, etc.) along with his experiences and reactions in his language learning journal. Although the Indonesians exposed to his planned eccentricity thought he was "a crazy Westerner," most of them went along with his antics and began to look forward to talking with him. Before too long, his circle of Indonesian friends and acquaintances began to widen rapidly. His conversational skills grew and eventually he was able to rent a house of his own and even purchase a car, using his newly developed language.

While many people might be reticent to pursue language goals in this way, they might feel comfortable with some of the strategies used: making friends with native speakers of the language, seeking a language helper, debriefing after participation in interactional situations, keeping notes in a journal, and so forth.

O'Malley and Chamot (1990) have helped to organize the myriad of strategies available to language learners by identifying and describing three major categories:

1. *Metacognitive strategies.* Self-regulatory strategies that help students to plan, monitor, and self-evaluate.
2. *Cognitive strategies.* Task-appropriate strategies that help students to actively manipulate the content or skills they are learning.

---

[8] Cognitive style relates closely to matters of culture and personality: high risk/low risk, cooperative/competitive, and so forth (see Chapter 5). It includes sensory modality preferences (auditory, visual, tactile-kinesthetic, etc.), field-dependence/independence, etc. (see Scarcella, 1990).

3. *Social and affective strategies.* Communicative and self-control strategies that help students to interact with others to enhance learning or control their own affective states.

A metacognitive strategy might be to be in control of one's own learning; a cognitive strategy might be to write down key ideas during a lecture; a social or affective strategy might be to use self-talk to lower anxiety. The authors are convinced that, through direct instruction, students can use such strategies, maintain them over time, and transfer them to new tasks when it is beneficial to do so (p. 499). Chamot (1990) states that students need to have experience with a variety of strategies in order that they may choose those that work best for them. She recommends that strategy instruction start at beginning levels by providing it in the students' first languages and that it be integrated within the curriculum rather than taught as a separate entity. She goes on to say that teachers should identify the strategies by name, describe them, and model them. Students who are not doing as well as they should be in the language learning process should be assured that their apparent failure is probably not due to a deficiency in intelligence but rather to a lack of appropriate strategies.

Oxford (1990) has developed a strategy inventory for students learning English that may be useful in helping to identify a few areas that may need focus. Similar inventories could be developed in any language and used in any situation in which they would be culturally appropriate. The students are to tell how true specific statements about strategies are for them. Here are just a few of the items to which they are asked to respond:

I actively seek out opportunities to talk with native speakers of English.
I ask for help from English speakers.
I try to relax whenever I feel afraid of using English.
I look for opportunities to read as much as possible in English.
I try not to translate word-for-word.
I say or write new English words several times, etc.

Just the survey itself may be enough to make students aware of many strategies that they can incorporate into their language learning practices. Other strategies may need to be expanded, modeled, and practiced before they can be incorporated.

Here I offer a few strategies that teachers may want to share and discuss with their students. They are categorized by skill area. The teacher may want to translate them into the students' first languages so they can benefit by using many of them right from the start.

LISTENING

- Focus attention as completely as possible on what is being said.
- Relax and let the ideas flow into your mind.
- Don't be upset if you don't understand everything.
- Relate what you hear to what you already know.
- Listen for key words and ideas.
- Look for overall meaning.
- Try not to be afraid to ask relevant questions about meaning when it is appropriate.
- Make guesses about what is being said.
- In conversation, check out your guesses by using confirmation checks (Is this what you are saying?, etc.).
- Whenever possible, pay attention to the forms fluent speakers of the target language are using (Do they match your own?).
- Keep a notebook to write down what you have learned, new words, meanings, concepts, structures, idioms, etc.

SPEAKING

- Think about what you are going to say.
- Think about the structures you are using but do not let them interfere with what you want to say.
- Do not be afraid to make mistakes (mistakes are normal as you are learning the language).
- When you are not understood, use repetition, gestures, synonyms, definitions, examples, acting out, whatever comes naturally as you begin to feel more proficient in the language, occasionally record on cassette and transcribe (write down) the interactions you have with fluent speakers (ask their permission, of course); afterwards, analyze the interaction (What was successful? Were there any breakdowns in communication? If so, what happened? Did you or your partner use any repair strategies to get back on track? Did you notice any errors?, etc.).[9] Ask your teacher or a peer to help you analyze the discourse.

---

[9] This idea was adapted from one that was described by Heidi Riggenbach during a presentation she gave at the Summer TESOL Institute in San Bernardino, California, 1993.

PRONUNCIATION

- Seek interactional opportunities with fluent speakers.
- Pay attention to the rhythm, intonation, and stress of fluent speakers.
- Realize that you will not always be understood (keep trying).
- Ask for modeling when desired and appropriate.
- Rehearse (make up a little song or chant—have fun with the language)
- Learn to self-monitor.
- You might want to use computer programs which can give you visual images of your speech (see Pennington, 1989).

Note: Not all students will desire nativelike pronunciation. Some will prefer to maintain certain prosodic elements of the first language in their speech, perhaps to retain identity with the first language culture (Morley, 1991) or for other reasons.

READING

- See what the reading material is about (look the text over; think about the title/subtitles; notice the pictures—if there are any), etc.
- Try to imagine what you might learn from the text.
- While you read, relax and feel the words and sentences flow together.
- Question yourself as you read (What is the author trying to say here? How does it relate to what you already know? What does it have to do with what the author has just said? What might come next?).
- Do not stop reading each time you find an unfamiliar word or phrase (the meaning may come as you read further).
- If a word seems critical but the meaning is not coming clear as you read further, check the glossary (if there is one) or look in a dictionary.
- You may want to talk about a new concept or phrase with a peer or the teacher.
- Make a note of any parts you do not understand; you can return later and reread for better understanding (Are the parts you, at first, did not understand more clear to you now? If not, discuss with a peer or the teacher.)
- Think about what you learned from the text; discuss it; write about it.

VOCABULARY DEVELOPMENT

- Make your own word bank or dictionary, using only those lexical items that you think will be useful to you.
- Group lexical items into logical categories.
- Use semantic maps or clustering to show relationships.[10]
- Try to focus on the units (or chunks) of meaning rather than only on individual words (see what other words are used with the lexical item).
- Use various dictionaries including bilingual ones.
- Use the new words or phrases in your own contexts.

WRITING

- Find out as much as you can about your topic.
- Brainstorm for ideas (discuss with peers, the teacher, family members, and others in the school or in your community).
- Make a plan; map out or cluster your ideas.
- Think about the structures you are using but do not let them interfere with what you want to say.
- Begin writing (do not worry about making mistakes); let your ideas flow.
- Rewrite making whatever changes seem necessary.
- Think of writing as a process through which the product develops gradually.
- Consult with peers, your teacher, etc.
- Rewrite and consult as many times as necessary.
- Share your writing with others.

Although the above lists may be useful to many students, it is important to remember that most strategies are too complex to be reduced to lists. Moreover, we must not assume that our students are not metacognitively aware. All one has to do is listen to students' conversations about what they are doing to find that they indeed are aware. Even children have very complex ways of self-regulation that they can often verbalize. It may be wise to ask students to share with others some of the strategies they use. In addition, after a task is completed, a debriefing session could be extremely valuable in focusing students on their strategies and providing them with the opportunity to learn from each other. Questions such as what did you do to get started or what helped you remember that, and so forth, can be used to stimulate discussion.

It is important that a focus on strategies not be so extensive or intrusive as to interfere with learning. Sometimes too much emphasis on strategies causes

---

[10]See example on p. 210.

students to lose the meaning of *what* they are learning as they become focused on *how* they are learning it. Furthermore, practice with strategies that may be inappropriate culturally (see especially LoCastro, 1994), or that students may not be ready for or do not need, could be a waste of precious time. On the other hand, instruction in strategies that is well timed and suited to the needs of the students can make a noticeable difference in the way they approach learning a second language.

SUMMARY

Vygotsky's Zone of Proximal Development and Krashen's $i + 1$ are similar concepts, both offering insights into the cognitive processes involved in language acquisition. Contrary to Piaget, who proposed one level of cognitive development, Vygotsky and Krashen implied two levels: an actual level and a potential level. While Vygotsky stressed the *importance* of social interaction, Krashen stressed the *nature* of the input.

The pivotal role of social interaction in second-language acquisition is supported by the following: John-Steiner's conclusions based on a study involving Finnish immigrant children in Sweden and on a study done by Lilly Wong-Fillmore of Mexican immigrant children in the United States; Seliger's research on the role of interaction in an intermediate English class at Queens College, C.U.N.Y.; Schumann's conclusions based on the Heidelberg Project; and Carroll's study of foreign-language students at several universities.

The nature of input is described not only by Krashen but by Brown, Cazden, and Bellugi, in addition to the many others who have looked at motherese and found that it emphasizes meaning rather than form. Applying this knowledge to second-language acquisition in the classroom, Sutherland and Yorio address the accuracy-versus-fluency controversy and its relative significance in instruction. Sutherland feels that the two should not be dealt with simultaneously at beginning levels, at which fluency should be the chief concern. Yorio addresses accuracy and offers some suggestions for dealing with systematic (not random) errors in the student's output.

Although the chapter focuses on the role of input in the interaction, that of output must not be ignored. Output can play a substantial part in the acquisition process. It not only aids in receiving comprehensible input, it offers opportunities for practice and appears to be an important means for testing hypotheses.

If Pienemann's learnability/teachability hypothesis is correct, instructed grammar can aid in the process of language acquisition, but only if the learner is developmentally ready to incorporate what is taught. Instruction in learning strategies, too, can be of benefit if it is well timed, suited to the students' needs, and is consonant with the students' cognitive styles and cultural expectations.

READINGS, REFLECTION, AND DISCUSSION

Suggested Readings and Reference Materials

Allwright, D., and Bailey, K. (1991). *Focus on the language classroom: An introduction to classroom research for language teachers.* Cambridge: Cambridge University. The goal of this book, according to the authors, was to demonstrate the relevancy of classroom research for teachers. In this effort it was successful. Particularly well developed and enlightening is the section on the treatment of oral errors. Other topics include input, interaction, and receptivity to the teacher, the methodology, peers, course content, and teaching materials.

Krashen, S. (1985). *The input hypothesis: Issues and implications.* London: Longman. In this book Krashen discusses the input hypothesis and its ramifications, including supporting evidence, the challenges it has faced, and its implications for teaching second languages.

Mehan, H. (1979). *Learning lessons.* Cambridge, Mass.: Harvard University. A fascinating, in-depth study of the structure of classroom interaction and the interdependence of its participants. The classroom is viewed as a "community" in which the members perform their roles to carry out its functions.

Oxford, R. (1990). *Language learning strategies: What every teacher should know.* New York: Newbury House. Here Oxford elaborates upon language learning strategies, both general and specific. Her analysis includes the naming, description, and application of learning strategies as well as strategy assessment and training.

Tharp, R., and Gallimore, R. (1988). *Rousing minds to life. Teaching, learning, and schooling in social context.* Cambridge: Cambridge University. Vygotsky's theories, particularly the Zone of Proximal Development, are explored within a comprehensive theory of education. Included are applications to the teaching of language and literacy.

Vygotsky, L. (1978). *Mind in society.* Cambridge, Mass.: Harvard University. Editors M. Cole, V. John-Steiner, S. Scribner, and E. Souberman spent several years compiling this volume of manuscripts and letters that might have been lost to us had it not been for their efforts. The collection highlights and clarifies Vygotsky's theories of the mind and its higher psychological functions.

Wells, G. (1981). *Learning through interaction: The study of language development.* Cambridge: Cambridge University. A valuable collection of papers on language acquisition and its inextricable relationship to interaction. Contains many examples of actual discourse between children and their caretakers. Identifies key communication strategies.

Questions for Reflection and Discussion

1. Considering Vygotsky's ideas with regard to learning and development, what do you think his reaction would be to the following:
   a. Homogeneous ability grouping for most activities
   b. A focus on audiolingual drill

c. An individualized program approach in which an individual works alone at his or her own rate

2. After visits to several beginning to early intermediate second- or foreign-language classrooms, answer the following questions:
   a. In which classrooms were the lessons focused on grammar?
   b. In which classrooms was meaningful interaction the focus?
   c. Did you notice any differences in student attitude between those involved in one type of lesson and those in another?

3. According to Freire, the relationship between teacher and student should be dialectical. What kind of classroom environment might foster this relationship? What sorts of activities might take place in such a classroom?

4. How, in your opinion, should student errors be handled in the classroom? Have your views changed now that you have read this chapter? Consider the following:
   a. Level of student proficiency
   b. The age of the student
   c. Systematic versus random errors
   d. Correction of oral versus written output

5. Do you see any parallel between Pienemann's Learnability/Teachability Hypothesis and Vygotsky's Zone of Proximal Development? If so, explain.

6. React to Macnamara's (1983) condemnation of language teachers in the quote:

   > Language is a particular embarrassment to the teacher, because outside school, children seem to learn a language without any difficulty, whereas in school with the aid of teachers their progress is halting and unsatisfactory.

   Assume that all the children to whom he is referring are learning a second language and are approximately the same age. If his statement has credibility in your opinion, give some possible explanations.

7. In your opinion, is there a place for the explicit teaching of grammar rules in the second-language classroom? If so, address the following questions and relate your discussion to the particular language you teach. Which rules would you teach? To whom? When? Under what conditions? How? Would it make any difference if the language is being taught in a second-language situation as opposed to a foreign-language situation? Explain.

8. If you have attempted to learn another language, what strategies did you use that you were aware of? Share a few of them with a small group. How effective do you think they were?

CHAPTER 4

Literacy Development and Skills Integration

> *. . . what people learn when they learn language is not separate parts (words, sounds, sentences) but a supersystem of social practices whose conventions and systematicity both constrain and liberate.*
>
> C. Edelsky, 1993

QUESTIONS TO THINK ABOUT

1. Think about your own experiences with learning to read and write in your first language. What do you remember about them? Were your experiences mainly positive? Do you have any negative recollections about them?

2. Now reflect upon experiences you may have had developing literacy in another language. Were they mainly positive? Why or why not?

3. Do you think there is a "natural" way to teach reading and writing? If so, what might it look like? How might it be different from other ways of teaching literacy?

4. To what extent is it wise to integrate reading, writing, listening, and speaking in the language classroom? How might you go about it?

Developing literacy and other abilities in a second or foreign language should involve students in very positive, authentic, and highly motivating experiences. It is when learning a language is equated with the mastery of separate sets of skills and subskills that students often run into difficulty. For example, learning to read in a first or second language is not a matter of stringing phonemes into words and words into phrases and sentences and so on. It is also not a matter of practicing such skills as scanning and skimming. K. Goodman in his article entitled "Acquiring Literacy Is Natural: Who Skilled Cock Robin" asserts:

> There is a comfort and orderliness that appeals to teachers in sequential skill hierarchies. They particularly lend themselves to very formal and structured classrooms. But the emptiness of such hierarchies and irrelevance to actual development in reading is observable in any skill-oriented classroom. In such classrooms, there are always two kinds of learners; one kind do well on the skill drills because they have enough control of the reading process to deal with the parts within the wholes. They don't need the skill instruction. The second kind have great difficulty with the sequenced skills because they are dealing with them as abstractions outside of the meaningful language process. Such learners can't profit from skill instruction unless they can transcend it and find their way to meaning on their own (1982, p. 247).

A NATURAL LANGUAGE FRAMEWORK

A natural language framework, frequently referred to in the literature as "whole language," has gained momentum in recent years. Learning to read in a first or second language is generally a matter of wanting to make sense of text.

Readers may have to be reminded that they need not understand every word and that trying to do so may interfere with their understanding. However, under normal conditions the reader is not even consciously aware that he or she is skimming or scanning or reading intensively. These are strategies that come naturally as the situation demands. Yet many exercises require that the reader learn the skills additively even if it means putting off a search for meaning until later. As F. Smith so aptly put it, "Programmed instruction can often be viewed as the systematic deprivation of information" (1982, p. 188). It is important to remember that reading can be as much part of the natural communication process as speaking and writing. It, too, is an active, creative process, not a passive one as has been commonly thought. Goodman reminds us:

> If you understand and respect language, if you understand that language is rule governed, that the most remarkable thing about human beings is that they learn a finite set of rules that nobody can teach, making it possible for them to say an infinite number of things, then it is also necessary to understand that you cannot chop language up into little bits and pieces and think

that you can spoon feed it as you would feed pellets to a pigeon or a rat. . .
Language doesn't work that way. . .We have learned a lot of things. One of
those things is that language is learned from whole to part. . . It is when you
take the language away from its use, when you chop it up and break it into
pieces, that it becomes abstract and hard to learn (1982, p. 238).

Goodman, along with many others, was instrumental in developing a
whole language perspective. He describes whole language as "the easy way to
language development." To make his point, he contrasts what makes language
learning easy with what makes it difficult. One might want to look at the two
columns below as ends of a continuum rather than as a dichotomy.

It's easy when:	*It's hard when:*
it's real and natural.	it's artificial.
it's whole.	it's broken into bits and pieces.
it's sensible.	it's nonsense.
it's interesting.	it's dull and uninteresting.
it's relevant.	it's irrelevant to the learner.
it belongs to the learner.	it belongs to somebody else.
it's part of a real event.	it's out of context.
it has social utility.	it has no social value.
it has purpose for the learner.	it has no discernible purpose.
the learner chooses to use it.	it's imposed by someone else.
it's accessible to the learner.	it's inaccessible.
the learner has power to use it.	the learner is powerless.

(Goodman, 1986, p. 8)

Let's first turn our attention to the right-hand column, which is most often
associated with *bottom-up approaches*. These approaches adhere to the idea that
acquiring literacy in a language begins at the most abstract level: sound and letter correspondences, syllables, words, and phrases. Students are expected to
use these as building blocks to move gradually to what is more concrete and
meaningful. Such approaches can be especially devastating for children who
are not yet ready to think metalinguistically. They can also be frustrating for
older learners, who, although they are cognitively highly developed, have not
had other means (i.e., books or other materials of interest) for accessing the
written language.

The left-hand column, on the other hand, is associated with *top-down
approaches*. Here the students are introduced to meaningful language right from
the beginning rather than to abstract bits and pieces. It may be a wordless book
for which the teacher helps the student write a story, using the student's own
words. It may be a short message addressed directly to the student. What child
or adult can resist trying to figure out a message with his or her own name on it?
Through top-down approaches, bits and pieces are internalized as the student

is engaged personally in the reading and writing process. The bits and pieces are learned as they are needed.

Unfortunately, some persons assume that whole language advocates are against bottom-up processing. Such an assumption is unfounded and misleading. It is approaches that *focus* on bottom-up processing to the exclusion of meaningful literacy events that they are against, not the process itself. They generally recognize the interaction between top-down and bottom-up processing and the importance of that interaction. As Edelsky, Altwerger, and Flores (1991) remind us, "Whole language teachers *do* teach children how to spell words they are using, *do* teach appropriate punctuation for letters children are writing, *do* teach strategies for sounding out particular combinations of letters under particular circumstances" (p. 38). However, what is taught and when may be different for each reader depending upon the task, the situation, and individual needs. It is interesting to note also that, according to Altwerger and Resta (1986), many good readers are not good at skills exercises and many poor readers are. What seems critical here is that developing readers be involved in *authentic* reading/writing activities that are meaningful (see Chapter 12 for descriptions of such activities).

SKILLS INTEGRATION

Within a natural language framework, integrating the four skills (listening, speaking, reading, and writing) is not difficult.[1] It should come as naturally for the teacher as it does for the students. See Figure 4.1. When one is listening, opportunities for writing evolve. When one is reading, opportunities for speaking make themselves felt. Flowing with these opportunities involves the kind of flexibility necessary to allow the skills to grow naturally. Often impetus for skill development comes from a need of the moment. For example, students may find themselves in situations in which writing is required to fulfill immediate obligations. For the foreign-language student in the later elementary grades or beyond, it may be that a response to a letter from a foreign pen pal is urgent. For a second-language student at the adult or secondary level it may be a job application that must be filled out in the target language. In these situations, the student cannot wait until the later stages in the language development process begin to emerge. The teacher and/or peers can aid the students in fulfilling these obligations. With guidance, students will frequently find themselves performing far above levels for which they are supposed to be "ready."

Integration can take place right from the beginning without causing an undue overload on the student's mental capabilities. Even during the silent

---

[1] The assumption is made here that the goal of any particular language program is to promote proficiency in all four skills. It should be noted, however, that not all language programs have this as a goal; some may be concerned with only one or two of the skills.

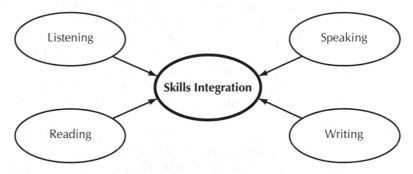

Figure 4.1

period, literacy in the new language can be introduced to second-language students who need to survive in school settings and on the street. Labels on various rooms throughout the school can be made clear, especially the words designating males and females on the lavatory doors. Words for the street are even more important: "stop," "danger," "keep out," and similar ones are crucial for survival. In the foreign-language classroom, labels can be placed on common objects around the room after their oral forms have been acquired or partially acquired. Story experience (see Chapter 10) can be highly motivating for beginners at any age, since it allows students to participate in a rich language environment even before they can utter a word in the target language. Later simple stories with accompanying pictures (see the same chapter) can be read in both second- and foreign-language classes. Speech development may be accelerated simply through the excitement of involvement in a character's conflict. Natural curiosity may push the students into higher and higher levels of communication, incorporating all the skills of which they are capable. If the teacher is there to take advantage of the *natural curiosity phenomenon,* he or she can guide the student in reading and writing far beyond what might have been considered possible in the traditional teacher-oriented, inflexibly structured classroom.

Before students begin to speak, they will already have begun their transition into literacy through their exposure to labels and other pieces of written language necessary for survival. At this point, it is important to let the reading and writing skills come, not only from simple, highly motivating reading materials, but from the students' own experiences and through the vocabulary and structures with which they are already familiar. Some strategies that seem to work particularly well with students of all ages who are cognitively able to handle literacy are associated with the "language-experience approach" (see Chapter 12). An adaptation of this approach may begin with a planned or spontaneous experience that the students all have in common (a story, a song, a picture, a trip to the local shopping center). After the experience, the students brainstorm while the teacher writes key words on the board or on a transparency. In some versions, each student then contributes to a group story or paragraph that is written by the teacher for all to see. Students can then read what has been written aloud as a group and copy it into their notebooks. Over a period of time, students can begin to read and write simple, short texts somewhat independently as they move to higher stages in the language acquisition process. Other helpful transitions are the matrices (see page 140), charts (see pages 139, 153, and 209), and other activities that involve the comprehension of written messages in the target language.

Nonliterates in second-language classes need special attention during the early stages. If possible, they should develop literacy in their primary languages first (if their languages have written traditions) and then apply this knowledge to literacy development in the second language.[2] It has been my experience that the more similar the first language and culture are to those of the target group, the more likely will be the transfer of specific as well as general reading skills. For example, if the L1 is a European language using the Roman alphabet and the L2 is English, specific transfer will probably involve many similarities in sound combinations, the written symbols, punctuation, the movement of the eyes from left to right while reading, and so forth. On the meaning level, specific transfer might involve cognates, organizational patterns, shared cultural knowledge, experiences, and expectancies.

On the other hand, when the language and culture are very different, the transfer appears to be more general. For example, if the L1 is an Asian language using an ideographic writing system, the transfer would tend to be limited to more general elements such as sensory-motor skills; the symbolic nature of written language; attitudes toward the reading process itself; general comprehension skills such as predicting, inferencing, coming to conclusions, etc. (see also Thonis, 1984). However, it must be remembered that knowledge gained in the content areas is always transferable across languages, regardless of the languages involved.

Learning to read in the first language is particularly important for language minority children, in order that their cognitive development not be arrested while they are trying to learn a new language system (Cummins, 1981). Nonliterates for whom an L1 mastery of literacy skills is impossible for whatever reason need to be introduced to the written form of their second language in much the same way that the other students are introduced to it, except that more preliminary work is necessary. The students need first to focus on the symbolic nature of language through such activities as role play (see Chapter 10) or game playing (see Chapter 11). During the course of these activities, objects can be made to represent people or things. The symbols are arbitrary, just as the words on the printed page are arbitrary representations of concepts. In addition, nonliterate students may need considerable exposure to multisensory input in order

---

[2] Note that this probably would not be true for a student in an immersion foreign-language situation (see Related Reading 4).

to develop a rich visual and kinesthetic representational system before they can be eased into literacy. Experience with real books, story experience and charts (both mentioned above), pictures to be labeled, maps, graphs, and actions associated eventually with the written word (such as one finds in the total physical response and the audio-motor unit—see Chapter 7) all form important preliminary steps leading into literacy at any age.

READING AS AN INTERACTIVE PROCESS

The term *interactive* has been used by many to describe the reading process. Some think of it as the interaction between top-down and bottom-up processing within the individual reader (see especially Carrell, Devine, and Eskey, 1988). Others think of it as a series of questions posed by textbook writers to ensure comprehension of a particular reading, as though its meaning were somehow static.

I prefer to think of interactive reading as a process during which meaning is created by the reader (see also Zamel, 1992), not only through interaction with the text, but, in case of the classroom, through interaction with others in the class and in the total school, community, and home environment. Rosenblatt (1985) draws a rather clear distinction between the word *interaction* as used in scientific paradigms and the word *transaction* as she uses it to describe the reading process (see also Dewey and Bentley, 1949). In scientific paradigms, interaction is seen in a mechanistic way involving separate entities acting upon one another but not affecting the nature of each other. She compares the entities to ". . . two billiard balls colliding and then going their separate unchanged ways" (p. 98). Transaction, on the other hand, indicates an ongoing process in which the entities are blended and changed as a result of the interaction. As explained earlier, my own definition and use of the word *interaction* includes a transactional quality. Figure 4.2 on the next page illustrates my conceptualization of reading as an interactive process (Richard-Amato, 1993). The focus of this interactive conceptualization is on the reader: the reader's values, relationships, experiences, prior knowledge, culture, dreams and goals, and expectations (or schema). The reader relates to the text, be it a story, a play, an essay, a novel, a poem, the lyrics to a song, and so forth.[3] Out of this relationship comes a preliminary interpretation or a "created meaning." This interpretation will either be accepted or rejected by the reader, either in part or as a whole, based on interaction with other readers. If

---

[3] Rosenblatt (1985) considers the text itself to be only a ". . . set of verbal signs" that comes into being only through transaction. Although I agree that the transaction gives it life, I believe that the text is more than ink on paper; it is a reflection of the thoughts, feelings, experience, knowledge, etc., of the author at a particular point in time and in a particular social situation.

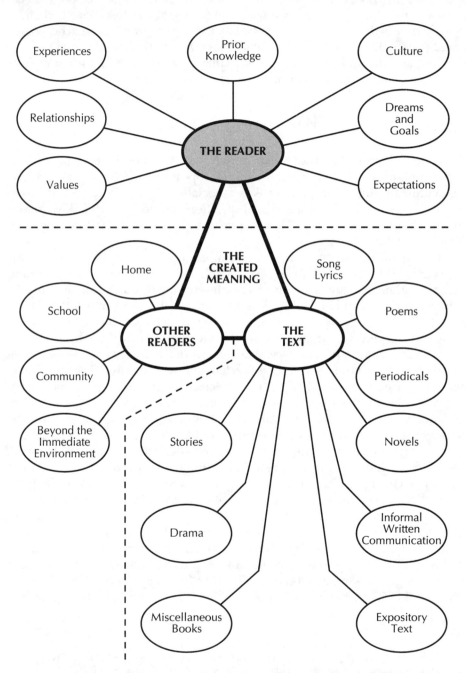

Figure 4.2. Reading as an Interactive Process

there appears to be a mismatch in interpretation, the reader may return to the text to reread or to reanalyze and *recreate* the meaning. All the while, skills are being internalized, hypotheses about the meaning are being tested, expectations are being adjusted, preconceived ideas are being reevaluated, and the student is reaching increasingly higher levels of understanding.

Others, too, have emphasized the role of the reader. For example, the French philosopher, Jacques Derrida (1976, 1981), who developed the deconstructionist point of view, insists that language has no "metaphysics of presence" of its own. In other words, it exists only when some other force gives it meaning. The reader (the "other force") reconstructs its meaning or "rewrites" it in effect.

Although I agree with Derrida's focus on the reader as a key component in the reading process, I am dubious about the way in which he and his followers (see Crowley, 1989, and her references) divide the world. On the one hand, they claim that the *traditional* view of reading should be avoided in that it adheres to rigid forms (e.g., the expository essay, the essay of comparison and contrast, etc.), that it stresses the finality of meaning as established by expert interpretation and the authority of the author. On the other hand, the *deconstructionist* view is presented as the view to embrace in that it focuses on deviating from rigid forms and static meanings and on the importance of reader interpretation as opposed to expert interpretation. While it is not the contrast itself I find questionable, it is the dichotomy they present that seems too simplistically drawn.

Who is to say that teachers should avoid the traditional view out-of-hand? Second- and foreign-language students, especially, may *want* to know about traditional "rigid" forms used in a society that may differ in many ways from their own. They may *want* (and may indeed *need*) to be familiar with conventional models so they can incorporate what they want of them into their own writing. The deconstructionists agree that both reading and writing are communal endeavors. Why then should we as readers and writers disregard the conventions of a particular community for whom we want to write or whose writing we want to understand? In addition, there may be times when readers (both native and nonnative) will want "expert" interpretation. But that does not mean they have to accept it and make it their own. By looking at the two views on a continuum, we can incorporate elements from both perspectives, even though we will undoubtedly lean one way more than the other.

Although the interactive conceptualization of reading presented in this chapter has elements of psycholinguistics (psychological influences within the reader's mind, particularly in respect to the READER component), it is basically a sociolinguistic representation in that the community of learners is the main influence. This is true also of the Interactive Writing Conceptualization presented later. Both representations are very rudimentary in that they do not seek to explain *how* the components work together (perhaps this is their greatest limitation). Instead they mainly identify and show the relationships of influences involved in an interactional process as I am defining it.

FACILITATING THE READING EXPERIENCE

In reading in both second- and foreign-language classes at almost any age level, the teacher can provide motivation by having students make predictions about what they are going to read and by asking questions that relate what they are reading to their own lives and to prior knowledge and experience (see additional elements in the READER component in Figure 4.2). Experiences can be provided to give the students a greater familiarity with new concepts involved in the reading selections. In the later elementary grades and beyond, the teacher can aid understanding by helping the students to map out ideas as they understand them, thus giving the content a graphic dimension (see examples in Chapter 12).

To further aid understanding, questions can be asked that call for reflection and inference. Rather than asking mainly questions requiring factual answers, teachers can ask questions requiring higher-level thinking skills and self-reflection such as those found in the interdependent categories below:

1. Predicting content and outcomes
   - What do you think the story (essay, poem, etc.) will be about? (Refer students to the title, pictures, subheadings, or other clues.)
   - In what sorts of dilemmas do you think the characters might find themselves?
   - What will happen?
2. Relating the text to prior knowledge
   - What does the author claim are the reasons for the occurrences of this incident (effect)?
     —Can you think of other examples in which similar incidents (effects) occurred?
     —What caused them to take place?
   - Are there alternative courses of actions that the author (character) might have pursued?
3. Making inferences and supporting conclusions
   - What is the author attempting to tell us here? (Refer to a specific line, paragraph, event, etc.)
   - How do you think the character (author) feels?
   - Why is the character (author) happy (angry, doubtful, relieved, etc.)?
   - Upon what evidence do you base your conclusions?
4. Relating to self and one's culture
   - What would you have done had you been in a similar situation (dilemma)?
   - Are similar situations (dilemmas) prevalent in your culture? If so, in what manner are they approached?
   - Does this event (fact, opinion) make you angry (glad, fearful)? Explain.

Additional questions can be asked about organizational strategies and patterns, use of literary devices, and whatever else is appropriate to the situation. The students can be asked to generate their own questions to ask one another.

Small-group discussions of readings can allow the students to share ideas within their own classroom community and to test their own hypotheses about what they are reading (see the OTHER READERS component). Because the other readers come to the discussion with their own values, prior knowledge, etc., this kind of activity becomes very potent in an interactive reading process.

Another consideration is the materials themselves (see the TEXT component). They must be of interest and they must be comprehensible semantically and syntactically, with some elements that are a little beyond the students' present levels (see other considerations for materials selection in Chapter 15). Students should be encouraged, too, to select their own materials for independent reading and for small-group participation.

WRITING AS AN INTERACTIVE PROCESS

Although it is artificial to separate writing from reading, for the purpose of this discussion they are considered separately even though their close relationship is evident. Like reading, writing is also an interactive process. See Figure 4.3 on the next page.

The writer (like the reader) brings to the process his or her own values, relationships, experiences, prior knowledge, culture, dreams and goals, and expectations. But, in the case of the writer, we have one additional category: hypotheses about the audience. It is important that the writer anticipate the possible reactions, backgrounds, etc., of those who will be reading and creating meaning out of what is produced.

The second component of the conceptualization in Figure 4.3 includes other writers (and readers) at home, in school (mainly the teacher and peers, some of whom will probably be more advanced) and in the community and beyond. Good writers often consult or conference with other writers to ask for their reactions, comments, and suggestions.

The third component is other texts (written and oral) including stories, drama, essays, novels, poems, formal speeches, informal written communication, song lyrics, periodicals, miscellaneous books, and so on that can serve both as sources of information and as models.

Because the process of writing is an interactive one, the evolving product therefore does not belong solely to the person who produced it; rather it belongs in varying degrees to all influences contributing to its development and to the reader who ultimately determines its meaning on a personal level. Thus, the product is truly reflective of a communal effort.

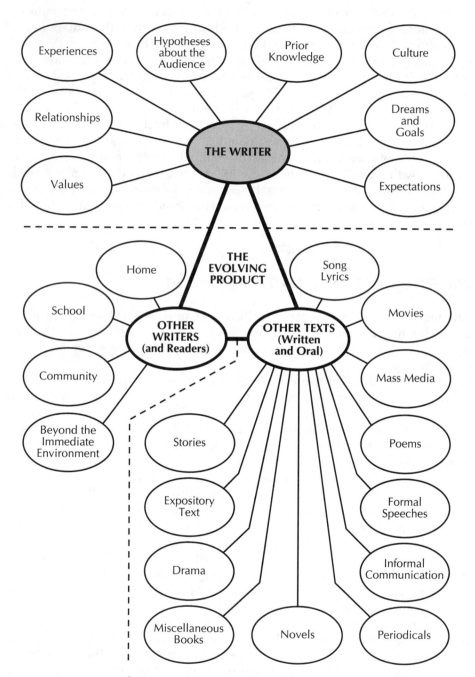

Figure 4.3. Writing as an Interactive Process

FACILITATING THE WRITING EXPERIENCE

When students are writing, motivation can come from numerous sources in second- and foreign-language classes. Experiences with music, poetry, story-telling, role play, drama, and affective activities often provide motivation and can lead into some highly relevant, exciting topics. Students need to begin the writing process with a certain amount of confidence, which can come in part from their exposure to versions of the language experience approach mentioned here and described in more detail in Chapter 12.

The writing itself can be very subjective (letters to pen pals, journal entries, simple poetry) or more objective (lists of various kinds, forms, charts, maps, compositions). The kinds of writing done will depend to a large extent upon the students' ages, needs, and proficiency levels. However, it is generally best to begin with short pieces of writing before proceeding to longer ones.

In all writing, students need to concentrate on the *process* and the evolving *product* simultaneously. Murray explains: ". . . You let the students write. . . Writing must be experienced to be learned" (1982, pp. 115–116). The writing process itself involves brainstorming for topics of interest, gathering information, allowing that information to settle into some sort of overall plan (clustering and other graphic organizers might be useful in planning), putting the words down on paper, consulting with others, and revising.

Revisions are particularly important to the writing process. According to Murray, they provide opportunities for the student to "stand back from the work the way any craftsman does to see what has been done. . . .The most important discoveries are made during the process of revision" (1982, pp. 121–122). Because the effective writer frequently has to pause, go back, reread, rethink, consult with other writers, rewrite, and write some more, he or she must be able to concentrate intensely on the composition without interference from the teacher or others who might want to help. Help may be needed before the actual writing begins in order to stimulate thinking, and again later once the student has had a chance to hammer out at least part of the piece alone. At that point the student can confer with the teacher and/or peers as needed. What points are coming across clearly? Questions can be asked to stimulate further development of ideas. What portions are not readily understood? Strategies can be discussed in an attempt to redress breakdowns in communication. Students then need a chance to reshape the writing if it has not communicated what was intended or if they feel challenged to move in other directions. Dialoguing with other writers, especially peers, can generate a great deal of enthusiasm for the writing process and can motivate thoughts and feelings that might otherwise remain unexplored.

Students need to be reminded that errors are perfectly normal during the writing process. An inductive approach to errors is often the most effective way to deal with them. In later drafts the teacher might underline or lightly circle the word or phrase in which a problem appears and ask the student to try to identify it. Many errors can be related to meaning on a more global level. The teacher can guide by asking pertinent questions. For example, in responding to errors in verb tense the teacher might simply ask *"When did this occur?"* Often the students will recognize the errors themselves without any lengthy explanation or further probing. In addition, if the teacher or the students quietly read aloud the writing during the individual conference sessions, the errors often become more salient and can be corrected more easily. However, sometimes brief explanations are needed in further dialogue with the students to lead them to a better understanding of their errors. Errors should be treated in a matter-of-fact way so that the students don't associate them with the quality of the ideas themselves. In addition it is best not to focus on too many errors at once; much depends upon what the students might be ready for at any given time. For some students, specific activities on recurring errors might help; for others, rewriting and a simple discussion of strategies may be enough to help them improve their writing.

Error correction may sometimes be handled indirectly in writing just as it is with oral production. For example, after students hand in their journals, instead of marking the errors, the teacher may simply react to the entry in the margin by repeating the words that the student has used, but in correct form. Thus, the teacher's comment serves as a model. For example, if the student writes "On Tuesday my mother sick," the teacher might respond with "I'm sorry your mother was sick." This particular type of correction often comes naturally to a teacher focused on the meaning and may work well, especially with reluctant writers during early stages of literacy development.

The teacher at times may want to demonstrate the writing process. By this means, the students can experience vicariously the frustrations and joys that go into writing and at the same time be exposed to the forms and conventions of various types of composition. For example, watching the teacher execute a well-developed paragraph on the board or on a transparency, can be highly motivating as well as instructive. The teacher will have to choose a topic (the students may want to make topic suggestions), brainstorm for ideas, map out a brief preliminary plan, begin a first draft, provide transitions, erase, move materials, modify, consult with the students, rewrite, and use the dictionary. If the teacher does his or her thinking out loud during the process, the students will more fully realize that even the teacher has to struggle to communicate.

It is a good idea to keep a portfolio for each student in which work can be saved so that all concerned can keep abreast of the progress that is taking place (see Chapter 6 for more information on portfolios). Periodic student–teacher evaluative conferences should be held to talk about progress made, strengths observed, and possible future areas of work. Students often find such conferences both informative and encouraging.

SUMMARY

An integrated approach to developing literacy and other learning skills in the target language can be dynamic and exciting in a natural classroom environment. Instrumental to the theoretical underpinnings of a natural language framework has been the whole language movement. This movement is one that has shifted our emphasis away from discrete skills and subskills to the natural processes inherent in learning to read and write for the purpose of communication.

Both reading and writing are interactional processes. My definition of *interactional* goes beyond the scientific use of the term and draws from a transactional perspective. From this perspective, not only does the interaction occur, but the components involved are changed, often in significant ways, by the interaction itself. The components of reading as an interactional process include the reader, other readers, and the text. Out of these the meaning is created. The components of writing as an interactional process include the writer, other writers (and readers), and other texts (both written and oral). Out of these comes the evolving product.

Error correction for developing writers should focus on meaning and go beyond a line-by-line, word-by-word analysis whenever possible. The teacher's modeling of correct forms through the relevant communication is one way to provide indirect correction and can be particularly effective with reluctant writers. By this means, the teacher's communication serves as a scaffold upon which students can build as they move progressively to more advanced levels of proficiency.

READINGS, REFLECTION, AND DISCUSSION

Suggested Readings and Reference Materials

Carson, J. G., and Leni, I., eds., (1993). *Reading in the composition classroom: Second language perspectives*, Boston, Mass.: Heinle and Heinle. This book presents an historical perspective of second-language literacy and an analysis of the issues involved in connecting reading and writing.

Edelsky, C., Altwerger, B., and Flores, B. (1991). *Whole language: What's the difference*. Portsmouth, N.H.: Heinemann. The authors clarify what it means to use a whole language approach to literacy. They discuss how whole language relates to language learning itself, and they challenge some of the practices often disguised as whole language.

Kroll, B. (1990). *Second language writing: Research insights for the classroom*. New York: Cambridge University. Presented here are numerous articles describing current research of the writing process of second-language learners, the variables influencing their performance, the relationship between reading and writing, and many other issues of interest to second-language teachers. Included are chapters by Andrew Cohen, Ulla Connor, Joan Eisterhold, Barbara Kroll, Ann Johns, Joy Reid, and many others.

Freedman, S., ed. (1989). *The acquisition of written language: Response and revision.* Norwood, N.J.: Ablex. This book made available several important contributions to writing pedagogy in the area of teacher and peer input into student revisions. Represented are the following authors, to name a few: Shirley Brice Heath, Courtney Cazden, Anne Gere, and Stephen Witte.

McKay, S. (1993). *Agendas for second language literacy.* New York: Cambridge University. The agendas for second-language literacy discussed here include sociopolitical, economic, family, and educational. All are examined through a sociohistorical perspective.

Wallace, C. (1988). *Learning to read in a multicultural society: The social context of second language literacy.* New York: Prentice Hall. This book explores the reading event itself, sources of miscues, the integration of language skills, case studies of learner-readers, and many other topics related to learning how to read.

Zamel, V. (1992). Writing one's way into reading. *TESOL Quarterly, 26*(3), 463–485. Here Zamel stresses the interdependence of reading and writing, and discusses both as creative processes. Her implications for instruction are particularly well-drawn.

Questions for Reflection and Discussion

1. What do you think Goodman means by "easy" and "hard" when he refers to language development (page 63)? To what extent do you agree with his conclusions?

2. Would you feel comfortable learning to read and write in another language within a natural classroom environment such as the one described in this chapter? Why or why not?

3. How do you think discrete points of language (e.g., spelling, sounding out consonant clusters, punctuation) should be handled within a whole language classroom?

4. Frank Smith (1982) argues that dyslexia (the inability to read) may actually be the result of an undue focus on abstract, meaningless elements of language rather than a physical problem. Once children begin to get meaning from print, the "disease" magically disappears. Do you think there might be some validity in his argument? Discuss. What implications might his argument have for language learning and teaching?

5. Create your own diagrams that show how you conceptualize reading and/or writing components and/or processes. Discuss them with a small group. Can you improve them in any way based on your group's feedback?

6. To what extent do you think a "traditional" approach should be used in teaching reading in a second or foreign language? Consider, in particular, the possible effects of an emphasis on organizational forms, expert opinion, and the authority of the author.

CHAPTER 5

The Affective Domain

If we were to devise theories of second-language acquisition or teaching methods which were based only on cognitive considerations, we would be omitting the most fundamental side of human behavior.

                                        H. D. Brown, 1980

QUESTIONS TO THINK ABOUT

1. Think about your own experiences while studying another language. To what extent did the following help or hinder your success?

                a. anxiety
                b. motivation
                c. attitude

2. What did you and/or your teacher do to lessen your anxiety, increase your motivation, and improve your attitude? How effective were these strategies?

3. What can you do as a second- or foreign-language teacher to lessen anxiety, increase motivation, and improve attitudes in your classroom?

The affective domain includes several variables that can either enhance second-language acquisition or hinder it, depending upon whether they are positive or negative, the degree to which they are present, and the combinations in which we find them.

Because these variables are difficult to isolate and are often so subtle they can scarcely be detected, it seems impossible to study them objectively with our current methods, although many have tried. How does one effectively measure inhibition, for example? Or empathy? Or attitudes, for that matter? All of these intangible concepts interact to form changing patterns usually operating out of the subconscious. We do know that factors or combinations of factors having to do with *attitudes, motivation,* and *level of anxiety* are central to the affective domain. These are strongly influenced by the process of *acculturation* and by certain *personality* variables.

ATTITUDES

Attitudes develop as a result of experience, both direct and vicarious. They are greatly influenced by people in the immediate environment: parents, teachers, and peers. Attitudes toward self, the target language and the people who speak it (peers in particular), the teacher, and the classroom environment all seem to have an influence on acquisition.

Attitude toward Self

Adelaide Heyde (1979) looked at the effects of three levels of self-esteem (global, specific [situational], and task) on the oral performance of American college students studying French as a foreign language. She found that students with high self-esteem at all levels performed better in French. Other studies have resulted in similar conclusions (Heyde, 1977; Oller, Hudson, and Liu, 1977).

In general, self-esteem leads to self-confidence. The degree of self-esteem and/or self-confidence may vary from situation to situation or from task to task. Both may increase as one performs well in a variety of situations. Oller (1981) argues that the relationship between affect and learning is probably bidirectional. We may perform well because our attitude toward self is positive; we may have a positive attitude toward self because we perform well (see also Gardner, Lalonde, and Moorcroft, 1985).

Stevick emphasizes the importance of *self-security,* an important facet of the attitude toward self. "Am I what I would like to be as an intellectual being and also as a social being? Do I have an adequate mind, and am I the kind of person that other people are willing to spend time with?" (1976b, p. 229). If the answer to all these questions is affirmative, then the individual is better able to engage in the often humbling process of acquiring a second language.

Attitude toward the Target Language and the People Who Speak It

The attitudes that an individual has toward the target language and the target group (especially peers) seem to have a very significant effect on motivation in particular. According to Gardner and Lambert:

> The learner's ethnocentric tendencies and his attitudes toward the members of the other group are believed to determine how successful he will be, relatively, in learning the new language (1972, p. 3).

Here stereotyping often plays a large role. Saville-Troike (1976) reports that the *in-group* often values characteristics that the *out-group* supposedly lacks, such as cleanliness, human traits (as opposed to animal), independence, self-reliance, appropriate behaviors concerning time, and the like. A major effect of stereotyping is to create or perpetuate social distance and social boundaries. Saville-Troike argues that stereotypes build "a social barrier which inhibits communication and learning and they affect the self-image of those who are typed."

When negative stereotypes are attributed to second-language students, they may become *internalized* and could undermine attempts at language acquisition. Not only do negative stereotypes affect the self-esteem of the group's members, but they often bring about negative reactions and encourage negative attitudes toward the target language and culture. Students who are considered linguistically deficient or disadvantaged because they have a different first language are particularly at risk. The second-language student's self-esteem is in jeopardy if the teacher and peers fail to show respect for the first language and the culture of which it is a part.

Attitudes toward the Teacher and the Classroom Environment

In classrooms in which mutual respect is lacking, differing values can meet head on. Conflicts are likely to develop between student and teacher and between student and peer. Students who cooperate on a project may be thought to be "cheating" or students who fail to guess on the true or false section of a test are thought to be "not caring." In the first case the students may not value competition as the teacher thinks they should; rather they value group cooperation in completing a task. In the second case, the students may not feel comfortable guessing when not knowing the answer; their motive may be not to get the highest possible score but simply to render a more accurate indication of what they actually know.

Scarcella (1990) addresses the issue of communication breakdowns and how to help students overcome them. She recommends the following:

1. Encourage the development of friendship.
2. Emphasize commonalities.
3. Create a place in which the experiences, capacities, interests, and goals of every classroom member are simultaneously utilized for the benefit of all.
4. Teach all students how their communications styles can be misinterpreted (p. 104).

We have all probably seen classrooms in which values clashed, student against peer. In one situation, for example, the students had been given a group task to identify problems that might be encountered on an American-style "date." Two fairly recent arrivals insisted that the couple must be chaperoned in order to prevent inappropriate behavior. A much larger number thought that the idea of a chaperone would be silly; they insisted that in a modern world one would never consider such a practice. The discussion resulted in a very angry exchange among the students. This incident might have been prevented had the majority of the students been given a chance to voice differences early on, discuss them, and through the discussion gain an appreciation of others and their differing worldviews.

To ease tensions that might result in unpleasant situations such as the one described above, some teachers might feel comfortable using affective activities or humanistic techniques (see Chapter 13). Those advocated particularly by Brown and Dubin (1975), Moskowitz (1978), and Simon, Howe, and Kirschenbaum (1972) seek to create good feelings on the part of the students toward the teacher, each other, and the resulting classroom environment.

Moskowitz sets out to gather evidence that the use of such techniques in language classrooms (both foreign and ESL) does indeed "enhance attitudes toward a foreign language, rapport with classmates, and the self-image of foreign language students" (1981, p. 149). She conducted two studies using the language students of eleven teachers enrolled at Temple University in courses on humanistic techniques of teaching a foreign language. The subjects were high school students studying a variety of languages: French, Spanish, German, Italian, Hebrew, and ESL. Each teacher chose one class (from beginners through advanced) in which to do the study. Often they chose classes that had been apathetic or difficult in some way. They gave three questionnaires prior to the humanistic activities and readministered the questionnaires two months later. Had the students' attitudes changed? In both studies there appeared to be significant positive increases in attitude toward themselves, toward the language, and toward each other.[1] The following four hypotheses were accepted (1981, pp. 145–150):

> Using humanistic techniques to teach a foreign language:
> 1. enhances the attitudes of foreign-language students toward learning the target language
> 2. enhances the self-perceptions of foreign-language students
> 3. enhances the perceptions of foreign-language students toward
>   a. the members of their language class
>   b. how their classmates perceive them
> 4. increases the acceptance of foreign-language students for members of the same sex and the opposite sex in their class, thus increasing their cohesiveness.

These studies indicate that humanistic activities may increase the development of positive student attitudes overall.

MOTIVATION

In much of the current literature, integrative motivation and instrumental motivation are differentiated. Gardner and Lambert (1972) describe *integrative motivation* roughly as a desire to integrate and identify with the target language group. They describe *instrumental motivation* as a desire to use the language to obtain practical goals such as studying in a technical field or getting a job.

The studies of French classes in Canada done by Gardner and Lambert (1959), and Gardner, Smythe, Clement, and Gliksman (1976) all concluded that integrative motivation is generally stronger than instrumental motivation in predicting French proficiency. In addition, Bernard Spolsky (1969) found that integrative motivation, as determined by a questionnaire that indirectly assessed attitudes toward the target language group, is among the strong predictors of proficiency in ESL students.

However, the evidence in this area frequently appears contradictory. There are cases in which integration appears *not* to be a strong motive but in which a certain urgency exists to become proficient in the target language for instrumental reasons. In such cases instrumental motivation becomes the main predictor (Lukmani, 1972; Oller, Baca, and Vigil, 1977). In addition, the study

---

[1] In the 1977 study the students' identities were not revealed and so the pre-post data were treated as though they came from two independent groups; in the 1978 study the identity of the students was retained in code so that pre-post data could be matched. Two questionnaires were administered: the Foreign Language Attitude Questionnaire and *My Class and Me* (see Moskowitz, 1981, p. 150). Sociometric data were collected from each student to see to what extent attitudes changed toward specific peers.

of Chinese-speaking graduate students in the United States (Oller, Hudson, and Liu, 1977) indicated that although the students' main reason for wanting to be proficient in English was instrumental, the subjects who characterized Americans positively performed better on a cloze test. Thus the studies are very inconclusive.

What appear to be contradictory findings may simply be evidence indicating that the various motivations studied are difficult if not impossible to isolate and are certainly not mutually exclusive.

Many questions need to be addressed. How do we distinguish the various motivations to begin with? For example, does "integration" mean to become part of the target language group or just to socialize on a casual basis with its members?[2] If the latter is true, then might not instrumental motivation be present as well? Imagine, for example, a person who desires to socialize with the target group in order to integrate but does so in a desire to curry political favor. How would one categorize such motives? Even if they could be isolated, how could they be measured? In addition, the person may not want to reveal his or her real feelings or may not even be aware of them.

Oller (1981) probes these and other thorny questions, particularly those involving the self-report questionnaire as the method of determination. How reliable can our data be if the information requested is potentially damaging to the student? For example, a student may indicate by certain choices a disloyalty to his or her first-language group. How reliable can the questionnaire be if the answers reflect the respondent's perception of what it is looking for? How reliable can it be if self-flattery (Oller and Perkins, 1978) is a tendency on the part of the examinee? By using the questionnaire, is it possible that we are, in fact, not even determining motivation at all? Obviously, the issues involved here are far from settled and probably will not be settled in the foreseeable future.

LEVEL OF ANXIETY

H. D. Brown (1987) distinguishes between two kinds of anxiety: *trait* anxiety (a predisposition toward feeling anxious) and *state* anxiety (anxiety produced in reaction to a specific situation). He also distinguishes between anxiety that is debilitative and that which is facilitative. Whether the anxiety is an aid or hindrance often depends upon the degree to which it is found in the individual.

---

[2]Graham (1984) attempts to clarify by adding yet another category: *assimilative motivation*. Assimilative motivation is present when one desires to "melt" into the target group to the extent that one becomes indistinguishable from the others.

For example, no anxiety at all might cause the person to be lethargic, whereas a small amount might bring the individual to an optimal state of alertness.

In a study using induced anxiety, MacIntyre and Gardner (1994) found that their control group, the members of which had not been exposed to anxiety-arousal, performed better than the experimental groups at all stages of the learning task set before them. They also concluded that whenever anxiety-reduction strategies are employed, they must be accompanied by reteaching strategies in order that students might have a second opportunity to learn what was missed during the time when anxiety was high.

In general, it appears that a lowered anxiety level is related to proficiency in the target language (Carroll, 1963; Chastain, 1975; Gardner, Smythe, Clement, and Gliksman, 1976). In the case of ESL, the teacher and peers can promote a lowered level of anxiety by providing a sort of surrogate family to serve as a buffer until independence is reached. Sheltered classrooms in the content areas (see Chapters 16 and 17) also provide temporary refuges in which students can receive comprehensible input in low-anxiety environments. Larsen and Smalley (1972), although they don't specifically mention the classroom as serving in this capacity, nevertheless do advocate such a haven. However, students who are sheltered for too long may fossilize early as a result of isolation from target group peers. A wise teacher involves students with native or nativelike speakers as early as possible and pushes the students into independence as soon as they become ready. In the case of foreign-language teaching, students can receive supplemental instruction, participate in a support group or foreign-language club, or learn how to apply relaxation strategies (see especially Campbell and Ortiz, 1991).

Additional potential causes of increased anxiety in both ESL and foreign-language classes include not providing a silent period, giving direct corrections, and so forth (see Chapters 2 and 3).

RELATED FACTORS

Acculturation

Acculturation may be an important predictor of target language acquisition (Stauble, 1980; Schumann, 1978a). Stauble argues that second-language learners will succeed "to the degree that they acculturate to the target language group" if no formal instruction is attempted. Although the procedures of her research may be open to dispute,[3] the following assumption appears reasonable:

> The assumption here is that the more social and psychological distance there
> is between the second-language learner and the target-language group, the
> lower the learner's degree of acculturation will be toward that group (1980,
> pp. 43–50).

Schumann (1978a) compared the linguistic development demonstrated by
six second-language learners of English—two children, two adolescents, and
two adults. The subject who acquired the least was Alberto, a 33-year-old Costa
Rican. Of all the subjects, he was the one most socially and psychologically distant from the target language group. He interacted predominantly with Spanish-speaking friends and made no attempt to socialize with English-speaking
people. He showed little desire for owning a television set and played mostly
Spanish music on his stereo. Although English classes were available, he
showed no interest in them. However, as Schumann points out, a Piagetian test
of adaptive intelligence revealed no gross cognitive defects that might prevent
him from learning a second language. The main reason for his low proficiency,
according to Schumann, was his lack of desire to acculturate.[4]

To explain the effect of acculturation on the second-language acquisition
process, Schumann developed the Acculturation Model (see Related Reading 2).
According to his way of thinking, L2 acquisition is dependent upon the amount
of social and psychological distance that exists between the learner and the L2
culture. When the distances are great, the learner's language tends to fossilize
during early stages of interlanguage development. The learner may not have

---

[3] In Stauble's study of the process of decreolization, she made a distinction between social distance
(domination versus subordination, assimilation versus preservation, enclosure, size, congruence,
and attitudes) and psychological distance (resolution of language shock, culture shock, and culture stress, motivation, and ego permeability). She measured the negation development of three
native Spanish speakers who had been living in the United States for over ten years. They were
classified along the Schumann (1979) continuum from Basilang (minimal skills in the target language) to Mesolang (intermediate skills) to Acrolang (nativelike performance).

In an attempt to account for their varying levels, she administered a questionnaire to determine their social and psychological proximity to English. She found that her subject Xavier (in the
lower Mid-Mesolang phase) had the least amount of social distance (12.5%) and greatest amount
of psychological distance (62.5%); her subjects Maria and Paz had the same amount of psychological distance (21%) but differed somewhat on social distance, 56% and 67%, respectively. From
this she suggested that psychological distance may be more important than social distance.
However, one might question this conclusion. Intuitively it would seem that the two factors
would be highly correlated with one another and would be difficult to separate so distinctly. She
mentions in passing that Paz demonstrated a higher degree of motivation than the other two.
Perhaps this should have been pursued as a causative factor. Stauble herself admits that the validity and reliability had not yet been determined on her measurement and that the results should be
considered speculative.

[4] It is interesting to note that, according to Schmidt (1984), the poorest learners in the studies
referred to by Schumann and Stauble were also the oldest. Age may have been, either directly or
indirectly, a contributing factor.

received the necessary input because of social isolation or may not have given the target language the attention necessary for acquisition because of psychological distance.

Andersen's Nativization Model (see Related Reading 2) also seeks to explain why the language of some learners fossilizes early. He considers the effects of what he calls "nativization" and "denativization" upon the learner. Through nativization, the learner tends to assimilate the target language into an already determined schema of how the L2 should be. Judgments are made based on a knowledge of the first language and culture. Denativization, on the other hand, is an accommodation process in which the learner changes the schemata to fit the new language. The learner who tends to denativize is the most likely to become proficient and nativelike.

Giles in his Accommodation Theory (see Related Reading 2) claims that motivation is the key and that it is closely related to in-group (the L1 group) and out-group (the L2 group) identification. He places importance on how the individual *perceives* social distance rather than on actual social distance as described by Schumann. Giles argues that feelings of identity are dynamic and are dependent upon continuing negotiations between and among individuals and groups. Schumann sees these feelings as being more constant and slower to change. Fossilization, according to Giles's model, occurs during what he calls "downward divergence," which takes place when the individual is not strongly motivated in the direction of the outgroup.

Schmidt's (1984) study of W seems to contradict a strong version of both the Acculturation Model and Accommodation Theory. His subject W was a 35-year-old native speaker of Japanese who had been living for five years in Hawaii. W was judged by the researcher to be intelligent, sophisticated, and uninhibited. In addition he appeared to be extroverted, socially adept, and self-confident but, at the same time, stubborn and domineering. He conversed readily in English and was not afraid of making errors. He was a successful businessman and had a great deal of professional and social contact with native speakers of English. Although he possessed a high level of integrative motivation to communicate in English, he had no interest in studying English or in analyzing the language and appeared to pay little attention to form during conversation. He made many errors in his speech but seemed not to be aware of them. Schmidt concludes that adults may actually require formal instruction in order to acquire the rules. Interaction may not be enough. However, it is more to the point to say that interaction without any attention to form (either conscious or subconscious) may not be enough. Even children acquiring a first language "pay attention" to form but at a subconscious level. W's ability to acquire normally may have been impaired for two reasons: (1) his inflexibility may have made a denativization process impossible and (2) his apparent success at being socially accepted without having to become more nativelike prevented him from undergoing the acculturation process in a normal fashion.

In his analysis of the literature, H. D. Brown (1987) describes the four stages that have been identified in the normal acculturation process. In the first stage the newcomer feels a type of *euphoria* mixed with the excitement of being in a new (sometimes exotic) place. As the reality of survival sets in, the newcomer moves into the second stage—*culture shock*. It is in this stage that frustration rises to its peak, the individual begins to feel alienated from the target culture, and self-image and security are threatened. The third stage signifies the beginning of recovery. The stress is still felt but the person is beginning to gain control over the problems that seemed insurmountable before. Brown refers to this state as *anomie* (see Srole, 1956), a state in which the individual begins to adapt to the target culture and lose some of the native culture. A feeling of homelessness might develop until the person fully adjusts to the new culture. This stage is considered a "critical period" in that the student is now able to gain a mastery over the new language. The fourth stage brings *full recovery*. The person has become reconciled to his or her role in the new culture. It is the critical period that Schmidt's subject W failed to experience and this failure may, in part, have accounted for his not acquiring the grammatical system of English.

Under normal conditions, persons becoming acculturated pass through all the stages at varying rates. Furthermore, they do not progress smoothly from one stage to the next; instead regression to previous stages is common, depending upon circumstances and the state of mind.

Personality

According to H. D. Brown, certain personality characteristics such as willingness to take risks (Rubin, 1975; Beebe, 1983) and relative lack of inhibition (Guiora, Acton, Erard, and Strickland, 1980; Guiora, Beit-Hallami, Brannon, Dull, and Scovel, 1972) can, in most cases, lead to proficiency in the target language. Extroversion and assertiveness, although not necessarily beneficial traits (Naiman, Fröhlich, and Stern, 1978; Busch, 1982), can be helpful to the degree that they encourage more output and hence more input. In addition, empathy, under normal conditions, can lead to greater proficiency. Being able to identify with members of the target language group is important to communication. Guiora, Brannon, and Dull (1972) feel empathy is essential in order that our ego boundaries be permeable. In other words, we need to be open to the new language and the new people. Schumann (1980) related empathy and ego permeability to a lowering of inhibitions.

> I would submit that empathic capacity or ego flexibility, particularly as operationalized under the concept of "lowering of inhibitions," is best regarded as an essential factor to the ability to acquire a second language (1980, p. 238).

It should be noted, however, that a person who is extroverted and assertive to the extreme will not tend to be empathic. The three characteristics need to be in balance in order to have a positive effect on language acquisition.

CREATING AN OPTIMAL SCHOOL
AND COMMUNITY ENVIRONMENT

Although a teacher may successfully establish an environment conducive to language acquisition in the classroom, what the students face outside of the classroom may have a greater impact on affect in general. For example, Bodinger-deVriate (1991) reports a disturbing increase in reported hate crimes across public school campuses in Los Angeles. Hate crimes have been reported at 33 percent of the county's schools. Unfortunately, ESL students are often the most likely to be subject to ridicule, prejudice, and sometimes outright hostility. This attitude can come not only from native-speaking peers but from teachers, administrators, and other school staff members, as well as from the community. The form that it takes among teachers and other school personnel, although perhaps subtle, can be especially devastating. Persons of influence can affect the attitudes found in the whole school setting, which often extend to the community itself. I remember an incident that occurred when I was an ESL teacher in a large public high school. One day in the teachers' lounge a fellow teacher asked me, "How's old 'Ho Hum' [a nickname he had given the Asian student we shared] doing today?" I pretended not to know to whom he was referring, although the student's identity was obvious since we had only one Asian student in common. He continued, "You know, what's his name" and then he gave the student's real name. "Oh, he's doing just fine," I replied. As it turned out, old "Ho Hum" went on to maintain close to a 4.0 grade-point average throughout school, won the top "Junior of the Year Award," and became a star member of the soccer team. Of course, not all ESL students achieve so much, and many are subject to the same learning and/or psychological problems as the rest of us.

Although we cannot hope to eliminate the prejudices of all insensitive persons with whom our students come into contact, we can perhaps through cultural awareness training make the overt expression of these prejudices unpopular. Through the inservicing of teachers and staff, and the sensitizing of entire student populations and groups within the community, we can achieve a school climate that will be supportive for all of our students, not only those in ESL.

The teacher inservice I would like to present here seemed to be particularly efficacious in exposing cultural biases. It began with the following scenario.[5]

> A man and woman dressed in clothes that represent a very "primitive" hypothetical culture walk slowly through the audience. The woman, who is carrying a basket filled with bread, walks a few paces behind the man (her husband). Once they reach the front of the room, they turn to face the audience

---

[5] Although I have not been able to locate the original source of this idea, I saw a version of it presented at the 1980 NAFSA Conference in El Paso.

and kneel down, side by side. The man places his hand on the woman's head while she bows her head down, touching it to the floor three times. She then rises, walks into the audience, and begins to lead people up to the front of the room as though she is preparing for a ceremony (in this case a wedding ceremony—her husband will take a second bride). First, she quietly leads two men (one at a time) from the audience to the front of the room. The only sounds she utters are pleasing "umms" from time to time. She motions for them to sit in the chairs she has set up previously. She repeats the same procedure except this time she takes two women from the audience. She motions for them to kneel on the floor. Lastly, she leads the new bride to a kneeling position beside the husband. She then passes out the bread from her basket. She gives it to the men first, waits a few moments, and then to the women.

The moderator asks the audience to describe this society. Usually the audience guesses that it is a patriarchal society supported by these facts: the man walked ahead of the woman upon entering, the women had to sit on the floor while the men got chairs, the men were fed first, and the husband pushed the woman's head to the floor three times. This reaction on the part of the audience is expected in that they had little choice but to react from their own world view or *weltanschauung*. Actually the hypothetical society being portrayed was set up as a matriarchal one. The men walked ahead of the women in case of danger lurking around the corner. The women were generally the only persons who could directly receive the spirits who were in the ground. Thus only the women could sit on the ground and bow their heads to it while the men could only receive the spirits indirectly through a hand gently placed on a woman's head. One exception to this rule occurred when a man married. Only at that time could he receive the spirits directly. The bread was served to the men first in case it had poison in it. That way safety for the women could be ensured.

A lively discussion usually follows about perspectives and how they color views of reality. Through activities such as this, people may begin to look at events from the viewpoints of others and may perhaps gain a more global perspective.

Other types of activities that promote cultural understanding involve cooperative learning (see Chapter 14) and other interactive strategies. Nieto (1992) points out that such strategies generally result in fewer racial comments and name-calling and in higher academic achievement overall. Yet another strategy is to take teachers, students, and community groups through the stages of ethnicity (Banks, 1990) by means of role-playing in hypothetical situations. Banks's typology applies to situations in which dominant and nondominant groups coexist in a variety of ways. His definitions of the stages are summarized as follows:

Stage 1: *Ethnic Psychological Captivity*
The member of a nondominant group feels rejection and low self-esteem and may avoid contact as much as possible with the dominant group. This individual has internalized the "image" that the dominant society has ascribed to him or her and may even feel shame.

Stage 2: *Ethnic Encapsulation*
The member of a nondominant group has reacted to Stage 1 by feeling bitterness and, in some cases, a desire for revenge. As a result the person may turn inward to the ethnic group and reject all other groups, particularly the dominant one. In extreme manifestations of this stage, other groups are regarded as "the enemy" and are often seen as racists with genocidal tendencies. Members of this group who try to assimilate into the dominant group are considered traitors.

Stage 3: *Ethnic Identity Clarification*
The member at this stage is able to clarify self in relation to the ethnic group of which he or she is a part. Self-acceptance and understanding are reached. The person is able to see both positive and negative aspects of the primary ethnic group and other groups. Usually, in order to attain this stage, the person must have gained a certain degree of economic and emotional security and must have had productive, positive experiences with members of other groups, particularly those in the dominant group.

Stage 4: *Biethnicity*
The individual is able to function successfully in two cultural groups, the primary group and a nonprimary group. Most individuals belonging to a nondominant group are forced to reach this stage if they wish to become mobile socially and economically in the society in general. Interestingly, members of the dominant group do not have to do this and can (and usually do) remain monocultural and monolingual all their lives.

Stage 5: *Multiethnicity and Reflective Nationalism*
The individual has learned to function successfully in several ethnic groups. The person still feels loyalty to the primary ethnic group but has developed a commitment to the nation state and its idealized values as well.

Stage 6: *Globalism and Global Competency*
The individual has developed global identifications and has the skills necessary to relate to all groups. This person has achieved an ideal but delicate balance of primary group, nation state, and global commitments, identifications, and loyalties.

The road to biethnicity is not easy (see especially Madrid, 1991). Individuals do not necessarily move from one stage to the next in linear fashion. Rather they tend to zigzag back and forth, and some may skip stages altogether. Fortunately, Stage 2 is often bypassed, although some feelings from it might exist temporarily, as the person moves from Stage 1 toward Stage 3. By role-playing in hypothetical situations, teachers, students, and community members can "experience" at least Stages 1–3. First the participants decide which groups they want represented, such as Latin-American, Korean-American, Vietnamese-American, American Indian, Japanese-American, and so on. Then they decide which group they want to join. Once in the group of their choice, they go through a set of planned activities to help them experience the various stages.

For example, in Stage 1 they might bring in pieces of literature, songs, pictures, or anecdotes depicting their people experiencing oppression at the hands of the dominant group. They may want to list negative feelings about the self and the ethnic group created by this experience and discuss how each feeling came about. There is a more general activity that will help the participants to feel the effects of being labeled. Give each participant a paper hat (a simple headband will do).[6] On each hat write a label such as "dumb," "smart," "good-looking," "unbathed," and so on. Place the hats on the participants in such a way that no individual will see the label he or she is wearing. Give the group an interesting topic for discussion and have them during the course of the discussion treat each other according to their labels. Most will be amazed at the intensity of the anger or joy they feel depending on the treatment to which they are subjected.

At Stage 2 the participants may want to discuss the negative feelings to keep them from festering to the point at which bitterness develops. Once these feelings are fully aired, the person is better able to begin to build a positive attitude toward his or her own ethnic group and the groups of others. This time the group may want to share literature and other cultural items that cause them to feel intense pride in their "own cultures."

Stage 3 involves a sort of sitting back just a little to look at the positive attributes and achievements of other groups (share their literatures, etc.) and to achieve a realistic view of their own ethnic group in relation to others.

Still other culture awareness activities can include celebrations, group discussions, films, and other events that bring school and community together. The rewards of such activities can be immeasurable in terms of increased human understanding.

SUMMARY

Because the concepts related to the affective domain are so intangible, they are difficult to define, describe, and measure. Yet despite their ephemeral quality, we cannot give up our attempts to understand what their role might be in second language development. Central to the affective domain are attitudes, motivation, and level of anxiety. They are strongly influenced by acculturation and personality factors.

Attitudes that are largely determined by what our students have experienced and by the people with whom they identify—peers, parents, teachers—influence the way students see the world and their place in it. Motivation also, whether it be integrative or instrumental, is a strong force in determining how proficient the students will become. In addition, level of anxiety has its effect. Have the students been given a chance to try out the language in a

---

[6] This activity was adapted from one shared with me by Leah Boehne.

nonthreatening environment where stress is kept at a minimum? If so, they will be more able to go through the stages of acculturation without its becoming a debilitating process.

The student's emotional well-being will be enhanced by a positive, accepting school environment. In spite of the fact that prejudices cannot be eliminated completely, much can be done to make the environment a better one not only for language learners but for all students. Cultural awareness activities can involve school personnel, students, and community members. They can sensitize people to the needs and feelings of others.

READINGS, REFLECTION, AND DISCUSSION

Suggested Readings and Reference Materials

Banks, J. (1988). *Multiethnic education: Theory and practice* (2nd ed.). Boston: Allyn & Bacon. A sensitive exploration of the nature of ethnicity and multiethnic education in the United States. Offers guidelines for promoting a more global, open society through education. A very readable and important book for all teachers.

Crookes, G., and Schmidt, R. (1991). Motivation: Reopening the research agenda. *Language Learning, 41* (4), 469–512. A review of the literature and research on the effects of motivation on the acquisition of a second or foreign language.

Gardner, R., and Lambert, W. (1972). *Attitudes and motivation in second language acquisition.* Rowley, MA: Newbury House. Research findings and the measures used in obtaining them are discussed in detail in this book, which has become a classic. Several studies on attitudes as they relate to second-language acquisition are presented.

Horwitz, E., and Young, D. (1991). *Language anxiety: From theory and research to classroom implications.* Englewood Cliffs, N.J.: Prentice Hall. A very comprehensive look at language anxiety and the effect it has on second- and foreign-language acquisition. Empirical research, students' perspectives, and teaching and program strategies are presented. Thomas Scovel, P. MacIntyre, R. C. Gardner, Harold Madsen, David Crookall, and Rebecca Oxford are among the authors included.

Richard-Amato, P., and Snow, M. A. (1992). *The multicultural classroom: Readings for content-area teachers.* White Plains, N.Y.: Addison-Wesley. Focusing on the needs of language minority students, this book addresses theoretical foundations for successful teaching in multicultural classrooms. It explores recommended classroom strategies and practices and later relates them to specific content areas such as math, social studies, science, and literature.

Questions for Reflection and Discussion

1. Several language students have mentioned that learning a second language makes them feel "helpless and ineffectual." What demands are typically

made on the individual in the following second-language situations that might contribute to this feeling?

    a. a child going to kindergarten in the new culture
    b. a tenth-grader in beginning Spanish as a foreign language
    c. an adult going to work in a new country for the first time
    d. a university ESL student attending a class oriented to native speakers

What affective factors will help or hinder the individual's ability to cope in each situation?

2. Savignon (1983) describes an incident involving her son Daniel, a new student in a Paris school. On the first day he met with more than a hundred students at his grade level in the school's courtyard. The school director called out the names of the students. They were to stand and tell what class they were in. When his name was called, he followed the procedure but was immediately chastised for having his hands in his pockets. When he went home that day, he vowed that he would never go back. He had had it with that school.

   Explain the incident in terms of what you know about the stages of acculturation, attitudes, values, etc. If you were Daniel's parent, what would you say to him to help him put this incident in perspective?

3. In what ways, other than those mentioned in the chapter, can you aid your own students in developing positive attitudes, strong motivation, and reduced anxiety? Consider kinds of activities, room arrangements, and the general ambiance in the school and classroom environment.

4. Plan a culture awareness inservice for the school personnel (including the secretaries, custodians, cafeteria help, etc.) in your school. Be very specific about the pre-inservice preparation, the inservice itself, and the follow-up.

CHAPTER 6

Language Assessment

> *To the extent that a test presents authentic language and communication tasks, with both verbal (discourse level) and an extralinguistic context, it will be evoking communicative performance, and thus approach as nearly as possible the evaluation of communicative competence.*
>
> M. Wesche, 1987

QUESTIONS TO THINK ABOUT

1. What have been your own experiences as a student (and/or as a practicing teacher) with language assessment? Were they mainly positive? Why or why not?

2. For what purposes do you feel second- and foreign-language students should be tested in the target language? In each case, what would you want to know?

3. What do you think a *pragmatic* test might be? How might it differ from other kinds of tests with which you are familiar?

4. Do you think it is possible to design a language assessment program that is both instructive and evaluative? What might it look like?

Often critical decisions are made concerning second- and foreign-language students based upon their performance on a single language test. Will the student be able to enter a program of choice? Will he or she be able to exit a basic language program and move on to more challenging course work? These are some of the more important judgments that are often based upon the very limited data provided by language tests whose scores mainly reflect a knowledge of grammar rules, vocabulary distinctions, and the like. Here I am reminded of the now classic story retold by Clark and Clifford (1988) about the scientific investigation of the bumblebee, carried out by an aerodynamic engineer.

> [He] carefully measured the wingspan, body weight, airflow pattern, size and placement of wing muscles, number of wing beats per second, and numerous other of the bee's physiology, and by means of elaborate diagrams, mathematical formulas, and computer-aided calculations, was able to demonstrate conclusively that the bumblebee is incapable of flight (p. 146).

In similar fashion we often examine students' knowledge of language to come to conclusions about performance capabilities. Does the student of German know the rule governing the subject-AUX inversion following fronted adverbials? Does the student of English know when and how to use the subjunctive? Does the student of French recognize meaning contrasts between the *imparfait* and the *passé composé?* Based on the data obtained from tests of such knowledge, we often determine that the student is incapable (or capable, as the case may be) of successfully functioning at the level expected.

Although some of these tests have been improved in recent years by including more authentic testing components (see especially the Test of English as a Foreign Language—TOEFL), they should never be used as the *only* criteria supporting decisions that have such impact on students' lives.

Although not all evaluative decisions may be as critical as those mentioned above, it is important that evaluation be based on a variety of assessment procedures, formal testing being only one of many from which we can draw. Moreover, it is important that our tests be as free as possible of cultural, sexual, and linguistic bias (see especially Mohan, 1992).

The aim of this chapter is to explore various assessment instruments including language tests and types of formative evaluative tools such as portfolios and performance checklists. It will also look at even less formal means by which we can determine how our students are doing and whether or not they have achieved general goals in language development. Performance data are discussed as they relate to decision making and the monitoring of our students' progression in the target language.

LANGUAGE TESTS

Generally language tests are given in an attempt to place students appropriately in programs; to diagnose their problems in the target language with a reasonable amount of accuracy; and/or to measure their achievement, in other words, measure to what extent they have reached course or program objectives.

Some distinctions made between tests involve *norm-referenced* tests versus *criterion-referenced* tests, *indirect* tests versus *direct* tests, and *discrete point* tests versus *integrative* tests.

Norm-Referenced Tests versus Criterion-Referenced Tests

Norm-referenced tests measure how the student does on the test compared to how others did on it. When administered on a large scale using accepted statistical procedures, we say that the test is "standardized." A standardized language test is a test that compares the performance of the person taking the test to the performance of others who have taken the same test. Results are given in terms of a percentile rank. For example, let's say that a student scores in the 96th percentile. This means that the student did better than 96 percent of the test takers upon which the norm was based.

Criterion referencing, on the other hand, refers to how well the student has met specific objectives or a level of performance in a certain area. A driver's license test is an example of a criterion-referenced test; either you pass or you fail. How you compare with others who have taken the test is not relevant.

Indirect Testing versus Direct Testing

Indirect testing is testing that does not examine the ability to perform in authentic situations. For example, a test of lexical items relating to history might be used to predict how well the student will be able to function in a history class with native speakers of the target language. Most would agree that such a test would probably not be a very good predictor in this situation. Indirect tests do not test actual performance; rather they test enabling skills or microskills which, in theory, are supposed to "add up" to what might constitute actual performance. Testing that is more *direct,* that is closer to testing the abilities needed to function will no doubt yield a better prediction. For example, tests that assess the ability to gather important ideas from a lecture, to write a summary or an essay expressing an opinion, to read and understand academic written discourse will tell us more about how the student will perform. Performance tasks might be used in such testing to increase its authenticity. In addition, we might observe the student in similar situations and use performance checklists to help inform our predictions about how the student will be able to perform (see later sections).

No less important in language testing than the distinctions mentioned above is the *discrete point* test versus the *integrative* test distinction. This distinction has profound implications not only for testing in second and foreign languages, but for teaching them as well.

Discrete Point Tests versus Integrative Tests

Discrete point tests grew out of a behavioristic/structural approach to language learning and teaching in which contrastive analysis was the main focus (see pages 11 and 26). *Discrete point* tests examine the knowledge of specific elements in phonology, grammar, and vocabulary in order to determine proficiency in the isolated skill areas of listening, reading, speaking, and writing. Can the student auditorally distinguish between "pill" and "bill"? Can the student recognize a past tense form or the present progressive? Does the student know the meaning of "chair" or "hippopotamus"?

Integrative tests, on the other hand, grew out of a developmentalistic/communicative approach to language learning and teaching. Integrative tests examine the student's ability to use many skills simultaneously when accomplishing a task. Can the student answer a question that is typical of conversation? Can the student determine the meaning of a certain passage? Can the student tell a story that can be understood? Can the student write an effective letter? These are the kinds of questions asked by teachers interested in knowing what the students can actually *do* in the target language.

These two kinds of tests are not dichotomous in nature but rather represent two ends on a continuum (see Figure 6.1 below).

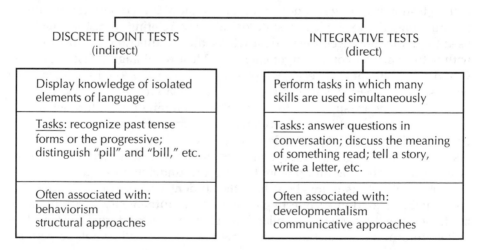

DISCRETE POINT TESTS (indirect)	INTEGRATIVE TESTS (direct)
Display knowledge of isolated elements of language	Perform tasks in which many skills are used simultaneously
Tasks: recognize past tense forms or the progressive; distinguish "pill" and "bill," etc.	Tasks: answer questions in conversation; discuss the meaning of something read; tell a story, write a letter, etc.
Often associated with: behaviorism structural approaches	Often associated with: developmentalism communicative approaches

Figure 6.1

Some tests are thought to be more discrete point, others more integrative. To complicate matters, a test may be integrative in task but discrete point in evaluation. For example, the student may be required to write an essay (integrative in task), but it may be evaluated on specific errors in grammar and vocabulary (discrete point in evaluation). Generally speaking, tests that are integrative both in task and in evaluation probably tell us more about the proficiency levels of the students, whereas tests that are integrative in task and discrete point in evaluation may be best used for diagnostic purposes.

Oller (1979) described a type of integrative test called *a pragmatic test*, which he defined as an integrative test meeting two naturalness criteria. A pragmatic test requires a natural sequencing of events and knowledge of the world and how it works (p. 70).[1] Pragmatic tests, according to Oller, include dictation (the teacher dictates sentences; the students write them down as they are being read), cloze procedures (passages are given in which every *n*th word is deleted; students are to supply the missing words), paraphrase recognition, question answering, oral interviews, essay writing, narration, and translation. It is interesting to note that pragmatic tests (even those of very different types) tend to correlate more highly with each other than they do with other tests. In other words, students who tend to do well on one pragmatic test will also tend to do well on others. Oller concluded that ". . .pragmatic testing seems to provide the most promise as a reliable, valid, and usable approach to the measurement of language ability" (1979, p. 71).

When choosing what kind of pragmatic test to use for general placement purposes, it might be wise to carry Oller's definition of such a test one step further. If we say that *the test tasks themselves have to approximate "normal classroom communication situations,"* then we would have to eliminate some of the pragmatic tests listed above except for certain kinds of question-answering tasks, oral interviews, essay writing, paraphrasing, and narration. This is not to say that cloze activities and dictation have no value. On the contrary, they do. In fact, Oller has pointed out that both correlate very highly with other pragmatic tests of proficiency. They can be useful, particularly in providing diagnostic information.

DETERMINING PLACEMENT

If our goal in placing students is to divide students roughly according to proficiency levels into beginning, intermediate, and advanced classes (see definitions on pages 99–100), then perhaps the combination of a listening comprehension task (with some simple total physical response activities—see Chapter 7), oral

---

[1] An example of an integrative test that is not pragmatic might be the writing of isolated sentences to demonstrate the use of a rule in the target language. The task is highly integrative in that many skills are called for simultaneously but it is not pragmatic for two reasons: (1) the sentences lack a normal sequential context and (2) extralinguistic data such as our perceptions of life, relationships between people, and so forth are not relevant.

interview (pictures depicting universal experiences may be referred to), some informal writing,[2] and a reading interpretation or paraphrasing section might be all that are needed to make a reasonable determination.

In the case of oral interviews, it is important that the tester flow with the student during the interview (adding a conversational quality) rather than ask a fixed set of questions designed to meet certain psychometric requirements. Anxiety levels are likely to be much lower in more natural, interactive situations and, although the evaluation will be highly subjective, the outcome will, in most cases, have greater applicability if it is communicative competence that we are assessing. Interaction between the tester and the student *can* indeed constitute *real* communication with varying degrees of conversational quality.[3]

A hierarchy of questions could be useful during the oral interview process. If a picture is used, the tester might begin with a general question that allows for elaboration such as "What is happening in this picture?" If there is little verbal response, the tester can move to something less general such as "What do you see in this picture?" If there is still little verbal response, the tester can move to a more specific, less difficult question such as "What is this?" (points to an object in the picture). If necessary, the tester can go down even further on the hierarchy and ask, "Is this a boat?" (points to a boat, assuming there is one in the picture). Much of what the tester says will depend upon what the student says. Information can be pursued to make the interview more conversational. For example, if the response to the question "What do you see in this picture?" is "I see boat and water. . . I live by water," the tester might pursue the latter utterance and make it temporarily the topic: "Oh, you live by the water? Where?" or "It must be nice to live by the water. Do you swim there?" It is important that the tester match the difficulty of his or her utterances approximately to those of the student. If the tester is an experienced language teacher and is able to accommodate effectively, then we can be fairly certain that he or she knows intuitively the level at which the student is operating. Once the teacher has reached the student's level of operation in each area (listening, speaking, writing, reading), it is important to terminate the testing at that point and move on to the next area.

It should be kept in mind that there will be a great deal of overlap between one placement level and the next and that the levels may vary depending on the tasks. However, this should not be disturbing, because when dealing with human beings one can never get a completely homogeneous unit. Even though the groups themselves will be fairly diverse, they will still be workable in that

---

[2] Here again, a picture depicting a universal experience might be used. In this case, the student is asked to write about the picture. What is happening in the picture? What does the student see? And so forth.

[3] Ross and Berwick (1992) present a study that indicates oral interviews can have characteristics that are typical of native-nonnative conversation. These characteristics need to be examined more carefully as they relate to authenticity. See also Van Lier, 1989, who addresses the same issue.

the "net" of input cast out will generally cover a fairly wide range of levels. This will be true particularly for the interactional classroom in which meaningful communication about some content of interest is the focus.

Although there are tests on the market that may yield a more detailed diagnosis than most teacher-made tests, unless they are pragmatic they often lead to a focus on discrete point teaching in separate skill and subskill areas. In addition, the tests on the market are often expensive and longer than necessary. Teacher-made tests, on the other hand, may be somewhat crude and highly subjective, but they are usually short, easy to use, and flexible. Furthermore, they can include exactly those items that are appropriate to a specific situation and thus be quite effective for the initial placement (and later reassessments) of students. The list in Table 6.1 may be of help in creating tests to place the students in workable groups. Similar to the ACTFL (American Council on the Teaching of Foreign Languages) list of proficiency guidelines, it contains language behaviors typical of students at various levels of proficiency. Unlike the ACTFL list, it is fairly concise and easy to use, and the items within it are expressed positively. In other words, it focuses on what the students can do at each level rather than on what they can't do.

TABLE 6.1. TYPICAL LANGUAGE BEHAVIORS OF STUDENTS AT VARIOUS LEVELS OF PROFICIENCY DURING THE NATURAL PROCESS OF LANGUAGE ACQUISITION IN THE CLASSROOM

Beginning Student	Typical Behaviors
	Low
	Depends almost entirely upon gestures, facial expressions, objects, pictures, a good phrase dictionary, and often a translator in an attempt to understand and to be understood
	Occasionally comprehends oral and written words and phrases
	Mid
	Begins to comprehend more, but only when speaker provides gestural clues, speaks slowly, uses concrete referents, and repeats
	Speaks very haltingly, if at all
	Shows increasing recognition of written segments
	May even be able to write short utterances
	High
	Is comprehending more and more in social conversation, but with difficulty
	Speaks in an attempt to meet basic needs, but remains hesitant; makes frequent errors in grammar, vocabulary, and pronunciation; often falls into silence
	Can read very simple text, including limited academic language
	Can write a little, but very restricted in structuring and vocabulary

Intermediate Student

Low

(same as high beginning above)

Mid

May experience dramatic increase in social and academic vocabulary recognition, both oral and written

Has difficulty with idioms generally

Often knows what he or she wants to say but gropes for acceptable utterances, both oral and written

Makes frequent errors in grammar, vocabulary, and pronunciation

Is often asked to repeat and is frequently misunderstood, orally and in writing

High

Is beginning to comprehend substantial parts of normal conversation but often requires repetitions, particularly in academic discourse spoken at normal rates

Is beginning to gain confidence in speaking ability; errors are common but less frequent

Can read and write text that contains more complex vocabulary and structures; experiences difficulty with abstract language

Advanced Student

Low

(same as high-intermediate above)

Mid

Comprehends much conversational and academic discourse spoken at normal rates; sometimes requires repetition; idioms still present difficulty

Speaks more fluently but makes occasional errors; meaning is usually clear; at times uses vocabulary or structures inappropriately

Reads and writes with less difficulty materials that are commensurate with his or her cognitive development; demonstrates some problems in grasping intended meaning

High

Comprehends normal conversational and academic discourse with little difficulty; most idioms are understood

Speaks fluently in most situations with fewer errors; meaning is generally clear but experiences some regression at times

Reads and writes both concrete and abstract materials; is able to manipulate the language with relative ease

Teachers might want to set up a rating scale by which to judge students in the various proficiencies. If each student is rated by four judges, an even more accurate placement is possible (see Hughes, 1989). This will be especially true once the judges have had adequate experience in assessing performance.

High rater reliability (both interrater and intrarater) is well documented in the literature (see especially Magnan, 1986; Shohamy, 1983; Mullen, 1980; and Clifford, 1978). This means that several raters judging the same individual's performance, tend to rate in very similar ways (interrater reliability) and the same rater tends to judge more than one performance by each individual in very similar ways (intrarater reliability). It is essential, however, that the raters be experienced in working interactively with second- and/or foreign-language students and that they be familiar with the type of scoring technique they are expected to use.

The two most commonly used scoring techniques are *holistic* and *analytic*.

Holistic scoring requires the rater to give a single impression of the student's performance such as "beginning," "intermediate," or "advanced" if one is using placement categories such as those found on pages 99–100. Another holistic scoring technique involves giving a number that corresponds to a particular description of a performance level within a given category. For example, if one is judging writing performance, a "10" might be the rating given to a writer who communicates effectively, who organizes logically, whose ideas flow effortlessly, and who make no semantic, syntactic, or mechanical errors. In contrast, only a "1" might be the rating given to a writer whose paper is very difficult to understand (no clear meaning comes through), whose ideas are just listed with no logical connection between them, whose semantic, syntactic, or mechanical errors are so numerous as to interfere with what is being said.

On the other hand, analytic scoring, usually used for diagnostic purposes rather than placement, requires the rater to make judgments of numerous individual aspects within a general category such as writing. The individual aspects of writing might include such items as syntax, organization, vocabulary, mechanics, fluency, etc. For example, the writer might receive a "1" in syntax if he or she makes so many errors that they interfere with meaning and a "2" in vocabulary if the range of words is very limited and/or if the words are frequently misused, and so forth. More specific categories within categories may be created. For example, mechanics could be broken down into spelling, punctuation, and capitalization and each of these could receive a rating that matches a particular description. Organization could be broken down into overall organization, organization within paragraphs, etc.

MAKING EVALUATION AN INTEGRAL PART OF THE CLASSROOM ENVIRONMENT

Many teachers and the language programs of which they are a part are beginning to move away from formal language testing as the sole criteria for placement, diagnosis, and measuring achievement. Language assessment for whatever purpose is becoming more and more authentic and direct as it involves students in the tasks with which they would normally be involved in communicative classrooms: expressing opinions, telling stories, asking and answering questions, creating meaning while reading and listening, role-playing, writing in journals, and so forth. The assessment in such situations is ongoing and instructive, in other words, formative as well as summative, process-focused rather than product-focused. It provides data, not only for the assessment of student progress, but for the continual informal evaluation of teaching practices and entire programs.

One way to manage such language assessment and make evaluation an integral part of the classroom environment is to use portfolios to gather student work, performance checklists, and other data.

Portfolios

Portfolios are individual collections of representative student work compiled over time.

Pierce and O'Malley (1992) remind us that there is no "right" way to design [and use] portfolios. The design and use of portfolios should grow out of needs felt in specific classrooms for which they are to be developed.

Portfolios may contain exemplary pieces of work and work in progress. The student might have a separate section of the portfolio for each. Exemplary pieces can be selected by the student independently or by the student and teacher together. What do you feel should go into this section of your portfolio? Why do you think this particular piece should go in? Why not that one? Even the selection of writing pieces itself becomes a learning experience.

Portfolios may also contain the teacher's observations and student self-evaluations. They may contain performance checklists in all skill areas (see examples on pages 105–108), preparation notes for writing and discussion (graphic organizers, brainstorming devices, and the like), materials that the student has read, summaries, illustrations, conferencing forms (see example relating to peer teaching on page 267), writing samples of various kinds, reading logs (students keep track of what they read and their reactions to what they read), performance logs (students note their reflections and intuitions about what they are doing while they are doing it), error analyses (see pages 26 and 50–51), oral production samples (transcribed or on cassettes), journal entries, anecdotal notes based on teacher observation, student learning journals (see page 223), questionnaires, videotaped performances, and so forth.

Portfolios may be used in the classroom for the same three purposes of testing already mentioned: placement (or to be more precise in this case, *re*placement, assuming that the students have already been placed initially); diagnosis; and informally measuring achievement (often used to determine grades). In addition, the data in the portfolios can be used to provide ongoing feedback to students, their parents, and other teachers. The portfolios can even go with the students to the next teacher(s), the next grade level, or the next school.

A word of caution here. The teacher and students in the classroom need to maintain control over the portfolios, their design and use. Moreover, the assessment itself, for whatever purpose, needs to be classroom-based in order to maintain the integrity of the portfolio. A portfolio is much more than simply a manila folder used to collect data for summative evaluation; it is an evolving thing that grows as the students grow and develop in the language learning process. It should not be reduced to rating scales and standardized pieces provided only to satisfy the requirements of large-scale testing programs.

As assessment instruments, portfolios can be instructive as well as evaluative, and they allow students, teachers, administrators, and parents to see the progress that has been made over time. It has been my experience that the students themselves are particularly pleased (and sometimes surprised) at the improvement they see in their work. By conferencing individually with the teacher about their portfolios, they often can come to their own conclusions about their progress, can see what their strengths are, and where they need to improve. Such conferences, if positive and nonthreatening, can be highly encouraging to students at all levels of proficiency.

The constructed dialogue below from Richard-Amato and Hansen (1995) shows a teacher and an adolescent student conferencing about the student's progress in reading-related activities. Some of the discussion is focused on a story the students have recently read entitled "Atalanta" by Betty Miles. It is about a young girl who decides that she wants to determine her own future rather than have it determined for her by her father.

Sample Dialogue

TEACHER: Well Alfredo, now that we can look back over the last nine weeks, maybe together we can see what has happened here. I can see that you have done a lot of work and, of course, we have talked about much of this before. What do you think is your best work in all of this?

ALFREDO: Well, I have been thinking about that. Let me see. I have to say that I think the letter I wrote to Atalanta's father is the best. I put it on top there (pointing to the portfolio). I told her father that she had to make her own decisions about her future.

TEACHER: Why do you like that one so much?

ALFREDO: Well, I think that it is because I will have to do that in my own family. My dad wants me to be a doctor. But me, I'm not so sure. I don't want to hurt my dad's feelings. But, you know, I think I really want to go into my own business. Like a store or something like that. You know, we talked about that before.

TEACHER: Yes, I know. And I think you are wise to talk to your dad about this.

ALFREDO: Thanks. I'm happy you agree. Now, let's see. . . .(looks back at his paper)

TEACHER: Are there any other reasons you like that piece? Maybe think about *how* you wrote it.

ALFREDO: Ummm . . . well . . . I don't know . . .

TEACHER: I see here that you put in a lot of good words to take your reader from one idea to another. See, here you used "not only that" (points to the paper) to give Atalanta's father another reason for why she wants to follow her dream. Remember, we talked about using what we called "transitions" to go from one idea to another. You needed to show how ideas were connected.

ALFREDO: I remember. I really tried to do that there . . .you know, what you told me. And I think I did that on other things too. See. (He points to another assignment.)

TEACHER: Yes, I noticed that too. That's why I have written it down here as a strength. See here (points to her list of his strengths), I wrote, "uses good transitions." Well, let's talk about some of the other improvements you have made and then we'll talk about how you can improve in a few other areas. I noticed that you are reading a lot more on your own. Your reading log here says that you have read two books since the last time we had a conference like this. . . ..

And so the discussion continues as both teacher and student talk about progress and areas for possible improvement. Together they lay out some strategies for weeks to follow.

Performance Checklists

Performance checklists are very helpful in language assessment and, as mentioned above, can be made part of the portfolios. It is important, however, that the criteria looked at be structured as general performance objectives rather than discrete-skill items. The examples in Figures 6.2 and 6.3. (Richard-Amato and Hansen, 1995) are intended for use in the assessment of reading and writing at intermediate levels. They include instruments for self-assessment in both areas. Similar instruments can be developed for teacher assessment based on observation.

Performance checklists such as those found in Figures 6.2 and 6.3 can be used to see informally what kinds of profiles emerge for each student and how they change longitudinally. Similar checklists developed by teachers can be used at other proficiency levels and for other skill areas such as listening and speaking.

When I read I . . .	usually	sometimes	not very often	comment
understand what the author is trying to say.				
understand most of the details.				
understand the vocabulary.				
read without stopping a lot.				
guess the meaning of a word by looking at the words around it.				
follow the way the author is moving through the text.				
connect what I read to my own life.				
connect what I read to what I already know.				
ask for help when I need it.				
After I read . . .				
I am able to tell someone else about what I read.				
I feel comfortable discussing the reading with others.				
I feel comfortable writing about what I have read.				

Name of Student _____ **Date** _____

Part I Check the box that best tells how often you do the things below:

My strengths appear to be:

Areas where I can improve:

Figure 6.2. Self-Assessment Reading Checklist Part I

<u>Part II</u> Put a check in front of the ones that answer the question best.

How many books did you read last month?

❑ a. none
❑ b. one
❑ c. two
❑ d. three
❑ e. more than three

What do you like to read the most? (You can check more than one.)

❑ a. books about science   ❑ g. books about the future
❑ b. books about math   ❑ h. books about the past
❑ c. books about history   ❑ i.   books about the present
❑ d. books about animals   ❑ j.   books about _____
❑ e. books about people   ❑ k. books about _____
❑ f.   books about places

What kinds of reading do you like most? (You can check more than one.)

❑ a. short stories   ❑ f.   essays that tell the opinions of others
❑ b. poetry   ❑ g. novels
❑ c. plays   ❑ h. textbooks
❑ d. autobiography   ❑ i.   _____
❑ e. biography   ❑ j.   _____

Where do you do most of your reading?

❑ a. in my classroom
❑ b. at home
❑ c. in the library
❑ d. _____

Which statements best tell how you feel about reading?

❑ a. Reading is one of my favorite activities.
❑ b. I am enjoying reading more and more.
❑ c. Reading is okay, but I like other activities better.
❑ d. I dislike reading and read only when I have to.
❑ e. I would like reading more if I could read better.

Figure 6.2. Part II

Name of Student _____ **Date** _____

<u>Part I</u> Check the box that best tells how often you are able to do the things below:

When I write I . . .	usually	sometimes	not very often	comment
plan beforehand the main things I want to say.				
say what I want to say clearly.				
organize my ideas so others can follow my thinking.				
am able to develop paragraphs.				
use bridges (transitions) to go from one idea to the next.				
use enough details to make myself understood.				
feel comfortable talking about my writing with my teacher.				
feel comfortable talking about my writing with my classmates.				
rewrite to make my ideas easier to understand.				
use words that say exactly what I want to say.				
spell correctly.				
punctuate and capitalize correctly.				

My strengths appear to be:

Areas where I can improve:

Figure 6.3. Self-Assessment Writing Checklist Part I

Part II Put a check in front of the ones that answer the question best.

How often do you write to tell about something or how you feel about something?

❑ a. almost never
❑ b. once a month
❑ c. once a week
❑ d. two or three times a week
❑ e. every day

What subjects do you like to write about most? (You can check more than one.)

❑ a. science   ❑ g. the future
❑ b. math   ❑ h. the past
❑ c. history   ❑ i.   the present
❑ d. animals   ❑ j.   _____
❑ e. people   ❑ k. _____
❑ f. places

What kind or kinds of writing do you like to do most? (You can check more than one.)

❑ a. journal writing   ❑ f. plays
❑ b. a single paragraph about   ❑ g. autobiography
        something I am interested in   ❑ h. biography
❑ c. letter writing   ❑ i.   essays that tell my opinion
❑ d. short stories   ❑ j.   _____
❑ e. poetry   ❑ k. _____

Where do you do most of your writing?

❑ a. in my classroom
❑ b. at home
❑ c. in the library
❑ d. _____

Which statements best tell how you feel about writing?

❑ a. Writing is one of my favorite activities.
❑ b. I am enjoying writing more and more.
❑ c. Writing is okay, but I like other activities better.
❑ d. I dislike writing and write only when I have to.
❑ e. I would like writing more if I could write better.

Figure 6.3. Part II

Other Assessment Procedures

Anything the student accomplishes, either in or out of school can be made part of the assessment process if that process is pragmatic and ongoing.

Not only that, but the very informal discussions that take place between student and teacher can serve as checks for comprehension (in the case of reading and listening) or as a means for finding out information about how the student is doing in all areas of language performance. A simple request, such as "Tell me about the book," and questions, such as "What do you think this story (or essay) is all about?," "What have you learned about _____ ?", "Do you feel comfortable writing about _____ ?" "Are you having any problems with _____ ?" will tell you a lot about how the student is doing and can be very helpful in completing the performance checklists. Moreover, knowing that the teacher is interested in what they are working on at the moment or what they have accomplished in the past can be extremely motivating to students.

Observing student behavior and providing anecdotal data are essential in an informed evaluation of student progress in the various areas of language performance. Has the student indicated that he or she has knowledge of a selected topic for writing? Is the student generally understood by other students when speaking? Do you usually understand what the student is saying orally and in writing? Do the student's questions about something read reveal logical thinking in the target language? Does the student appear to understand what you and others say? The answers to these and similar questions (although subjective in determination) will be extremely beneficial in coming to decisions during the evaluative process.

SUMMARY

Several types of language assessment have been presented and discussed in this chapter: norm-referenced versus criterion referenced tests; indirect versus direct tests; discrete point tests versus integrative tests. Also included in the discussion was the pragmatic test, a type of integrative test in which two naturalness criteria are relevant to the testing situation: a normal sequential context and extralinguistic data involving perceptions of life, relationships between people, and so forth.

Language assessment does not have to be a mysterious and remote activity accomplished in isolation from what is done in classrooms. The way we test does not have to be that much different from the way we teach; in fact assessment should be *an integral part of what happens in the classroom.*

Portfolios are a means by which testing can become part of the instructional process. Using portfolios, we can collect performance data to use as a basis for ongoing language assessment. Portfolios can include student work, self-evaluations, performance checklists, oral production samples (transcribed or on cassettes or video), anecdotal records, and so forth gathered over time. Portfolios can be used to inform decisions made, not only about students and how they are doing in our classrooms, but about our own instructional practices. By making language assessment an integral part of our classroom environment, we are making evaluation a formative, authentic, direct, and pragmatic process.

READINGS, REFLECTION, AND DISCUSSION

Suggested Readings and Reference Materials

Bachman, L. (1991). What does language testing have to offer? *TESOL Quarterly,* 25(4):671–698. A detailed historical overview of language testing is presented here. Included also is an interactional model of language test performance and a highly developed characterization of authenticity.

De George, G. (1988). Assessment and placement of language minority students: Procedures for mainstreaming. *Focus* 3:1–15. Occasional Papers in Bilingual Education. National Clearinghouse for Bilingual Education. Guidelines for mainstreaming students in second-language programs are presented in this paper. Teachers and administrators of second-language programs will find its contents particularly useful.

Mohan, B. (1992). What are we really testing? In P. Richard-Amato and M. A. Snow, eds. *The multicultural classroom: Readings for content-area teachers.* White Plains, N.Y.: Longman, pp. 258–270. The author talks about the problem of content validity in relation to a variety of factors. He offers examples to illustrate how language and content tests overlap and may be confused and the ways in which language tests may be culturally biased. He points out that many such tests may be, in fact, tests of cultural knowledge.

Oller, J. (1979). *Language tests at school: A pragmatic approach.* London: Longman. This now classic textbook focuses on creating, giving, and interpreting the results of pragmatic language tests. It stresses the importance of having the test reflect the teacher's general teaching philosophy.

Short, D. (1993). Assessing integrated language and content instruction. *TESOL Quarterly,* 27(4):627–656. This article presents a wealth of ideas for assessing student performance in classes in which language and content are integrated. It includes a discussion (including advantages and disadvantages) of assessment matrices, skill and concept checklists, anecdotal records, inventories of various kinds, performance-based tasks, portfolios, etc., with examples in several categories.

Wesche, M. (1987). Communicative testing in a second language. In M. Long and J. Richards, eds. *Methodology in TESOL: A book of readings.* Rowley, Mass.: Newbury House, pp. 373–394. A clearly written overview of test types in general and the objectives, issues, and characteristics of communicative tests in particular. Recommended for those readers interested in an introduction to language testing.

Yancey, K. (1992). *Portfolios in the writing classroom.* Urbana, Il.: National Council of Teachers of English. Although this anthology is intended for mainstream language arts classes and focuses on composition, it is, nevertheless, a valuable resource for teachers wanting to incorporate portfolios into their teaching. It discusses such topics as increasing student autonomy through portfolios, the teacher as a team member, and evaluation as learning. In it several teachers share their own experiences with the use of portfolios.

Questions for Reflection and Discussion

1. What would you include in a test for placing students in a language program? Create a short test that would be useful to you in a specified situation. Explain how you would use it to determine levels.

2. How might you construct a test for diagnostic purposes? How would you use it? You might consider the discussion of error analysis in Chapter 3, pages 50–51.

3. Would you feel comfortable as a language teacher using the data in portfolios as your chief means of evaluation? Why or why not?

4. Portfolios, as evaluative instruments, have been criticized for being "messy," much too subjective, and overly time-consuming. What would you say to educators making such judgments? Are any of these criticisms justified, in your opinion? Explain.

5. If you wanted to use portfolios in a typical classroom in which you might find yourself, what kinds of performance data would you want included in them. Design a plan for the use of portfolios in a hypothetical classroom. First decide who the students are and what their goals are for learning the target language. Share your plan with a small group. Ask for their feedback.

PART II

Exploring Methods and Activities: What Can We Learn?

In the literature about what can be done in classrooms, terms such as "approach," "method," and "technique" are often confusing, at best. Anthony's (1963) definitions, while general, seem adequate for the purposes of this book. He sees the relationship among these concepts as being hierarchical in nature. An *approach* (at the top level) consists of an axiomatic group of related assumptions about language teaching and learning. A *method* is an orderly plan giving direction to the presentation of materials. It must be consistent with the approach under whose umbrella it falls. A *technique* is the lowest level on the hierarchy. It is used to implement a method and accomplish immediate objectives.

Applying this terminology to the book, one could say that Part I describes a fundamental approach which teachers can utilize in developing their own language teaching principles. Part II presents the methods and activities that form a reservoir from which teachers can draw, in some way or other, whatever seems appropriate to the teaching situation. I have added the term "activity," which describes content and a set of procedures falling somewhere between the method and technique levels. Some activities, now in their embryonic states, are capable of becoming methods (e.g., "Story Experience" on pages 174–176); others will never develop into methods but will remain closer to the level of technique. The important thing to keep in mind is that all of the content and strategies suggested (regardless of their labels) are consistent with an interactional approach to second language teaching. In varying degrees, they call for high-quality input, negotiation for meaning, and creative language production in non-threatening environments.

Generally, the activities are intended specifically for elementary, secondary, and/or university second- or foreign-language programs (see Chapter 16 for descriptions of program types and Part IV for "Programs in Action"). However, many of the activities, when given modified content, could be used in language programs for special purposes such as preparing students for various technical occupations.

It should be noted that although a majority of the activities are recommended for specific age and proficiency levels, they can, for the most part, be adapted to other levels (see pages 278–280 for sample adaptations).

The particular methods or activities chosen for incorporation into a specific program will depend upon several factors: the student, the situation, and teacher preference. Not all the methods and activities are for everyone and every situation. They must be chosen carefully to form a workable program and a developing teaching methodology (see Chapter 14). The activities, for the most part, can be successfully integrated with grammar lessons when such lessons are appropriate, particularly for older learners (see Chapter 3). However, it is important in most programs to keep the main focus on meaningful communication.

CHAPTER 7

The Total Physical Response and the Audio-Motor Unit

If the training starts with explicit learning such as audio-lingual that emphasizes error-free production, correct form, and conscious rule learning, the risk is that most children and adults will give up before even reaching the intermediate level.[1]

J. Asher, 1972

QUESTIONS TO THINK ABOUT

1. Think of some examples of how children are involved physically in learning their first language. To what extent do you think learning a first language depends upon such involvement?

2. How do you think it may be possible for older children, teenagers, and/or adults to become physically involved with learning another language? What do you think the effects might be?

3. Recall a time when you may have studied another language. To what extent were you involved physically in learning that language? Do you wish you had been involved to a greater or a lesser extent with such activities? Why?

---

[1]Asher (1972) bases his opinion on the conclusions of Carroll (1960) and Lawson (1971).

THE TOTAL PHYSICAL RESPONSE

It was in the 1960s when James Asher first offered the total physical response (TPR) as one alternative to the audiolingual approach. His method, based on techniques advocated much earlier by Harold and Dorothy Palmer (1925), involves the giving of commands to which the students react. For example, the teacher might say, "Point to the door," and all the students will point to the door. The imperatives are designed to bring the target language alive by making it comprehensible and, at the same time, fun. The students are asked to act with their bodies as well as with their brains—in other words, with their total beings. Thus, the cognitive process of language acquisition is synchronized with and partially facilitated by the movements of the body.

Asher offers theoretical justification for his basic approach by looking at the process by which children master the first language. Mother or caretaker directs the child to look at an object, to pick it up, or to put it in a specific place. Production is naturally delayed until the child's listening comprehension has been developed and the child is ready to speak. Thus the child gradually becomes aware of language and what it means in terms of the environment and the situation.

It is recommended that the students, too, remain silent until they are ready to speak, usually after about ten hours of instruction. At first they jump, run, sing, or do whatever is necessary to show that the request has been comprehended. Advancing gently, at their own rates, they eventually achieve a productive command of the target language. Through this process, they evolve from silent comprehenders of language to full participants in its nuances. After a few weeks of instruction, a typical class might consist of approximately 70 percent listening comprehension, 20 percent speaking, and 10 percent reading and writing (Asher, Kusudo, and de la Torre, 1974).

The commands are given to the class as a whole, to small groups, and to individuals. Once the student has acquired some basic commands, he or she might be asked to perform a double action such as, "Walk to the window and open it." The teacher or another student generally demonstrates the appropriate behavior first, making the actions very clear. Then the student is expected to carry out the request. If he or she does not respond at first, the teacher should repeat both the words and the demonstration rather than demand that the student comply with a repetition of the words alone. Gradually, the requests gain complexity as the student becomes more proficient. For example, the teacher might say, "When Lamm opens the window, Maria will run to the door and close it."

The students, when ready, move into the production phase by volunteering to give the commands while the teacher and other students carry them out. The students are allowed to make mistakes when they first begin to speak; thus anxiety is lowered. It is expected that their speech will gradually take on the shape of the teacher's as they gain confidence with their new language.

Although Asher recommends a grammatical sequencing of the materials, the lessons themselves are not focused on grammar; instead they are focused on meaning, especially at beginning stages. The grammar is internalized inductively. It is expected that certain forms will be more suited than others to the method and will therefore be repeated over and over in the natural course of events.

Concerning the method itself, Asher admits that a few teachers may be skeptical of his basic approach for one reason or another. Although some have accepted TPR for the teaching of simple action verbs, they have questioned its use for teaching some of the nonphysical elements of language—past and future tenses, abstract words, and function words. To defuse this kind of skepticism, Asher (1972) and Asher, Kusudo, and de la Torre (1974) offer a number of studies such as the two field tests described below.

The first field test involved adults who had taken about 32 hours of German with an instructor using the total physical response. It was found that most of the linguistic forms of German could indeed be incorporated into the commands. Tenses were combined by using clauses in sentences such as "While John is closing the door, Annette will turn out the light." Function words were not a major problem because they were ubiquitous and were acquired naturally through repetition in a variety of situations. Abstract words such as "honor" and "justice" were manipulated as though they were objects. The words were written on cards. The instructor gave commands in German such as "Andy, pick up 'justice' and give it to Sue."

Although the experimental group had had only 32 hours of training, it did significantly better in listening comprehension than a group of college students who had received 75 to 150 hours of audiolingual/grammar-translation instruction in German. It is interesting to note that the experimental group, even though it had no systematic instruction in reading, did as well in that area as the control group which had received such training.

Asher (1972) surmised that if students can internalize listening comprehension of a second language, they can make the transition to oral production, reading, and writing with a fair amount of ease.

The second field test reported by Asher, Kusudo, and de la Torre (1974) involved undergraduate college students in beginning Spanish. After about 10 hours of concentration in listening comprehension, the students were invited but not coerced into switching roles with the teacher. As each student became ready to do so, he or she assumed the teacher role and gave the commands for brief periods of time. Reading and writing were also accomplished at the student's individual pace. The teacher wrote on the chalkboard any phrases or words that students wished to see in writing. Skits were created and presented, and problem solving was attempted, all in the target language.

After 45 hours of instruction, the experimental group was compared with the control groups whose hours of instruction ranged from 75 to 200. The group exposed to the total physical response exceeded all other groups in listening skill for stories.

After 90 hours of instruction, the group was given a form of the Pimsleur Spanish Proficiency Test that was intended for students who had completed about 150 hours of college instruction, audiolingual style. Even with almost no direct instruction in reading and writing, the students were beyond the 75th percentile for level I and beyond the 65th percentile for level II.

According to Asher, the studies clearly indicated that TPR training produces generally better results than the audiolingual method. He attributes the success to the fact that TPR utilizes implicit learning, whereas the audiolingual approach relies on explicit learning. These two concepts roughly parallel Krashen's acquisition/learning distinction (see Chapter 2). However, Asher suggests that an alternative model of teaching might begin the instruction in the implicit mode and end it in the explicit mode. At later levels he feels that a student's skills may be advanced to the point at which teaching rules and correcting errors may be beneficial.

Even though Asher (1982, 1993) sees his method as being the focus of classroom activity rather than a supplement, he does recommend that it be used in combination with other techniques such as skits, other kinds of role play, and problem solving.

The commands themselves may be arranged around several topics of interest. For example, lessons may be organized around parts of the body, numbers, spatial relationships, colors, shapes, emotions, clothes, giving directions, and so forth. Asher recommends that only a certain number of new concepts be given at one time depending upon the students' levels of understanding and other factors.

Below is a list of a few typical commands to use with beginners.[2] These may be modified, expanded, or combined in a variety of ways. Some possibilities for modification are suggested in parentheses.

Stand up.

Sit down.

Touch the floor (desk).

Raise your arm (leg).

Put down your arm (leg).

Pat your cheek (back, arm, stomach, chest).

Wipe your forehead (face, chin, elbow).

Scratch your nose (knee, ankle, heel).

Massage your arm (neck).

Giggle.

Make a face.

Flex your muscles.

Shrug your shoulders.

Wave to me (to_____).
(name of student)

Tickle your side.

Clap your hands.

Point to the ceiling (door).

Cry.

Mumble.

Talk.

---

[2] These commands were adapted from a mimeographed sheet (author unknown) distributed by the Jefferson County Schools, Lakewood, Colorado.

Turn your head to the right (left).	Whisper.
	Hum.
Drum your fingers.	Stand up.
Wet your lips.	Hop on one foot (on the other foot, on both feet).
Pucker your lips.	
Blow a kiss.	Step forward (backward, to the side).
Cough.	Lean backward (toward me, away from me).
Sneeze.	Make a fist.
Shout your name ("help").	Shake your fist (head, hand, foot, hips).
Spell your name.	_____ , walk to the door, (window).
Laugh.	(name of student)
Stretch.	_____ , turn on (off) the lights (radio).
Yawn.	(name of student)
Sing.	

It is important to note that Asher intended a lighthearted, relaxed approach to his method, one in which students are encouraged to take on some of the playfulness of childhood, a time when learning language could easily be made a game and "losing oneself" in it was a natural consequence. Therefore, a "barking" of commands, army sergeant style, would not be appropriate. Instead, the commands should be given in an easy, nondemanding manner.

A sample lesson for rank beginners might look like this:

The teacher has one or two volunteer students, peer teachers, or lay assistants (see Chapter 14) come to the front of the room. They are offered chairs through gesture. They sit in them. The teacher also sits in a chair. He or she gives the following commands:

1. Stand up. (The teacher demonstrates by standing.)
2. Sit down. (The teacher demonstrates by sitting.) (two repetitions of 1 and 2)
3. Stand up. (The teacher motions to the two volunteer students or teacher assistants to stand up. They stand.)
4. Sit down. (The teacher motions to them to sit down. They sit down.) (two repetitions of 3 and 4)

The teacher turns to the class.

5. Stand up (motions to everyone to stand up and they all stand).
6. Sit down (motions to everyone to sit down and they all sit). (two repetitions of 5 and 6)

The teacher compliments with a simple "good" at various points and with a lot of smiles. Then he or she continues by giving the commands minus the gestural clues to see if the students are indeed comprehending the words. Gradually other commands are added following similar procedures. For example, the next commands might be "step forward" followed by "step backward." And on it goes until the students have a rather large repertoire of commands that they can comprehend. Often the order of the commands is varied to ensure that students are not simply memorizing a sequence of actions.

I personally like to give commands to volunteers or to the whole class (as in the example above) rather than single out individuals. I feel that anxiety is lowered if students are allowed some anonymity, especially at the very beginning stages.[3] In addition, I prefer to use the method in small doses, perhaps for fifteen minutes or so three or four times a week at beginning levels. Otherwise, the technique becomes too tiring for the students and for me. Also, if I use it extensively, there is the danger that the students will get the impression that the main function of the target language is to give commands. For these reasons, it makes sense to combine it with other kinds of activities that *reinforce* what is being taught. Activities such as cutting and pasting, drawing, painting, jazz chants, story experience, songs, and others (see later chapters) can all be effective ways to increase possibilities for acquisition. Another means of reinforcement is to incorporate key concepts during a common classroom ritual such as grouping students for other activities (see also pages 194 and 213). For instance, the teacher might want to reinforce colors: "All students with the color red on come to table 1; all students with blue on go to table 2." Or, using the same method, the teacher might reinforce months of the year: "All students born in May or June come to table 1." The teacher can continue reshuffling students by giving similar commands until each group has the necessary number of students in it.

Below are some TPR-based activities that can readily be adapted to almost any age level (provided the students are cognitively ready) or to the teaching of any language.[4] Possible alternative words are given in parentheses.

Total Physical Response-Based Activities

THE POINTING GAME

With a small group of students, use a collection of pictures such as those one might find in a mail-order catalog to reinforce concepts that have been taught. Ask students to point to various specific body parts (a head, an arm), to colors (something green), or to items of clothing (a dress, a sweater).

IDENTIFYING EMOTIONS

After the class has acquired simple commands such as "cry" or "laugh," pictures can be placed across the front of the room of people clearly demonstrating such emotional reactions.

---

[3] It is interesting to note that even those students who only observe seem to internalize the commands (see Asher, 1982).

[4] I would like to thank Sylvia Cervantes, Carol Gorenberg, and Cyndee Gustke for the basic notions involved in "Dress the Paper Doll," "Working with Shapes," and "Following Recipes."

Students can be asked to take the picture of a person displaying a specific reaction (someone crying, someone laughing). Later this same procedure can be extended to other kinds of descriptions of emotions, perhaps more subtle ones (someone who is sad, someone who is angry).

DRESS THE PAPER DOLL

A large paper doll man, woman, or child with a set of clothes can be made and mounted on a bulletin board. Velcro can be used to make the paper clothes stick to the figure. Students are then asked to place various items of clothing on it. Concepts such as checked, polka-dotted, and striped can be taught in the same manner along with a variety of fabrics and textures (wool, cotton, velvet, or rough, smooth, soft). For teaching the fabrics and textures, different kinds of materials can be cut in the shape of the paper clothes and glued to them.

MANIPULATING RODS

Rods of various colors such as those used in Gattegno's Silent Way can provide realia for teaching numbers, spatial relationships, colors, and the like (take the *blue* rod, take *three* red rods, put the blue rod *beside* a red rod). Rods can be used also in advancing students to more complex structures (take a red rod and give it to the teacher).

BOUNCING THE BALL

Concepts such as numbers, days of the week, and months of the year can be acquired or reinforced simply by having the students bounce a ball (Richard-Amato, 1983, p. 397). For instance, each one of twelve students in a circle could represent a month of the year. The "March" student would be directed to bounce the ball and call out "March, June." The student who is "June" would have to catch the ball before it bounces a second time. Conscious attention is centered on the act of catching the ball while the language itself is being internalized at a more or less peripheral level of consciousness.

WORKING WITH SHAPES

Another idea is to cut squares, rectangles, triangles, and circles out of various colors of construction paper and distribute them to the students. Shapes (hold up the triangle), colors (hold up the green triangle), and numbers (hold up three triangles) can be taught or reinforced. Ordinal numbers can also be introduced by placing several shapes in various positions along the chalkboard. A student can be asked to place the green triangle in the third position or the eighth position, for example. Each student in the class can then be given a small box of crayons or colored pencils and a hand-out with rows of squares, rectangles, triangles, and circles drawn on it. Commands such as "Find the first row of circles. Go to the fifth circle. Color it red" can be given to reinforce not only the shape, but the ordinal number and the color.

As a follow-up, students can cut out of magazines pictures of objects that have shapes similar to those mentioned above. Another follow-up might be to have students cut the various shapes from colored poster board, newsprint, or wallpaper. Have them arrange the shapes into a collage.

FOLLOWING RECIPES

At much later stages, making holiday rice cakes, baking valentine cookies, or preparing enchiladas can provide a TPR experience and can also involve students in the cultures of other countries and those within the United States. First display all the ingredients for any given recipe and introduce each item, one by one. Then present each student with a written recipe. An extra large version to which you and the students can refer can be placed at the front of the room. While you or a student reads the recipe, other students can measure, mix the ingredients, and so on. As a follow-up, students can bring in favorite recipes to share. These can be put together to form a class recipe book to which others can be added.

INFORMATION GAPS

Information gaps (Allwright, 1979; Johnson, 1979) can be created in which one student has information that another does not have but needs. One student may give a set of directions or commands to another student, who will carry them out to meet some stated goal. For example, Student A goes to the chalkboard and Student B goes to the back of the room and faces the back wall, with a drawing in hand (simple geometric shapes usually work best at first. Student B then gives step-by-step directions to Student A so that A can reproduce the drawing. This activity can be followed by a debriefing if the directions have not produced a configuration fairly close to the original. If the directions have been written down by a teacher assistant as they are given, the specific steps can be analyzed to see how they might be clarified (Richard-Amato, 1983, p. 399).

An alternative might be to have Students A and B seated across from one another at a table with a divider between them, high enough so Student B cannot see what Student A is doing. Next give Student A some blocks of various sizes, shapes, and colors. Student B gets a duplicate set of blocks. Student A then is asked to build an original configuration or structure with the blocks. While Student A is accomplishing the task, he or she gives directions to Student B so that B can build a similar configuration or structure. Again a debriefing can take place if there has been a breakdown in the communication.

Although the advantages are obvious, there appear to be a few potential drawbacks in using Asher's method. The first concerns the teaching of words representing abstract concepts. Although words such as "honor" and "justice" might be briefly remembered through use of Asher's technique, it is difficult to see how their meanings would become clear unless they are used repeatedly in some sort of meaningful context based on experience. It should be noted, however, that Asher has attempted to remedy the problem by placing translations of the words into the students' first languages on the back of cards.

Another possible difficulty is the lack of intrinsic sequencing. Although some of the applications suggested in this chapter do involve a logical sequencing, the method itself does not call for it. It is probable that students, particularly those who are operating at the high beginning levels and up, will lose interest in the activities unless some sort of logical sequencing of events is present in the commands. No matter how much fun or how fast paced they may be, something is lost if they remain isolated from one another and from what we know about human experience. For example, suppose a student is asked to "turn off the light and shout 'help'" (as suggested in the list of commands earlier in this chapter). What motivation does the student have for performing these actions other than to demonstrate that he or she is comprehending? If at some point a context could be provided for such behavior, then perhaps the action would become more meaningful and thus more memorable to the progressing learner. Consider the following situation. A blind person (such as in the Audrey Hepburn classic *Wait Until Dark*) has discovered an intruder in her apartment. Cleverly, she turns off the light so that she and the intruder will be equally handicapped. In spite of this maneuver, she soon realizes she is definitely in a "no-win" situation. She might shout "help" in order to attract her neighbors. Now the commands have taken on another dimension for a student who might be asked to play the part of the blind person. Strings of seemingly unrelated sentences have now taken on meaning and become part of motivated, logical discourse (see Chapter 15).

Often TPR-type activities can begin with a simple story, read and acted out by the teacher and one or more teacher assistants. Later the teacher can act as a director and the students can perform the parts. Directions might include commands such as "Sit down in the chair" or "Shake hands with Mr. Kim (a character in the story)" or "Tell Hong (another character) to take the book from the shelf." The key words and phrases eventually can be written on the chalkboard or placed on cue cards. When the students are ready, they can take turns being the director while the teacher and other students act out the parts. The students can move from predetermined scripts to ones that they create themselves. Perhaps they can even perform their own creations for other groups. (For more ideas involving role play and drama, see Chapter 10.)

THE AUDIO-MOTOR UNIT

Kalivoda, Morain, and Elkins (1971) also recognize the lack of meaningful sequencing as a weakness in the TPR method at later stages and suggest alternative ways of combining commands. Although their ideas may not be as dramatic as the one offered above, they nevertheless add a contextual dimension to the utterances. They call a particular sequence of commands an *audio-motor unit*. A 10-minute tape is played on which a native speaker issues a series of commands for twenty actions, all centering on a single topic. The teacher demonstrates the appropriate responses to the commands, using whatever realia are available to make the actions comprehensible. An audio-motor unit might include such pantomimed or real sequences as "go to the cupboard," "open the cupboard door," "find the largest bowl," "take it out," "set it on the table," and so on. The students are then invited to comply with the commands. Actions may be pantomimed when it is not possible or advisable to use props. For example, climbing a real ladder could prove a difficult and even dangerous task, but a pretend ladder could be almost as effective if one uses a little imagination.

Kalivoda, Morain, and Elkins like to consider the audio-motor unit as supplemental to a larger program (which, unfortunately, they do not describe) rather than as the focus. Although one unit generally lasts only about 10 minutes, it can be made longer or shorter depending on student needs and on the amount of time available from day to day.

They also like to include cultural learning in the lessons. Various customs involving eating, preparing food, telephone conversations, and introductions can be taught through a series of commands given in the context of real or pretend situations.

To examine the effectiveness of the audio-motor unit, they looked at the results of a pilot program in the Southeastern Language Center at the University of Georgia (Kalivoda, Morain, and Elkins, 1971.) The students were given intensive six-week courses in Spanish, French, or German. Beginning classes received one 10-minute lesson each day; advanced classes were given only one or two 10-minute lessons a week. The eight participating teachers had received only enough special instruction to make the presentations similar in execution. After the courses were over, the students filled out questionnaires so that their attitudes toward the audio-motor strategy could be studied. Of the 180 students who took part, 90 percent revealed positive attitudes. They thought that the method improved their listening comprehension and increased their vocabularies. Furthermore, they seemed to like the change of pace that it gave to the daily lessons, and they found it stimulating and entertaining. However, a few of the remaining 10 percent found it not difficult enough, boring, or silly. Some students and teachers felt that the written form of the commands should have been given and a few students thought that they should have been able to participate orally in the lesson.

Six of the eight teachers reacted positively. The benefits they reported are paraphrased below:

1. The vocabulary, structures, and syntax of the language used in their lessons were reinforced by exposure to the audio-motor strategy.
2. Students became strongly interested in the lessons through the physical acting out of cultural aspects.
3. The lessons, even though designed for the development of listening skills, had a real impact on oral production. The teachers noticed increased spontaneity and better pronunciation although they admitted the latter was difficult to verify.
4. The nonnative teachers of the various languages felt that they improved their own skills with the languages they were teaching.

In spite of its qualities, the audio-motor unit may suffer somewhat from its dependence on a tape to give the commands. The activities could become less personalized and less flexible than those in Asher's approach, in which teachers use students' names and react to their changing needs from moment to moment. This is not to say that it is not a good idea to expose students occasionally to taped voices for which there may be no visual clues to meaning.

It must be pointed out that in both methods the teacher is the controlling force. The interaction must be almost completely teacher structured and controlled until the students gain enough proficiency to have more influence. At that time, activities such as "information gaps" mentioned earlier can be implemented, allowing students to have a more significant role in the interactional process.

SUMMARY

Asher's total physical response involves giving a series of commands to which the students respond physically. The students themselves remain silent until they are ready for oral production. At that time, they have the option of giving the commands. The students gradually develop their interlanguage, which becomes more and more like the language of their teacher. The main disadvantage, which becomes most apparent at later stages, is that the commands do not, except in some adaptations, adhere to a logical sequence based on experience.

Kusudo, Morain, and Elkins, while following the way led by Asher, enlarged upon the basic method by adding meaningful sequence. In addition, they considered their method to be an adjunct to a much larger program rather than the focus. A disadvantage may be that by recommending the use of a tape to give the commands, they take away some of the personalization and flexibility that seem to be an integral part of the Asher method.

In spite of their drawbacks, effective adaptations of either approach can pay large dividends in terms of student interest, spontaneity, and language development. Students' chances for becoming more proficient in their new language seem to increase when they are allowed to listen first, speak when ready, and be involved in the target language physically.

READINGS, REFLECTION, AND DISCUSSION

Suggested Readings and Reference Materials

Asher, J. (1982). *Learning another language through actions: The complete teachers' guidebook.* Los Gatos, Calif.: Sky Oaks. A must for anyone intending to use total physical response methodology in the classroom. Covers related research and discusses in depth the techniques themselves. The lessons can be readily adapted to teaching languages other than English.

Francois, L. (1983). *English in action.* Southgate, Calif.: Linda Francois. Offers very explicit instructions on using the total physical response for teachers who have never experienced it before. Combines the total physical response with such activities as acting out, songs, and chants. Includes greetings, colors, shapes, body parts, time, numbers, the alphabet, and directions.

Glisan, E. (1993). Total physical response: A technique for teaching all skills in Spanish. In J. Oller, Jr., ed., *Methods that work: Ideas for literacy and language teachers,* 2nd ed., Boston, Mass.: Heinle and Heinle, pp. 30–39. The author offers suggestions for taking the language learner far beyond the beginning proficiency levels in the target language. In addition, she presents the outline of a sample lesson in Spanish.

Larsen-Freeman, D. (1986). The total physical response method. In D. Larsen-Freeman, *Techniques and principles in language teaching.* New York: Oxford University Press, pp. 109–122. The principles and techniques of the total physical response are discussed and the reader is invited to "experience" it through a description of its implementation in a constructed classroom setting.

Segal, B. (1984). *Teaching English as a second language: Shortcuts to success.* Paso Robles, Calif.: Bureau of Education and Research. Although Segal comes to questionable conclusions concerning right- versus left-brain function, she does offer helpful guidelines for teachers who want to develop units around total physical response lessons. She has created similar books for teaching Spanish, French, and German.

Questions for Reflection and Discussion

1. How serious is the problem of a lack of logical sequencing in the Asher method applied at later stages?

2. How might the total physical response foster lowered anxiety levels (refer to Chapter 5)? Discuss.

3. Kalivoda, Morain, and Elkins (1971) state, "Careful structuring of the audio-motor units provides for reentry of materials at regular intervals." How might you incorporate reentries into a previous lesson from a present lesson? Create one or more examples of effective uses of this technique.

4. Prepare a 5-minute TPR or audio-motor unit lesson to try out on a small group of fellow students. If the commands are simple enough, you might want to demonstrate in a target language with which the group is unfamiliar. In what ways was the lesson successful? How can it be improved? Discuss with class members.

CHAPTER 8

The Natural Approach: How it Is Evolving

The essence of language is human activity—activity on the part of one individual to make himself understood, and activity on the part of the other to understand what was in the mind of the first.

O. Jespersen, 1904

QUESTIONS TO THINK ABOUT

1. What do you think a "natural" approach to acquiring another language in a classroom might entail?

2. To what extent was any experience you may have had with another language "natural"?

3. What do you think the role of grammar might be in a natural language classroom?

AN OVERVIEW

Tracy Terrell was careful to make no claim for the natural approach that other methods could not match if they relied on real communication as their *modus operandi*. Like Asher (1982), he reminded us that students must acquire the second language in much the same way that people acquire language in natural situations (therefore the term "natural approach"). Some argue that what was being recommended is not really a method at all but is, in a more general sense, an approach. However, Krashen and Terrell (1983) developed the natural approach as a method, and so, for the purposes of discussion, that is the way it will be presented here. They based their method on four principles.

The first principle states that *comprehension precedes production*. As in the total physical response, the teacher observes the need for a silent period. During this time, the teacher uses the target language predominantly, focuses on communicative situations, and provides comprehensible input that is roughly tuned to the students' proficiency levels.

Second, *production must be allowed to emerge in stages*. Responses will generally begin with nonverbal communication, progress to single words, then to two- and three-word combinations, next to phrases and sentences, and finally to complete discourse. Students speak when they are ready, and speech errors are generally not corrected directly. However, a teacher focused on communication will give many indirect corrections as part of the natural process of checking for understanding. Thus, the student's interlanguage is allowed to develop normally as the student begins to incorporate such corrections into his or her own utterances through communication.

The third principle asserts that *the course syllabus be based on communicative goals*. Grammatical sequencing as a focus is shunned in favor of a topical/situational organization. Discussion centers on items in the classroom, body parts, favorite vacation spots, and other topics of interest. It is felt that the grammar will be acquired mainly through the relevant communication.

Fourth, *the activities themselves must be planned so that they will lower the affective filter* (see description on page 30). A student who is engrossed in interesting ideas will be less apt to have anxiety than one who is focused mainly on form. In addition, the atmosphere must be friendly and accepting if the student is to have the best possible chance for acquiring the target language.

The natural approach and its extensions used in conjunction with many other methods and activities with which it is compatible (total physical response and the audio-motor unit, jazz chants, music, games, role play, storytelling, affective activities) can produce extremely rich environments where concepts are reinforced through a variety of ways. The natural approach and all the methods with which it is used should blend to form a well-integrated program if it is to work. Although recycling is not emphasized in the natural approach literature, it is important that concepts be recycled in many different ways in order for them to be mastered.

Because the focus of the natural approach is on real communication, many demands are made upon the time and energy of the teacher. He or she must present a great deal of comprehensible input about concrete, relevant topics, especially at beginning levels. It is not unusual to see the natural approach language teacher trudging across campus with sacks filled with fruits to talk about and eat, dishes with which to set a table for an imaginary dinner, oversized clothes to put on over other clothes, and additional paraphernalia to demonstrate the notions involved. This teacher can no longer just ask students to open their books to a certain page, say "Repeat after me," or assign the students to endless exercises in rule application. According to Krashen and Terrell, the teacher's chief responsibility during class hours is to communicate with the students about things that are of interest and relevance to them.

Even though other topics might be more appropriate depending upon the goals of the students, the following outline adapted from Krashen and Terrell (1983, pp. 67–70) may be useful in planning units for beginning to low-intermediate students who appear to be mainly interested in improving personal communication skills.

Preliminary Unit: Learning to Understand

Topics

1. Names of students	5. Clothing
2. Descriptions of people	6. Colors
3. Family members	7. Objects in the classroom
4. Numbers	8. Parts of the body

Situations
1. Greetings
2. Classroom commands

I. Students in the Classroom

Topics
1. Personal identification (name, address, telephone number, age, sex, nationality, date of birth, marital status)
2. Description of school environment (identification, description and location of people and objects in the classroom, description and location of buildings)
3. Classes
4. Telling time

Situations
1. Filling out forms
2. Getting around the school

II. Recreation and Leisure Activities

Topics

1. Favorite activities
2. Sports and games
3. Climate and seasons
4. Weather
5. Seasonal activities
6. Holiday activities
7. Parties
8. Abilities
9. Cultural and artistic interests

Situations

1. Playing games, sports
2. Being a spectator
3. Chitchatting

III. Family, Friends, and Daily Activities

Topics

1. Family and relatives
2. Physical states
3. Emotional states
4. Daily activities
5. Holiday and vacation activities
6. Pets

Situations

1. Introductions, meeting people
2. Visiting relatives
3. Conversing on the phone

IV. Plans, Obligations, and Careers

Topics

1. Future plans
2. General future activities
3. Obligations
4. Hopes and desires
5. Careers and professions
6. Place of work
7. Work activities
8. Salary and money

Situations

1. Job interviewing
2. Talking on the job

V. Residence

Topics

1. Place of residence
2. Rooms of a house
3. Furniture
4. Activities at home
5. Household items
6. Amenities

Situations

1. Looking for a place to live
2. Moving
3. Shopping for the home

VI. Narrating Past Experiences

Topics

1. Immediate past events
2. Yesterday's activities
3. Weekend events
4. Holidays and parties
5. Trips and vacations
6. Other experiences

Situations

1. Friends recounting experiences
2. Making plans

VII. Health, Illnesses, and Emergencies

Topics

1. Body parts
2. Physical states
3. Mental states and moods
4. Health maintenance
5. Health professions
6. Medicine and diseases

Situations

1. Visiting the doctor
2. Hospitals
3. Health interviews
4. Buying medicine
5. Emergencies (accidents)

VIII. Eating

Topics

1. Foods
2. Beverages

Situations

1. Ordering a meal in a restaurant
2. Shopping in a supermarket
3. Preparing food from recipes

IX. Travel and Transportation

Topics

1. Geography
2. Modes of transportation
3. Vacations
4. Experiences on trips
5. Languages
6. Making reservations

Situations

1. Buying gasoline
2. Exchanging money
3. Clearing customs
4. Obtaining lodging
5. Buying tickets

X. Shopping and Buying

Topics

1. Money and prices
2. Fashions
3. Gifts
4. Products

Situations
1. Selling and buying
2. Shopping
3. Bargaining

XI. *Youth*

Topics
1. Childhood experiences
2. Primary school experiences
3. Teen years experiences
4. Adult expectations and activities

Situations
1. Reminiscing with friends
2. Sharing photo albums
3. Looking at school yearbooks

XII. *Giving Directions and Instructions*

Topics
1. Spatial concepts (north, south, east, west: up, down; right, left, center; parallel, perpendicular, etc.)
2. Time relationships (after, before, during, etc.)

Situations
1. Giving instructions
2. Following instructions
3. Reading maps
4. Finding locations
5. Following game instructions
6. Giving an invitation
7. Making appointments

XIII. *Values*

Topics
1. Family
2. Friendship
3. Love
4. Marriage
5. Sex roles and stereotypes
6. Goals
7. Religious beliefs

Situations
1. Making a variety of decisions based on one's values
2. Sharing and comparing values in a nonthreatening environment
3. Clarifying values

XIV. *Issues and Current Events*

Topics
1. Environmental problems
2. Economic issues
3. Education
4. Employment and careers
5. Ethical issues
6. Politics
7. Crime
8. Sports

  9. Social events   11. Minority groups
 10. Cultural events   12. Science and health

Situations

  1. Discussing last night's news broadcast
  2. Discussing a recent movie, etc.

The students move through three overlapping stages in the natural approach: (1) comprehension, (2) early speech production, and (3) speech emergence. Beyond speech emergence is a fourth stage later recognized by Terrell and others as *intermediate fluency*. According to natural approach advocates, the length of time spent in any one stage varies greatly depending upon the individual, upon the amount of comprehensible input received, and upon the degree to which the affective filter has been lowered. Some students begin speaking after just a couple of hours, while others need several weeks. Children may need several months. The second stage, early speech production, may take anywhere from a few months to one year or longer. The third stage, speech emergence, can take up to three years, but usually the student is reasonably fluent in personal communication skills long before that, if the input has been of high quality, if it was given in sufficient quantity, and if the student has been receptive to it. Generally the teacher does most of the talking to provide the needed comprehensible input. However, as the students become more proficient, they take over and the teacher's role becomes predominantly that of an organizer and a facilitator.

THE COMPREHENSION STAGE

During this first stage, the students are allowed to go through a silent period. They receive comprehensible input usually from the teachers and, in some classrooms, from peer teachers and lay assistants (see Chapter 14). Often the total physical response or versions of it are used. Although the students' main goal is to develop listening skills, many of the activities overlap into the next higher level, early speech production. Simple responses to the comprehensible input may be made by gesturing, nodding, using the L1, answering "yes," or "no," giving names of people or objects as answers to questions such as "Who has on a yellow dress?" (Kim) or "Do you want an apple or an orange?" (apple). A lot of visuals, explanations, repetitions, and so forth are used. The teacher's speech is a little slower than usual. The intonation is reasonably normal except that key words receive a bit of extra emphasis. Students are not called upon to respond individually. Instead, questions are directed to the whole group, and one or several can respond. Key terms can be written on the board, perhaps on the second or third time the students are exposed to them. If the student is exposed to written forms of the words too soon, he or she may experience a cognitive overloading that could interfere with acquisition.

Total physical response (TPR) activities may be used to get the students into some basic vocabulary. For example, students can acquire names ("Give the book to Hong"), descriptions ("Take the pencil to a person who has short hair"), numbers ("Pick up three pieces of chalk"), colors ("Find the blue book"), and many other concepts. Notice that aspects of the total physical response will be involved to some degree in almost every activity suggested for this level. From my own experience with the natural approach, I found that at this stage it is important that new concepts be introduced gradually and that frequent checks for understanding be made before adding other new concepts. In the sample dialogue that follows, the teacher is teaching four colors (red, blue, green, yellow) and has a strip of construction paper for each color. Notice that the language is very simple for rank beginners when they are first being exposed to the relevant concepts. However, the language will become *much richer* quickly, as the teacher begins to build upon these concepts.

TEACHER: (*holding up the red strip*) This is red. This is red. (*The teacher then points to a student's red sweater.*) Is this red? (*The teacher begins to nod her head, softly uttering*) Yes.

STUDENTS: (*nodding their heads*) Yes.

TEACHER: (*pointing to a student's red skirt*) Is this red?

STUDENTS: (*nodding their heads*) Yes.

TEACHER: (*pointing to a green sweater*) Is this red? (*She begins to shake her head softly uttering*) No.

TEACHER: (*The teacher points to the red strip again.*) Is this red?

STUDENTS: Yes.

TEACHER: Yes. This is red. (*again points to the red strip*)

TEACHER: (*holding the blue strip*) This is blue. This is blue. (*The teacher points to a student's blue scarf.*) Is this blue?

STUDENTS: Yes.

TEACHER: (*pointing to a blue door*) Is this blue?

STUDENTS: Yes.

TEACHER: Good. Yes, this is blue. (*The teacher points to the red strip.*) Is this blue?

STUDENTS: No.

TEACHER: No. (*pointing to the blue strip*) This is blue and this (*pointing to the red strip*) is red.

And so the teacher continues, adding one color at a time while returning to check for understanding of the colors already introduced. After working through the four colors, the teacher then gives the strips to various students, with the following requests: "Give me the red one." The teacher reaches for the red one, and then adds, "Give me the blue one," and so on. The students may not understand all of the teacher's words at first, but chances are they will remember the key concepts that were emphasized, and they probably will note (perhaps subconsciously at first) other elements (usually function words) in the utterances. Gradually they will begin to comprehend and then use the concepts in many different meaningful contexts.

It is important not to introduce too many new concepts at once. In addition, it is important to reinforce the ones introduced immediately. For example, the teacher may want the students to cut out of magazines objects of each of the four colors, paste those of the same color on a sheet of paper, and label the sheet with the name of the color. Or the teacher may ask the students to draw and color with crayons various objects in different colors. A day or so later the teacher may bring in pieces of clothing that are of the same colors taught, to see if they are remembered. At that point, the pieces of clothing themselves may be the new concepts to which the students are introduced in a similar manner.

Once the students can identify simple concepts, then the teacher can reinforce these and introduce some new ones by using a stream of comprehensible input: "Look at Maria's feet. She is wearing shoes. Look at Jorge's feet. He is wearing shoes, too. His shoes are brown. Look at his hair. His hair is brown. How many students have brown hair?" (nine) "What is the name of the student with red hair?" (Carolina) "Who is behind the person with the red shirt?" (Yung) "Does Yung have on a shirt or a sweater?" (sweater) "What color is the sweater?" (yellow) The teacher can carry on in this fashion about a wide variety of concrete subjects stimulated by a picture, an object, a map, and so on.

Other sample activities, which are extensions of the natural approach, are described on the next few pages.[1]

Extensions of the Natural Approach Activities

WHERE DOES IT BELONG?

On a chalkboard, sketch and label the rooms of a house (see Figure 8.1). Then briefly talk about the house and the various rooms in it. (*Look at the house. It is big. It has many rooms. Here is the kitchen. Food is kept in the kitchen. People eat in the kitchen. And so forth.*) A few typical household items including furniture can be roughly drawn in each of the rooms to help the students correctly identify them. Other household items can be cut from heavy paper, to be placed in the appropriate rooms. Pieces of cellophane tape can be rolled up and placed on the backs of the pictures to make them stick to the chalkboard. (Later the tape can be removed so that the pictures can be reused). Commands such as "Put the stove in the kitchen" or "Put the dresser in the bedroom" can be given. An alternative might be to use a large doll house with miniature furniture for the same kind of activity or a magnetic board.

Items typical of other places can be incorporated in similar activities. Simulated settings such as zoos, farmyards, hospitals, libraries, various work sites, cafeterias, and university campuses can be the focus.

---

[1] Many of these activities can be adapted to several age levels, provided students are cognitively able to deal with the tasks (see Chapter 14). They can also be adapted for teaching any language, second or foreign, and for most programs: English for Academic Purposes (EAP), English for Special Purposes (ESP), and others.

Figure 8.1

PUT IT ON!

Bring in a variety of oversized clothes. Talk about the clothes. (*These are pants. They are blue. Here is the pocket. Point to the pocket.*) Have the students put the clothes on (over their own) according to the directions you give. The oversized clothes can be taken off using a similar procedure. A camera can come in handy for recording the highlights of this activity. The photos can be displayed in the classroom and used at a later stage to stimulate discussion.

A follow-up might be to provide the students with clothing catalogs, scissors, paste, and blank sheets of construction paper.[2] Then demonstrate the activity for the students. Take articles of clothing (which you have previously cut out) as well as a cut-out head, arms, and legs. Show the class how easy it is to create a figure by gluing these items to the construction paper. The figure will probably look very humorous, especially if you have chosen such things as enormous shoes, a little head, and a strange assortment of clothing. Have the students make their own funny figures. Through a cooperative effort, students locate the items each needs to complete a creation. In the process, the same words are repeated over and over, and a great deal of laughter is generated, lowering anxiety.

GUESS WHAT'S IN THE BOX[3]

Have a box filled with objects whose names are already familiar to the students. Describe a particular object and have the students guess which object is being described. Once the object has been correctly named, remove it from the box and give it to the student temporarily. Once all the objects have been handed out, you can then ask that the objects be returned: "Who has the rubber band?", and so forth.

---

[2] I wish to thank Teri Sandoval for the follow-up idea.

[3] Thanks to Esther Heise for introducing this idea to me.

GETTING AROUND

For ESL students, make a large map of the campus or school using strips of butcher paper taped together (an alternative might be to block off the various locations with masking tape placed on the floor). The total area should be large enough so the students can stand on it and walk from place to place. Label rooms, buildings, or whatever is appropriate. Make sure it is clear what the various rooms in the buildings are. For example, you might place a picture of medicines in the clinic or pictures of food in the cafeteria. Using TPR, have students move around to various places. Take a tour of the campus or school itself, pointing out these same places. When the students feel familiar with the area, ask them to act as guides to new students of the same L1 backgrounds. In order to survive the first few days, new students need to know where things are before they are fluent enough to ask about them.

THE PEOPLE IN OUR SCHOOL

Take photos of personnel within your school. Show them to your students and talk about the job that each one does. You may want to act out the various roles: custodian, cafeteria helper, secretary, nurse, counselor, teacher, and orchestra director. Have the students point to the picture of the custodian, the principal, and so on. Now ask a volunteer student to act out the roles. See if the others can guess which roles are being acted out. (See Chapter 10 for other role-play activities that would be appropriate to this level and would help reinforce concepts.)

CLASSIFYING OBJECTS

Have each student make a classification booklet. Any categories can be used, depending upon the objectives you have in mind. For example, one page could be for household items, another for clothing, and a third for sports or camping equipment. Give the students several magazines or catalogs, and have them cut out pictures to be categorized. Then ask them to glue the items to the appropriate pages. You can provide comprehensible input about the pictures and do some individual TPR with each student. (*Point to the _____.* *Name two objects that belong in a kitchen, etc.*) Previously acquired concepts can be reinforced by this means.

FOLLOWING A PROCESS

Through a series of simple commands, students can learn to make things to eat (guacamole, onion and sour cream dip, sandwiches), items for play (kites, puppets, dolls, pictures), fascinating projects such as papier-mâché maps or miniature cities. You need to demonstrate first before taking the students through the step-by-step processes. Students are not expected to speak; they simply carry out the commands in TPR fashion.

MATCHING

Students can match pictures of objects with words placed on heavy paper and cut into puzzle pieces (Figure 8.2). Thus, the student can use the kinesthetic matching as a clue if necessary and the word itself will be more easily acquired. Or the student can use the word only and the matching of the puzzle pieces will simply reinforce the choice.

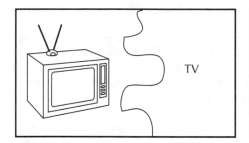 

Figure 8.2

The above represent just a small sampling of the many activities that can be used with students at this stage. Of course, some are more applicable to certain ages than others. However, it has been my experience that activities that one might consider "childish" for older learners are often enjoyed by children and adults alike. A lot depends upon the degree of comfort the students feel in the setting that has been established.

Success in internalizing concepts is strongly influenced by a freeing environment and made possible through their continued recycling. In addition, the teacher needs to make optimal use of manipulative visuals; to act out, model, or demonstrate expected responses; to make full use of body language in order to clarify meaning; to use high-frequency vocabulary, short sentences, yes/no questions, either/or questions, and other questions that require only one-word answers; and to rely heavily on getting the students physically involved with the target language in order to facilitate its acquisition. At the same time, types of activities need to be varied within any given time period for two reasons: Students' attention spans are often short, and the teacher's stamina is limited.

THE EARLY SPEECH PRODUCTION STAGE

Getting into Speaking

The transition into the second stage generally begins with an extension of many of the activities used in the comprehension stage. The teacher gradually begins to see changes in the length of the responses. For example, to a question such as "Who has on a blue dress?" the teacher might get the answer "Ashwaq has dress" instead of just "Ashwaq." Once the expansions begin to appear, they come naturally and abundantly, especially if the students are feeling comfortable with the teacher and the ambiance of the classroom. The speech at first will contain many errors, which should be dealt with *only* indirectly. To the omission of words in the student's utterance above, the teacher might respond with "Yes, Ashwaq has on the dress" instead of "No, you should say, 'Ashwaq has on the dress'" (emphasizing *on* and *the*). It is felt that if allowed to develop their interlanguage naturally, the students will continue expanding their utterances to include a wide variety of structures and eventually complex language.

Some of the activities that can be added to the teacher's repertoire at this stage (or before) are described below.

Speaking-Focused Activities

CHARTS AND OTHER VISUALS

Krashen and Terrell (1983) recommend the use of charts and other visuals that will make discussion easier and will serve as transitions into reading. The following can be written on the board as aids to conversation.

Numbers

How many students in the class are wearing
rings _____
tennis shoes _____
belts _____
glasses _____

Follow-up questions: How many students have on tennis shoes?
Are any students wearing glasses?
How many?

Clothing

Name of Student	Clothes
Carlos	jeans
Sung Hee	dress

Follow-up questions: Who is wearing jeans?
What is Sung Hee wearing?

Below is an example of a chart used in an ESL class to encourage interaction and to help the students to get to know one another.
First the students interview partners to fill in the chart below:[4]

	Partner 1	Partner 2	Partner 3
What's your name?			
Where are you from?			
What language do you speak?			

---

[4] This chart is adapted from one supplied by Linda Sasser of the Alhambra School District in California.

Follow-up questions: What country is _____ from?
                                        (name of student)
                    What languages does _____ speak?
                                            (name of student)
                Who speaks _____ ?
                            (name of language)

GROUP MURALS

Each student can be given a space on a huge piece of butcher paper that has been strung across a wall in the classroom. The students, who have been given pencils, rulers, wide felt-tip pens, paints, and brushes, can use their spaces to draw pictures. Have the students put their signatures at the bottom of their pictures. The butcher paper is displayed for a week or two, then rolled up and saved. As the students progress in the target language, the butcher paper can be brought out for different kinds of activities. At first simple questions can be asked about each picture: "Look at Juan's picture. What color is the wagon?" (green) "How many apples did Jenny paint?" (three) Later, when the students are into the stage of speech emergence and beyond, they can tell about their own pictures and those of their friends or they can make up an oral group story incorporating each picture in some way.

OPEN-ENDED SENTENCES

Extend the streams of comprehensible input to include utterances that the student completes.
On Saturdays I _____.
My family likes to _____.
Ho likes to eat _____.

        Or students can bring in family photos to share. Using open-ended sentences, they can talk about their relatives pictured in the photos:
My sister likes _____ .
My brother is _____ .
My cousins are _____ .

MATRICES

Open-ended sentences that are used in certain combinations for specific situations are called *matrices*. Below are a few situations in which they might be used.

First Meetings

        Hi there, my name is _____ .
        Nice to meet you. I'm _____ .
        Are you a new student too?
        Yes, I came from _____ .

On the Telephone
Hola.
Hola. Soy _____ . ¿Con quién hablo?
Con _____ .

At an Office
May I help you?
My name is _____ . I have an appointment with _____ .

The matrices should not be drilled in audiolingual style. Instead they should be used in role-playing situations in which a variety of responses can be given. Students simply use the matrices as aids and "starters" for as long as they need them (see Chapter 10 for more ideas). The matrices can be placed on cue cards, which can serve as transitions into reading (see Chapters 4 and 12) or they can be incorporated into jazz chants or lyrics (see Chapter 9).

ASKING FOR THE FACTS

Students can be shown simple sale advertisements (Figure 8.3) from local newspapers (in second-language classes) or foreign-language newspapers (in foreign-language classes). An alternative might be to show the students pictures of forms that have been filled out: a hospital record, an application for welfare, or a passport (see Figure 8.4). Pertinent questions can be asked about each.

Figure 8.3

Sale Advertisement Questions
1. What is being sold?
2. How much was it?
3. How much is it now?
4. How much will you be saving?

```
  _____
 /                                                           \
|                  SAM'S HARDWARE STORE                       |
|            _____                |
|                   Job Application Form                      |
|            _____                |
|                                                            |
| Name _____Mohamed Abdullah_____ Date ___5-24-97____ |
|                                                            |
| Address _____120 Maple Drive_____ Phone _(218) 543-7841_|
|                    (street)                                |
|         _____  _____                  |
|            Mentor            Minnesota   Sex (M or F) __M__ |
|             (city)            (state)                      |
|         _____                                   |
|            56702                                           |
|             (zip)                                          |
| Birth date __3-20-53__ Social Security number |4|8|0| |2|2| |3|9|6|7| |
|                                                            |
| Position you are seeking ___Salesclerk_____ |
 \                                                           /
  _____    _____    _____    _____    _____    ___/
```

Figure 8.4

Job Application Questions:

1. What is the person's last name?
2. What job does the person want?
3. Where does the person live?
4. What is the person's telephone number?
5. When was the person born?

Getting into Reading and Writing

Even though speaking is their major thrust, most of the above activities can be used as transitions into reading and writing (see also Chapter 12). Key words written on the chalkboard, TPR commands that students may have listed in their notebooks, cue cards with matrices written on them, words on charts, and other visuals, all lead to reading and writing in the target language. Of course, nonliterate learners of all ages, and students whose L1 writing system is vastly different from that of the target language will need special attention (see Chapters 4 and 12). However, the teaching should always be done through meaning rather than through a stringing together of isolated elements such as phonemes, orthographic symbols, and the like. The natural approach, as first described by Krashen and Terrell, was concerned mainly with oral communication skills. However, they believed for the most part that skills—listening, speaking, reading, writing—should be integrated rather than taught as separate entities.

THE SPEECH-EMERGENCE STAGE AND BEYOND

Because speech has been emerging all along, to distinguish *speech emergence* as a separate stage seems artificial. Perhaps this is the reason Krashen and Terrell replaced it with the term *extending production* in their book *The Natural Approach*. During this third stage, the utterances become longer and more complex. Many errors will still be made but, if enough comprehensible input has been internalized, they should gradually begin to decrease as the students move beyond this level toward full production. If undue attention has been paid to developmental errors, the process of acquiring correct grammatical forms in the new language could be impeded (see Chapter 3).

At this stage a large number of activities can be used that are somewhat more demanding and challenging but still within reach cognitively: music and poetry (Chapter 9), role-playing and drama (Chapter 10), affective activities (Chapter 13), and problem solving or debates at higher levels (Chapter 13). Many of the activities already recommended in this chapter for earlier stages can be extended to provide additional opportunities for development. For example, instead of simply answering questions about an application form, the students can now fill one out; instead of just following directions, they can begin to write their own sets of simple directions to see if others can follow them. Below is a sampling of other activities that might be typical at this stage and beyond.

Speech-Emergence-Stage Activities

THE PEOPLE HUNT

Give the students the following list and ask them to find a person who:
  has shoelaces
  wears glasses
  is laughing
  speaks three or more languages
  is wearing black socks
  hates carrots
  has on a plaid blouse or shirt
  lives north of Maple Street
  has five letters in his or her last name
  lives with a grandparent
  has a six in his or her phone number
  plays a guitar
They must get the signature of a person in each category.

As the students become more advanced, they can find a person who:
  has parents who drive a Toyota
  has been to Hong Kong within the last five years

has a family with more than six people in it
has a sister who likes to ice-skate or roller skate
has lived in more than three countries
hopes to be an actress after completing high school

CARTOONS

Take several cartoons from the newspaper and cut out the words in the bubbles. Place the cartoons on a blank sheet of paper, providing a place for students to write their own dialogue in the bubbles. They can exchange cartoons and end up with several versions of the action. (See Chapter 10 for more storytelling activities.)

DRAW THIS!

Divide the students into groups of four or five. Give one student per group a picture with simple lines and geometric shapes on it. Have each student give directions to his or her group so that they can reproduce the picture without seeing it. The student who comes closest to the original picture gives directions for the next picture. You may want to brief the group on the kinds of directions that will help by giving some words that may be key: horizontal, vertical, diagonal, perpendicular, parallel, a right angle, upper-left corner, lower right, etc. (see Figure 8.5). Pictures should become progressively more difficult as the students become more proficient.

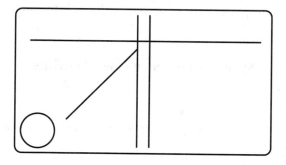

Figure 8.5

SHOPPING SPREE[5]

Set up one corner of the room as a grocery store. Stock the shelves with empty Jell-O boxes, egg cartons, milk cartons, cereal boxes, cleaning supplies, magazines, and so forth. Mark prices on the items. Have the students make out a shopping list (see Figure 8.6) and go shopping; fake money can be used. Students can take turn being shoppers, salespersons, and cashiers. Various situations can be set up to add variety to the shopping expeditions: A shopper may have to ask where a particular item is on the shelves, may need to exchange an item, may have been given wrong change, and so forth. Similar public places can be

---

[5] Thanks to Cyndee Gustke, who introduced me to a similar idea.

SHOPPING LIST
bread
cereal
eggs
milk
flour

Figure 8.6

simulated: a doctor's office, a bank, the post office, a drugstore, a clothing store, a garage. Various lists can be compiled, depending on each task. The situations can be an extension of matrices (see page 183).

WHOSE NAME IS IT?

Write the name of a student in large letters on a piece of paper. Tape it on the back of a student volunteer. The volunteer needs to guess whose name is on his or her back by asking *yes* or *no* questions of the class (they are in on the secret). "Is the person a female?" (yes) "Is she in the first desk? (no) "Does she like to sing?" (yes) "Is it _____ ?" (no) And on it goes until several volunteers get a chance. A variation of this activity is "Guess What's in the Box," described earlier in this chapter. One student could be given the box, which would have only one object in it. The rest of the class would ask *yes* or *no* questions until the object is named. (See Chapter 11 for similar activities.)

FOLLOWING THE WRITTEN DIRECTIONS

Give students sets of simple directions to follow. The directions can be on many topics of interest: how to make a model car, how to make paper flowers, how to decoupage, and so on. See if the students can read the directions and follow them. Have students work in pairs on some projects and in groups on others. (See also "Following Recipes" in Chapter 7.)

MAP READING

This activity could be an extension of "Getting Around," described earlier in this chapter. Helpful phrases could be written on the chalkboard: turn right (left), go south (north, east, west), go around the corner (straight), on the right (left, north, south, east, west) side of the street, in the (middle, far corner) of the block, down (up) the street, until you see a mailbox (fire hydrant, bus stop), between the drugstore and the bank, across from the hardware store, and so on. Give the students maps such as the one in Figure 8.7 and have them follow directions as you give them by tracing the route with a pencil. First do a demonstration with the class. Place the map on the overhead projector and trace a route while reading a set of directions aloud. For example, "Start at the bank, go north on Second Street until you get to Central Avenue, turn left, walk straight ahead to the gas station. It's between the grocery store and the bakery." Then divide the students into pairs and have them give each other directions while they trace the routes on their own maps.

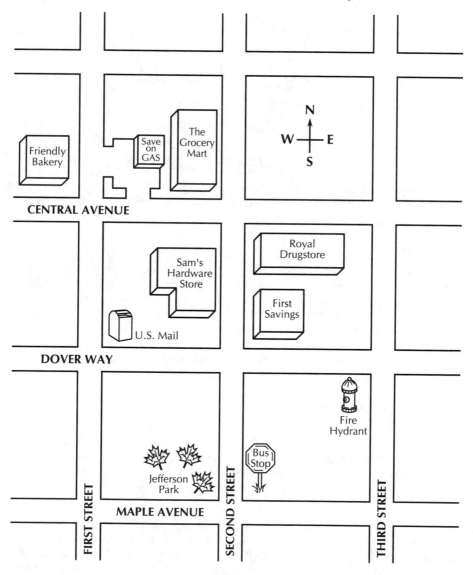

Figure 8.7

An alternative might be to combine storytelling with the activities.[6] For example, create a story about a fugitive who moves from place to place in different ways: he walks, runs, darts, crawls, skips, and drives. The students trace the route on their individual maps as you read. Instead of drawing only straight lines, the students can draw broken lines for "walks" (----------), zigzag lines for "runs" (∧∧∧∧∧∧), sideways carets for "darts" (>>>>>>), wavy lines for "crawls" (∼∼∼∼∼∼), arches for "skips" (ⱤⱤⱤⱤⱤ), and a series of plus signs for "drives" (++++++).

Follow-ups could include having the students draw maps of sections of their own communities and write sets of directions to the various places within them. They may even want to write ministories to go with the directions. Eventually the students can participate in similar activities using real street maps of cities or highway maps of whole states or countries.

SHARING BOOKS: THE CLASSROOM LIBRARY

Place several comfortable chairs in the corner of the classroom along with several bookcases set up at right angles to form a little library. Give students time to spend in this area where they can read individually, read to each other, and/or discuss books. Books might even be checked out through a system similar to that used in a public school or university library.[7] Students may even want to contribute their own books to the collection.

WRITING MEMOS

Set up situations in which students can write memos. Some suggestions are given below (see Figure 8.8):

Your mother is at work. You are leaving for a baseball game. You and some of your friends want to go out after the game for pizza. Write a memo to your mother and tape it to the refrigerator door. Tell her you will be home a little late.

You are at home. Someone has called for your brother. He is still at school. Write a note asking him to return the call.

You have a job as a receptionist. A salesman has come to sell paper products to your boss. Your boss is not in. The salesman asks you to leave a message. It should say that the salesman will be back later.

You have an appointment with your professor. You must cancel it because your mother is coming to visit that day. Write a note to give to the professor's secretary. Explain the situation.

USING LOCAL OR FOREIGN-LANGUAGE NEWSPAPERS[8]

1. Ask the students to find, cut out, and paste on butcher paper a sample of each of the following. Students can work in groups or individually. This kind of activity could begin at much earlier stages if the items are simple enough.

   the price of a pound of ground meat

---

[6] I wish to thank Braden Cancilla for this idea.

[7] Cyndee Gustke suggested this idea.

[8] These activities have been adapted from the pamphlets "Newspapers in Education," *Albuquerque Journal/Tribune.*

the low temperature in a major city
a number greater than a thousand
a face with glasses
the picture or name of an animal
a sports headline
a letter to the editor
the price of a used Honda Accord
a city within 50 miles of your own
a movie that starts between 1:00 and 4:00 P.M.
an angry word
the picture of a happy person
a ten-letter word
the picture of a bride

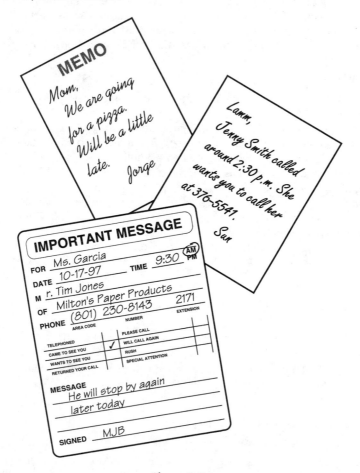

Figure 8.8

2. Have the students go through the ads in a recent paper. Ask them to find three things that were produced in other countries. Ask them to find three things that were produced in the state or city in which they now live.

3. Students can look for suitable jobs, apartments, and other items of interest in the want ads. They can discuss what they have found and tell why the ones they have chosen fit their needs.

4. They can also look in the want ads to find items for sale. Have them play the roles of potential sellers and buyers. For example, the buyers can make "telephone calls" to the sellers to gather more information about the content of the ads. A fist held to the ear makes a good pretend phone.

   They can then write want ads advertising things they want to sell. They can even bring these items to class. Have them consider the following questions before writing: What do you want to sell? Who do you think will buy it? Why would someone want to buy it?

   Once they have written their ads (restrict number of words and dollar value), collect them, duplicate them, and distribute them among the class. Let them buy, sell, or trade at will.

5. Finding articles about interesting people in the news can be exciting. Students can plan a "celebrity" party and make a list of those they would like to invite. Have them tell why they would like to meet those they have selected.

6. Ask students to choose a headline and write an alternative story to go with it.

PEN PALS

Mainstream English classes or organizations within or outside of the school can write personal letters to ESL students. After several exchanges of letters have taken place, the groups might get together to meet for a party or outing.

In foreign-language classes students can write to each other on a regular basis in the target language, they can write to students studying the same language in another school, or they can obtain pen pals in the countries where the target language is spoken.

You might want to establish a mailbox center in a quiet area of the classroom. Directions and information about the area can be displayed. A table with three or four chairs can be provided along with several types of paper, envelopes, and writing tools. To encourage letter writing, the teacher, teacher assistants, and advanced students can first write letters so that each student receives one. Then time can be scheduled regularly to receive, read, and respond to the letters as students become involved in writing to each other as well. If students have access to computers, they might correspond through electronic mail (see Chapter 15).

The three stages of the natural approach flow into one another and it is difficult to tell where one ends and the next begins. If one were to compare these stages with the traditional levels, beginning, intermediate, and advanced, their relationship might look like this (see Figure 8.9 below).

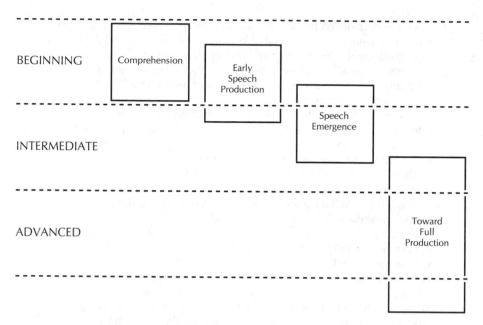

Figure 8.9. Classification of Proficiency Levels

At the comprehension stage, students develop the ability to understand spoken language and to react to simple commands. During this time students experience their "silent period" when they are not expected to speak, although they may respond with a word or two. At the early speech-production stage, students are able to produce a few words and can often recognize their written versions. At the speech-emergence stage, they begin to use simple sentences and can read and write simple text in the target language. As students become capable of fuller production (sometimes referred to by natural approach advocates as the period of "intermediate fluency"), they can express themselves in a variety of ways and can understand much of what is said. (See pages 99–100 for a more comprehensive list of typical language behaviors found at each level.)

It should be noted that there is much overlap between one level and the next and one stage and the next. Students may be beginners at some tasks but advanced learners at others. In addition, an intermediate or advanced student might be thrown back temporarily into the comprehension stage typical of beginners whenever new concepts are introduced. It has been my observation that students need several "silent periods" as they move from one group of concepts to another.

EXPANSIONS OF THE NATURAL APPROACH

Although the natural approach as originally proposed seems to have many strengths and has gained many advocates, particularly in the United States, it does appear to have some limitations. One of these is that the method itself is oriented to oral development with beginning- to low-intermediate students. While this is not a fault in and of itself, teachers need to be aware that literacy skills require more emphasis than they were given at first. In addition, advanced students need to be challenged through an increased emphasis on higher thinking skills and on tasks that are likely to promote proficiency at higher levels.[9]

Another limitation is that it did not adequately address the formal teaching of grammar. Originally it was intended that grammar develop naturally by exposing the students to sufficient amounts of comprehensible input. Although it was acknowledged that formal grammar should have some role, it was not made clear what that role should be.

In 1991 Terrell revealed an evolution of his thinking about the formal teaching of grammar, especially in the foreign-language classroom. In an article entitled "The Role of Grammar Instruction in a Communicative Approach," he acknowledged that instruction "…is beneficial to learners at a particular point in their acquisition of the target language" (p. 55). He goes on to say that instruction can give students structures to use as advance organizers to aid in the comprehension of input. It can help students focus on less noticeable features of language such as word endings. And it can serve as a basis for conscious monitoring and the creation of utterances using structures not yet acquired. However, he did *not* advocate a return to the use of a grammatical syllabus. (See also the grammar discussion beginning on page 47.)

A third limitation lies in the area of content and tasks. With the natural approach, the content and tasks in the early stages of acquisition are mainly related to everyday survival topics (foods, colors, body parts, interests, and so forth). While these may have been fine for many students, they are inadequate for those who wish to reach academic proficiency sooner in the new language. In practice, many teachers have introduced subject-matter content relating to math, science, social studies, literature, and so forth early on and have involved students in tasks that were more likely to lead to earlier success academically.

In addition, many teachers have related the new concepts taught to meaningful larger contexts to provide a cognitive hierarchical framework for them. Look again at the dialogue about colors at the beginning of this chapter. Think about how it might differ if it were related to a science unit on flowering plants, for example. Consider the dialogue below, which again is oriented to rank beginners.

---

[9] Krashen (1995) expands this notion in *What is Intermediate Natural Approach*. In P. Hashemipour, R. Maldonado, M. VanNaerssen, eds. *Studies in Language Learning and Spanish Linguistics in Honor of Tracy D. Terrell*, New York: McGraw-Hill, pp. 92–105.

TEACHER: Flowers come in many colors. Here is a red flower. (The teacher holds up a red flower or a piece of one, then holds up another red flower just like the first one.) Is this a red flower?

STUDENTS: Yes.

TEACHER: (holding up the same kind of flower, only this time it is yellow) Is this a red flower?

STUDENTS: (shaking their heads) No.

TEACHER: (pointing again to a red flower) No. Good. *This* is a red flower.

And thus the dialogue continues in much the same way as the first one did. The language becomes more enriched (maybe within a day or two) by relating to other qualities that flowers have and by talking about *where* they grow and *how* they grow.

In the first dialogue, the focus was on colors only. In the second dialogue, although the focus is still on colors, the teaching of them is part of a larger hierarchical unit: Flowering Plants. Flowering Plants might be part of a still larger unit: Plants. The largest unit including plants and flowering plants might be labeled Living Things. See Figure 8.10.

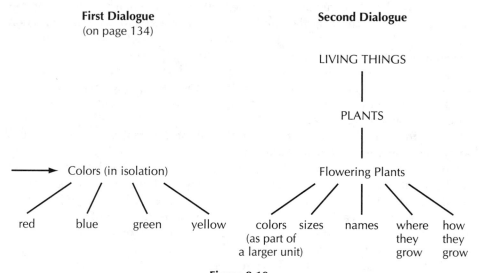

Figure 8.10

It should be noted that the other activities mentioned in this chapter can also be parts of larger units and themes, depending upon their content. For example, "Guess What's in the Box" can be used for recycling math vocabulary if the box contains items such as a ruler, a compass, a pocket calculator, and the like. "Following a Process" can be part of an art lesson if it involves a process such as creating hanging mobiles. And "Charts and Other Visuals" can be used in a geography lesson comparing various countries. See Figure 8.11 below from Richard-Amato and Snow (1992).

Country	Location	Climate
Argentina	South America	Warm Summers Temperate Winters
Canada	North America	Warm Summers Cold Winters
Vietnam	East Asia	Hot Summers Temperate Winters

Figure 8.11. A Chart Used to Clarify a Geography Lesson

It must be remembered that a hodgepodge of activities thrown together does not a curriculum make. The activities must be carefully selected and adapted, and they must logically fit into a well-planned, but flexible, hierarchy of units and themes. Within this hierarchy, key concepts will need to be reinforced sufficiently to be acquired. Unfortunately there appears to be no mechanism inherent in the method itself for the recycling of key concepts.

Yet an additional limitation appears to be the natural approach's penchant for putting the teacher on center stage. Of course, at beginning levels the teacher's input is of utmost importance while the students are beginning to develop proficiency in the language. However, students even at early stages need to begin communicating with one another more and with peers (or others) who are fluent speakers of the language being learned. An emphasis on group/pair work should not be relegated to later stages.

SUMMARY

According to Krashen and Terrell, the foundation of the natural approach rests on four principles: (1) comprehension precedes production, (2) production must be allowed to emerge in stages, (3) the course syllabus must be based on communicative goals, and (4) the activities and classroom environment must work together to produce lowered affective filter. Its evolution has had to do with the development of literacy skills, the inclusion of academic themes, group/pair work during the early stages; its handling of instructed grammar; and the contextualization of learned concepts into broader, hierarchical units.

But ultimately it is the teacher in the classroom who draws from the method and makes it work in a particular situation by combining many strategies. This method (like the other methods and activities described in this book) is dynamic and will evolve in different ways in different classrooms and with different teachers. Under optimal classroom conditions, students can move with relative ease from comprehension to early speech production and eventually into speech emergence and beyond.

READINGS, REFLECTION, AND DISCUSSION

Suggested Reading and Materials

Baltra, Armando (1992). On breaking with tradition: The significance of Terrell's natural approach. *The Canadian Modern Language Review, 48*(3), 265–583. The author discusses the impact of the natural approach on how we view language teaching in both second- and foreign-language classrooms. He makes us aware of its contribution to the movement toward interactive approaches, a contribution that is often downplayed and sometimes even ignored in the literature.

Christison, M., and S. Bassano (1981). *Look who's talking*. Englewood Cliffs, N. J.: Alemany/ Prentice-Hall. Adults and teens in the speech emergence phase and beyond can learn interactive techniques through the activities presented in this book. The suggested lessons, which include games and problem solving, begin with low-risk kinds of activities and progress to more personal, higher risk ones as the students become more proficient.

DLM Teaching Resources Comprehensive Catalog. Allen, Tex.: DLM Teaching Resources. Catalogs are not normally included in annotated reading lists such as this. However, because this particular catalog contains a wide variety of realia, I have included it even though not all of the materials contained are compatible with a natural approach classroom. The following manipulatives, pictures, games, and other activities are especially effective for language teaching: colorful photo library sets; picture cards depicting opposites and categories of different kinds; sequence and spatial relation picture cards; map games; colored cubes for teaching cognitive skills; math games; plastic clocks; play coins and bills; association cards; functional signs.

Gill, M., and A. Hartman. (1993). *Get it? Got it!: Listening to others, speaking for ourselves*. Boston, Mass.: Heinle and Heinle. A communicative book for developing listening, speaking, and pronunciation skills in low-intermediate speakers of English. Topics are oriented toward both survival and academics and are highly appropriate for young adults.

Krashen, S., and T. Terrell. (1983). *The natural approach: Language acquisition in the classroom*. Englewood Cliffs N. J.: Alemany/Prentice Hall. Essential reading for any one planning to draw from the natural approach. The book clearly describes the method, offers theoretical justification for its use, and presents suggested activities for making it work.

Ligon, F., and E. Tannenbaum. (1990). *Picture stories: Language and literacy activities for beginners*. White Plains, N.Y.: Longman. This book for young adults presents survival stories told in pictures. Students begin by talking about what is happening in each picture and end by writing the story. A few of the relevant topics are washing clothes, going to the doctor, following directions, and making phone calls. Students find many of the stories humorous as well as instructive.

Shoemaker, C., and Shoemaker, F. (1991). *Interactive techniques for the ESL classroom*. Boston, Mass.: Heinle and Heinle. Presents many interactive activities including warm-ups and mixers, puzzles, games, role plays, and simulations. Also included are ways of adapting and creating interactive techniques. A firm theoretical background is laid out to support the use of interaction in general.

Winn-Bell Olsen, J.(1984). *Look again pictures*. Englewood Cliffs, N. J.: Alemany/Prentice Hall. This book contains twenty-two picture pairs (which can be duplicated) and student exercises to accompany them. Within each pair, one picture is different in eight ways from the other. Students are to search for the differences. The materials, which are designed for teenagers and adults, can stimulate a great deal of interaction.

Questions for Reflection and Discussion

1. Reflect on the process by which you became proficient in a second language. How closely did your progress approximate the stages described in the natural approach? Did your teachers appear to help or hinder your acquisition of the language? Explain.

2. Often listening, speaking, reading, and writing are treated as isolated skills by language teachers. How might you integrate them by using the natural approach? Give some specific activities as examples.

3. How might you incorporate natural approach strategies into a short lesson? Create a ten-minute demonstration of the natural approach or an extension of it to try out on fellow students. The demonstration may be in a language unfamiliar to your group if it is simple enough. After your presentation, ask the group in what ways it was effective and in what ways it could be improved.

4. Terrell (1983) claimed that one of the conditions that fosters acquisition is a low-anxiety environment. In what ways can the natural approach foster such an environment? Are there any situations in which anxiety might aid acquisition? Think of situations in which one might experience the anxiety associated with anger, for example. LaForge (1971) found in his experimental language classes that an overt display of anger seemed to make students more uninhibited and freer in their communication. Thus, the acquisition process was actually helped by anxiety. Do you see this as being a possible refutation of Terrell's claim or only a surface discrepancy that can be explained through a deeper analysis of anxiety and its ramifications?

CHAPTER 9

Jazz Chants, Music, and Poetry

Rhythm and rhyme, assonance and pun are not artificial creations, but vestigial echoes of primitive phases in the development of language, and of the even more primitive pulsations of living matter; hence our particular receptiveness for messages which arrive in rhythmic pattern.

A. Koestler, 1964

QUESTIONS TO THINK ABOUT

1. What role do you think chants, music, and/or poetry play in the acquisition of a first language? What do they have in common? How important do you think they are to the success of first-language acquisition?

2. Do you think older children, teenagers, and adults learning a second or foreign language might benefit from them also? If so, in what ways?

3. Think about the experiences you may have had learning another language. To what extent were you exposed to chants, music, and/or poetry during the process? What effects did they have on your own success?

4. Do you think chants, music, and poetry should be incorporated into a second- or foreign-language program? If so, how?

Second-language learners, just like first-language learners, should have the opportunity to play with language. Children and adults alike can receive considerable enjoyment from indulging in such frivolity. Through word/sound play, many "chunks" of useful language can be incorporated into the individual's linguistic repertoire at almost any age or level of proficiency. The use of prosodic elements, redundancy, and sometimes thoughtless repetition can produce lowered anxiety and greater ego permeability.[1] One might call the process a sort of "palatable audiolingualism." However, unlike audiolingualism, its rhythms and sound repetitions carry the student into sensually appealing activities that can go far beyond mere drill. The subject matter does not have to be frivolous but can be directly anchored in meaningful experience. The meanings can be rich and multileveled, and discussions can follow that would challenge even the most proficient among the group.

Second-language students can be exposed to meaningful word/sound play through jazz chants, music, and poetry, all of which can provide them with a few tools for communication, especially valuable at beginning levels. Through these genres, students can internalize routines and patterns with or without consciously committing them to memory. Students do not even have to understand the meanings of the words within the chunks in order to use them to participate (albeit in a limited fashion) in social events and to encourage input from others. One possible drawback here is that others may at first assume that students are more fluent than they really are. However, it doesn't take long for these people to realize the approximate levels of second-language students and adjust their speech accordingly.

The use of routines and patterns can provide a stopgap strategy that students can use to gain entry into the new culture before being considered "ready." Even though the process in developing routines and patterns is thought to be very different from that used in developing creative speech (Krashen, 1981b; Lamendella, 1979), they can become part of creative speech once the student's proficiency matches his or her need for communication.

JAZZ CHANTS

Jazz chants were developed by Carolyn Graham, an ESL teacher and jazz musician, in order to provide language learners with a rhythmic means for improving speaking and listening skills. Through the chants, students can be exposed to natural intonation patterns and idiomatic expressions in often provocative, sometimes humorous situations. Feelings are expressed in the playing out of the common rituals of everyday life. Because the chants are often in dialogue

---

[1]Guiora, Brannon, and Dull (1972) discuss the concept of *language ego,* which refers to the self-identity intricately involved with the risks of taking on a new language. It is responsible for boundaries that can make us extremely inhibited if too strong and impenetrable.

form, students can learn the cultural rules of turn-taking and appropriate ways to communicate specific needs in a variety of situations. The dialogues generally include three kinds of conversational patterns: question/response, command/response, and provocative statement/response.

Graham (1978) suggests that certain steps, summarized below, be taken.

1. The teacher needs to make sure that the students understand the situational context of the chant. Vocabulary items and cultural ramifications inherent in the situations themselves will need clear explanations.

2. Initially, the teacher in a normal conversational voice gives each line of the chant once or twice as needed and the students repeat in unison. Graham advises the teacher to stop at any point to correct pronunciation or intonation patterns.

3. The teacher then establishes a beat by snapping the fingers (students seem to prefer this means), counting, clapping, or using rhythm sticks. Step 2 is then repeated, but this time with a firm beat.

4. The teacher now divides the class into two parts (the numbers of students in each part do not seem to matter). Using the beat established above, the teacher gives the lines. The two groups of students alternately repeat the lines as they are given.

5. The dialogue of the chant is then conducted between the teacher and the class. The teacher takes the first part in the dialogue, the students take the other (without the teacher to model). The teacher can use the tapes (optional) that accompany the jazz chants books (see Suggested Readings at the end of this chapter).

In my own experience with jazz chants, I have found it unnecessary to stop and correct students' pronunciation as Graham suggests. Students pick up the modeled pronunciation through the repetitions. In addition, stopping for corrections seems to place the focus on form rather than meaning.

Jazz chants can be used to help students internalize matrices (see Chapters 8 and 10) and, at the same time, reinforce specific vocabulary items. In the sample jazz chant excerpt below, sound play is embedded through the use of rhyme. The matrix includes various structures for offering and refusing food. Substitutions can be made to include the names of the common foods one wants reinforced. Follow-ups might include total physical response activities involving food preparation (see Chapter 7) or role play taking place at the dinner table (see Chapter 10).

Would you like a fried egg?
Would you like a fried egg?

No thanks. I'm on a diet.
Please don't fry it.
Please don't fry it.

Jazz chants can also be used to introduce some of the topics recommended in the natural approach and its extensions (see Chapter 8). For example, the chant below was written to introduce a unit on sports events. Typical pictures of the events can accompany the chant. Follow-ups can include total physical response activities (involving basic actions of the sport), sports demonstrations, local news reporting of sports events, or a trip to a sporting event as part of a "Language Experience" activity (see Chapter 12). The matrix in the following chant offers a means for talking about sports. Word substitutions can easily be made to include a wide variety of events.

Where do you go? Where do you go?
Where do you go to see
a ball go in a basket,
a ball go in a basket?

Where do I go? Where do I go?
To a basketball game.
To a basketball game.
That's where I go to see
a ball go in a basket.

All you have to do is ask it.

Where do you go? Where do you go?
Where do you go to see
a ball kicked all around,
a ball kicked all around?

Where do I go? Where do I go?
To a soc-cer game,
To a soc-cer game.
That's where I go to see
a ball kicked all around.

You keep it on the ground.

Where do you go? Where do you go?
Where do you go to see
a girl fly through the air
a girl fly through the air?

Where do I go? Where do I go?
To a gym-nas-tics meet,
To a gym-nas-tics meet.
That's where I go to see
a girl fly through the air.

Would you do it on a dare?

There are many ways in which jazz chants can be orchestrated. The two parts can be used to pit males against females, those born in January through June against those born in July through December, those wearing green against the others, and so forth. To add variety, parts might be assigned to individuals who volunteer or to small groups of differing sizes.

Some chants can be partially improvised by the students. For example, in the following one, all the students sit in a circle on the floor.[2] A rhythm is set by the snapping of fingers. The teacher begins the chant with something like "My name is _____. What's your name?" The teacher looks at the student on the right, who responds, "My name is _____. What's your name?" The student looks at the next student on the right, who will be responding, and so on around the circle. Variations could follow that overlap into affective activities (see Chapter 13). "My name is _____ and I like _____" and "My name is _____ and I feel _____" are two examples of matrices that would lend themselves to this kind of activity.

Although the jazz chants above are oriented to beginning students, (see pages 99–100) intermediate and advanced students are exposed to idiomatic expressions through this means. Subtle forms of humor, decisions about the appropriateness of utterances, and symbolic content are only a few of the things to which students at higher levels can be introduced. Through the cadences, the students' pronunciation and intonation can become more native-like and natural without conscious drill.

MUSIC

Music, also, reduces anxiety and inhibition in second-language students. Furthermore, it is a great motivator in that its lyrics are often fraught with meaningful input. Human emotions are frequently expressed in highly charged situations. Through music, language easily finds roots in the experience of students at any age or proficiency level. Often awareness is heightened through its prosodic elements. Kahlil Gibran once said, "The reality of music is in that vibration that remains in the ear after the singer finishes his song and the player no longer plucks the strings." Music can break down barriers among those who share its rhythms and meaning. Its unifying effect can extend across time, nations, races, and individuals.

At beginning levels, music can be used to teach basic vocabulary. Colors, body parts, simple actions, clothes, and names of people are only a few of the concepts that can be taught through music. The teacher doesn't have to be talented in music to make it a memorable experience. A gravelly voice can exude as much enthusiasm as a euphonious one. Records or cassettes can provide the

[2]I wish to thank Linda Cobral for sharing this idea with me.

accompaniment in some situations. Words can be created and students' names can be inserted into the stanzas that are coordinated with easy-to-learn melodies. For example, below are some lyrics that could be sung to "You Are My Sunshine."

> Your name is Car-los.
> Your name is Car-los.
> You come from Per-u,
> so far away.
> And now you're with us
> Until the summer.
> And it is here
> we want you to stay.

> Your name is Sung Lee.
> Your name is Sung Lee.
> You're from Kor-e-a,
> so far away.
> And now you're with us
> Maybe forever
> Even after your hair turns
> gray.

> Your name is Ni-kom.
> Your name is Ni-kom.
> You come from La-os,
> so far away.
> And now you're with us
> We are so happy.
> We want to sing with you today.

Although Carlos, Sung Lee, and Nikom may not understand all the words the first few times they hear them, they will be highly motivated to find out what is being sung about them. Thus acquisition will be highly likely.

Specific matrices can be reinforced through music. Notice the lyrics of the following song, written to the tune of "Mary Had a Little Lamb."

> Danella says, "Come on, let's go.
> Come on, let's go. Come on, let's go."
> Danella says, "Come on, let's go.
> To the zoo on Friday."
> Hung an-swers, "That's fine with me.
> Fine with me. Fine with me."
> Hung an-swers, "That's fine with me.
> Let's go to the zoo on Friday."

Friday comes and off they go.
Off they go. Off they go.
Friday comes and off they go.
To see the an-i-mals.

First they see the elephants.
El-e-phants. El-e-phants.
First they see the el-e-phants.
In the mud-dy waters.

Then they walk to the lion's den.
Lion's den. Lion's den.
Then they walk to the lion's den.
To find him pacing back and forth.

And on the song goes through as many stanzas as the teacher wants to create. Once students become more proficient, they can add their own stanzas. The words written down and duplicated along with pictures can aid the students' understanding. Total physical response can be used, with students pointing to the pictures of the animals while the song is being sung. A trip to the zoo can stimulate all sorts of additional meaningful experiences with the target language.

For those who prefer songs of a more "professional" nature, Hap Palmer[3] has provided several in a series of songbooks and records (see Suggested Readings at the end of the chapter). Figure 9.1 presents one that he wrote on body parts and actions for beginning students.

Although these songs are mainly of benefit to beginning students, there are many songs popular today that are particularly effective for intermediate to advanced students. Even the "top ten" can provide one or two. It is interesting to note that a serious study has been done on such music. Murphey (1992) looked at the characteristics of fifty pop songs in relation to second-language acquisition. He found them to be repetitive, basically simple, conversation like, and vague enough to allow for their being interpreted in personal ways. He argues that "these discourse features and the song-stuck-in-my-head phenomenon make them potentially rich learning materials in and out of the classroom" (p. 771). If one decides to use appropriate pop songs as text, the lyrics should be duplicated so that each student can have his or her own copy. Students will probably want to take the words home so they can sing the songs to themselves or with their families and friends.

When a song is presented in class, it is usually a good idea to let the students just listen to the song first as it is played on the CD or tape. Then hand out the words and play the song again. The third time the song is played, the students will no doubt sing along with you and the recording. Students should

---

[3] Thanks to Raquel Mireles for making me aware of these songbooks and records.

be given the opportunity to have words or phrases explained to them during the course of the activity. A discussion should follow during which the students can relate the song to their own lives and to the lives of others.

Figure 9.1. (From Hap Palmer, 1971)

Put your hands   in   your lap.

Bow   your   head and   take a   nap.

Bow   your   head and   take a   nap.

Figure 9.1   (Continued)

POETRY

Although poetic elements are contained in jazz chants and music lyrics, poetry can be treated as a separate category. Poems range in length anywhere from a few words to a whole book. They are generally concise, sometimes deceptively simple, and often highly charged with emotional content. They can be used at a variety of levels to reinforce ideas and introduce new ones.

The following poem by Jack Prelutsky[4] is a favorite, especially among elementary schoolchildren. It reinforces the names of concrete objects in the classroom as it presents a fantasy that we all may have had at one time or another.

The Creature in the Classroom

It appeared inside our classroom
at a quarter after ten,
it gobbled up the blackboard,
three erasers and a pen.
It gobbled teacher's apple
and it bopped her with the core.
"How dare you!" she responded.
"You must leave us . . . there's the door."

The Creature didn't listen
but described an arabesque
as it gobbled all her pencils,
seven notebooks and her desk.
Teacher stated very calmly,
"Sir! you simply cannot stay,
I'll report you to the principal
unless you go away!"

But the thing continued eating,
it ate paper, swallowed ink,
as it gobbled up our homework
I believe I saw it wink.
Teacher finally lost her temper.
"OUT!" she shouted at the creature.
The creature hopped beside her
and GLOPP . . . it swallowed teacher.

It is important to remember that poems such as this one may not at first be understood in their entirety. In fact, the students, when initially exposed to them, may understand only a few words. However, upon subsequent exposures to and discussion of the poems, the students will begin to understand more and more.

The next poem, by Edwin Arlington Robinson, is for students in university or adult programs. It can be used at high-intermediate to advanced levels to reinforce various emotions such as happiness, love, envy, loneliness, and desperation and to teach literary devices such as symbolism and metaphor.

---

[4] From *The Random House Book of Poetry for Children* (1983). Thanks to Norma Ramirez, who introduced me to this poem.

The poem leads naturally into a discusson of Richard Cory's life and the seeming irony of his death. What was missing in his life that was essential to his happiness? The cultural ramifications and the social taboos concerning suicide might also be relevant to the discussion. A good follow-up to the poem is the narrative song of the same title from the Simon and Garfunkel recording *The Sounds of Silence* (1965, Eclectic Music Company). In the song, Richard Cory owns a factory and the narrator, who works for him, envies his lifestyle and is shocked at his death, just as we are. Both poem and song are very powerful and can stimulate not only discussion but the writing of short papers as well.

Richard Cory

Whenever Richard Cory went down town,
We people on the pavement looked at him:
He was a gentleman from sole to crown,
Clean favored, and imperially slim.

And he was always quietly arrayed,
And he was always human when he talked;
But still he fluttered pulses when he said,
"Good-morning," and he glittered when he walked.

And he was rich—yes, richer than a king—
And admirably schooled in every grace:
In fine, we thought that he was everything
To make us wish that we were in his place.

So on we worked, and waited for the light,
And went without the meat, and cursed the bread;
And Richard Cory, one calm summer night,
Went home and put a bullet through his head.

In addition to listening to and reading poems written by others, the students who are ready may want to write some of their own even at beginning levels. Christison in her book *English Through Poetry* (1982) recommends concrete poetry, formed from pictures and words. For example, students can be asked to draw large butterflies such as the one in Figure 9.2. Once the butterflies have been drawn, words and phrases such as "light," "flying," "beautiful," "in the air," "a dream" or whatever can be written on the wings or the bodies, following the forms of the butterflies. A butterfly for a student at an intermediate to advanced level might look something like the one in Figure 9.3.[5]

---

[5]This poem and illustration are by Jane Decock and come from *Harbinger*, published by the Advanced Creative Writing Classes at Jefferson High School in Edgewater, Colorado.

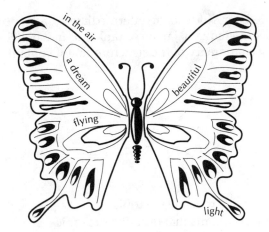

Figure 9.2 (adapted from Christison, 1982)

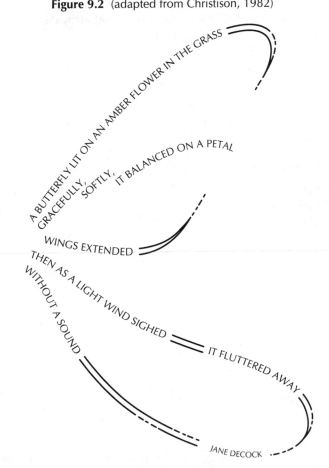

A BUTTERFLY LIT ON AN AMBER FLOWER IN THE GRASS
GRACEFULLY, SOFTLY, IT BALANCED ON A PETAL
WINGS EXTENDED
THEN AS A LIGHT WIND SIGHED
IT FLUTTERED AWAY
WITHOUT A SOUND
JANE DECOCK

Figure 9.3

Also recommended for students at intermediate to advanced levels are verse forms such as word cinquain, Japanese tanka, or haiku. Below are examples, each followed by a summary of the structure that it contains.

Word Cinquain

A cat
Full of mischief
Charges, dances, pounces
Brightens my longest days
A wonder

1st line: a word or two to name the topic
2nd line: two or three words that describe the topic
3rd line: three or four words that express action
4th line: four or five words that express personal attitude
5th line: a word or two to rename the topic

Tanka

Drifting in the sky
Clouds come and go in patterns
I look to the sun
The darkness hovers around
Slowly rain begins to fall

1st line: 5 syllables
2nd line: 7 syllables
3rd line: 5 syllables
4th line: 7 syllables
5th line: 7 syllables

Haiku

Flowers wave to me
As I pass them in the field. . . .
Gentle, swirling wind

1st line: 5 syllables
2nd line: 7 syllables
3rd line: 5 syllables

(Note: There is generally a break in thought between the second and third lines.)

The verses can be written at first in groups with the help of the teacher or teacher assistants using pictures to stimulate ideas. Later the students may want to try a few verses on their own.

Whether students are working in groups or individually, it is important that they not be held to exact numbers of words or syllables for structured verse unless they can be shown at the more advanced levels how a poem might be improved by doing so.

Christison (1982) suggests that the events in the students' lives provide some of the impetus for writing and sharing poetry of various kinds. For example, greeting cards can be created to give to others for special occasions. Birthdays, marriages, graduations, holidays, and other celebrations are ideal times to write and/or illustrate poetry. If the students don't want to write their own poetry, they can search in books for appropriate poems to put on their cards, giving credit to their sources.

Another idea she recommends is to have students draw or paint pictures and then find or write poems that seem to go with them. Activities such as these can give the students important reasons for reading and writing poetry, thus increasing their exposure to meaningful language.

SUMMARY

Jazz chants, music, and poetry often produce lowered anxiety and greater ego permeability among second-language learners. Beginners are often able to internalize chunks of language that allow them to participate in social situations early on. During initial stages of language development, students often have the desire to communicate but do not have the necessary skills. By having a repertoire of ways to be communicative (however limited), the students are able to form bonds with native speakers and thus be in a position to receive more input.

Intermediate and advanced students also gain benefits from jazz chants, music, and poetry. Idiomatic expressions, subtle forms of humor, decisions concerning appropriateness, and symbolic content can be internalized through these media. Pronunciation and intonation patterns can take on a more nativelike quality through use of word/sound play. Students can be exposed to situations in which highly meaningful content can be dealt with on many different levels.

READINGS, REFLECTION, AND DISCUSSION

Suggested Readings and Reference Materials

Christison, M. (1982). *English through poetry.* Hayward, Calif.: Alemany. Includes criteria for the selection, presentation, and creation of poetry in ESL classes. In addition, the incorporation of simple poetic forms, choral readings, and readers' theater is described. The book ends with several poems appropriate for second-language students.

Dunleavy, D. (1992). *The Language Beat*. Portsmouth, N.H.: Heinemann. Includes ways to incorporate music into classroom instruction. The book offers original songs with related activities involving choral reading, drama, creative writing, and much more.

Graham, C. (1978). *Jazz chants and jazz chants for children*. New York: Oxford University. Still popular collections of chants that teachers can use with beginners learning English as a second language. Often humorous dialogues are presented based on commonplace situations and events. Includes cassettes.

Graham, C. (1986). *Small talk*. New York: Oxford University. The jazz chants presented in this book focus on specific tools for communication. Topics such as one might find in typical matrices (see Chapters 8 and 10) are in abundance. Greetings, introductions, saying goodbye, talking about food, money, and the weather are among the many relevant topics included. Available on cassette.

Graves, D. (1992). *Explore Poetry*. Portsmouth, N.H.: Heinemann. Both the reading and writing of poetry for children are explored here. The author encourages teachers to integrate poetry throughout the curriculum.

Kind, U. (1980). *Tune in to English: Learning English through familiar melodies*. New York: Regents. Functions in English are taught by the use of familiar tunes. For example, "I'm Glad to Meet You" is sung to the tune "La Cucaracha," "My Father Has a Sister" to "Row, Row, Row Your Boat," and "Where's My Key" to "Jingle Bells." A songbook and cassette are part of the package.

Palmer, H. (1971). *Songbook: Learning basic skills through music I*. Freeport, N.Y.: Educational Activities. A cassette accompanies this lively, action-packed book of songs, which can still be found in children's book stores and music stores. Although it is meant for teaching children, it can be used successfully with beginners of all ages. It includes such topics as colors, body parts, animals, numbers, clothes, names, and the alphabet. This particular volume is just part of a large collection of songbooks and records by Palmer on a wide variety of topics at many different levels.

Silverstein, S. (1981). *A light in the attic*. New York: Harper and Row. This book of humorous poems with unexpected twists keeps students of all ages enthralled. A cassette tape is available.

Questions for Reflection and Discussion

1. Compare the use of repetition and imitation in the audiolingual method with the use of similar strategies in jazz chants, songs, and poetry. In what ways do the latter render the strategies more "palatable"?

2. Krashen (1981b) argues that routines and patterns play a "minor, though significant role" in the second-language acquisition process. Do you feel that a difference in the method of exposure to such prefabricated forms might make a difference in the role they play? Think about the level of proficiency at which the student might be exposed to them. Would the role of routines

and patterns change in any way for an intermediate student? For an advanced student?

3. Choose a topic that you might wish to include while using the natural approach or an extension of it (see Chapter 8). Find a jazz chant, some lyrics set to a popular song, or a poem to introduce or reinforce some of the key concepts. You may write your own if you wish. Present it to a group of your fellow students. Inform them about what other activities you might use to reinforce the same concepts. Discuss with them the strengths of your presentation and ways in which you might improve it.

CHAPTER **10**

Storytelling, Role Play, and Drama

Drama is like the naughty child who climbs the high walls and ignores the "No Trespassing" sign. It does not allow us to define our territory so exclusively; it forces us to take as our starting-point life not language.

A. Maley and A. Duff, 1983

QUESTIONS TO THINK ABOUT

1. How important do you think storytelling is to children acquiring a first language? What about role play and/or drama?

2. Do you think older children, teenagers, and adults learning a second or foreign language might also benefit from storytelling, role play, and/or drama? If so, in what ways? What is there about these activities that might facilitate the language learning process?

3. Recall your own experiences with one or more of these activities in learning another language? What effects do you think they may have had on your own language development?

4. Think of some ways storytelling, role play, and drama can be incorporated into a second- or foreign-language program.

Second-language students can easily become absorbed in the dramatic playing out of life's experiences and, through them, forget the self-consciousness often associated with learning another language. Drama-based activities can heighten the students' abilities to acquire. By losing themselves in the struggles and conflicts of others, they seem better able to make the target language part of their memory store (see Episode Hypothesis in Chapter 15).

In the results of a questionnaire given to UCLA teachers and students, Susan Stern found support for her theory that drama has a positive effect on second-language learning by encouraging the operation of certain psychological factors that facilitate oral communication: heightened self-esteem, motivation, and spontaneity; increased capacity for empathy; lowered sensitivity to rejection (1983, p. 216). Storytelling, role play, and other forms of drama can be used in the second-language classroom to help bring about such results. These activities allow students to explore their inner resources, empathize with others, and use their own experiences as scaffolds upon which to build credible action. As a result, each student may be able to improve his or her ability to produce the target language, lower anxiety, acquire many of the nonverbal nuances of the language, and improve the ability to work cooperatively in group situations.

Before the teacher involves the students in the main body of activities presented in this chapter, a series of warm-ups is recommended to reduce anxiety and to create a warm, active environment.

WARM-UPS

The warm-ups included here require almost no verbal language and therefore can be used with rank beginners. In addition to the benefits mentioned above, they help to establish trust and understanding among the group members and to lower their inhibitions. The teacher may want to begin with a series of simple exercises involving stretching, bending, and the tightening and relaxing of specific muscle groups before proceeding to the activities below.

Warm-Up Activities

CIRCLE MIMICS

Students form a circle. The first student is asked to make some sort of movement such as hopping on one foot. The second student repeats the movement and adds a new one such as shaking a fist in the air. The third student hops on one foot, shakes a fist in the air, and adds a third movement, and so on around the circle.

BASEBALL MIME

Throw a make-believe ball across the room to one of your students. After the student "catches" it, motion to the student to join you in a game of catch. Then throw the ball to other students and motion to them to join you also. The game can remain simply a game of catch or it can develop into a full baseball game if the students are familiar with it. Give one student a make-believe bat and station the others around the room at pretend bases. Let the students take over the game.

Once students have worked out tension and seem to have lowered inhibitions, they may be ready to attempt storytelling.

STORYTELLING

Stories have traditionally been used to teach, to entertain, and to explain the unknown. The activities offered here can be coordinated with several of the methods recommended in this book (total physical response, the audio-motor unit, the natural approach, etc.) Some of the activities are more appropriate to beginners; others, to more advanced levels. Most can be adapted to any age level provided they are within the students' range cognitively.

Allowing students to be exposed to a story before fully understanding the words is highly motivating for beginners at any age.[1] The same story can be used from time to time in different ways until a full understanding is achieved over a period of perhaps several months. Activities such as those presented below enable the students to participate in the language *before* actually becoming proficient in it, just as children do when they are being read to in their first language. Through these activities, curiosity in the target language is stimulated.

Storytelling Activities

STORY EXPERIENCE[2]
Level: Beginning

Have the students form a large circle. Choose a story or a narrative poem such as the one that follows (this particular poem is oriented to children, although adults have been found to enjoy it too). Pick out the concrete words that can be easily acted out. Assign to each student a word to act out. Help the students understand what the word means by demonstrating its meaning or by showing a picture to illustrate. Then read the story aloud with much feeling. Each student is to listen carefully for his or her word. When the word is read, the student is to go across the circle, acting it out as he or she moves across. Students on the other side will have to make room as the actors come across.

---

[1] Note that this recommendation appears to fly in the face of the arguments favoring comprehensible input. It is true that if the story were simply read aloud with little expression of feeling and if there were no physical involvement on the part of the student, then it probably would be as meaningless as most other input that is not understood.

[2] This activity has been adapted from one presented by the Barzak Institute of San Francisco at a workshop done for the Jefferson County Public Schools of Colorado in 1979.

For the following story excerpt, the teacher will need these words acted out: a fly, a spider, a bird, a cat, a dog, a cow, and a horse.

Excerpt from *There Was an Old Lady Who Swallowed a Fly*[3]

There was an old lady who swallowed a *fly*.
I don't know why she swallowed a *fly*.
Perhaps she'll die.

There was an old lady who swallowed a *spider*,
That wriggled and wriggled and jiggled inside her.

She swallowed the *spider* to catch the *fly*.
I don't know why she swallowed a *fly*.
Perhaps she'll die.

There was an old lady who swallowed a *bird*.
How absurd, to swallow a *bird*!
She swallowed the *bird* to catch the *spider*.

There was an old lady who swallowed a *cat*.
Well, fancy that, she swallowed a *cat*!
She swallowed the *cat* to catch the *bird*.

There was an old lady who swallowed a *dog*.
What a hog, to swallow a *dog*!
She swallowed the *dog* to catch the *cat*.

There was an old lady who swallowed a *cow*.
I don't know how she swallowed a *cow*!
She swallowed the *cow* to catch the *dog*.
She swallowed the *dog* to catch the *cat*.
She swallowed the *cat* to catch the *bird*.
She swallowed the *bird* to catch the *spider*,
That wriggled and wriggled and jiggled inside her.
She swallowed the *spider* to catch the *fly*.
I don't know why she swallowed a *fly*.
Perhaps she'll die.

There was an old lady who swallowed a *horse*.
She's dead of course.

    The next story experience activity is oriented toward teenagers and adults. This time the students in the circle are to hold cards of various colors: red, yellow, blue, white, and so on. Work with the students to make sure they are able to associate the words with the

---

[3] Those who would like the story in its entirety can refer to the version by Ruth Bonne, illustrated by Pam Adams, and published by Child's Play (International). I wish to thank Ernestine Saldivar for introducing me to this version.

particular colors to which each has been assigned. They are to listen very carefully to the words as the story is read. When the names of their colors are read, they are to walk across the circle, holding up the colored card. More than one student may have the same color. The number of students holding each color will depend upon how many persons the teacher would like to involve at any given time.

A Spring Day

The door opens wide. It is Sasha. Sasha comes to my house every morning at six o'clock. We walk to work together. Today is such a beautiful, warm day. We walk on the long sidewalk. A YELLOW sun peeks through the trees. It is spring. The flowers are opening up—RED flowers, YELLOW flowers, BLUE flowers. We see a man in the street. He is riding a RED bicycle. He is wearing boots and a BLUE hat. He stops riding. He asks, "Have you seen our rabbit? He's WHITE and BLACK, mostly BLACK. He got out of the cage this morning and must have come this way." He points toward the grass behind us. We look in the direction he is pointing. Then at each other.

"No, we haven't," we say at the same time. "Sorry." The man looks very worried. He gets back on his bicycle. He begins to ride away. "Wait," I yell. "I see something here . . . behind the bush. I think . . . I see fur . . . it's WHITE and BLACK—why it is. It's a rabbit and it looks very scared. Look, it's all hunched over." The man turns around and rides back. I pick up the frightened little ball of fur and hand it to him. "Oh thank you so very much!" exclaims the man. "My little boy will be very happy." He cuddles the rabbit in one arm as he rides away.

Once the students are familiar with the colors and feel comfortable with the activity, they can pretend to be the objects as they go across the circle. One can, for example, be the sun, others can be flowers, and so forth. Even the characters and main actions of the story can be acted out once a fuller understanding is achieved.

During the time that I have worked with story experience since the first edition of *Making It Happen* was published, two alternatives have evolved:
(1) Story experience can begin with a core story (the simplest form of the story) that can be gradually expanded by adding more complex syntactic structures and more and more abstract vocabulary as the students move forward in the language, or (2) Story experience can begin with the fully developed story and the students can "grow into it" over time.

The latter was the original intention of story experience. The process of letting students grow into the story is similar to the one that children go through in learning to read in their first language. At first they only understand bits and pieces and gradually, over time, they come to a full understanding of it. My student, Tom Cook, once compared story experience to a language puzzle, the pieces of which are given to students over time until the completed puzzle emerges.

SOUND EFFECTS
Level: Beginning

Demonstrate the sound effects that accompany the following story.[4] Beginning students only have to listen for the words that cue the appropriate effect (blanks have been inserted where the sound effects should go). Once the students understand the whole story (perhaps at an intermediate level), they can act it out. If they want, they can change the ending or rewrite it completely.

Rosita's Night to Remember

Rosita is alone in the house. Outside she hears the wind blow through the trees _____(hooing noises). Rain begins to fall _____ (patting of fingertips on the desks). There is a scratching at the door _____ (light touch of fingernails scratching on desks). Maybe it is a lion (roaring). Maybe it is a mouse _____ (squeaking). Maybe it is a monster _____ (howling). She is scared. She turns on the radio to drown out the scratching . The radio is playing a song _____ (singing—it doesn't have to be a particular tune). She turns it low _____ (the singing softens), high _____ (it becomes very loud), off _____ (it stops). At the door the scratching continues _____ . She opens the door _____ (creaking). Her dog comes in, jumps up, and gives her a big kiss _____ (kissing sound).

As the students become more proficient, they can write their own scenarios complete with sound effects. At advanced stages the minidramas can even become part of full-blown radio shows complete with commercials and newsbreaks.

IDENTIFYING OBJECTS IN STORIES
Level: Beginning

Ask advance-level volunteers, peer teachers, or lay assistants (see Chapter 14) to read very simple stories with lots of pictures in them to small groups of beginners (two or three in a group). Have the readers stop reading aloud from time to time and ask students to point to various specific objects in the pictures. Some of the volunteers or assistants might want to make up their own stories centering around a series of pictures. A book corner could be set up in your room where students can go to read stories aloud to small groups (see also Sharing Books—the Classroom Library).

STORY ACT-OUT
Level: Beginning to Intermediate

Read a favorite story aloud while the students listen. Give students a chance to ask questions, then read the story again. Ask for volunteers to take the parts of the characters. Pin a sign with the character's name on each volunteer. Read the story a third time as students act it out, action by action. Then give other volunteers a chance to be the actors.

---

[4]This story is an adaptation of one shared with me by Sylvia Pena.

WHAT'S THE TITLE?
Level: Intermediate

Read a story to students but leave out the title. Once the students understand the story, let them make up a title for it. Eventually the author's title can be revealed and discussed in relation to the meaning of the story.

SPINNING STORIES[5]
Level: Intermediate

Take a ball of yarn and tie knots in it at varying intervals. Some knots will be close together, others far apart. Tape a stimulating picture with people in it to the wall. After placing students in a circle, ask them what they see in the picture. Write the words on the chalkboard as they give them to you so that they will have some starters. Have students make up names and short biographical sketches for the people. Give the ball of yarn to one student in the circle. Ask him or her to begin a story about the picture while unraveling the ball of yarn. The student continues to tell the story until he or she reaches the first knot. Then the ball of yarn is passed to the next person, who continues the story until reaching the next knot. The activity continues until every student in the circle has had a chance to contribute.

GROUP STORY
Level: Intermediate

Using a language-experience type of activity (see Chapter 12), have the students create a group story. As each student makes his or her contribution, write the utterances on the board, making any necessary corrections indirectly. The stories will probably be very brief at first but will evolve into longer and more complex plots as the students gain proficiency. A series of pictures can be used to stimulate ideas.

SILLY STORIES[6]
Level: Intermediate to Advanced

You and your students can create a story together while a teacher assistant writes it on the chalkboard. Begin by offering the first half of a sentence and have a volunteer student finish it. Other sentences can be produced in the same fashion. For example:

> TEACHER: The elephant knocked at . . .
> STUDENT 1: . . . the door to my house.
> TEACHER: He asked . . .
> STUDENT 2: . . . "Can I borrow a cup of straw?"

GHOST STORIES BY CANDLELIGHT
Level: Intermediate to Advanced

Ask each student to bring a scary story to tell the class in the target language. Have the students sit in a circle on the floor. Light a candle, place it in the center of the circle, and turn

---

[5] Adapted from an activity shared with me by Esther Heise.

[6] This idea has been adapted from Wright, Betteridge, and Buckby (1984, p. 99).

off the lights. Students are told that they can volunteer by taking the candle from the center and placing it in front of them so it lights up their faces. Then they proceed to tell their stories. The candle is returned to the center as each student finishes his or her story. The teacher should demonstrate the procedure first. Background music, the volume of which can easily be adjusted to fit the situation, can be used to fill the silence between volunteers while adding to the mood. Because this activity may be a little too frightening for young children, you will probably want to limit its use to older children, teens, and adults. A flashlight may be used to substitute for a candle as a safety measure, especially for preadolescents.[7]

FINISH THE STORY
Level: Intermediate to Advanced

Present part of a story, and have students finish it orally and/or in writing. At first most of the story can be given. Later only a few lines such as those below may be necessary to launch students into building a climax followed by the denouement.

The boys see a dark shadow fall across the sidewalk. They look up and see . . .

The first day of her trip went well. Then she opened her suitcase. She discovered . . .

ORAL HISTORY
Level: Intermediate to Advanced

As part of a study of local history, students may want to tell their own stories and those of their parents, grandparents, friends, and neighbors. Where did they come from? How did they get here (to this town, suburb, city, state, country)? The project can be as broad as the students want to make it. They can include stories about their experiences in the particular locale, how certain buildings came into being, how traditions developed, and so forth. Collections can be made of these stories to share with each other, with other classes, and/or with visitors to the classroom.

STORY INTERPRETATION
Level: Intermediate to Advanced

The following story is one that is sure to interest ESL students in particular because it involves the mixed feelings that seem to accompany returning to one's homeland.

At first it is necessary to motivate the students to read the story by offering what I call "mind grabbers." Questions about their own longings to return home or about what they think it might be like to return home will serve well in preparing them for the experience in store for them. Following the story are relevant activities that can heighten its impact.

Excerpt from "Blue Winds Dancing," by Thomas S. Whitecloud

Morning. I spend the day cleaning up and buying some presents for my family with what is left of my money. Nothing much, but a gift is a gift, if a man buys it with his last quarter. I wait until evening, then start up the track toward home.

---

[7] I want to thank Cesar Montes for suggesting this precaution to me.

Christmas Eve comes in on a north wind. Snow clouds hang over the pines, the night comes early. Walking along the railroad bed, I feel the calm peace of snow-bound forests on either side of me. I take my time; I am back in a world where time does not mean so much now.

I am alone—alone but not nearly so lonely as I was back on the campus at school. Those are never lonely who love the snow and the pines, never lonely when the pines are wearing white shawls and snow crunches coldly underfoot . . .

Just as a light snow begins to fall, I cross the reservation boundary. Somehow it seems as though I have stepped into another world. Deep woods in a white-and-black winter night. A faint trail leading to the village.

The railroad on which I stand comes from a city sprawled by a lake—a city with a million people who walk around without seeing one another; a city sucking the life from all the country around; a city with stores and police and intellectuals and criminals and movies and apartment houses; a city with its politics and libraries and zoos.

Laughing, I go into the woods. As I cross a frozen lake, I begin to hear the drums. Soft in the night the drums beat. It is like the pulse of the world. The white line of the lake ends at a black forest, and above the trees the blue winds are dancing.

I come to the outlying houses of the village. Simple box houses, etched black in the night. From one or two windows soft lamplight falls on the snow. Christmas is here, too, but it does not mean much—not much in the way of parties and presents. Joe Sky will get drunk. Alex Bodidash will buy his children red mittens and a new sled . . . The village is not a sight to instill pride, yet I am not ashamed. One can never be ashamed of his own people when he knows they have dreams as beautiful as white snow on a tall pine.

Father and my brother and sister are seated around the table as I walk in. Father stares at me for a moment. Then I am in his arms, crying on his shoulder. I give them the presents I have brought, and my throat tightens as I watch my sister save carefully bits of red string from the packages. I hide my feelings by wrestling with my brother when he strikes my shoulder in token of affection. Father looks at me, and I know he has many questions, but he seems to know why I have come. He tells me to go on alone to the lodge, and he will follow.

I follow the trail to the lodge. My feet are light, my heart seems to sing to the music, and I hold my head high. Across white snow fields blue winds are dancing.

Before the lodge door I stop, afraid. I wonder if my people will remember me. I wonder—"Am I Indian, or am I white?" I stand before the door a long time. I hear the ice groan on the lake, and remember the story of the old woman who is under the ice, trying to get out, so she can punish some runaway lovers. . . .

Inside the lodge there are many Indians. Some sit on benches around the walls. Others dance in the center of the floor around a drum. Nobody seems to notice me. It seems as though I were among a people I have never seen before. . . . I look at the old men. Straight, dressed in dark trousers and beaded velvet vests, wearing soft moccasins. Dark, lined faces intent on the music. I wonder if I am at all like them. They dance on, lifting their feet to the rhythm of the drums. . . .

The dance stops. The men walk back to the walls and talk in low tones or with their hands. There is little conversation, yet everyone seems to be sharing some secret . . . they are sharing a mood. Everyone is happy . . . the night is beautiful outside, and the music is beautiful.

I try hard to forget school and white people, and be one of these—my people . . . we are all a part of something universal. I watch eyes and see now that the old people are speaking to me. They nod slightly, imperceptibly, and their eyes laugh into mine. I look around the room. All the eyes are friendly; they all laugh. No one questions my being here. The drums begin to beat again, and I catch the invitation in the eyes of the old men. My feet begin to lift to the rhythm, and I look out beyond the walls into the night and see the lights. I am happy. It is beautiful. I am home.

FOLLOW-UP ACTIVITIES TO "BLUE WINDS DANCING"

1. First, ask the students if there are any words or phrases that they do not understand. Ask them to guess at the meanings by using the context. Discuss.
2. Have volunteers retell the story to a guest who is not already familiar with it (you may want to invite someone in for this purpose).
3. Divide the students into pairs. Have one person take the part of the man who comes home and the other the part of one of the older men who is at the lodge. Have them make up a dialogue, write it down, and practice it. Ask volunteers to share their scenes with the class.
4. Divide ESL students into groups of three. Have them speculate about what it would be like to return to their homelands. Encourage them to share the problems they might have as well as the delights.

STORY WRITING
Level: Advanced

Students can be given time to write and share their own stories. They may want to make their stories autobiographical, biographical, or fictional. As a culminating activity, they may want to put copies of all the stories together in a book with illustrations and a table of contents. The books can be shared with other classes or placed in the school's library to be checked out by anyone who wants to read them.

ROLE PLAY

Role play has high appeal for students because it allows them to be creative and to put themselves in another person's place for a while. As Atticus Finch says in Harper Lee's *To Kill a Mockingbird*, "You never really understand a person until you consider things from his view—until you climb into his skin and walk around in it." Role play can be just "play" or it can have serious social implications, such as in sociodrama.

Scarcella (1983) defines sociodrama as being student oriented rather than teacher oriented. Students act out solutions to social problems, generally defining their own roles and determining their own courses of action. The enactment is open-ended but centers around a clearly stated conflict that is relevant to the students. Only those students who demonstrate a special interest in particular roles are chosen to play them. The steps, which she adapts from Shaftel and Shaftel (1967), include introducing topic, stimulating student interest, presenting new vocabulary, reading a story that clearly identifies a problem, stopping the story at the climax, discussing the dilemma, selecting students to play the roles, preparing the audience to listen and later offer advice, acting out the rest of the story, discussing alternative ways of dealing with the problem, and replaying the drama using new strategies if necessary. Some sample mini-sociodramas (one might call them simply "role-play situations") are below.

Role-Play Situations

FOR ADULTS OR TEENAGERS

Sun Kim comes home from school all excited. Jeff, an Anglo-American boy, has asked her for a date. She tells her mother. Her mother is very upset.

"In Korea you do not do any such thing," her mother reminds her.

"But, Mother, this is not Korea. This is America."

"But we are Korean," her mother insists. "You are Korean. This is not what we do. In time you will be ready. Your father and I will arrange a nice Korean man for you. We will not let you go alone with this man."

"Oh, Mother . . . but . . . I . . ."

FOR PREADOLESCENTS

"Look. I'm as big as you," Anita says to her brother John. She stretches up on her tip-toes. "Why can't I go to the movie with you?"

"Look, Squirt, you stay home this time, okay. The movie is not for you because . . . "

FOR YOUNG CHILDREN

"Mom, come here. Come here. The cat is stuck up in the tree. He won't come down. Come quick."

Mother sticks her head around the door. "Now just a minute, Sally. Don't panic. The first thing we'll do is . . ."

It's important that the students be gradually worked into the above role-play situations. The teacher can get them into their roles by asking questions such as, "How old are you, Anita? What kinds of movies do your parents want you to see?" When the students seem to feel comfortable in their roles, the teacher can reread the situation and let the actors take it at the point where the story leaves off.

Another activity for the more proficient students that can be adapted to various age groups is acting out roles of characters from literature. Literature can come alive when students play the role of a character with which they are familiar. For example, if they have just read *The Pearl* by John Steinbeck (1947), one student may want to play Juana and another Kino. The characters could be interviewed as they might be on the David Letterman show or they might be part of a panel discussion on what money and greed can do to one's life. In addition, people from history might be brought back to life for a day or two. For example, one student might play Abraham Lincoln and another Susan B. Anthony. After students read up on their lives and times, these characters can be brought together for a TV show such as Steve Allen's "Meeting of the Minds," popular during the 1970s. Other characters from history could be pitted against each other in a debate about a current topic. It would be interesting to see how Henry VIII might feel about divorce or how Joan of Arc might react to women's liberation issues.

Mid-beginners also can participate in role play. Tools for communication can be taught through role-play situations. Students can be given matrices on index cards to be used as cues. Short scenes can begin with total-physical-response activities in which the teacher plays the role of the director and directs students in their parts (move to the right, sit down, walk to the table, say, "Are you ready to order?"). Matrices such as those below can be tailored to fit different situations. It is suggested that similar matrices first be incorporated into jazz chants and lyrics (see Chapter 9).

In a restaurant:

(Menus are given to two customers by the waiter.)
Are you ready to order?
Yes, I will have the _____.
And you? (looks at the second person)
I will have the _____.

At a produce store:

(A clerk is setting out baskets of strawberries. A customer approaches from behind.)
Excuse me. Can you please tell me where the _____ is/are?
Oh, yes. It's/they're by the _____ .
Thank you.

Typical greetings, simple compliments, frequently asked questions, and often-used comments can be introduced or reinforced in this manner. Other public places can be simulated to serve as settings (a post office, a doctor's office, a library, a hospital). Eventually the students can simply be given an oral description of a situation (no cue cards this time) to which they can respond through role play.

You are in a restaurant. The waiter comes to take your order. You look at the menu and tell the waiter what you want.

You are in a produce store. You can't find what you want to buy. You ask the clerk for help.

The most beneficial kind of role play, however, is that in which the *teacher plays a key role*. For example, if the teacher is the waiter in the restaurant or the clerk in the produce store, he or she can provide comprehensible input to extend the conversation. The teacher can prompt, expand, or offer help as needed. By this means groups of mixed abilities can be included in the same role-play situation. Starters are offered to some, explanations provided to others, and others are given no help at all if they don't need it. Below is an illustration to show how this can work.

At a produce store—(The students have been given play money and have had prior experience counting it.)

> Pedro stands in front of the strawberries.

TEACHER:	(or teacher assistant playing the role of the clerk) Strawberries? For you, Pedro? (She holds up a basket of strawberries.)
PEDRO:	Aaa. . . Straw . . .
TEACHER:	Strawberries? Do you want strawberries?
PEDRO:	. . . Strawberries . . . (nods his head)
TEACHER:	(offering the basket to him) Do you want to buy the strawberries? Yes? (points to some play money in the box which serves as a cash register)
PEDRO:	Yes . . . buy.
TEACHER:	One dollar. Give me one dollar. (Pedro takes some play money from his pocket but looks puzzled.)
TEACHER:	One dollar (points to a dollar bill in his hand).
PEDRO:	One dollar (gives the teacher the dollar bill).
TEACHER:	Thank you (takes the money and gives him the basket).
PEDRO:	Thank you.
TEACHER:	(turning to the next customer) Do you want some strawberries, Nor?
NOR:	I want oranges.
TEACHER:	Oranges, huh (moves to the oranges). I've got juicy ones for you.
NOR:	Juicy?
TEACHER:	Yes. Juicy. Lots of sweet juice (squeezes one to show its softness).
NOR:	Oh yes. Juice.
TEACHER:	They cost $1.50 a bag. Do you want a bag?
NOR:	Yes. I'll take a bag (gives the teacher the money and takes the oranges).

Thus the teacher is able to adjust the input to fit the approximate level of each student. *No cue cards are needed.* With sufficient input the students will begin to acquire the structures through the interaction.

DRAMA

To some it may seem artificial to make drama a separate category since it is an integral part of storytelling and role play. However, for the sake of clarity we will use this term for activities with roles, plots, and dialogues that are written down in play form to be memorized and acted out on the stage or read aloud. Some of the introductory activities recommended here can be used as warm-ups for storytelling and role play as well.

At beginning levels students can first be introduced to the simple emotions involved in dramatic action. The teacher or teacher assistant can model the emotions, using exaggerated facial expressions and other movements to illustrate words such as *joy, anger, fear, sadness,* and *doubt.* Students can model the emotions themselves as a group (see also "Identifying Emotions" in the Total Physical Response section of Chapter 7). They can refine their abilities to recognize and reproduce emotions by learning to draw them. (See Figure 10.1.) For further reinforcement, they can find pictures in magazines of people expressing specific feelings. The pictures may be cut out and pasted in a book of emotions (one page can be labeled "Joy," another "Fear," another "Anger," and so forth).

Figure 10.1 (adapted from Evans and Moore, 1982)

Later when the students are a little more proficient, each can be asked to write the name of an emotion on a piece of paper to be put into a grab bag. Each student will then take an emotion from the grab bag and act it out while the rest of the class guesses which emotion is being portrayed. At another time the names of specific activities can be written on pieces of paper, and students can pantomime the activities while the class guesses what is being acted out.

Yet another technique is to choose a segment of a TV soap opera to put on videotape. Find one that you feel will interest your students. Show it without sound and let the students decide the emotions that the actors are feeling. Later you can show the same segment, again without sound, and let your students figure out what they think is happening just from facial expressions and actions. Then replay the same segment and listen to the words. How close did the students come to guessing the reality? Discuss it with them. It is not necessary that they understand all the words this time. You may play it again in a few months and let them write and act out additional segments. Eventually, they may want to write and stage their own soap operas.

Students, particularly younger ones, can each make a puppet out of heavy construction paper and a tongue depressor (see Figure 10.2).[8] For the head, they can cut out two identical shapes from construction paper and staple the edges together, leaving an opening at the neck. Placing a small wad of newspaper inside gives the puppet a three-dimensional effect. They can then place the tongue depressor where the neck should be and staple the paper to it. Yarn can be used for hair. Eyes, a nose, and a mouth can be drawn with a felt-tip pen. The puppet can be given a name and can become part of a series of dramas or mini-scenarios that the students write and act out. One alternative might be to have the students make flannel-board characters to move about on a large flannel board.

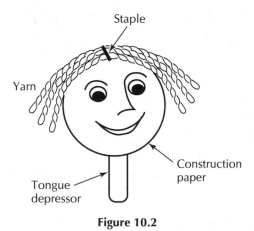

Figure 10.2

---

[8] This idea came from a handout distributed at a presentation by Susan Andrews during the Spring COTESOL Conference 1980, Denver, Colorado.

Another activity (this one can be used during the upper elementary grades and later) is an adaptation of an idea called "The Prop Box," which comes from Winn-Bell Olsen.[9] Each student is asked to bring something from home that isn't wanted anymore. It can be from any room in the house but it must be something that the teacher can keep. All the items should be placed in a large box (the prop box). The class should be divided into groups of two, three, or four students. Each student is asked to reach into the prop box without looking and draw out an item. The groups then write short dramas or skits that incorporate all the items as props. The plays can be rehearsed with the help of peer teachers or lay assistants (see Chapter 14) and presented to the whole class.

Finally, Goodman and Tenney (1979) recommend readers' theater as a vehicle for acquiring a second language. The name "readers' theater" comes from the fact that the actors hold their scripts and read from them with expression and feeling. The actors and the narrator generally sit on tall stools arranged in a semicircle in front of the audience. It might help them to imagine that the wall in back of the audience is a mirror. The actors talk directly to the "images" of the other characters rather than address them directly. In fact, they more or less ignore the presence of the other characters except as they appear in the "mirror." Characters who are supposed to be offstage also sit on stools, but keep their backs to the audience, facing the audience only upon their entrances. The narrator, who addresses the audience directly, plays a large role: He or she sets the scene, introduces the characters, and gives running comments about actions, feelings, and moods. In other words, the narrator provides the glue that holds the dialogue together and makes it comprehensible.

Because readers' theater involves a great deal of repetition as students are rehearsing a presentation, the words become part of the students' repertoires without conscious memorization. The whole class, even the audience, begins to internalize the lines. Reading also can be enhanced if members of the audience are able to look at the scripts as the lines are being read. Goodman and Tenney feel that creating a script and putting on a play can be a good culminating activity for almost any unit of study. Through it, concepts and structures can be acquired or reinforced. However, they recommend teaching the techniques of readers' theater through a prepared script first. Below is a sample.

An Unusual Birthday Celebration

NARRATOR: It is mid-afternoon. Two elderly women and a dog are on the sidewalk. They are in front of the ice-cream store on Maple Street.

MABEL: Well, Nettie, what will we get today?

---

[9] She gives credit to the Creative Environment Center, SFUSD workshop for this suggestion. Prop boxes can be used to teach other lessons, particularly in conjunction with the natural approach (see Chapter 8). For example, one box could include household items, another camping equipment, and so forth.

NARRATOR: She smiles at Nettie. Their eyes are dancing.

NETTIE: I want something very special today . . . something new.

NARRATOR: Nettie tugs at her dog's leash.

NETTIE: Now you be a good boy and lie down.

NARRATOR: She points to the sidewalk in front of the glass door. The dog lies down obediently. The two women go into the store.

MABEL: Something new? You're going to try something new? You always want the same old thing. A cone with one scoop of chocolate. You always get that.

NETTIE: But today I want something special. Today is my birthday, you know. Seventy-six years old.

NARRATOR: She looks at all the pictures on the wall. There are ice-cream sundaes everywhere. Chocolate and caramel drip from them. They are covered with nuts, whipped cream, and cherries. Her mouth waters. Mabel says . . .

MABEL: Did you hear from your son today? Did he wish you a happy birthday?

NARRATOR: Mabel's hands flutter in the air. Nettie's smile fades.

NETTIE: No. I'm afraid he hasn't . . .

CLERK: What will you have, Ma'am?

NETTIE: I think I'll have that . . .

NARRATOR: She points to a caramel sundae.

NETTIE: I'll have . . . that caramel sundae . . . with whipped cream and nuts. No cherry, please. I'm allergic to cherries. They give me hives.

CLERK: Yes, Ma'am. Right away.

NARRATOR: She turns to look at Mabel. She catches a glimpse of the glass door and the sidewalk outside. Something is wrong. Her eyes open very wide. She screams . . .

NETTIE: My dog. Where's my dog?

NARRATOR: She runs out the door. She looks up and down the street. But she can't find him. She calls and calls . . .

NETTIE: He-re Lad-die. He-re Lad-die.

NARRATOR: . . . in a high voice. A stranger comes out from behind the building.

STRANGER: Ma'am, is this the dog you're looking for? He's right here eating ice cream. A little boy dropped his cone . . .

NARRATOR: Nettie runs around to the side of the building. Sure enough, there in front of her is the dog. He is lapping up the last bit of ice cream from the ground. He makes slurping sounds. Nettie is overcome with joy. She says . . .

NETTIE: Oh, my Laddie. Thank goodness he's safe.

NARRATOR   She rushes over and hugs him. The dog is now licking his chops.
            Mabel is right behind her.
NETTIE: Oh, my sweet Laddie.
MABEL: I guess he wants something special on your birthday too. Just
            like a dog, you know. They all think they're people. Come on,
            let's get our ice cream. I don't have all day, you know.
NARRATOR: The three of them head back to the door of the ice cream store.

Goodman and Tenney suggest that the teacher first have selected students read
the dialogue aloud and then ask the audience what they think was especially
effective about the way it was read. Then the teacher can discuss the drama
with the students to create interest in the problems of the characters. The
teacher as director should model the roles with much enthusiasm to encourage
the students to put aside some of their own inhibitions. Then the students
should read the parts one more time with added expression and feeling. The
audience might then be called on for suggestions, which might include the
addition of various sound effects or other elements. All the students should be
made to feel that they are part of the drama in some way.

   Later, students might be encouraged to write and perform their own
scripts based on pictures or other forms of mental stimulation (musical lyrics,
poetry, TV shows, and so forth). The productions can then become whole-class
projects from beginning to end.

SUMMARY

Storytelling, role play, and drama, through their attention to human experience,
can involve students in highly motivating activity. Because students can lose
themselves in the characters, plots, and situations, they are more apt to receive
the benefits of reduced anxiety levels, increased self-confidence and esteem,
and heightened awareness.

   Even beginning students can enjoy the pleasures of dramatic action right
from the start. They can join in on the prelanguage activities or warm-ups,
"Story Experience" and various other physical responses, sound effects production, or simple recognition of emotional states.

   As they progress, the students can improve their abilities to comprehend
and later produce the target language, and can learn to work cooperatively in
group situations toward mutual goals. Eventually students can tell their own
tales, interpret stories, deal with problems through sociodrama, and write, read
aloud, and even produce minidramas.

READINGS, REFLECTION, AND DISCUSSION

Suggested Readings and Reference Materials

Garvie, E. (1990). *Story as vehicle: Teaching English to young children.* Clevedon, England: Multilingual Matters Ltd. Here the story is presented as a way to increase intrinsic motivation in children and thereby make language acquisition more likely.

Ladousse, G. (1987). *Role play.* Oxford: Oxford Press. Preparing students for role play, and ideas for role play that are suitable for classes, both large and small, are highlighted in this book.

Maley, A., and Duff, A. (1983). *Drama techniques in language learning: A resource book of communication activities for language teachers.* Cambridge: Cambridge University. Presents a useful selection of dramatic activities for the language classroom. The authors are careful to point out that their book is not about putting on plays for audiences. In fact, many of the activities appear to have little to do with dramatic performance. Instead, they are dramatic in that they pique student curiosity and interest by capitalizing on the unpredictable events that can occur when people are placed in contact with one another.

Rowland, P. (1990). *Happily ever after big book packages.* Reading, Mass.: Addison-Wesley. Includes classics such as "Little Red Riding Hood," "La Tortuga," "The Three Bears," and "Peter and the Wolf." Intended for lower grades, each package contains one Big Book and four Little Books of the same title. A teaching guide, story script, and activity suggestions accompany each package.

Smallwood, B. (1991). *The literature connection: A read-aloud guide for multicultural classrooms.* Reading, Mass.: Addison-Wesley. A helpful guide for teachers searching for read-aloud materials and guidelines (grades K–8). Of particular interest is the extensive annotated bibliography which arranges books by theme. Along with the annotations is information about grade level, proficiency level, cultural group, vocabulary, and so forth.

Scarcella, R. (1983). Sociodrama for social interaction. In Oller and Richard-Amato, *Methods that work*, pp. 239–245. A discussion of the ways in which sociodrama can be used to teach the target language. Activities include the enactment of solutions to social problems.

Questions for Reflection and Discussion

1. How might dramatic experiences help to make the ego more "permeable" in the sense that Guiora uses the term? (See Chapter 5.)

2. What might be some advantages to the language acquisition process of drama that has been improvised by the students over drama written by playwrights to be memorized by actors (the students)? Any disadvantages? What about advantages and disadvantages of preparation for an actual performance before audiences? Is it better, for example, for the students simply to perform for themselves and each other?

3. DiPietro (1983) points out that a scenario that is appropriate in one culture may be inappropriate in another. What role should cultural constraints play in your selection of content? What might be the consequences if such constraints are ignored? Give examples.

4. Plan a lesson using storytelling, role play, or drama. Be specific about the age levels and proficiency levels of the students with whom you might use it (beginning, intermediate, or advanced). Share the lesson with members of your class and get their feedback.

CHAPTER **11**

Games

Game playing, having apparently originated as a form of instruction, now appears again to be coming into its own as an instructional activity.

T. Rodgers, 1978

QUESTIONS TO THINK ABOUT

1. Do you remember a favorite game you played as a child that you think helped you to learn your first language? What was that game? In what ways do you think it helped you to learn language?

2. Do you think teenagers and adults are too old for games that might help them learn a second or foreign language? Why or why not?

3. What advantages might games have in learning another language?

4. Would you incorporate them into a second- or foreign-language course you might be likely to teach? If so, how would you go about it? To what extent would you use games to teach language?

Games are often associated with fun. While it is true that games *are* usually fun, one must not lose sight of their pedagogical value, particularly in second-language teaching. Like most of the other activities recommended in this book, games can lower anxiety, thus making the acquisition of input more likely. In addition, they are often highly motivating, relevant, interesting, and comprehensible.

Games are sometimes used in classrooms to develop and reinforce concepts (e.g., colors, shapes, numbers, word definitions), to add diversion to the regular classroom activities, and even to break the ice, particularly in the case of rank beginners. Occasionally they are used to introduce new ideas. Perhaps their most important function, however, is to give practice in communication skills. Although some are quiet, contemplative games, others are noisy and require much verbal or physical involvement. Some are meant for small groups, others for large groups. Often classes can be divided into smaller units and several games can be played simultaneously. The teacher, peer teachers, or lay assistants (see Chapter 14) can facilitate in the individual groups.

The games recommended here may involve a certain amount of group competition, but competition is generally not the focus (except perhaps in some of the nonverbal games). Games in which individuals may be singled out and embarrassed in front of large groups of peers are avoided.

It is important that the rules of the games be very few and clearly explained. In some cases students can begin the games and have the rules explained as the game progresses. Demonstrations also can be very helpful.

Most of the games discussed below can be adapted to any age level, provided students are cognitively able to handle the content. In addition, most can be adapted to several proficiency levels (beginning, intermediate, or advanced) according to the difficulty of the tasks involved. None of the games require large outlays of money. Usually the materials needed can be easily collected or made by the teacher or an assistant.

Even though the categories often overlap, the games are divided into the following types depending on their emphasis: nonverbal games, board-advancing games, word-focus games, treasure hunts, and guessing games.

NONVERBAL GAMES

Games such as relays or musical chairs can help students become acquainted with each other, even before they can speak. Used sparingly, they can serve as ice breakers and can be used to bring together students of mixed levels. After hearing the directions for a specific game given in the target language, the more proficient students of various language backgrounds might be able to translate the directions into the L1 of other, less proficient students.

Nonverbal games can also be used to form groups for other games and activities. For example, at Christmas time, trees may be made of construction paper and cut into puzzle pieces to be matched (Figure 11.1). The number of trees will depend on how many groups are necessary for the game that is to follow and on how many students are in the class. For example, if the class is going to play classroom scrabble (described later in this chapter) and fourteen students need to be divided into four teams, four trees will be necessary (two trees will be cut into three puzzle pieces and two into four puzzle pieces). The students will each draw a puzzle piece out of the grab bag and find the students who have the missing pieces to make a complete tree. Thus a group is formed. The same can be done with hearts on Valentine's Day, pumpkins on Halloween, shamrocks on St. Patrick's Day, and so on. Another alternative is to cut several pictures (one for each group desired) into puzzle pieces, mix them up, and have each student take one piece and find the other people with the pieces that will complete the picture. (For more ideas about forming groups, see pages 120 and 213.)

Figure 11.1

BOARD-ADVANCING GAMES

Using game pieces (such as buttons or little plastic cars) to represent the players, students can perform certain tasks or simply roll the dice to move forward a certain number of spaces. The board itself can be as imaginative and colorful as the teacher wants to make it. The spaces must form some sort of pathway from a starting point to a finishing point, which is the goal, as in Figure 11.2.

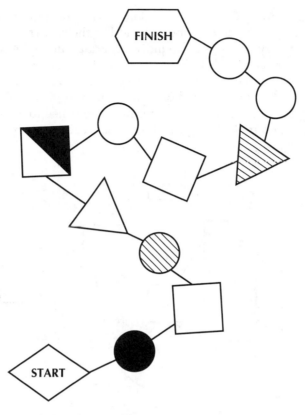

Figure 11.2

Students might also take turns drawing cards with specific commands on them (jump three times, write your name on the chalkboard, sing a song from your country). Once the student has completed the task (other students can help in interpreting and carrying out the command), he or she can move forward the number of spaces indicated on the card. Additional tasks can include giving synonyms or antonyms for specific words, identifying objects on pictures, doing simple math computations, or any kind of task that will reinforce what the teacher wants the students to learn. The "winner" is the one who reaches the goal first.

WORD-FOCUS GAMES

Students can be given words to see how many other words they can make from them. For example the following words can be made from the word *teacher:* ear, her, teach, reach, cheer, each, hear, here, arch, tea, and eat. By working with others in a team situation, the student can learn new words from the other members in the group. Group competition to see which group can make the most words in a certain time period may add to the excitement and probably will not raise anxiety levels since no individuals are put on the spot.

An alternative activity is to have teams of students see how many words they can make from a letter grid such as the one shown in Figure 11.3. Students must move along the connecting lines without skipping any letters. A single letter cannot be used twice in succession but can be returned to if there is an intervening letter. For example, in Figure 11.3, *regret* is acceptable but *greet* is not.

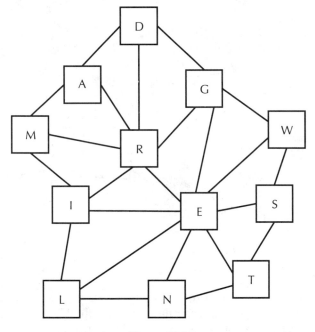

Figure 11.3

The bean bag toss suggested by Evans and Moore (1982) can be adapted to teach antonyms, synonyms, or categories of words. They suggest that the teacher make a large playing area on tagboard with a felt-tip pen. The teacher draws circles all over the area, and puts one word in each circle (see Figure 11.4). The teacher should make sure that each word has its opposite (if working on antonyms), that each word has a corresponding word that means the same thing (if working on synonyms), or that each word has a corresponding category to which it belongs (if working on categories). The student stands behind a line that has been marked with masking tape and tosses a bean bag. After reading the word on which the bag lands, the student takes a second bean bag and tries to toss it so it will land on the antonym, synonym, or a category member.

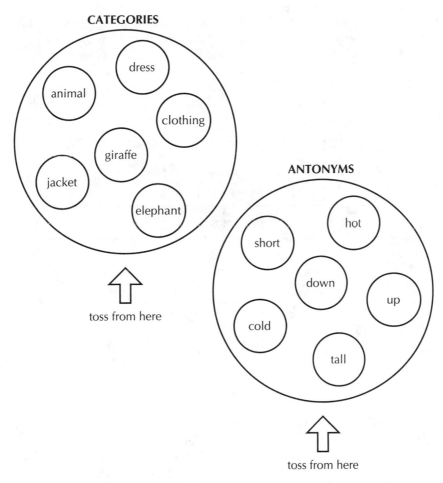

CATEGORIES

ANTONYMS

toss from here

toss from here

Figure 11.4 (adapted from Evans and Moore, 1982)

Classroom scrabble[1] is a particularly effective word-focus game. Students are divided into teams, three to four students per team. A scrabble board is drawn on the chalkboard (see Figure 11.5). Notice that some squares have been shaded; letters placed on the shaded areas receive double their normal count. Two to four teams are given letters cut from index cards (four consonants and three vowels per team), on which point values have been written—lower point values for frequently used letters, higher point values for the rest. The teacher begins by writing a message in the middle of the board, such as "Peace." The students must build their words off the letters in the message. Cellophane tape is rolled up and put behind each letter to make it stick to the chalkboard (later

---

[1] I wish to thank Deborah Floyd for this game idea.

the tape can be removed so the same letters can be used again). The teams take turns, making as many words as they can. All words must connect to a word already on the board, either horizontally or vertically. Each team's letters are replaced after the turns, a vowel for a vowel and a consonant for a consonant. They are drawn at random by a team member from a reserve guarded by the teacher. To keep the game moving, it is a good idea to place a time limit of about two or three minutes to complete a turn.

Figure 11.5

One commonly used word-focus game that I choose to avoid is "scrambled word." The students are given words with the letters scrambled. They are supposed to unscramble them to form the intended word. For example, "cesenic" can be unscrambled to form "science." Although native speakers might find this fun, second-language students tend to find such games frustrating. To most of them, the language may appear to be "scrambled" to begin with, so it seems senseless to cause them additional anxiety.

TREASURE HUNTS

A treasure hunt is a favorite game among second-language learners. It allows them to work cooperatively in a group effort to find the items required. At the same time communicative competence can be increased. Often the items will call for a group consensus. For example, the students may have to find something beautiful, so they have to agree on what is beautiful. Condon (1983) suggests that the following steps (paraphrased below) be taken in organizing a treasure hunt. The hunt can take anywhere from ten minutes to an entire day, depending on the number and kinds of items listed.

1. Divide the class into groups of from three to six members.
2. Give an identical list of treasures to each group.
3. Read the items aloud for children or less proficient students to make sure they understand the vocabulary.
4. A time limit should be given.
5. Say "Go" to indicate when the groups can begin their searches.
6. At the end of the time limit, or when the first group returns, everyone gets together to check each item, giving points (five points are suggested) for each completed item. Points are taken away for incomplete ones.

Here are a few of the more interesting tasks in which Condon involves her students.

1. List five countries the members of your group would like to visit.
2. What is the largest shoe size in your group?
3. Find something useless.
4. Make a dinner menu in English.
5. Find a photograph.
6. Collect the autographs of three people not in your group.
7. Find something that smells good.
8. Make a crazy hat for your teacher.
9. Write down six ways of making people laugh.
10. Find a picture of something good to eat.

GUESSING GAMES

Guessing games can be painless ways to develop or reinforce any number of concepts. "Guess What I Am" or "Guess Who I Am," for example, can be used to teach about animals, professions, or people in different age groups (baby, child, teenager, young adult, middle-aged adult, elderly person). Each student can pantomime a particular role, and the class guesses which role is being acted out. The student who guesses the role correctly is "it" and takes the next turn. A time limit should be set so not too much attention is devoted to any one person.

"Guess What I'm Doing" can be used to teach recognition in the target language of activities such as taking a bath, going fishing, doing homework, and so forth. "Guess What I Have" is even more focused on verbalization. The student gives verbal hints as to what object is being described, or the students ask questions about the object (as in "Twenty Questions"). The object may be hidden or in full view. It is important that the class not know the name of the object beforehand.

Alternatives include "Whose Name Is It?" or "What Am I?" In either case, one person is "it," and a sign, which the person cannot see, is placed on his or her back. On the sign has been written the name of a classmate or the name of a specific occupation. The person with the sign asks *yes* or *no* questions of the class until the correct response is arrived at. (Do I wear a hat? Do I climb ladders?) The students take turns being "it."

Games come in many different forms and can be gathered from a variety of sources: books on the subject, young people's magazines, department store game sections. However, one important source that must not be overlooked is the second-language students themselves. Having students share games from their countries or cultural backgrounds can be a very exciting experience for everyone and can provide many opportunities for practice with the target language.

SUMMARY

Games can be used to develop or reinforce concepts, to add diversion to the regular classroom activities, or just to break the ice. However, their most important function is to give practice in communication.

It is recommended that competition be downplayed for most games, that the rules be few, and that they be clearly explained and demonstrated where possible.

Although the categories can overlap, the games offered here are divided basically into the following types depending on their emphasis: nonverbal games, board-advancing games, word-focus games, treasure hunts, and guessing games.

Various sources for game ideas are mentioned, but teachers are reminded that one of the best sources is the students themselves.

READINGS, REFLECTION, AND DISCUSSION

Suggested Readings and Reference Materials

Crookall, D., and Oxford, R., eds., (1990). *Simulation, gaming, and language learning.* New York: Newbury House. Developing learning strategies through simulation/gaming, using simulation/gaming as a language testing device, and simulations on computers are only a few of the topics discussed. Included are selections by Martha Cummings and Rhonda Genzel, Robin Scarcella and Susan Stern, and many others.

McCallum, G. (1980). *101 word games.* Oxford: Oxford University. This explicit, easy-to-use book includes word games that can aid students in developing proficiency in the target language. Activities involve listening practice, conversation, spelling, and vocabulary building. Helpful suggestions accompany the game descriptions.

Schultz, M., and Fisher, A. (1988). *Games for all reasons: Interacting in the language class-room*. Reading, Mass.: Addison-Wesley. Among the games described in this collection are language structure games; vocabulary games; pronunciation, number, and other listening games; role plays and total physical response games; and debate games.

Wright, A., Betteridge, D., and Buckby, M. (1984). *Games for language learning.* Cambridge: Cambridge University. A wide array of language games is presented, similar to those mentioned in the descriptions above. They can be used to teach many different target languages and can be quite easily adapted to various age levels.

Questions for Reflection and Discussion

1. Form a set of criteria that you might use in the selection of a game for classroom use. Give examples of games that might or might not fit particular situations based on the criteria you have developed.

2. How can a game such as a treasure hunt be used to reinforce the teaching of a story? Choose a particular story, describe the story, and tell what "treasures" you might incorporate in order to reinforce the concepts.

3. Recall a favorite game that you played as a child. How might it be adapted to a second-language class?

4. Select several topics for use with the natural approach or its extensions (see Chapter 8). Find and adapt, or create, two or three games that you could use to reinforce each topic. Try one game out on members of your class. To what extent was it successful?

CHAPTER 12

Ways to Promote Literacy Development

> *... writing like a reader becomes inextricably bound up with reading like a writer.*
>
> V. Zamel, 1992

QUESTIONS TO THINK ABOUT

1. What kinds of activities do you think will best promote reading and writing in second- and foreign-language learners? Relate their use to your own experiences with developing literacy in your first or second language. You may want to consider experiences you already have had as a teacher.

2. Are there any types of activities that you would avoid? Again try to relate their use to your own experiences.

3. Do you think it is important for reading and writing to be taught simultaneously? Why or why not? To what extent do you feel they should receive separate treatment?

Although all the chapters in this section promote the development of literacy in one way or another, this chapter more directly focuses on it. The ways to promote the development of literacy suggested here are extensions of the natural language framework developed in Chapter 4. They are based on the premise that learning to read and write is a communal process. They assume that the student's major goal in developing literacy is to effectively create meaning either as a writer or a reader. They assume that the learner comes to the classroom community with a rich fund of knowledge and experience to share with others.

In this chapter, the following topics will be discussed:

• The Language Experience Approach
• Literature-Based Curriculum
• Writing Workshops
• Advanced Academic Reading and Writing

THE LANGUAGE EXPERIENCE APPROACH

The language experience approach (Van Allen and Allen, 1967), was a precursor to the whole language movement (see Chapter 4). Even though it originally lacked a well-developed theoretical base, its apparent efficacy established it as a viable means for teaching reading to native speakers. Later several versions of this approach were suggested for use with second-language students (see especially Moustfa, M., 1989, and Dixon and Nessel, 1983). The language experience approach is predicated on the notion that students can write by dictating to the teacher what they already know and can express verbally, and that they can then read that which has been written. Thus, the students' first reading materials come from their own repertoire of language.

Although applications differ for various age levels and needs, the process begins with the students' experiences. It may be a trip to the countryside, a movie, a food-tasting session, a picture, poem, story, and so on. The students first discuss the experience with the teacher and/or fellow students and then dictate a "story" about that experience to the teacher individually. The teacher writes down exactly what the student says, including the errors. The teacher then reads aloud each sentence after it is written, giving the student a chance to make changes (some may notice their own errors and want to correct them). The teacher may want to wait until the story is finished before reading it back, making sure that the student sees the correspondence between what is being said and what was written. The student is then encouraged to read the story either silently or aloud to the teacher or to another student and then to rewrite it, again making changes that seem necessary.

An interesting alternative, which changes the dynamics considerably, is for the whole class or small groups within the class to dictate a "group" story while the teacher writes it on the board, flip chart, or overhead transparency. What makes this alternative particularly interesting is that the students scaffold upon each other's utterances and create Zones of Proximal Development for each other (see previous discussion on pages 38–39).

The stories, once they are ready, can be placed in story collections and displayed in the classroom for all to read and reread. Students can also provide illustrations to accompany their stories, adding another dimension to the printed page. As the students become more proficient reading their stories, they can be gradually introduced to textbooks and other materials that are easy and are within their reach cognitively.

Some applications of the approach break the story into its discrete elements, perhaps a misapplication of Goodman's "whole to part" versus "part to whole" distinction (see page 63). For example, teachers have been known to place the story on poster board, cut the story into sentence strips, and ask the students to put them together again to form the whole. Then teachers sometimes cut the sentence strips into sentence parts or phrases, followed by words, syllables, and finally letters and again ask the students to form the whole again, using increasingly smaller units. Other teachers have had students identify letter-sound correspondences by matching them (e.g., find the [*b*'s] in the story). Although for some students, this kind of activity might be helpful, for others it might simply be tedious repetition. But the greatest danger in this type of application is that students might find it disconcerting to see their stories turned into frustrating scrambled word/sentence/letter puzzles (I always hated those myself) or into endless *phonics* lessons.

Other teachers use the story as a lesson in semantics (e.g., Which word means "to walk slowly"? Which word is the opposite of "dangerous"?). While some students might find this of benefit, most students probably would be more motivated to answer questions concerning the meaning, at least at first. For example, if the students have just written a story about a picture they have been shown of a man packing his suitcase, questions answered by the story could be asked (e.g., Where is the man going? Point to the sentence that tells that. Why is he going there? How do you know? and so on).

Applications of the language experience approach can be used in many other kinds of classroom writing activities other than story writing and at many different levels of proficiency. Charts can be created with the information supplied by students, comparisons can be drawn in chart or paragraph form, and idea maps or clustering devices can be generated, just to name a few.

Advantages of the Language Experience Approach

Perhaps the biggest advantage is that the text is appropriate both cognitively and linguistically since it comes from the students themselves. Moreover, it reflects the culture of which the students are a part. The students' own ideas are encouraged and validated, thereby enhancing self-concepts and fostering independence. The unit of study is the created story or product rather than isolated sound and letter correspondences, words, and sentences. Grammar and other discrete point instruction can be individualized and used as needed and small groups can be formed of students needing similar instruction. In the case of a group-created product, students can learn from one another and scaffold upon each others' contributions. The teacher serves as a facilitator in the entire process rather than mainly as an editor of what is produced.

Possible Limitations of the Language Experience Approach

Writing down student errors as part of the dictation procedure might be considered by some to be a limitation. Teachers often express reservations about this practice in the belief that they are reinforcing errors. Advocates of the more "pure" versions of the language experience approach feel that this fear is unjustified and that the benefits of such a practice far outweigh the disadvantages, especially for children and for beginners of any age who are in special need of encouragement.

A second possible limitation is that through dictation, students might get the mistaken idea that writing is simply recorded speech. Of course, it is much more than that. Through the act of writing itself, students create meaning, adjust, rewrite, move forward, reread, rewrite, and so forth.

Closely related to the above is yet another potential problem that has to do with the teacher acting chiefly as a transcriber, when in fact the teacher could be playing a far more facilitative role. One way to make the experience more than simply a dictation is for the teacher and students to become integral parts of a composing process. However, care must be taken that the students be given the chance to contribute as much as their abilities will allow and that the teacher not overshadow their efforts. Thus the benefits of the more pure forms of the language experience approach can remain reasonably intact.

Below is an example of an alternative application during which the teacher takes on a more facilitative role and out of which a collaborative product is created.

TEACHER: (referring to a story she has just read aloud to the students) Let's write our thoughts about the story. Did you like the story?

ASSAD: I didn't like the story.

TEACHER: You didn't? Why? Why didn't you like it?

ASSAD: I didn't like when Maria keep the ring. It didn't belong to her.

TEACHER: Do the rest of you feel the same way? Did you not like it when Maria kept the ring? (Five students raise their hands.) How do some of the rest of you feel?

JORGE: It's okay.

TEACHER: What's okay?

JORGE: To keep the ring. It was her mother's ring.

ASSAD: But her mother give it to the neighbor.
TEACHER: How many of you agree with Jorge that it was all right to keep the
          ring? (Three students raise their hands.) Okay, what should we write?
JORGE: Write "Some of us want Maria keep the ring. It belonged to her
          mother."
TEACHER: Some of us wanted Maria to keep the ring? (She looks at Jorge as
          she begins to write. Jorge nods. She writes "Some of us wanted
          Maria to keep the ring. It belonged to her mother.")

And so the writing continues as the teacher guides the students, bringing out their ideas and helping them to shape the language. The teacher, in a sense, becomes a coauthor, as well as a facilitator who asks questions, clarifies meaning, and makes a few contributions of his or her own. Moreover, the teacher is providing language upon which the students can scaffold. Note also that indirect corrections are made through modeling. By this means, a teacher who feels uncomfortable writing errors doesn't have to.

Gradually, students begin to write more independently and need less and less guidance by the teacher. Soon students may be able to finish, on their own, the compositions begun as collaborations. Later students may be able to work with partners to create compositions. And eventually they will able to write independently, with help available as needed from the teacher and peers (see Writing Workshops discussed later in this chapter).

LITERATURE-BASED CURRICULUM

Even at beginning proficiency levels, teachers can use literature as the pivot around which curriculum can revolve. Story Experience (see page 174) can bring students into the excitement of literature before they can even utter a word. Other activities using stories (found in Chapter 10) can help students as they begin and continue their journey through the language learning process. All the while, writing, speaking, and listening can be incorporated as they relate to the literature used. Often speaking and/or reading events can be turned into writing events, and so forth. In addition, the language experience approach just described can make a major contribution to the development of literacy by providing students with materials they themselves have written or have helped to write.

Why Use Literature as a Pivot?

Literature is authentic. It generally is not written solely for the purpose of teaching specific structures or vocabulary (unless we are talking about basal-type readers). The structures and vocabulary are allowed to grow naturally out of the ideas developed, the plots, dialogues, and situations.

Literature can provide optimal input for language acquisition. Because literature (particularly literature using plot lines and characters) often completely absorbs students in the things they really care about, it engages them, not only cognitively, but emotionally as well. Through it, they can become intimately involved with the characters, their fears, their joys, their inner hopes. Often they become so absorbed that they, at least momentarily, lose the inhibitions and other barriers generally associated with learning another language. I can remember my own elation in being introduced to the legendary Marianela in Spanish. In most versions she falls in love with a blind man named Pablo, who is about to have an operation that may restore his sight. Because Marianela thinks of herself as ugly, she becomes very afraid that Pablo will see her ugliness and not love her anymore, once he regains his vision. So she runs away. According to some versions of the story, she takes poison; according to other versions, she dies of a broken heart. For the first time in my formal study of Spanish, I became totally involved in the language. In just those few weeks with Marianela, I felt as though I had acquired more Spanish than I had in all my previous years of formal study put together.

Literature (again, referring to those pieces involving plots and characters) can provide contexts for language learning in which the language itself (its syntax, semantics, and pragmatics) becomes more memorable. To support this argument John Oller offered the Episode Hypothesis, which states that "text (i.e., discourse in any form) will be easier to reproduce, understand, and recall, to the extent that it is structured episodically" (1983b, p. 12). Episodic organization requires both the motivation created by conflict and the logical sequencing that is necessary to good storytelling and consistent with experience.

Schank and Abelson (1977) go even further and relate episodic structure to the very way in which memory is organized. It is their view that humans not only store information in episodic form, but that they also acquire it in that way.

Literature exposes students to a variety of cultures and subcultures within a given society. By reading *The Diary of Anne Frank*, for example, students learn about the Jewish culture within Nazi-occupied Europe. From the biography *Isamu Noguchi: The Life of a Sculptor*, they learn what it was like to be a struggling Japanese-American artist during the same time period. From *The Me Nobody Knows*, they learn through poetry about the frustrations of children in the black ghettos of America. By using literature in the classroom, teachers can help students vicariously experience the cultures of others and the struggles of persons within those cultures. Some may be going through similar experiences themselves.

Components of Literature-Based Units

Literature-based units are comprised of three basic components: Prereading, reading, and postreading. In this section, each component is discussed along with suggested activities and strategies. Most of the examples come from

Worlds Together and its accompanying *Teacher Resource Book* (Richard-Amato and Hansen, 1995) and *Exploring Themes* (Richard-Amato, 1993b).

The Prereading Component

There are three main purposes for prereading activities: (1) to help the student relate the text to prior knowledge and experience both in L1 and L2, (2) to heighten motivation for the reading, and (3) to gain cultural knowledge that can be helpful in more fully comprehending what it is that the writer is trying to say.

Schema theory (see especially Carrell, 1984, 1985) has been called a "theoretical metaphor" by Grabe (1991), who sees it as a useful way to describe the reader's prior knowledge. He goes further to say that the idea that long-term memory is organized by *stable* schema structures appears to be a myth and is not strongly supported by current research. Moreover, there is evidence that there may not be as much difference in schema across cultures as was once thought (see, in particular, Mohan and Au-Yeung Lo, 1985).

In spite of the criticism of schema theory itself, we know that there are expectations that readers bring to a selection that can either help or hinder the understanding of what an author is trying to say and that make significant contributions to the created meaning of what is read.

In order that students be able to get the most out of what they read, it is important to aid them in relating text to what they already know and have experienced, and to attempt to prepare them for elements of the text that may be particularly puzzling.

To facilitate this process, prereading activities such as the following can be developed.

Prereading Activities

1. ASKING SPECIFIC AND OPEN-ENDED DISCUSSION QUESTIONS

An example of these kinds of questions comes from *Exploring Themes,* designed for intermediate to advanced young adults. The book begins with a unit entitled "To a Distant Shore," which includes autobiographical sketches of four new arrivals. Below are the discussion questions that begin the unit.

Think about your own situation. Have you recently arrived on a "distant shore"? Are you planning to make such a move? Even if you cannot answer yes to either question, try to imagine what it might be like to leave your home and live far away. What joys are experienced by persons going from one culture to another? What problems do they face? Discuss with your class.

Instead of discussing the questions with the class, the students may want to discuss them in smaller groups, each of which can share its conclusions. Such questions help give direction to the students' reading and thinking without being authoritative.

The next example comes from *Global Views: Reading About World Issues* (Sokolik, 1993). The specific questions here are part of a poll to be taken of the class before they read an article from the *Houston Chronicle* about manned space flights.

The following reading consists of letters to a local Houston newspaper concerning the issue of sending people into space. Before you read this passage, take a poll of your class, asking everyone these questions.

a. Do you think space exploration is a worthwhile endeavor?
b. If there is limited funding, do you think money should go to programs on earth first?
c. Do you think space exploration benefits everyone? Why or why not?

---

2. USING DEVICES FOR GRAPHICALLY REPRESENTING IDEAS (CHARTS, CLUSTERS, AND SO FORTH)

A learning chart such as the one below can be used to find out what the students already know and what they think they will learn from the reading. The following is adapted from *Worlds Together* (intended for adolescents at intermediate levels) and appears before a selection about Martin Luther King, Jr.

A Learning Chart

WHAT WE KNOW ALREADY ABOUT MARTIN LUTHER KING, JR.	WHAT WE'D LIKE TO KNOW ABOUT MARTIN LUTHER KING, JR.

After the students finish the selection, they fill in a third column, WHAT WE LEARNED ABOUT MARTIN LUTHER KING, JR.

The next example of a prereading device, in this case a cluster, comes from the same textbook. It begins the unit "What Makes a Hero?"

What do you think it means to be a hero? Perhaps a hero is someone who is unusually brave or has uncommon strength or speed. With your class, name people you think are heroes. They may be famous people (past or present). They may be people you know in your own neighborhood. They may even be make-believe people in movies you have seen or in stories or cartoons you have read. Think about what it is that makes them heroes. With your class make a cluster such as the one below in Figure 12.1. Display it in the classroom. You and your classmates may want to add heroes to your cluster after reading this unit.

THE HEROES WE KNOW ABOUT

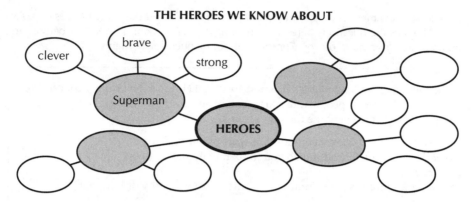

Figure 12.1

3. EXPLICITLY PRESENTING KEY WORDS

The teacher might want to write a few key words from the selection for all to see. The students can then brainstorm or say what comes to mind about these words while the teacher forms a cluster out of the ideas.

The teacher or the students may want to ask questions to clarify and/or extend meaning.

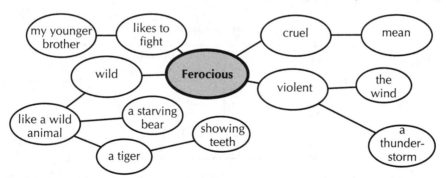

Figure 12.2

4. USING PREDICTION STRATEGIES AND ANTICIPATION GUIDES

Students can predict what is going to happen or what they think they might be introduced to in a particular selection. Helpful in this process might be the title, subtitles, illustrations, photos and other artwork, or a sample excerpt from the reading. To add interest, the teacher or a student may want to write down some of the predictions as they are given and refer back to them after the reading to see which ones come closest to what actually happens or what is learned.

An anticipation guide (Readence, Bean, and Baldwin, 1981) is yet another device to help students build relevant expectations. Such a guide presents the students with statements to which they are to react. The one below precedes the essay "Romantic Deceptions and Reality" in *Exploring Themes*.

Anticipation Guide

It is not unusual for people to have many misconceptions about love and what makes it thrive. Read the following statements. Check the ones you think are true.

a. When you feel that the romance has left your relationship, it is time to move on to a new relationship with another person.
b. It is a bad sign when one partner in a love relationship wants to make changes in the relationship itself.
c. A strong physical attraction for one's partner is necessary in order for a love relationship to blossom.
d. In a lasting relationship, partners have enough in common that they don't need outside activities with other people to lead happy, fulfilling lives.
e. Conflict should be avoided if one wants a love relationship to last.

Now read the following essay. After you read it, you will be asked to look back at your answers to this activity to see if you still feel the same way.

Students are surprised to learn from reading the essay that all of the above statements are false, at least according to the authors. When writing statements for an anticipation guide, the teacher needs to first consider what important concepts are to be learned from the reading and then write statements that will determine whether or not the students already know these concepts. Such an activity is highly motivational as students seek to check out their preconceived notions.

5. WRITING IN JOURNALS

In journals (see also page 222), students can write down their prereading thoughts about the issues or topics related to a specific selection or unit. They may describe their own experiences or those of others, they may express opinions, or they may write their predictions and then react to them later.

6. GIVING STUDENTS METACOGNITIVE STRATEGIES FOR DEALING WITH NEW SELECTIONS

Before You Read

1. Look the book over. Think about the title. Notice the cover of the book. Is there a picture there? Are there other pictures in the book? Look at a few of them. Do they give you any ideas about what the book will be about? If the book tells a story, do the pictures give you any clues about what might happen in the story?
2. What do you think you will learn from this book?
3. Have you already learned some things from personal experience, other books, or classes that might help you understand this book?

While You Read

1. Relax and feel how the words and sentences flow together.
2. Ask questions of yourself as you read. Does this seem real? Have you experienced this yourself? What does this have to do with what the author has just said or what has just happened? What is coming next?
3. Do not stop reading every time you find a word you do not understand. The meaning may come to you as you read further.
4. If a word seems important and the meaning is not coming clear as you read further, then look in the glossary (if there is one) or check a dictionary. You may want to discuss the word's meaning with a classmate or your teacher.
5. If there are parts you do not understand, make a note of them so you can return later.
6. Reread for better understanding. Return to the parts you did not understand. Reread them. Are they more clear to you now? If not, discuss them with a classmate or with your teacher.

After You Read

1. What did you learn from this book? Has it changed the way you thought before?
2. Did the book turn out as you expected?
3. Talk about it with others who have read the same book. Maybe you can start a discussion group.

One word of caution about prereading activities in general—they should not be too lengthy. Sometimes teachers, in an attempt to cover all possible unknowns, expose the students to overly lengthy explanations and too many activities, thereby postponing the reading itself. Although students usually appreciate having their curiosity piqued and having a cognitive scaffold established upon which to build meaning, they do not appreciate putting on hold whatever motivation they may have already gained to read a given selection. Sometimes, too, teachers will impose their own interpretations upon the students, making it difficult for them to create meaning for themselves.

The Reading Component

The Reading Component refers to what happens *while* the students are reading. The selections themselves will often contain illustrations, photographs and other artwork, subtitles, glossaries, and footnotes that offer clues to meaning and, in the case of visuals, establish the mood and/or give added life to any characters and situations that might be found in the selections.

Particularly important to second- and foreign-language students are glossaries that are sometimes found at the bottoms of the pages. The more effective glossaries will offer not only definitions, but also common root derivations and clues to help students use the context to determine meaning. Although they may not seem a significant feature, they are extremely valuable in that they provide help *while* the students are reading, when the need to understand is immediate and the motivation is strong. However, students should be encouraged to first use the context and not concern themselves with every unknown element.

Scheduling reading times during class is essential. Again, the teacher can act as a facilitator and a guide by being available to students needing help, as long as such help is not disruptive to others. It should be remembered, however, that a wise teacher will also be seen as a reader, reading silently during these times. Thus the teacher serves as a role model for the students to emulate.

Once the students have completed the silent reading of a literary piece, they will often benefit (especially at beginning to intermediate levels) from hearing the selection read aloud by the teacher or others, or by listening to it on a cassette. They need to hear the intonation, the pauses, the rhythm, and the pronunciation of the words. If the selection has been placed on a cassette, students will often want to hear it again and again.

Concerning reading aloud, I must give a warning. Being read aloud to can be an exhilarating experience; being *forced* to read aloud in front of a group is often the opposite. It can create needless anxiety and sometimes even fear in those students who do not read aloud well. Moreover, it is often difficult for nonnative readers to attend to meaning while reading aloud. Reading aloud is a specialized skill and should be expected only of volunteers. It is important to remember that reading is generally a quiet activity accomplished in a comfortable environment either at school, in a library, or at home.

The Postreading Component

Postreading activities should enable the student to further create meaning and extend it beyond the context itself. Here students test their hypotheses about the selection and reread when it is beneficial to do so. They share their interpretations with peers and with the teacher in an effort to express themselves and, at the same time, stretch progressively to higher levels of understanding.

Grouping for Discussion and Short-term Projects. Groups can consist of the whole class and the teacher, or of smaller numbers of students. The teacher can move from group to group, serving as a facilitator and a guide. The groups can either be formed randomly or carefully planned (see also pages 120 and 194).

Of the two, planned groups have at least two major advantages: Ethnic and cultural diversity within the groups can be ensured and students of varying abilities can be assigned to a single group. Thus each group's work will be more likely to reflect a variety of perspectives and proficiency levels. The latter is important in that students will have a greater chance of being exposed to the language and the thinking of others operating at more advanced levels. However, most teachers recognize the fact that sometimes homogeneous groups are just what's needed in a given situation, e.g., when the task pertains to a particular ethnic or cultural group or when it is intended only for those having specific goals not shared by everyone.

Letting students choose their own groups often works well with adults and mature adolescents. Like the planned groups, it can produce the desired diversity of perspective and ability in some situations. However, it can sometimes result in hurt feelings and bruised egos. Inevitably there will be some who are left out for one reason or another. In order to allow students more freedom of choice and, at the same time, preserve self-esteem, it may be wise for the teacher to ask students to write down the names of those students with whom they would most enjoy working. Consideration then should be given to those choices when planning workable groups. While this alternative requires more time and effort, it does pay dividends in terms of self-esteem and motivation. Most students will assume they have been "chosen" by someone and will be more inclined to put forth their best efforts.

Questions for Discussion. Two basic types of questions are discussed here: knowledge-based questions and reflective/inferential questions.

KNOWLEDGE-BASED QUESTIONS. Often these kinds of questions are discussed by the whole class and the teacher. Their main purpose is to ensure that the students have comprehended the main facts or points of the selection. Often they begin with who, when, where, and how. They allow the students, under the guidance of the teacher, to know what is essential to the creation of meaning. For example, *Life, Language, and Literature* (Fellag, 1993) includes the following knowledge-based questions about Bret Harte's "The Luck of Roaring Camp."

---

1. What interesting thing happened in Roaring Camp in the beginning of the story?
2. What happened to the baby's mother?
3. What did the citizens of Roaring Camp decide to do with the baby?
4. Who was declared chief caretaker for the infant?
5. How did the baby fare in the camp?
6. How did the town change as a result of the baby?
7. What happened to the baby in the end?

It is important to remember, however, that this kind of information can be brought out (perhaps more effectively) through reflective and inferential questions.

REFLECTIVE AND INFERENTIAL QUESTIONS. Discussion questions requiring more thought and reflection can perhaps best be handled in small groups in which students have more opportunities for interaction. The teacher can circulate among the groups, guiding when necessary. The examples below come from "Making Friends in a New World" in *Worlds Together.* They follow the story about a Vietnamese boy, San Ho, who comes to the United States after the Vietnamese War. Notice that, in this case, cultural expectations are directly referred to.

- How does San Ho know that he and Stephen [his new stepfather] will be good friends? What does it mean to San Ho to be a good friend? Do you agree with him? What does it mean to be a good friend in the culture you know best? List some words that you think describe a good friendship.
- San Ho was so filled with fear that he cried in the story. Is it all right to cry? Does the culture you know best encourage or discourage crying? Does age make a difference? Is it different for boys and girls? If so, why do you think it is different?

A spokesperson from each group shares the group's ideas with the class later. The teacher may want to summarize the ideas for all to see, as they are shared.

If the questions are quite personal in nature, then pairs of students usually work best. For example, after the same story referred to above, one or more of the following questions are discussed with a partner.

- Why do you think San Ho felt alone in the crowd of people in the gym? Have you ever felt alone in a crowd? Why do you think this happens sometimes?
- Our friends are sometimes much older or younger than we are. For example, Stephen, an adult, was San Ho's friend. Have you ever had a friend who was much older or younger than you? Talk about your friend. Why do you think you became friends?

When students are working in small groups, it is important that they be able to select or create the questions they want to deal with. There are some questions that the students might prefer to write about privately rather than discuss. This option should always be available.

Discussion questions generally promoting the expression of opinions and feelings about the selections should lead to higher-level thinking skills (application, analysis, synthesis, and so forth). In addition, students should be encouraged to form their own questions. Being able to pose good questions is as important as being able to answer them and is extremely beneficial to cognitive as well as language development.

Short-term Group Projects and Activities. Short-term group projects and activities (also see cooperative learning beginning on page 270) can be effective in increasing student involvement and motivation. Often such projects and activities require the sharing of information. An example of this is found following "Blue Winds Dancing" in *Exploring Themes*. It is the story of a Native American who returns to his reservation with great anxiety as well as anticipation (see the story on pages 179–181). Will his people accept him or has he become too "white"?

Once the story is discussed, it is suggested that students research a particular tribe of Native Americans, including the problems they have had. They may want to look at the tribe's history, culture, and contributions to society. Eventually they might share the information they find with a small group.

Other short-term group projects and activities might include:
• acting out the story
• adapting the selection for readers' theater (see page 185)
• forming round-table groups to discuss related problems and possible solutions
• role-playing the characters in pretend situations
• forming collections of student writings about or related to the story
• sharing favorite literature about related themes, genre, and so forth

It should be remembered that, although suggestions are made by the teacher or a textbook, short-term projects and activities generated by students themselves are often very effective in that they involve the students maximally right from the start.

Short-term group projects and activities that are teacher- or textbook-generated are best when they are tied very closely to the selection and are critical to creating its meaning. The chart below follows the excerpt from *Sarah, Plain and Tall* in *Worlds Together*.

Finding Details to Support an Idea

We know from the story that it has been several years since Mama's death. How do we know that this family still deeply misses her? Give the details from the story that show that each of the following characters misses Mama. With your group, make a chart similar to the one below. Have one member of your group do the writing.

	Details
Caleb	
Anna	
Papa	

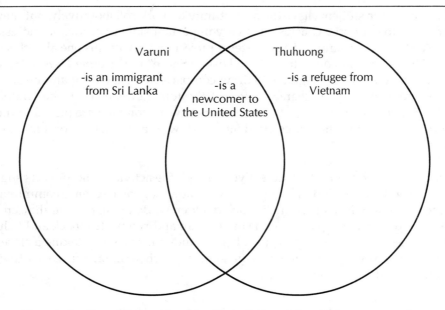

Now work with a partner and use the Venn diagram below to draw a comparison between two newcomers of your choice.

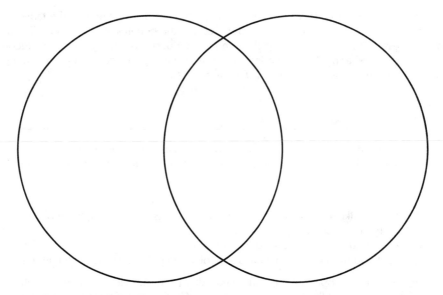

Form a group with at least two other people and share your diagrams. You may want to make changes in them based on what you learn from the others in your group.

Figure 12.3

Not only do the students have the opportunity to work collaboratively, but they learn how to support a conclusion, a very important skill for academic success.

And the last example of a short-term project or activity, this one also closely tied to a selection, comes from "To a Distant Shore" in *Exploring Themes*. Here the students use Venn diagrams to draw comparisons. They compare the situations, goals, and other characteristics of the four newcomers to the United States. Notice that the things the newcomers have in common are placed in the overlapping area of the circles. Students work with a partner to complete the diagrams. See Figure 12.3.

Individual Activities and Projects. Even though the activities and projects suggested below may be individually executed, they, too, are in essence communal to the extent to which others are involved. Often students share what they create with the teacher, a partner, or a small group and receive feedback and help when necessary. The examples given here include interviewing, taking a closer look at literature, writing in a specific genre, speech writing, journal writing, and independent reading.

Individual Projects and Activities

INTERVIEWING

One way for students to interact with each other and with people fluent in the target language is to interview them. Students not only receive the benefits inherent in the interactional process, but they also develop skills in posing questions, asking questions, recording answers, and sharing that which is learned from the experience. Here is an example from "Between Two Cultures," a unit in *Exploring Themes*.

Are you learning English in a country where it is a commonly used language? If so, write several questions to ask fluent speakers of English. Following are a few sample questions:

-Have you ever been between two cultures? If so, what were the two cultures?
-What was it like for you to be between two cultures? What were the problems? Were there any advantages?
-Were there times when you were fearful? Explain.
-How did you overcome the problems involved in being between two cultures?

Interview several people outside your class. After each interview, write down what you can remember of the answers you received. Share a few of the more interesting answers with your class.

Taking a Closer Look at Literature

Discovering more about literature, including characteristics of various genre types, expository formats, descriptive language, and so forth, can aid in the creation of meaning and can enhance the appreciation and enjoyment of literature in general.

The next two examples both come from *Worlds Together*. The first one, which follows the story of San Ho, explores the concept of plot or chain of events; the second one, which follows the excerpt from a biography about Martin Luther King, Jr., explores the concept of time line (or chronology).

The Plot or Chain of Events

A plot or chain of events is all the things that happen in a story. It tells which thing happens first, which one happens second, and so forth. See the sample chain below. Like all chains, it is made of links. Notice that the links are joined together. Each link contains an event that is important to creating the meaning of the story. The first four links are filled in for you already. Use as many links as you need.

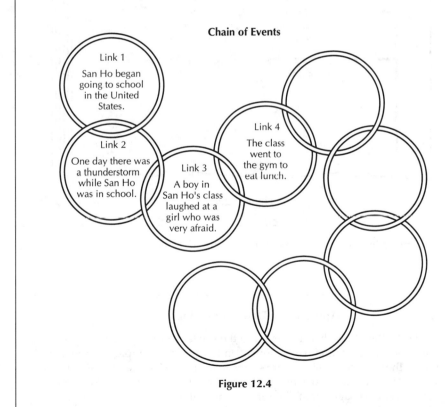

Chain of Events

Link 1
San Ho began going to school in the United States.

Link 2
One day there was a thunderstorm while San Ho was in school.

Link 3
A boy in San Ho's class laughed at a girl who was very afraid.

Link 4
The class went to the gym to eat lunch.

Figure 12.4

A Time Line

Biographies are often written in the order of the events that happened. This order of events is called a time line. The time line may begin with the person's birth and end with the person's death.

With a partner, make a time line on your paper of Martin Luther King, Jr.'s life. See the example started for you on the next page.

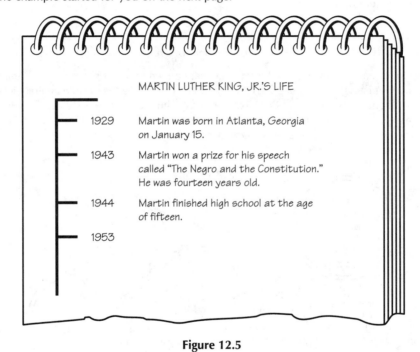

MARTIN LUTHER KING, JR.'S LIFE

1929   Martin was born in Atlanta, Georgia on January 15.

1943   Martin won a prize for his speech called "The Negro and the Constitution." He was fourteen years old.

1944   Martin finished high school at the age of fifteen.

1953

Figure 12.5

The last examples in this section come from activities developed around John Steinbeck's *The Pearl* in *Exploring Themes.* All four have to do with appreciating descriptive language.

Appreciating Descriptive Language

1. Authors often draw their readers into the excitement of a story by appeals to the senses: sight, sound, smell, touch, and taste. For example, John Steinbeck makes the night come alive by appealing to the reader's sense of sound with the words "the little tree frogs that lived near the stream twittered like birds . . ." Find several passages from the story that appeal to the senses listed below and place each in the appropriate category. There may be categories for which you can find no examples.

sight: _____

sound: _____

smell: _____

touch: _____

taste: _____

Discuss your examples with a small group. You may want to add other examples to your list based on what you learn from your classmates.

2. Descriptive language often involves a comparison between two things that are not usually thought to be similar in any way. For example, the statement *"your bicycle leaped forward like a cat"* uses such a comparison. Bicycles and cats are not usually compared to one another. Look at the following comparisons from the story in the chart below. Explain each one in the column provided. Then find one additional example of your own to place in the last space.

Comparison	Explanation
Example: *". . . Kino was a terrible machine"*	Kino is compared to a machine because he seemed to be fighting without any human feelings or pity for the trackers.
". . . two of the men were sleeping, curled up like dogs"	
"And Kino crept silently as a shadow down the smooth mountain face"	

Figure 12.6

Discuss each comparison with your class and the teacher.

3. What does Steinbeck mean when he talks about the "music of the pearl," the "Song of the Family," and the "music of the enemy"? Why does he compare the movements of people's lives to music? Does this increase your enjoyment of the story? If so, how?

4. Steinbeck uses many words whose sounds suggest their meanings. The forming of such words is called *onomatopoeia* (pronounced ŏn-ä-mat-ä-pē'-ä). For example, Steinbeck uses onomatopoeia when he says that the baby "gurgled and clucked" against Juana's breast. Find several other examples of onomatopoeia in the story.

WRITING IN A SPECIFIC GENRE

Students often like to try their own hand at writing in a specific genre, be it a poem, a short story, a play, and so on. It is often helpful to use what they have just read as a model. For example, following the reading of the poem "Desiderata" in *Exploring Themes,* students are highly motivated to express their own feelings and opinions about what is important in life. One of the postreading suggestions is the following:

> Write your own "Desiderata." Include all of the things that you think are important to leading a full and rich life. Share your paper with a partner. Ask your partner to write a brief response, including areas of agreement or disagreement. You may want to react in writing to your partner's response, thus continuing the dialogue.

SPEECH WRITING

Writing a speech on a topic about which one has strong feelings can be quite exhilarating, especially if it is well-received by one's peers. Following the autobiographical piece about Martin Luther King, Jr., in *Worlds Together* (which includes an excerpt from his "I Have a Dream" speech), the students are encouraged to write a speech and share it with a small group.

> Write your own "I Have a Dream" speech. It may be about one dream or about several dreams. You may want to repeat the line "I have a dream . . ." or "I wish . . ." or similar phrases in your speech. Think about what you would like the world to be like. It could be a world without hunger, a world without war, and so forth.

With a small group, the student is asked to share his or her speech. The student can either read it to the group or record it on a cassette and play it for the small group. The members of the group are then asked to make a list of the ideas they feel to be most important in the speech. These ideas are then discussed. Do they agree with what has been expressed? Why or why not? What do they like about the speech? Do they have any questions about it? The student is then asked to rewrite the speech based on what is learned from the small group.

JOURNAL WRITING

Journals provide students with the opportunity to express their thoughts in writing and to relate what they read to their own lives. They may keep their entries private or share them with others. In a standard journal, students often describe their ideas and experiences, express their feelings and opinions, and/or talk about hopes and dreams. Often students write about what happens on a given day in a diary; other times they choose or are given a specific topic, usually related to what they are reading or studying. But there are alternative kinds of journals. A few are described below.

The Reaction Journal

In a reaction journal, the student reacts to something very specific: a story, a poem, a picture or a song (Richard-Amato, 1992b). These may have been selected and presented by the teacher or by fellow students. Special days may be set aside as "reaction days," when students bring in and present items to which others react in their journals.

Or the reaction may be to something even more specific such as a line from a story, poem, or essay; a quote from a character in a story or play (see Figure 12.7); a description of an event; an expressed opinion; or the like. It should be something that the student finds interesting or thought-provoking. By dividing the page into two columns in a double-entry journal, the item to which the student wishes to react can be written in the left column; in the right column can be the reaction. The student might react by questioning, agreeing or disagreeing, analyzing, and so on.

Lines from the Reading	My Reaction
Martin Luther King, Jr. said, "I am a citizen of the world." (p. 197)	I was glad that he called himself "a citizen of the world." Too often people think only about themselves and their own country. They do not think of what is best for the world. For example, . . .

Figure 12.7

The Dialogue Journal

Using a standard format or a double-entry format like the one described above, the students may write about a topic related to what is being read or studied. The student expresses his or her opinion or feelings in the left column; in the right column, a partner or the teacher responds. Thus the writing itself becomes a social event and takes on interesting social ramifications through its dialectical nature. Often by the means of dialogue journals, relationships are built and bonds are formed.

Peyton and Straton (1992) feel that the following are a few additional benefits that can accrue to those participating in dialogue journal writing. They say that such writing:

-makes available discourse adapted to the students' "linguistic, cognitive, and emotional levels,"

-facilitates the acquisition of advanced language functions and structures of reasoned discourse, and

-presents students with texts that are individualized and progressively more demanding.

The Learning Journal

Again the double-entry format is used. Only this time the student lists in the left column those things that he or she has learned from a given selection. In the right column the student can write what he or she still wants to learn *or* how the learned information can be applied.

Journal entries, regardless of type, can be used as the roots from which longer, more formal writings can grow. Many a poem, story, or expository piece has sprung from a journal entry. Thus, the usefulness of the journal is extended. In this way, the journal serves as a brainstorming mechanism, a means for generating and clarifying ideas and sorting out information.

INDEPENDENT READING

Through independent reading, students can pursue subjects of interest, perhaps expanding their knowledge and vicarious experiences in areas to which they have been introduced in their lessons.

Book Reviews

Book reviews can become an integral part of the independent reading process. They can provide a means whereby students can share their impressions and make recommendations to others. Below is a sample form.

BOOK REVIEW

Title of book:
Author: Type of book:
Name of reviewer: Date:

- -

What did you feel this book was about?

What did you like about this book?

Was there anything you did not like about this book? Explain.

Do you think your classmates should read this book? Why or why not?

The reviews can be written or typed on index cards which can be filed in an accessible place in the classroom. Or the reviews can be put into a computer data base which is shared by all the members of the class.

Reading Journals

Somewhat more personal in nature are reading journals. In them students can reveal generally their feelings about what a character says or does. They can state their reactions to the author's ideas, relate to their own experiences, and so forth. Moreover, they can talk about *how* they are reading. Is reading becoming any easier for them in their new language?

What strategies are they using to help them comprehend? Have they discovered new means for adding to their repertoire of language, both semantically and syntactically?

Coauthored Reading Journals

An interesting alternative is for partners to select a book of the same title. During the period of time that they are reading the book, they may write in a coauthored journal (also called a "buddy book journal," Gillespie, 1993). This is a shared journal that is passed back and forth between them. Some of the things mentioned previously may be discussed, i.e., feelings, reactions, reading strategies, and so on.

WRITING WORKSHOPS

Transforming the classroom into a writing workshop can be an effective way to utilize all important resources, including peers, and to reinforce the notion that writing is indeed a communal process. The teacher and peers can give input when needed at whatever stages the students are ready for: coming up with an idea; gathering information; working out the idea on paper, perhaps graphically at first; expanding and developing aspects of the idea; getting some semblance of order (moving things around, deleting, replacing); providing transitional elements where needed; rendering the draft more coherent as well as cohesive; polishing; sharing with an audience.

A word of caution here. Sometimes setting up a workshop results in writing as an isolated activity, removed from other events of the classroom and other language experiences. Care must be taken to ensure that the writing will be an integral part of the total curriculum and will be related to what the students are reading, listening to, and talking about.

Conferencing with the Teacher and with Peers

Conferencing, although often treated in the literature as being a separate activity, can be made an integral component in a workshop approach to teaching writing.

Conferencing with the teacher and with peers should not be disruptive to those needing a quiet place in which to think and write. Therefore the conferencing itself should take place in out-of-the-way places, perhaps at conferencing stations at the periphery of the classroom (see Figure 14.2 on page 268) or in private corners. Not everyone is going to be ready to conference at the same time, and so those who are ready can go to a station when one is available or set up a new one if needed. It should be noted here that some students may be reluctant to join in the conferencing at first. Those not wishing to participate should not be forced to. It has been my experience that eventually almost everyone becomes caught up in the excitement generated by working with others, especially if the environment is generally positive. Students often receive a better sense of the reader through conferencing. Nevertheless, some students might need a little extra encouragement occasionally from the teacher and from peers.

The conferencing groups can be organized in several ways:

(1) A few students can be selected by the teacher to serve as peer consul-
     tants (the ones chosen can be different for each workshop, until all who
     want to, can serve at least once). Each peer consultant can be assigned
     a station. Students can either be assigned to specific consultants, can
     select those with whom they feel most comfortable, or can go to
     whomever might be available at the time of need.
(2) Students can be paired by the teacher to serve as consultants for each
     other.
(3) Students can form their own partnerships.

The way in which the conferencing groups are organized may vary from
workshop to workshop, depending on the task to be accomplished and on the
outcomes desired. At first the writings will probably be rather personal, short,
and elementary—a listing of ideas or a cluster, a chart, a paragraph, a simple
poetic form (see Chapter 9). Later the writings can be more academic in nature,
longer and/or more complex—perhaps an essay, a report, a critique, a short
story, a poem, a one-act play.

The purpose of the conferencing will probably be different at each stage of
development in the writing process. During early stages, when ideas are first
taking shape, students will want to express their ideas orally and receive feedback. At other points in the process, students will want reactions to what they
have written and may ask or be asked specific questions about what they write.
At some point they may want an editing of surface forms from the teacher or a
peer with whom they have established rapport. Usually this occurs toward the
end of the writing process; however, those who are anxious about errors may
request editing earlier. The important thing is to give this kind of feedback
when the student is ready.

It is essential that all the students go through a preparation phase before
any conferencing begins. Respect for one another's ideas needs to be stressed
and a focus on the positive needs to be emphasized. Some role play demonstrating effective conferencing should take place, during which all students
have access to the sample piece of writing being talked about. Such role play
can prevent many of the problems often associated with peer conferencing, i.e,
overly severe criticism, a focus on "being correct," a failure to offer positive
support, and overall lack of preparation (see Leki, 1990; Hedgcock and
Lefkowitz, 1992; Yoshihara, 1993).

As part of the preparation for conferencing, the following suggestions can be discussed and/or used in a role play.

What the *Writer* Can Do During the Conference

Read the paper aloud to the teacher or peer (you may see some problem areas yourself). You may be asked to read it aloud more than once.
Ask questions such as the following:

  -Which idea or ideas do you find of interest in my paper?

  -Is there a main idea that holds it together?

  -Are there any ideas that might be best put in another paper?

  -Do you have any questions about what I am saying?

  -Is there anything you would say more about if you were me?

What the *Teacher or Peer* Can Do During the Conference

Listen carefully as the paper is being read. Take a few notes if you want to. If you have trouble understanding the reader, look at the paper with the reader while it is being read. Ask the writer to read it again, if necessary.
Ask questions such as the following:

  -What part do you like the best about your paper?

  -What idea do you think is the most important?

  -Are there any ideas that might be best put in another paper?

  -Why did you choose this topic?

  -How do you feel about . . . ?

  -Can you tell me more about . . . ?

  -When did this happen?

  -Should this go first or last?

  -What kinds of details might you add here?

  -What do you want the reader to learn from this?

  -What do you plan to do now?

The following form could be filled out by the writer as a result of the conference.

Date:_____ Name of Writer: _____

Name of the conference partner: _____

What did you learn from the conference?

What changes do you plan to make on your next rewrite?_____

The effectiveness of peer conferences has been associated with the quality of the interaction itself. Nelson and Murphy (1993) found in their study of ESL students in a writing course at a large urban university that a particular student was more likely to use a peer's suggestions in rewrites when the interaction was cooperative. When the interaction was defensive or when a negotiation for meaning was nonexistent, the student was less inclined to use the peer's suggestions. The latter was also supported by Goldstein and Conrad (1990), who looked at a similar population.

Feedback on Errors

It is interesting to note that the quality of the revisions may depend on the type of feedback that the student is given. Kepner (1991) found that students studying Spanish in an intermediate class at Wheaton College who had received meaning-focused written feedback rather than error-focused feedback did not "sacrifice accuracy for content." In fact, those receiving surface-error correction feedback wrote subsequent journal entries of far lower ideational quality than those receiving meaning-focused feedback. She concluded:

> Correction of discrete errors should occur only at the final stages of editing, when the piece is prepared for "publishing" or other forms of public display (p. 306).

Zamel (1985), found in her study that when the written feedback was mixed (contained both meaning-focused and error-focused feedback), the students tended to focus on the surface errors at the expense of content, the improvement of which was often ignored. It is my feeling that, as a general rule, when error-focused feedback is given, it should come near the end of the writing process unless the student specifically requests it earlier.

In this section I have offered suggestions for teacher and peer conferencing within a workshop approach based on what has worked in the classroom situations I have facilitated. It should be noted that there are many other ways in which this type of activity can be carried out, some of which may be more effective than what you have read about here. For further ideas on a similar subject, the reader might take a look at the section on page 265 detailing peer teaching. Although the role of the peer is different in peer teaching situations, many of the ideas may be appropriate to teacher and peer conferencing and can be easily adapted.

Information on Assessment tools, including portfolios (their development and use) can be found in Chapter 6 on Language Assessment.

ADVANCED ACADEMIC READING AND WRITING

Academic goals need to be pursued right from the beginning in second- and foreign-language classroom settings, especially if the students expect to be able to function successfully in academic environments (see also Chapter 16).

Many of the already mentioned strategies and activities can be adapted for advanced academic applications. For example, the language experience approach can yield a group-generated analysis of an experiment on the effects of one chemical on another. Prereading, reading, and postreading strategies and activities can be applied to a seminal article on pre-World War II influences on modern political thought, a writing workshop approach can be used to develop a critical paper on Jungian philosophy, and so forth. The applications are virtually limitless.

At advanced levels within a second- or foreign-language program, students need to be exposed to the kinds of reading and writing (and listening/speaking) tasks that will be expected of them in later coursework: reading abstract materials, getting down the key ideas from lectures, writing critiques and summaries, and so forth. And once students are in a mainstream academic environment, they will need a place where they can go for assistance and support, perhaps in the form of an adjunct program or a learning center (see related programs described in Chapter 17).

Within a second- or foreign-language academic program, students need to gain knowledge and experience (including guided experience) in areas that are likely to lead to academic success. These areas include but are not limited to the following:

1. *Text-structure schema and conventional text-constructing devices*

It is important for students to have a knowledge of the text-structure schema and the text-constructing devices commonly used by the academic community within a given society and within a given field of study. Being familiar with the structures associated with argumentative composition, chronological development, definition, procedural description, and analysis, to name a few examples, is useful to students studying in a variety of fields. The related text-constructing devices such as specific introductory elements, conclusions, headings, transitions, and other organizational signals, aid the students in gaining perspective on what they read, in seeing relationships, and in following lines of thought. In addition, there is evidence that students who have text-structure knowledge appear to comprehend and recall more of what they read than those who do not (see especially Carrell, 1983, 1984, 1985, 1987). Not only is such knowledge beneficial to students as readers (and listeners), but it can help students construct their own compositions, so that they can be better understood by academic audiences.

2. *Cognitive and metacognitive strategies for reading and writing as it relates to the academic content being studied (see also Chapter 16)*

Important strategies for reading as an aid to learning include underlining, highlighting, paraphrasing in the margins, outlining, idea mapping, using the dictionary, identifying key ideas, using context to determine meaning, and many more.

Strategies for writing include brainstorming mechanisms, researching, using quickwrites[1] and graphic representations of ideas (see clustering devices used earlier in this chapter), drafting compositions, combining text-structures, and so forth.

Additional tasks such as answering questions, posing questions, anticipating questions, reacting in various ways, summarizing, using specific composition formats and combinations of formats, collecting information for specific writing tasks, test-taking and preparation, and notetaking involve a wide variety of strategies of their own. Talking about strategies in "What Works for Me" sessions can be extremely beneficial. So can practice with such strategies. However, it should be remembered that such practice should not be isolated from the content with which the students are currently involved; on the contrary, the strategies experienced should be an integral part of what the students are learning.

3. *Synthesizing information from a wide range of reading materials in a single area of study (Krashen, 1981, calls this "narrow reading"; see also Shih, 1992)*

Such reading is more akin to the kind of reading students will be doing in their academic coursework. Shorter, less complex readings can be used first, followed by those that become progressively longer and more complex. These

---

[1] Quickwrites allow students to write down whatever comes to mind without stopping to make corrections or worry about format. It is one way to get preliminary ideas down on paper. Peter Elbow (1993) calls the quickwrite an "evaluation-free zone" and strongly encourages its use in getting students to take risks, follow hunches, and increase their fluency in writing. Students can return later and restructure their quickwrites, making them more palatable to potential readers.

readings can then become the basis for a variety of academic writing (and speaking) experiences. Thus the students will have the background knowledge necessary to the intelligent, logical treatments of related assignments.

4. *Other areas*

In addition to synthesizing information in a single area of study (number 3 above), Horowitz (1986) has identified 6 other categories. Based on an examination of actual writing assignment handouts and essay examinations given to students at Western Illinois University, he found that out of 54 examples the following types of tasks emerged:

Category	Number of Examples
Summary of/reaction to a reading (in psychology, communication arts and sciences, history, home economics, special education, and learning resources)	9
Annotated bibliography (biology)	1
Report on a specified participatory experience (anthropology, psychology, educational foundations, and home economics)	9
Connection of theory and data (communication arts and sciences, psychology, economics, and home economics)	10
Case study (administrative office management, marketing, and psychology)	5
Synthesis of multiple sources (communication arts and sciences, psychology, biology, geology, sociology, accounting, zoology, management, special education, and marketing)	15
Research project (communication arts and sciences, psychology)	5

Figure 12.8

In studies such as this, the departments from which the examples come and the number of examples will vary from term to term and from campus to campus. It is critical that the language instructor to know the kinds of tasks that his or her students will be expected to carry out. Not only that, but knowing the specific nature of the tasks provides valuable information for the instructor who really cares about preparing students for what is to come. Horowitz found that out of the 54 tasks, 34 of them were highly controlled and accompanied by detailed instructions, calling for specific content organization. Related to these tasks, Horowitz emphasized the importance of the student's being able to select relevant data from sources that will be appropriate for the task, reorganize the data in response to questions, and encode data into academic forms of the language.

Rose (1983), in a study similar to the one Horowitz completed, looked at assigned topics for composition and take-home test questions given by faculty members in 17 departments at the University of California, Los Angeles. The topics and questions generally required a knowledge of expository and argumentative modes and the ability to synthesize information and relate to the theoretical assumptions associated with a given field of study.

Concerning writing for an academic audience, in particular, Reid (1993) stresses the importance the academic community places on traditional formats and accepted conventions of expression. In her discussion of surface errors in English, she refers to Vann, Meyer, and Lorenz's (1984) survey of academic readers, which found that respondents tended to be least accepting of those errors that were generally associated with the writing of nonnative speakers (e.g., word order and word choice, *it* deletion, tense and relative clause errors). Perhaps the academic audience needs to become more informed about the nature of errors typically made by nonnative writers so that they can see them in light of the normal language development process. But, in the meantime, students need to be prepared for the kinds of feedback they may receive from an audience that may or may not respond in way that is helpful. It may be beneficial, too, to give students the opportunity to write for *real* audiences from time to time (see especially Johns, 1993).

Finding out as specifically as possible what it is that students will need to be able to do seems essential to any serious academic preparation program (see also Tarone and Yule, 1989). Not only that, but while the students are in preparation, the instructors should be working closely with the content-area teachers/professors—that is if they are known and available. This collaboration, in all likelihood, will make the transition much easier for students. See Chapter 16 for other ideas about transitioning into academic programs.

SUMMARY

There are many ways to promote literacy in a second or foreign language, some of which are better than others. In this chapter I present a few ways that have worked for me, not only as a language learner myself, but as a teacher of first and second languages. Using versions of the language experience approach, we begin where each student is. By involving the students in a literature-based curriculum, we use the power of language to heighten awareness and fully engage the mind. By these means, the reading-writing connection can be more fully realized. Motivation and guidance is provided through a workshop approach to writing in which the students can take full advantage of the classroom community they and the teacher have established. At later levels, the students take on progressively more advanced academic reading and writing tasks in an effort to be prepared to function in an academic environment, if functioning in such an environment is the goal. All the while, skills are integrated and experience with them is allowed to grow naturally out of what is being learned.

READINGS, REFLECTION, AND DISCUSSION

Suggested Readings and Reference Materials

Atwell, N. (1987). *In the middle: Writing, reading, and learning with adolescents.* Portsmouth, N.H.: Heinemann. Although this book is intended for teaching reading and writing to native-speaking adolescents, many of its ideas are applicable to second- and foreign-language learners at all age levels. It is an honest account, told by a teacher, of her own experiences setting up writing and reading workshops. It includes many specific examples of activities and student work.

Connor, U., and Kaplan, R. (1987). *Writing across languages: Analysis of L2 text.* Reading, Mass.: Addison-Wesley. Cultural thought patterns, argumentative patterns, and contrastive schema are among the topics covered in this anthology. Included also is the current research related to text analysis.

Dixon, C., and Nessel, D. (1983). *Language experience approach to reading (and writing).* Hayward, Calif.: Alemany. This book presents an extensive literacy program for ESL students based on the language experience approach. Combined are both theoretical and practical ideas for teachers.

Johnson, D., and Roen, D., eds., (1989). *Richness in writing: Empowering ESL students.* White Plains, N.Y.: Longman. Enriching task contexts in second-language writing, computer networking, bilingual issues as they relate to writing, parallels between speaking and writing acquisition processes, planning effective assignments, peer review, topic development, evaluation of composition are only a few of the topics included in this anthology. Many of its insights can be applied to foreign- and as well as a second-language teaching.

Leki, I. (1992). *Understanding ESL writers: A guide for teachers.* Portsmouth, N.H.: Boynton/Cook Heinemann. The author takes a close look at the writing behaviors of ESL students and the ways in which instructors can effectively respond to their attempts at writing.

Shih, M. (1992). Beyond comprehension exercises in the ESL academic reading class. *TESOL Quarterly, 26*(2), 289–318. The author looks at current research on comprehending and learning from texts, at the selection and sequencing of text materials, at the wisdom of allowing reading assignments to be determined by criterion tasks rather than by reading skill factors, and at strategies that can benefit both reading and learning.

Questions for Reflection and Discussion

1. What is your opinion of the more "pure" applications of the language experience approach? To what extent do you think the teacher should take on the

role of a facilitator? Might there be a danger in the teacher's contributing too much? Explain.

2. Try out a version of the language experience approach with a small group of peers. Ask them to play the role of students operating at high-beginning to low-intermediate levels (see page 99 for behaviors typical of those levels). What experience will you give them about which they can write? Decide what your role will be and how you will handle errors. Ask your group for feedback.

3. Select a piece of literature that you think will engage the minds of your students and develop several prereading and postreading activities around it. Share your plans with a small group. What is their reaction? Can they suggest any additional activities you might incorporate into your plans?

4. Devise a way to use a writing workshop that relates to and is an extension of a unit you are developing. How will you set it up? What will you do to prepare your students so that the workshop has the best possible chance for success? Discuss your ideas with a group.

5. How might you go about preparing your students for a mainstream academic environment, if that is their goal? Make a list of the tasks you would include. What if their goal were something other than an academic environment? What if their goal were to have the skills necessary to succeed in a specific trade or vocation? What would your list look like in this case? Share your list with a small group and ask for their input.

CHAPTER 13

Affective Activities

When given the opportunity to talk about themselves in personally relevant ways, students tend to become much more motivated. The result is that they want to be able to express their feelings and ideas more in the target language. They want *to communicate. When this happens, growth becomes a reciprocal process: enhancing personal growth enhances growth in the foreign language.*

G. Moskowitz, 1978

QUESTIONS TO THINK ABOUT

1. Think back about what you learned in Chapter 5, The Affective Domain. In your opinion what were the most important factors discussed there? What do you think "affective activities" might entail?

2. Have you ever personally participated in affective activities? If so, what activities? What were the circumstances? What effect did they have on you?

3. How do you think affective activities might be used in a second- or foreign-language class? Do you think they can be of benefit to language acquisition? If so, in what ways?

BACKGROUND INFORMATION AND DESCRIPTION

Many of the affective activities found in this chapter have grown, either directly or indirectly, from an earlier interest in values clarification. Raths, Merrill, and Simon (1966) asserted that valuing is made up of three categories of subprocesses: prizing beliefs and behaviors, choosing beliefs and behaviors, and acting on beliefs. The approach that they recommended did not include the inculcation of any specific set of values. Instead the aim was to help students work through the process of valuing in order to reach a clarification of what it was that gave meaning to their lives. It was felt that exploring beliefs that had already formed and those that were emerging could be a very rewarding experience for students of all ages and could greatly enhance their self-esteem and confidence.

Many teachers today feel that, for second-language learners, especially those at intermediate to advanced proficiency levels, affective activities (including values clarification) can add another dimension to the language learning process. If used appropriately by an impartial, accepting teacher, such activities not only can provide meaningful dialogue in the target language, but can serve as an important means of bonding between students. This can be particularly important in ESL classes in which many different values systems are brought together (see Chapter 5). An environment that fosters an appreciation of differences tends to encourage individual growth and decrease hostility.

It must be pointed out, however, that in spite of their potential benefits, affective activities are not for everyone. They are not for the teacher who feels uncomfortable with sharing feelings and opinions. They are not for the teacher who wants to treat them as therapy sessions, although, as Moskowitz (1978) points out, they may be therapeutic. And they are certainly not for the teacher who wants to use them as a way to change the beliefs of others.

If they are to be effective for language teaching, they must be used by a teacher who has read in depth (see suggested readings) or who has completed a training program. Moreover, the activities chosen must be compatible with the students' age and proficiency levels, and they must be appropriate to the cultural environment in which they are to be used. In some cultures it is considered offensive to reveal oneself or to probe the thoughts of others.

For the teacher who decides to implement affective activities, Moskowitz lays down a few ground rules: Students must be given the right to pass, meaning they must not be forced to answer questions or contribute; they must have the right to be heard; and they must have the right to see their own opinions respected (no put-downs are allowed). She recommends further that the students have a chance to express afterwards how they felt about specific activities and what they learned from them.

In addition Moskowitz advises that the activities accentuate the positive and that they be of low risk so that the teacher and students will not feel threatened by them. In other words, instead of asking students what they dislike about themselves, ask them what they like; rather than asking them what they feel guilty about, ask them what makes them feel proud. Of course, negative feelings cannot be denied when they do arise. They should be treated like any other feelings, unless, of course, they are used to diminish someone else. At the same time, it must be remembered that not all the items in the activities can be positive in all respects. For example, we may want to ask students what they would want changed in the world or how something might be made better in their lives. What Moskowitz is saying, I believe, is that the overall focus should be positive in that it is constructive.

Although there appears to be some disagreement in the early literature (Simon, Howe, and Kirschenbaum, 1972; Galyean, 1976, 1982; Moskowitz, 1978) as to the role of the teacher in the affective activities, all seem to agree that the chief duty is one of facilitator. As facilitator, the teacher needs to encourage honest responses, to establish an aura of trust, to listen with genuine interest to what the students say, and to invite sharing, but only what students want to share. Furthermore, the teacher should clarify what they say by responding with questions such as "Is this what you're saying?" and by paraphrasing what has been said with statements such as "I think you're saying . . . " In addition, the authors all seem to agree that the teacher should be free to reveal his or her feelings and opinions in the discussions. However, Simon, Howe, and Kirschenbaum believe that these revelations should occur only at certain times.

> The best time for the teacher to give his view is toward the end, after the students have had a chance to think things through for themselves and to express their own points of view. The teacher should present himself as a person with values (and often with values confusion) of his own. Thus the teacher shares his values, but does not impose them. In this way, he presents the class with a model of an adult who prizes, chooses, and acts according to the valuing process. The teacher gets a chance to share his actual values as does any other member of the class. The particular content of his values holds no more weight than would anyone else's (1972, pp. 26–27).

On the basis of my own experience with affective activities, I agree that it is important for the students to realize that teachers,[1] like other people, are engaged in the valuing process themselves. However, it may be naive to think that the teacher's point of view can be downplayed to the extent that it holds no more weight than anyone else's, particularly when the teacher is acting as a facilitator. The problem then appears to be how teachers can make it known that they are developing and refining their own values without their belief systems' having an undue influence on the students. Perhaps the answer lies in how we view a *facilitator's role* as opposed to a *participant's role*. It is my opinion that the

---

[1] When I use the word *teachers* here, I also mean peer teachers and lay assistants if they are included in the program (see Chapter 14).

teacher should not attempt to be a facilitator *and* a participant simultaneously. As a facilitator, the teacher should remain objective throughout the activity. It is the facilitator's job to prepare and lead the students into a particular activity, to enforce the ground rules, to listen thoughtfully and nonjudgmentally, to clarify, to accept each student as he or she wants to be accepted, and to provide transitions as well as closures at the end of each activity.

The participant's role also includes listening thoughtfully and nonjudgmentally, clarifying others' ideas, and accepting others on their own ground, but it does not require that one remain impartial. A participant has the right to state his or her opinions and feelings about the subject as long as others' rights to opinions are respected.

In order for the teacher to be in a position where his or her ideas can find expression without being given undue weight, a switching of roles generally needs to take place. The teacher can become a participant on occasion and volunteer students can become facilitators (somewhat akin to the dialectical relationship between student and teacher described by Freire in Chapter 3). This role switch provides a chance for teachers and students to maximize the benefits of the activities and creates a great deal of excitement and motivation for students when they realize that they too can take on the responsibility of being facilitators.

There are also other ways in which a teacher can express opinions without being overly imposing. For example, the teacher can step down from the role of facilitator without reversing roles. However, it may be prudent to do this only when the students ask for the teacher's opinion on a certain issue of interest and only *after* students have had a chance to express themselves fully, as Simon, Howe, and Kirschenbaum suggest. The teacher also may want to use himself or herself as an example in a demonstration as part of the preliminary instructions, especially if the issue involved is not a controversial one.

Affective activities can be used in the classroom at almost any time. However, there are some situations in which they can be particularly beneficial. On days when students are feeling especially tense or somewhat down emotionally, such activities can have comforting effects. For example, when tensions seem to be very high, before final exams or other somewhat threatening events, the teacher can attempt an overt enhancement of self-concepts. Seating the students in a circle and having them concentrate on one person at a time, each member of the group, including the teacher, can say one thing he or she especially likes about that person. During the session someone (perhaps an advanced student) can record on separate sheets of paper what is said about each person so that the students can go home at the end of the day with the comments in writing (Richard-Amato, 1983).

On lighter occasions the teacher may want to center on a theme such as "exploring career options" with teenagers and adults or "choosing a pet" with children. In addition there are times when a particular activity is very compatible with what is being discussed in reaction to a story, song, or poem (described later in this chapter). For instance, if a character in a story being studied has to decide between marrying for love and marrying for money, an affective activity on related choices might be in order. In this way the content of the various genres can be related to the lives of the students. Flexibility helps the teacher recognize these moments and take advantage of them in a way that will maximize the benefits of each activity. Particularly at advanced levels, the teacher may want to use several activities to stimulate thought for writing assignments. Similar activities may also serve as appropriate means for culminating library research.

Most of the activities presented in this chapter are for small groups (two, three, or any number up to ten). Groups can be formed by many different means. Students can be grouped sociometrically. The teacher can have students write down the names of students with whom they feel most comfortable. After collecting their papers, the teacher can plan what might be some workable groups. In an ESL class the teacher might want to have the various cultures represented in each group. In addition, the teacher might want to make the act of grouping an affective activity in itself by setting up groups on the basis of favorite colors, seasons, foods, and the like. For example, the teacher might say, "Today we will have four groups. The group to which you belong will be determined by your favorite season of the year. All people who like fall come to this table; spring to that table . . . " Or random units might be formed by simply having the students number off. The method used for forming groups depends on the activity chosen, the number of groups needed for the activity, the number of students in the class, and/or whether or not the groups need to be of equal numbers (see also pages 120, 194, and 213).

Most of the activities suggested in this chapter are intended for intermediate to advanced levels although some, particularly those recommended in the next section, can be accomplished with beginners. It should be kept in mind that most of the activities can be modified to accommodate several different proficiency levels and can quite easily be adapted to various age groups simply by changing the content (see Chapter 14). Many of the questions and statements used as examples in the exercises that follow are oriented toward the interests of teenagers and adults. However, they can be changed to reflect the interests of children. Topics appropriate to children might include animals, toys, being the youngest or oldest in the family, discipline at home, holidays such as Halloween and Valentine's Day, TV cartoons, allowances, what you want to be when you grow up, and so forth. The activities must always be tailored to the needs, interests, and capabilities of the students. In addition they must be activities with which the teacher feels comfortable.

PREPARATION OF THE STUDENTS

It is important at beginning stages of language development to expose students to some of the basic vocabulary that will be particularly useful for the affective activities later on: emotions, feelings, favorite things to do, preferences in foods, colors, clothing, occupations, classes, and so forth. These can be taught through several of the methods presented in previous chapters. For example, using the total physical response, students can be introduced to emotions by having them demonstrated and by being asked to display them (to cry, to laugh, etc.); to foods by preparing various foods according to directions; to clothing by putting on and taking off sweaters, jackets, and other garments; to colors by manipulating objects of various colors. Through discussion, students can hear and talk about these same concepts. During warm-ups for role play, they can have similar notions reinforced.

As the students move into the early speech production stage, they can begin to express feelings and preferences through an activity such as one of the jazz chants described in Chapter 9. The students can be asked to supply the missing words. Once the beat has been established by snapping of the fingers, the teacher begins and the students follow suit: "My name is _____ and I feel _____ (happy, sad, tired, etc.)" or "My name is _____ and I like _____ (apples, pizza, movies, dancing, to read, etc.)."

Eventually, as the student begins to move into the speech emergence stage, the vocabulary becomes a little more sophisticated. Words such as *beautiful, stubborn, smart, safe,* and *selfish* may have become part of the student's repertoire, although several of these words may have appeared sooner. As the student approaches full communication, he or she may pick up such words and phrases as *self-confident, self-conscious, ridiculous, secure, spiteful, stimulated, enthusiastic, open-minded, to know oneself,* and *to lay it on the line.* Many similar words and structures commonly used in expressing feelings and opinions will come naturally through participation in the affective activities themselves. There may be times, however, when the teacher may want to provide supplementary vocabulary and perhaps even some open-ended sentences (Moskowitz calls them "stems") to reinforce certain vocabulary and structures by building exercises around them:

If I were older, I would . . .
One thing I do well is . . .
I want my friends to . . .
I wonder if . . .
I like you because . . .
My brother (sister) makes me feel . . .
People seem to respect me when I . . .

People can't force me to . . .
One thing I like about my family is that . . .
When people tease me, I . . .
If I could have one wish come true, I would wish for . . .

In addition, students should be encouraged to get assistance when attempting to share something that is temporarily beyond them rather than simply to pass. Thus they will expand their repertoires even more. Students should be invited to consult with more proficient peers or with the teacher. Thus, others can serve as counselors similar to those used in conjunction with Curran's counseling learning approach.[2]

If intermediate to advanced students seem reluctant to use affective activities, it may be a good idea to start with activities involving characters in literature. For instance, one might have the students read a story with well-developed characters and have them role-play the characters, revealing what they think the character's values might be. It is easy then to slip into a "and what would you have chosen in this situation?" kind of activity. For example, the students may be reading about a couple who fight because one wants to buy an expensive home, own a flashy car, and take frequent trips to Europe whereas the other would rather live moderately, drive a simple car that runs well, and vacation in the Sierras in a camper. Students can participate in affective activities while role-playing the characters. Once comfortable in role-play situations, they may be ready to do the same activities without role-playing. An alternative might be to have the students make up a story about the people in a picture shown to them and then role-play those characters while using appropriate affective activities. Once the students feel at ease when expressing feelings and preferences that belong to someone else, it may not seem so difficult to express their own.

Another aid for reluctant students (all students may be a little reluctant at first) is to warm up for each activity by beginning with issues not very close to the heart. For example, instead of asking, "Describe a moment when you were really embarrassed," the teacher might begin with something less personal, such as "Tell us about your favorite movie." Several of the ideas presented below may also serve as warm-ups to the other activities.

---

[2] Curran (1972) describes an approach whereby the teacher or others proficient in the target language serve as counselors and linguistic models for the students. At the beginning the students are completely dependent on the counselors, who help them translate their utterances from L1 to L2. As they become more and more proficient in the new language, it is expected that they will work toward complete independence.

AFFECTIVE ACTIVITIES

Suggested Ideas

VALUES SURVEY[3]

Students are asked questions and are given three or four choices from which to select the answer. Place the items on a ditto and distribute to the class. When giving the instructions, stress that *there are no right or wrong answers.*

Which would you rather be?
___ an astronaut
___ a business person
___ a teacher
___ a mechanic
___ a social worker

If you had $2,000, what would you do with it?
___ give most of it to some worthy cause
___ put it in the bank or invest it
___ buy a nice present for yourself

Where would you like to spend your vacation?
___ by the ocean
___ in New York City
___ at a ski resort
___ on a camping trip

Which is most important in choosing a spouse?
___ looks
___ personality
___ interests

___ values

What kind of gift do you prefer?
___ something someone made
___ money so you can buy something you want
___ a gift that somebody buys for you

How would you most like to spend an afternoon with a friend?
___ on a picnic in the mountains
___ at the movies
___ bowling

Which do you like least?
___ a person who is loud and obnoxious
___ a person who is dishonest
___ a person who gossips

---

[3] Adapted from Simon, Howe, and Kirschenbaum (1972, pp. 58–93).

What would you most like to do alone?
___ eat at a restaurant
___ attend a party
___ go to a movie
___ visit the zoo

Which car would you buy if you could?
___ a small, compact car
___ a sports car
___ a medium-sized, comfortable car
___ a pickup truck

Which is most important to you?
___ to plan for your future
___ to show others that you care about them
___ to get all the possessions you can

It is interesting to the students to complete the same survey several months later to see if their values have changed over the months.

THE SEARCH[4]

Place the following on a ditto and distribute to the students (see "The People Hunt" in Chapter 8 for a similar activity):

Find someone who . . . (write the name of the person in the blank following each item).

likes to go to libraries _____
has eaten okra _____
has been to a water polo game _____
would like to have a cat as a pet _____
saw a funny movie in the last week _____
is trying to break a habit _____
would like to be an actor _____
wants to take a trip to Mars some day _____
plays a guitar _____
went swimming recently _____
likes to tell jokes _____
owns a computer _____
can tap dance _____

Give the students about five minutes and then call time. Ask the whole class questions such as the following: Who likes to go to libraries? Who has eaten okra?, and so forth.

An alternative might be to have the students take similar search sheets home to use with family members, neighbors, or friends.

---

[4] Adapted from Moskowitz (1978, pp. 50–52).

Values Voting[5]

One sure way to get all the students involved in affective issues is to use this rapid-fire activity. Begin with the question "How many of you _____?" The blank can be filled in with items such as those below. Students raise their hands if the phrase is true of them.

> have a dog
> are afraid of storms
> think parents should be stricter with their kids
> do not like movies
> enjoy loud music
> plan to go to college
> have been in love
> wear seat belts in the car
> like to eat chocolate
> disapprove of smoking cigarettes
> want to end all wars
> think school is exciting
> work part-time
> want to get better grades in school
> like to sing

My Favorite Possession

Have the students decide which objects in their households are the most valuable. Tell them to imagine that their houses are about to be destroyed by a natural disaster (earthquake, tornado, hurricane, or fire) and that they are each allowed to save only one thing (all humans and animals are already out of danger). What one thing would they save and why? Have them talk about their answers in small groups.

A Collage about Me

Give students several magazines out of which they can cut pictures. Have them paste pictures together on individual poster boards of things that are particularly revealing about themselves. Items can include favorite activities, colors, foods, clothes, products, sayings, poems, jokes, and so on. After dividing the students into groups of about six, have them talk about their collages and what each item reveals. The collages can then be hung around the room for all to see.

An interesting follow-up might be to have students find someone else's collage that comes closest to revealing their own values.

---

[5] Adapted from Simon, Howe, and Kirschenbaum (1972, pp. 38–57).

My Own Space

If the room is large enough, you might want to give each student (especially younger ones) some bulletin board space. Freestanding bulletin boards work well for this purpose. Each student can use the space for things that are important to him or her but that could be replaced if lost or damaged: favorite sayings, reprints of family pictures, art work, compositions, poetry, and pictures from magazines. Students may want to rearrange their spaces from time to time and put up new things.

Pretend Pen Pals

Ask the students to pretend they are writing to pen pals for the first time. In the letters have them talk about such topics as their physical appearance, family, pastimes, favorite classes, and activities. Ask them to include questions they want to ask the person with whom they are corresponding. Divide them into groups of four, and have them share their letters. The group might want to suggest additions to each letter. A follow-up could be the real "pen pal" activity suggested in Chapter 8.

An alternative might be to have the students (particularly teenagers) describe themselves to a "blind date." This could be done orally in small groups.

A Helping Hand[6]

With your assistance, the students can make two separate lists: one for the things they know how to do that they can teach others, the second for the things with which they need help (Figure 13.1). Collect these lists, choose those tasks that can be worked on in class, and give the students time to help and be helped as appropriate. The activity could be repeated at various times throughout the year and could involve many different tasks.

Students can follow up the activities by answering the following questions:

What is one new thing I learned today?
Who helped me?
What would I like to learn tomorrow?
Who can help me?
What did I help someone do today?

You can get into the act if you wish. Learning from the students such things as how to fold paper birds Japanese style or how to count in Korean can be very challenging and exciting.

---

[6] Adapted from Farnette, Forte, and Loss (1977, p. 25).

Figure 13.1

Dear Abiwail[7]

Tell the students to play the role of assistants to the famous personal advisor, Abiwail. Have them write answers to the following letters (these particular letters are oriented toward teenagers).

Dear Abiwail,

I can't seem to get this boy at school to talk to me. I try to get his attention by wearing clothes I think he will like and by saying things to attract him. Nothing seems to work. I did catch him staring at me one day, but when I am near him, he ignores me. What can I do? I think I am in love with him.

Love Sick

---

[7] Adapted from Farnette, Forte, and Loss (1977, p. 59).

Dear Abiwail,

Last week I did a terrible thing and I feel very guilty. In fact, I can't do my school work. I just think about what I did all the time. When I was in the hardware store near my house, I was looking at some tools. The next thing I knew, I put a small wrench in my pocket and walked out with it. No one saw me do it, but I feel just awful. My parents always taught me never to steal. How can I make myself feel better?

Guilty in Memphis

Dear Abiwail,

I can't seem to make any friends. Everyone around me has many friends and they laugh and talk all the time. But, me, I'm alone. I think maybe I'm boring. I just can't think of anything interesting to talk about when I'm with someone. I try to act cool so no one will know what I'm really feeling. I think I'll go crazy if I can't have at least one friend.
Help me please.

Only the Lonely

THE MOST INFLUENTIAL PERSON

Have students decide which persons have affected their lives the most. Ask them to write about these people and include information such as descriptions (they may have pictures to share), how long they have known these people, and what these people did that made such an impact. Divide them into groups to share their writings.

REACHING THE GOAL

Ask students to decide on a goal (either academic or social) and map their approach to it, trying to anticipate possible obstacles (see Figure 13.2). Work out one to use as an example. When the students have completed the exercise, divide them into small groups for a discussion of their goals and the steps they will take to overcome the obstacles.

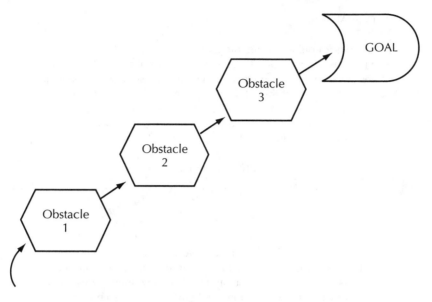

Figure 13.2

A Quote to Live By[8]

Have students choose a favorite quotation such as "To have a friend, you must be a friend" or "If you love something, you must set it free." Provide a few books of quotations from which the students can select their sayings, or give them the option of creating their own. Make available felt-tip pens with which to illustrate the sayings they have chosen. Give each student a poster board that can later be displayed in the room. Divide the class into small groups to discuss the meanings of their sayings. At the high school or university level, the teacher might ask the students to develop effective paragraphs or essays using the quotes as topics.

Journal Keeping

Daily journal entries are one means by which reactions, feelings, and experiences can be recorded in the target language. Encourage the students to make "I" statements, such as "I was angry when I found out that . . ." or "Today I knew that . . ." From time to time the students can hand in their journals for your reaction. It is recommended that the journals not be corrected for mechanical errors. However, space should be provided for you or your assistants to write positive and encouraging comments.

---

[8] Adapted from Moskowitz (1978, pp. 232–234).

GETTING TO KNOW YOU THROUGH INTERVIEW

Below are listed a few interviewing situations that can be used to provide practice with the target language and to aid students in the process of clarifying values. Remind students of their right to pass.

1. Even though most of the students in the class may already be acquainted, new students who are at intermediate or advanced levels come in from time to time and need to be introduced. One effective way to do this is to write questions on cards (one or two per card) and distribute them. Pair the students up and have them briefly interview each other, allowing about three minutes for each member of the pair. During the interview, the students can include the questions on the card. Then have each student introduce the person he or she interviewed and tell about the answer that was given to the questions on the cards as well as other information received. Below are some sample questions:

   What place do you like to go to when you're all alone? Describe it.
   What person do you admire most? Tell about that person's qualities.
   If you could choose any time period in which to live, which would you choose? Give your reasons.
   Where would you like to take your next vacation? Explain your choice.
   Which famous person would you like to have as a personal friend? Why?

2. Ask students to bring to class questions to ask each other (you can provide them with a list of sample questions to help them get started). On the day of the interviewing, place the students in a circle and have one volunteer begin by asking a question. Allow people to volunteer to give an answer. The person who volunteers to answer then has the privilege of asking the next question.

3. Have two volunteers go to the front of the room to be interviewed. Either one or both can answer the questions as they are asked by the teacher. It is important that the questions be reasonably nonthreatening in nature.[9] Here are a few possibilities:

   Who is your favorite female athlete? Explain your choice.
   What do you think is the best thing one person can give to another person?
   What kind of person do you usually choose as a friend? What characteristics must he or she have?
   What is the funniest situation you've ever found yourself in?
   Out of all the people in the world, past and present, who is the one you most admire? Why?
   Have you ever made a choice that surprised everyone? What was it?
   Do you have any advice to give us that you think would be good for us to hear?
   Which has been your best year in school? Why?

---

[9] It must be pointed out that what might seem nonthreatening to one student may not be to another. Sometimes even an innocent question such as "Where does your mother work?" might bring tears to one who has just lost a mother. The teacher simply has to use his or her best judgment and encourage the students to do the same in asking questions. As teachers and other facilitators become more experienced and skillful in using affective activities, they may want to take higher risks in some situations in order to maximize the results.

Has any news in the paper or on TV really worried you lately? If so, what was it and why did it disturb you?

How would you change this school if you could?

If you could have one question answered about life, what would your question be?

It is important before going on to the next question to follow up answers with other appropriate questions or react by simply repeating what the students say in order to ensure that the intended meaning comes across. Once you complete the interview, the class should have a chance to ask questions also.

An alternative might be to have the volunteers select topics about which they would like to be interviewed. You might post a list somewhere in the room to suggest possible categories: sports, movies, vacation, school, dating, and so on.

4. Invite students, teachers, and administrators (who speak the target language) from outside the class to come in to be interviewed. Students, with your help, can prepare questions beforehand. Other questions will grow out of the interviews themselves.

5. Send the students out into the school or university campus to interview other students (this is especially appropriate for an ESL class). Have them form the questions beforehand and return to report the most interesting answers they received. One alternative is to have students write up an opinion poll and ask students outside of class to respond orally while their opinions are recorded. Questions calling for a "yes," "no," or "maybe" answer, such as "Do you think most drugs should be legalized?" would be the easiest to tabulate. The results can be tallied once the students return to class.

STAND UP AND BE COUNTED![10]

Place five large signs around the room far enough apart so groups have room to form by them without crowding. Label the signs "Strongly Agree," "Agree Somewhat," "Neutral," "Disagree Somewhat," and "Strongly Disagree." Read a statement. The students move to the sign that best describes their reaction. Then volunteer spokespersons from each group tell the whole class why they have chosen that particular position. Each group is heard out fully before a verbal exchange among groups is allowed. Only one person should talk at a time and all the ground rules mentioned previously must be adhered to. Below are sample statements to which students can react:

Childhood is the happiest time of life.

Men and women should share equally the chores of running a household.

Grades in school should be outlawed.

Pets should be allowed in homes for the elderly.

Most people are dishonest when given the chance.

This activity could be followed up with advanced writing activities and in many cases library research, particularly if the issues are ones about which a great deal has been written.

---

[10] Adapted from Simon, Howe, and Kirschenbaum (1972, pp. 252–254).

Concentric Circles[11]

Students sit on the floor in two concentric circles with equal numbers in each circle. The members of the inner circle face outward toward corresponding members of the outer circle, who face inward. The activity begins with a question such as "What do you find especially difficult about learning a second language?" The students in the outer circle answer the question first, and as soon as a lull in the conversation becomes apparent (after a minute or so),[12] the students in the inner circle answer the same question. Then the inner circle remains stationary while the outer circle rotates clockwise until each student is aligned with the next person to the left. A different question is asked. This time the inner circle answers first, and after those in the outer circle answer also, the inner circle rotates counterclockwise to the next person, and so on. Make sure to give students time to think about the question before you begin the timing.

An alternative, with somewhat different interpersonal dynamics, uses groups of three. One person in each group answers the question while the others listen. When time is called, the second member of each group answers the same question, and then the third member.

Below are a few sample questions:

Describe one thing you would like to learn to do well.
Is there anyone in the world with whom you would like to change places? Explain your answer.
If you could run this school or university, what would you change about it?
What do you really like about the person (or people) sitting across from you?
What is the biggest problem faced by the younger generation living at home?
If you were the President of the United States, what is the first thing you would try to do?
What was the nicest thing anyone ever did for you?
What is one thing you wish you had the courage to do?

Problem Posing

The following is an adaptation of Wallerstein's (1983) approach to language teaching based on Freire's philosophy (see Chapter 3). She presents the activity as a means of developing critical thinking through group dynamics. However, it can also be used as a means of clarifying values. Begin by listening to the students to discover what issues seem to be important to them. Then attempt to find a codification (a story, a dialogue, a photograph, a picture) to tap into what is truly meaningful. For example, the students in an advanced ESL class may have recently been discussing the difficulties they faced when first coming to this country. As a codification for a problem posing activity, you might show the

---

[11] I first heard of this activity from another teacher (whose name is unknown to me) at a workshop several years ago. Later I came across a version of it in Moskowitz (1978, pp. 78–79).

[12] During some affective activities, time is called after each response to indicate that it is now someone else's turn to react. The turn should stay with only one person until the facilitator says that time is up. If that person finishes his or her response early, the group can either use the remaining time to ask questions to clarify or its members can simply reflect silently until it is the next person's turn.

students a picture of a lone woman waiting with her suitcases near the departing taxis at an international airport in the United States. She is dressed in native garments from India. Ask a series of inductive questions about the codification to try to pinpoint the problem as the students see it.

> What is happening here?
> Is there a problem?
> Have you or someone you have known experienced a similar problem?
> To what causes can you attribute this problem?
> What can we do?

In answering the questions, the students decide that the woman, who does not speak English, has been forgotten by those who were to meet her. She must survive on her own, at least for a while. A discussion ensues about the students' own experiences in similar situations and about the causes of such dilemmas. They decide, as a group, that they can do something to help others who find themselves in similar predicaments. They outline some steps for preparing pamphlets in a variety of languages to place at an international airport in the area. The pamphlets will clearly explain important procedures (finding the restrooms —a map of the airport will be included, converting one's money into dollars, using the telephone, finding a hotel or alternative lodging, taking a taxi or a shuttle bus, and so on).

Problem posing, as a process, has three major components: listening, dialogue, and action. It is important that only one problem be the focus at a time so that the issues do not become clouded. In addition, care must be taken to flow with the students when pinpointing the problem rather than lead them to one that has been predetermined. Issues can be dealt with on several different fronts: home, school, community, nation or state, world. Actions can run the gamut from speaking frankly with those who are in charge on the local level to writing letters to members of Congress or leaders of countries. The teacher and the students need to determine what actions would be effective and appropriate in each situation. Problem posing may require considerably more time than the teacher anticipates, but the benefits of increased student interest and the subsequent gains in language acquisition can make it very worthwhile.

SUMMARY

One important reason for using affective activities in the classroom is to help students reach an understanding of those beliefs and behaviors that give meaning to their lives. At the same time, these activities can provide motivating dialogue in the target language and serve as a way to bring individuals and groups closer together.

Although many benefits can accrue from use of affective activities, they are not suited to everyone. Teachers who are not comfortable sharing feelings and opinions, teachers who want to turn them into therapy and/or sensitivity training sessions, or teachers who are interested in imposing their own belief systems on others are not good candidates. Before attempting to use them, teachers should be familiar with the literature and, if possible, be specially trained in the techniques.

The activities themselves must be appropriate to the proficiency and age levels of the students as well as to the cultural environments in which they are used. They should be nonthreatening and generally positive in nature. Certain ground rules must be adhered to concerning the right to pass, the right to be heard, and the right to have one's opinion respected. If the classroom atmosphere is warm and accepting and the teacher wise and caring, affective activities can carry the students far in the language acquisition process.

READINGS, REFLECTION, AND DISCUSSION

Suggested Readings and Reference Materials

Galyean, B. (1982). A confluent design for language teaching. In R. Blair, ed. *Innovative approaches to language teaching* (pp. 176–188). Rowley, Mass.: Newbury House. Galyean calls for a merging of subject skill mastery and humanistic goals. Although her approach may be too grammar oriented for some, she does offer several ideas that can be adapted in the second-language classroom.

Hooker, D., and Gallagher, R. (1984). *I am gifted, creative, and talented*. New York: Educational Design. EDI 331. A collection of self-development activities centering around self-awareness, working with others, sharpening mental gifts, creativity, and talents (teens/adults). Includes activities on personal opinions, family expectations, dreams, fears, peer-group influence, trusting others, and much more.

Moskowitz, G. (1978). *Caring and sharing in the foreign language class*. Rowley, Mass.: Newbury House. A sourcebook on humanistic methods. Presents a wide array of ideas on relating to others, discovering the self, expressing feelings, and sharing values.

Schoenberg, I. (1989). *Talk about values: Conversation skills for intermediate students*. White Plains, N.Y.: Longman. Topics such as honesty, views toward growing old, gift-giving, and choosing a mate are to stimulate discussion about values. There are no right or wrong answers. The book is intended for adults, both young and old.

Simon, S., Howe, L., and Kirschenbaum, H. (1972). *Values clarification: A handbook of practical strategies for teachers and students*. New York: Hart. Contains a series of activities and explains how to use them for furthering the process of values clarification. Includes decision making, problem solving, and many other means for confirming and developing values. Even though a few of the topics suggested in this book may be a little high risk for most teachers and students, many of the activities lend themselves readily to successful language teaching.

Questions for Reflection and Discussion

1. To what extent do you feel our values are culturally determined? Is there a set of values basic to all cultures? Explain. What role does individual experience seem to play in the process of the development of a values system?

2. Green (1983) stresses the characteristics of a successful values clarification teacher.

> Use of values clarification in the classroom requires a teacher who (1) is willing to examine his or her own values; (2) can accept opinions different from his or her own; (3) encourages a classroom atmosphere of honesty and respect; and (4) is a good listener (1983, p. 180).

What might be the consequences in the classroom for the teacher who tries to use values clarification, but who lacks even one of these characteristics?

3. What are several situations in your own teaching for which affective activities could be adapted? Plan in detail a few such activities for at least two situations. You might consider using them as part of a literature or history unit of some kind, as a follow-up to the study of the lyrics of a song, as a unit to commemorate a special holiday, or for any other situation in which such activities might be appropriate.

4. Choose one of the affective activities planned above and try it out with the members of your class. State clearly the situation, the proficiency and age levels for which it is intended, and the possible follow-ups you would use. Give the class members a chance to express their feelings about it afterwards. In what ways was it successful? How can it be improved?

PART III

Putting It All Together: Some Practical Issues

It is the teacher in the classroom who has the task of putting it all together and making it work. No book can dictate a program or a methodology. What may be good for one group of learners in one particular setting may not be appropriate for those in other situations. The following types of programs and a few of their implications are presented below for your consideration (see Chapter 16 for a fuller description of these types in relation to bilingual education and/or sheltered adjunct classes).

SECOND-LANGUAGE PROGRAMS

Second-language programs were referred to in the Introduction (see footnote 1) as programs in which the target language is a dominant language in the area where it is being taught. Generally, students in such programs are interested in learning to survive physically, socially, and often academically in the new culture. They are, in most cases, surrounded by the target language in the community, the workplace, and the school or university campus. Sometimes, however, second-language students live in communities in which their first language and culture are predominant. This means that, although they have the advantages of L1 language and cultural maintenance, they may lack the target language input available to those in more integrated situations. For them, having considerable contact with native or nativelike speakers as part of the curriculum would be especially important to their interlanguage development.

FOREIGN-LANGUAGE PROGRAMS

Foreign-language programs were referred to in the Introduction as programs in which the target language is not the dominant language in the area where it is being taught. Students have a variety of reasons for being in these programs. Sometimes their goals are integrative ones. For example, they may want to communicate with people from another language group or survive in another culture. Often their goals are instrumental. For example, they may want to get a job which requires that they be bilingual. Other times, the goal is simply personal enrichment. The environment outside of the classroom, however, does not usually give foreign-language students the opportunity to be immersed in the target language. They are in special need of meaningful interaction since the classroom may be their only source. On the other hand, because they may not receive a sufficient quantity of high-quality input in the classroom to become proficient (many foreign-language classes meet only one hour a day), they may find a judicious formal application of rules to be necessary in facilitating the acquisition process. This presents the teacher with somewhat of a dilemma.

Other factors come into play as well. The culture of the students may prevent some methods or activities from being as effective as they might be in other circumstances. For example, in many Asian cultures it is considered rude to talk of oneself. In such cultures affective activities such as those found in Chapter 13 may be highly inappropriate. Yet another problem has to do with motivation. Students in foreign-language programs generally have less motivation to function in the target language because they do not have to know it to survive on a daily basis.

Additional foreign-language programs have their own implications for curriculum planning. For example, instrumental programs that are offered strictly for a single academic purpose (e.g., interpreting research findings in another language) or for other specific purposes (e.g., becoming acquainted with a new medical procedure used in another culture) may not include the development of communication skills at all. In these programs learning to read and being familiar with a certain technical vocabulary may be all that is necessary.

CHAPTER 14

Classroom Management

Just as there is no one set of ideal teaching materials, so there is no universal teaching method suited to the many contexts of language learning. . . . The most effective programs will be those that involve the whole learner in the experience of language as a network of relations between people, things, and events. The balance of features in a curriculum will and should vary from one program to the next, depending on the particular learning context of which it is a part.

S. Savignon, 1983

QUESTIONS TO THINK ABOUT

1. Think about the kind of program in which you are teaching or will be teaching. Is it a second- or a foreign-language program? What do you think some of the organizational problems might be due to the kind of program it is?

2. Can you think of ways to involve native-speaking or near-native-speaking peers with your language students in your classroom?

3. Have you ever experienced cooperative learning either as a teacher or as a student? If so, what was your reaction to it as a management technique? To what extent was it effective?

4. How teacher-dominant do you think language classrooms should be? Do you think proficiency level of the students would make any difference? If so, how?

A single method by itself will probably not provide an adequate language teaching program. Neither will the concatenation of several methods and activities. What we need is an interweaving of courses of action, each providing what is required at the moment, all working together to form a highly integrated curriculum. There will be times when activities most typically related to the total physical response and the natural approach are well suited, other times when jazz chants and role play are more appropriate, and still others when affective activities fit the situation best. Grammar exercises may have their place, once students have enough competence to benefit from grammatical analysis (see Chapter 3). Much depends on whether the goals are integrative and/or instrumental (see Chapter 5), what concepts and proficiencies are needed, what the learning and teaching preferences are, cultural factors, and the age and competency levels of the students. No longer can a teacher depend upon a single book or a single course of action to get the job done.

INTEGRATION OF METHODS AND ACTIVITIES

A program utilizing an integration of methods and activities could be organized at beginning stages around basic topics and situations similar to those suggested by Krashen and Terrell (1983): body parts, physical actions, clothing, occupations, emotions, recreation, going shopping, etc. Early on, the program might ease into subject-area concepts and themes, including their related proficiencies.[1] The subject areas might include art, math, business, computer processing, physical education, social and natural sciences, and literature. Whatever the content, it must be relevant to the students and their needs. In addition, it must include areas of knowledge in which the teacher has some expertise, although most areas can be explored together (see especially theme cycles on page 277).

Students might at first be introduced to many key concepts during low-beginning levels, through aspects of the total physical response or the audio-motor unit (Chapter 7). The *same* concepts can be reinforced while new ones are introduced through activities typical of the natural approach and its extensions (Chapter 8). As students move toward mid- and high-beginning levels, jazz chants, simple poetry, and/or music lyrics (Chapter 9) can be added and used occasionally either to introduce a set of concepts or to reinforce them. During this period, techniques from storytelling, role play, and drama (Chapter 10) can be highly motivating while providing the many passes through the material necessary for acquisition to occur. Games (Chapter 11) can be effective if played occasionally to develop or reinforce concepts or to teach the

---

[1] Most of the suggestions here are applicable in all second- and foreign-language teaching situations in which content is the focus (see Chapter 16 and Related Reading 4).

vocabulary and structures of game playing itself. During the high-beginning through advanced stages (see pages 99–100), the teacher may want to involve the student to a greater extent in the planning process. At these levels, the teacher can introduce and reinforce concepts through affective activities (Chapter 13) and through more advanced applications of the above methods. All the while, literacy in the target language (Chapter 12) and the related proficiencies can be taught in an integrated fashion rather than as separate sets of skills and subskills (see Chapter 4).

Various methods and activities could also be combined on a much smaller scale, either within a unit (several lessons about the same topic) or within a single lesson. In the two examples following, we have several methods and activities merged *within a unit*.

Susan Ashby, a teacher in the Alhambra School District of California, illustrates how storytelling, music, affective activities, and poetry can be integrated with aspects of the total physical response and the natural approach. All can work together to produce a unified whole—in this case a subject-area unit on birds. She suggests that the unit (intended for use with children at intermediate levels) begin with the Mexican folktale, "The Pájaro-cu." It is the story of a bird who, at the beginning of the world, appeared before the eagle (the king) stark naked because he had no feathers. The eagle was so offended that he sent the featherless bird into exile. A dove took pity on him and began a campaign to clothe him. Each bird willingly contributed a feather. The result was a bird so colorful and beautiful that he became vain and would have nothing to do with the other birds. He decided to leave the country. The other birds were sent to look for him. In their search, the various birds began to sing out the different calls by which they are now known. Although the lost bird (called the *pájaro-cu*) has never been found, the other birds still sing their characteristic songs but no longer expect an answer.

By using an extension of the natural approach, the teacher and students discuss the meaning of the story. Questions such as these are asked:

1. Do people, like the Pájaro-cu, ever get sent away—into exile? If so, why?
2. Once the Pájaro-cu became more colorful and beautiful than the other birds he would have nothing to do with them. Why do you think he would have nothing to do with them? Do people ever behave this way? Explain.

In addition, the teacher displays a series of colored pictures of birds and talks with the students about the different types and the features that most birds have in common. By including elements of the total physical response, the teacher has the students pantomime to the beat of a drum the movements of various birds: big birds, delicate birds, birds that run, walk, and soar. Using movements to music (see Chapter 9), the children dance, playing the roles of different types of birds. Then following a lesson in watercolors (again using aspects of the total physical response), the students sketch and paint the bird, perhaps combining crayons and watercolors to give the hues a jewel-like appearance. An affective activity comes into play when the students are asked to find sayings such as "Birds of a feather flock together" and "A bird in the hand is worth two in the bush." After discussing the meanings of the sayings, the students can use them to label their pictures. Ashby suggests a poetry lesson as a follow-up. One poem she finds particularly effective and stimulating for discussion is "Gooloo" by Shel Silverstein.

> The Gooloo bird
> She has no feet
> She cannot walk
> Upon the street.
> She cannot build
> Herself a nest,
> She cannot land
> And take a rest.
> Through rain and snow
> And thunderous skies,
> She weeps forever
> As she flies,
> And lays her eggs
> High over town,
> And prays that they
> Fall safely down.

The second example of an integrated unit is provided by Heather Robertson, an instructor in the American Culture and Language Program at California State University, Los Angeles. It combines affective activities and role play to provide a cultural awareness unit for English as a Second Language students in a course entitled "Readings in Sociology." The course is intended for advanced students who will soon be seeking admission to the university.

In the first lesson, the students are given a minilecture on how appropriateness of behavior is judged in many cultures. Students are asked to listen and take notes. They are then given a quiz during which they are encouraged to use their notes. As homework for that evening, they are to read a section from a college-level sociology text reinforcing the same concepts. During the next lesson, students discuss what sorts of behaviors are considered appropriate in their cultures but not appropriate in the United States. They share opinions on how native speakers might react to persons deviating from the norm. Homework for the second evening consists of coming up with situations in which specific behaviors are incorporated for the purpose of bringing about overt or subtle reactions among native speakers. The behaviors might include such actions as facing the "wrong" way in an elevator and standing "too close" to someone while speaking.

On the third day the students decide which situations they would like to act out at various spots around the campus. The students who feel uncomfortable with being actors can volunteer to be observers and recorders of the reactions of native speakers. Once the roles have been decided, the students predict the kinds of responses they expect to get and how the responses might make them feel. The observers and recorders are told to watch the native speakers carefully and record in writing their reactions. Even a wry smile or raised eyebrow should be noted.

The last day is reserved for reporting the results and for a discussion aimed at achieving some sort of perspective. Did the native speakers react as predicted? What were the feelings of the actors? The observers? Had they been in similar situations before? How had they reacted the first time? Through a sharing of such responses, students seem better able to deal with the feelings, whatever they might be.

In the next example, Sandy Nevarez, a resource teacher in the ABC Unified School District of California, combines characteristics of several approaches *into a single lesson* that is part of a subject-area unit on insects or bugs. She incorporates elements of the natural approach, total physical response, and some elements from poetry to produce a "soup fit for toads." She tells the students (primary children at beginning levels) that they are about to prepare a real delicacy—toad soup. Prior to the activity, the students are introduced to the names of various insects or other bugs and are given small pictures of them (run off on a ditto and cut out). The teacher has provided a pot in which to make the soup, along with the various ingredients needed: a raw egg, water, honey, cooked spaghetti noodles, and sand mixed with small rocks. Each ingredient should be kept out of view until it is needed, thus increasing anticipation. The dialogue can go somewhat like this:

TEACHER: What are some bugs that toads like? Put them in the pot. (The teacher looks at each picture and says its name as the students put them in the pot.) Very good. Now we have many bugs in the pot. We have spiders, bees, flies, mosquitoes, ladybugs, and many others. The soup should be very good, don't you think? (The students nod but with some doubt.) Could our soup use a raw egg? (She breaks an egg into the soup, adds water, and stirs the mixture around with her hand.) Ooooooh, it feels slimy. It feels sliiiimy. (She lets the students feel in the pot.) How does it feel? Does it feel slimy?

STUDENTS: (muttering while grimacing) Slimy. Slimy.

TEACHER: Okay. Could our soup use some noodles? Yes, it could use some noodles. (She dumps in a fistful of noodles and stirs it around, again with her hand.) Squishy. It feels squishy and ishy and soooo slimy. (Again she lets the students feel.) How does it feel? Squishy and ishy?

STUDENTS: Yes.

TEACHER: Slimy?

STUDENTS: Yes.

TEACHER: Sooooo squishy and ishy and slimy. (The students make faces to indicate their disgust.)

The teacher continues in this manner adding the other ingredients and using other rhyming words: sticky, icky (for honey), and lumpy, bumpy (for sand with rocks). Through the highly comprehensible input, the physical involvement, and the sensual quality of the words and actions, the students become completely absorbed in the activity, making acquisition highly probable.

DECIDING THE FOCUS OF THE PROGRAM

Now that we appear to have moved away from grammar-based programs, there seems to be some confusion about the proper focus of communicative programs. Some say we should focus on proficiencies/competencies (Omaggio, 1986); others say we should focus on tasks (Long, 1985, and Nunan, 1989, 1991); yet others say we should focus on content (Brinton, Snow, and Wesche, 1989).[2]

Proficiency/Competency-Based Instruction

This focus refers to the "mastery of basic and life skills necessary for the individual to function proficiently in society" (National Center for Educational Statistics, 1982, p. 80). Often the syllabus is organized around learning outcomes that have been divided into skills and subskills: (1) being able to recognize and write common abbreviations, (2) being able to auditorially distinguish certain vowel sounds, (3) being able to spell a list of two-syllable words, (4) being able to verbally produce and write the alphabet, (5) being able to correctly punctuate a dialogue, (6) being able to use negatives in obligatory positions, (7) being able to distinguish between "some" and "any," (8) being able to correctly use prepositions of location, etc. Often checklists are used to make sure students have these proficiencies or competencies before they can move on to the next task or the next level.

---

[2] In addition there are many other alternatives, including product-based instruction, theme-based instruction, literature-based instruction, etc. Most can be directly related or subsumed by the three foci described above. For example, product-based instruction relates closely to task-based instruction in cases in which a product is a result of the task at hand. Theme-based instruction and literature-based instruction can both logically be subsumed under content-based instruction.

Task-Based Instruction

Long (1985) defines tasks as ". . . the things people will tell you they do if you ask them and they are not applied linguists" (p. 89). They might include filling out a form, typing a letter, checking a book out of the library, and so on. Task-based instruction, according to its advocates, can (and should) be guided by second-language acquisition research. A task-based syllabus first requires a needs identification. Once the needs have been identified, they are classified into task types (e.g., tasks related to working in a bank or tasks related to driving a car). Task difficulty is assessed within each task type and a syllabus is prepared. Meaning is negotiated as the learners try to accomplish goals related to each task.

Nunan (1991) relates task-based instruction to experiential learning. He gives an example using steps to develop a pedagogic task (p. 282):

1. Identify target task (e.g., giving personal information in a job interview).
2. Provide model (e.g., students listen to and extract key information from an authentic or simulated interview).
3. Identify enabling skill (manipulation drill to practice *Wh*-questions with *do*-insertion).
4. Devise pedagogic task (interview simulation using role cards).

Nunan claims that this procedure provides students with the opportunity to accomplish the following: (a) develop language skills meeting their needs, (b) be exposed to native-speaker or user language, (c) receive explicit instruction and guided practice, (d) mobilize emerging skills by rehearsing.

Brown (1994) asserts that some tasks may be synonymous with teaching techniques (e.g., a role-play task/technique or a problem-solving task/technique). According to him, "It [task-based instruction] views the learning process as a set of communicative tasks that are directly linked to the curricular goals they serve, and the purpose of which extend beyond the practice of language for its own sake" (p. 83). He presents for teachers important questions such as: Do the tasks specifically contribute to communicative goals? Are their elements carefully designed and not simply haphazardly or idiosyncratically thrown together?

Content-Based Instruction

Brinton, Snow, and Wesche (1989) define content-based instruction as

> ". . . the integration of content learning with language teaching aims. More specifically, it refers to the concurrent study of language and subject matter, with the form and sequence of language presentation dictated by content" (p. vii).

Content-based teaching is usually associated with the *academic* course content found in school subjects such as math, science, history, literature, etc. Survival topics taught at beginning levels of second-language development such as getting a job, going to the doctor, and so forth, are not generally considered "content-based." Rather they are "task-based" (see Long's definition above). What Brinton, Snow, and Wesche are advocating (among other things) is that academic content be used in second-language classes and that it integrate language skills around a content topic such as ocean fish, travel destinations, the effects of drugs on society, and so on. Any of the topics, depending upon the students' needs and interests, could last for a short time period or be extended over a long time period. Such topics would probably be most appropriate for students operating at high-beginning to advanced levels (see pages 99–100), although preparation for them could begin at much earlier stages. The academic content is generally selected by the teacher and the modified input is specially tailored to their needs. A language course based on academic content in second-language situations (as opposed to foreign-language situations—see page 255) is transitional in nature. Students expect to be placed eventually in sheltered, adjunct, or mainstream courses in the content areas for which they are being prepared (see Chapter 16 for a description of each type of course).

Which Focus is Best?

When addressing this question, at least two subquestions need to be considered.

1. Will any of them lead to a syllabus concentrating on isolated elements of language for study? If so, these should be avoided.
2. Which one would make the most sense cognitively to learners in a particular teaching situation?

To answer the first question, it is my opinion that the only focus described above that leads to a syllabus concentrating on isolated elements of language for study is proficiency/competency-based instruction. It is not much different in this respect from the grammar-based approaches of the past. Here I am reminded of Newmark's seminal article, "How Not to Interfere with Language Learning" (1983). He says that we learn language in natural chunks, exponentially, rather that additively. The "interference" occurs when we artificially isolate parts from wholes. This is exactly what a proficiency/competency-based curriculum appears to do. This is not to say that proficiencies and competencies are not important. On the contrary, they should be *part of* the curriculum, but not *the focus* of the curriculum.

Concerning the second question, although a focus on task-based instruction would make sense cognitively to learners, particularly its applications intended for those operating at rank beginning levels and for those in special programs,[3] I would have to say that, overall, content-based instruction appears

---

[3] An example would be an English for Special Purposes (ESP) program whose goals are often highly specified for a particular technical field such as medicine or computer technology. In such programs, a task-based approach might work best.

to make the most sense as a focus for situations in which successful communication and/or academic competency are the goals. In such situations, tasks generally need something to belong to in the way of content. A course that jumps from task to task may lack both cohesion and a reason for being.

For a workable hierarchy in which the three foci are integrated into a program, see Figure 14.1 below:

Figure 14.1

If the content were ocean fish, for example, then the tasks might involve finding out as much as possible about ocean fish and sharing that information with a small group; helping the class and the teacher set up an aquarium in the classroom to study; describing the animals in the aquarium; and so on. Proficiencies and competencies might involve being able to spell the names of various ocean fish, being able to correctly punctuate a paragraph about the habitat of various ocean fish, and so forth.

UTILIZING PEER TEACHERS AND LAY ASSISTANTS

An ideal teaching situation would be one in which each student receives

1. An adequate amount of meaningful, relevant input aimed roughly at the $i + 1$ or the Zone of Proximal Development (see Chapter 3)
2. A sufficient number of opportunities to enhance the self-image and develop positive attitudes
3. Regular encouragement, motivation, and challenge
4. Plenty of opportunity for output
5. Continual feedback
6. Appropriate linguistic models (native or near-native speakers of the target language are best)

The quantity or amount of each of these necessary to the acquisition of the target language depends on the individual student and on each situation.

Peer teachers and/or lay assistants may prove to be necessary additions to the program in order to help meet the students' individual needs in the above areas. They, like the teacher, can facilitate communication through a negotiation for meaning, offer comprehensible input, and give encouragement and feedback. They can provide a social link to the rest of the students in the school and to the community. In addition, they can serve as linguistic models to help prevent early fossilization. Potential peer teachers who are fluent in the target language are usually available within the schools themselves. For example, in the foreign-language class one can draw from the advanced students in the language; in ESL at the junior and senior high schools and at universities, one can draw from the student body at large; in elementary schools, from the upper grades except in cases in which the tasks are not very demanding cognitively. In those cases, peer teachers can be much younger. (However, younger peer teachers will require a lot more supervision from the teacher than will older ones.) In adult programs, one can draw from the community. Lay assistants who are fluent in the target language can be invaluable at all levels. They are often an overlooked community resource.

Peer teachers and lay assistants should meet certain qualifications: They must have the necessary skills, enjoy aiding others, have a lot of patience, be supportive, and be willing to work hard. In addition they will need preparation workshops (especially effective at secondary and adult levels) to aid them in the following areas:

1. Development of cultural sensitivity (see also Chapter 5)
2. Knowledge of the instructional procedures the teacher chooses to use
3. Familiarity with the methods and materials with which they will be working (role play might help here—they can gain practice in the techniques by trying them out on each other)
4. Pertinent background information on the students with whom they will be working—cultural information, common problems, and so on
5. Strategies for creating friendly, supportive relationships

Below is a collection of strategies for helping others that could be discussed at a preparation workshop.

Strategies for Helping Others

1. Become familiar with the student's name and use it frequently.
2. Have an easy smile.
3. Be friendly. Get to know the student.
4. Be a good listener. Encourage the student to talk. Ask questions to find out more or to clarify what the student is saying.
5. Show recognition of and enthusiasm for the student's accomplishments no matter how small. Praise genuinely. Make it as specific as possible. Try to build intrinsic motivation by getting the student to

reflect on what he or she has done. Questions such as "How does it make you feel to have _____ ?" or "You must be very proud of _____ " encourage the student to be self-motivating.

6. Find out about the student's culture.
7. Be accepting of the person's right to his or her own opinions and beliefs. Avoid put-downs.
8. When asking questions, give the student enough time to respond. Be patient.
9. Give the student sufficient time to work at his or her own pace without feeling hurried.
10. Instead of responding with a flat "No, that's wrong," say something more encouraging such as "You're giving it a good try. But maybe we should look at it in a little different way. . . ."
11. If the student does not understand a concept after several attempts, go to something that you know the student can do with success. Later when you return to the more difficult task, it may come more easily.
12. If the student is obviously troubled or upset, give him or her a chance to talk to you about it. The task at hand can wait.
13. Use language that the student can understand. Repeat frequently. Use pictures and/or act out concepts whenever necessary.
14. Keep your directions short and simple.
15. Be honest with the student. If you don't know the answer to a question you have been asked, be willing to admit it. Often you and the student can pursue information about an area of mutual interest together.
16. Remember that the teacher is there to help you when you need it. Do not hesitate to ask for assistance when there is something you can't handle.

In addition to preparation workshops, the peer teachers and lay assistants need to meet with the teacher regularly to make flexible lesson plans and to talk about possible problems and various approaches. The following is an evaluation checklist to ensure frequent communication between the teacher and peer teacher or lay assistant concerning the progress of the students.

EVALUATION CHECKLIST

Name of peer teacher or lay assistant _____ Date _____

Name of student _____

1. What did the student accomplish today?

2. Were there any problems?

3. What activities will you work on tomorrow?

4. Can the teacher help you in any way?

Comments:

Room Arrangements[4]

As far as room arrangements are concerned, there are two plans that have worked well for me to incorporate peer teachers and lay assistants (see Figures 14.2 and 14.3). In Figure 14.2, *a private work station* has been set up for each peer teacher and lay assistant where the students to whom he or she has been assigned go for assistance. While working on their own, these students remain at the tables in the center of the room. This particular configuration works well when the tasks are mainly one-to-one, requiring a certain degree of privacy. Figure 14.3, on the other hand, illustrates the *flexible cluster work station* where

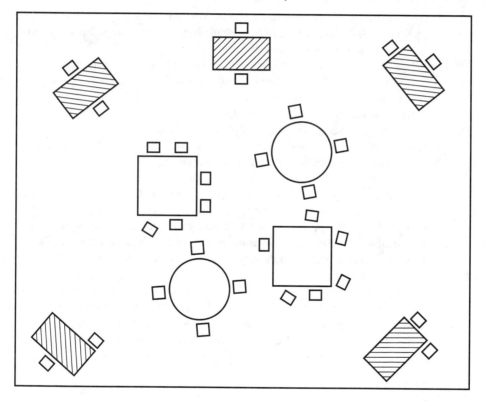

Figure 14.2. Private Work Stations
Comfortable chairs are found at each table. The tables with diagonal lines running through them are work stations for the peer teachers and lay assistants. The teacher, too, might have a work station. Note that for whole-class activities, the students can all be at the tables in the middle.

the students assigned to a particular peer teacher or lay assistant sit together, with the peer teacher at the apex. This arrangement is ideal when group instruction or a group project is undertaken. However, the cluster is flexible

[4] From Richard-Amato (1992a, pp. 282–283).

enough so that by rearranging the desk, the peer teacher and lay assistants can still work somewhat privately with one or more members of the group.

In addition to the work stations mentioned, other areas can be clearly defined for special purposes. For example, an elementary classroom might include one

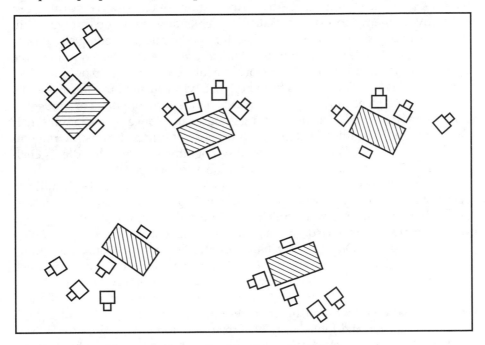

Figure 14.3. Flexible Cluster Work Stations
Movable desks cluster around the tables which serve as work stations for peer teachers and lay assistants. A similar station may be set up for the teacher. Note that for whole-class activities, the tables can be moved to the periphery of the room and the movable desks can be moved to the center to form a circle or any other configuration needed.

corner for story reading, another for free play, yet another for working on spontaneous art projects related to some unit of study. In a secondary classroom, there might be a book corner for comfortable, private reading, a writing station with a typewriter or computer for student use, a hands-on display area, and so on.

The task of organizing a program utilizing peer teachers and lay assistants may at first appear overwhelming. However, once they are prepared in the methods that the teacher chooses to use and are assigned to workable groups (perhaps three or four students of similar proficiency levels), the program seems to take on a momentum of its own. At that point, the time and talents of the teacher can be put to optimal use. The teacher is able to concentrate on students needing special help, peer teachers and lay assistants wanting additional guidance, whole-class activities, and overall structural concerns.

COOPERATIVE LEARNING AS A MANAGEMENT TECHNIQUE[5]

In cooperative learning, students help other students within groups of four to five persons in an effort to reach goals. Adaptations of cooperative learning can be effective at many age levels from the late elementary grades up through adult levels. It can be used in both second- and foreign-language teaching situations.

In cooperative learning there is an *interdependence* established among the students in each group as they strive for the achievement of group or individual objectives. This technique draws from both behaviorism and humanism. On the one hand, it frequently offers group rewards (in the form of points or grades) as its prime motivation; on the other, it urges students to develop more fully their own individual identities while respecting those of others. It must be remembered, however, that the students should be cognitively able to handle its challenges in whatever situations the teacher wishes to incorporate it.

The results of studies done on cooperative learning (Slavin, 1983) indicate great potential for some aspects of the method to produce academic success, especially in classes of mixed ethnicity. In almost all the studies (89%) in which group rewards were based on individual achievement, there were noted achievement gains. On the other hand, in studies in which only individual grades were given, or a group grade was given based on a group product, achievement was roughly the same as that found in the control classes. Moreover, several studies indicated that medium to low achievers seem to benefit most and that their accomplishments were not made to the detriment of high achievers (Martino and Johnson, 1979; Armstrong, Johnson, and Balow, 1981).

One drawback of cooperative learning, if it is used extensively at beginning to intermediate levels with second- or foreign-language students, is the possibility of early fossilization (see Chapters 3 and 5). Wong-Fillmore (1985) reports that students who are not proficient in the target language do not provide adequate models for each other. This was true also in the immersion programs. This is not to say, however, that all nonnative peer grouping should be avoided. On the contrary, such groups can provide comfortable environments in which the students can practice giving output and negotiating for meaning (see Long and Porter, 1984; Pica and Doughty, 1985; Porter, 1986). The danger, it would seem, comes when nonnative peers are the *major* source of input during the language acquisition process. Perhaps it is Porter who sums it up best:

> Though learners cannot provide each other with the accurate grammatical and sociolinguistic input that native speakers can provide them, learners can offer each other genuine communicative practice, including the negotiations for meaning that may aid second language acquisition (1986, p. 220).

---

[5] I wish to thank Carole Cromwell, Linda Sasser, and Leslie Jo Adams for sharing their ideas about cooperative learning with me. However, it is improbable that each will agree with every one of my conclusions.

Versions of cooperative learning can be incorporated very successfully in almost any subject area, especially in intermediate to advanced language classes and in mainstream content-area classes. It is particularly effective in the latter, where ESL students can be grouped with native or near-native speakers.

Kagan (1986) describes five distinct types of cooperative learning, which I have briefly summarized below. The examples for possible use are mine. Types 2–5 seem to work best when groups of mixed ethnicity (in the case of ESL) and mixed ability levels are created. It should be noted that there are many other versions of these basic types that have evolved over the past few years.

1. *Peer Tutoring.* Teammates teach each other simple concepts. This type is often used for math or language arts. It would be particularly applicable in a mainstream content-area class that includes ESL students.

2. *Jigsaw.* Each member of the group is given the chief responsibility for a specific portion of the learning unit. These members work with the members of other groups who have been given the same assignment. They form "expert groups." However, eventually each member must learn the whole unit by sharing information with the others in the group. This type of cooperative learning is often used in the mastery of text material in social sciences. For example, a unit on the contributions of women in the United States might be studied by each group. One group member might be responsible for women's contributions to science, another on their contributions to literature, a third on their contributions to politics, and so forth. Each student is graded individually on his or her understanding of the whole unit.

3. *Cooperative Projects.* The members of the group work together to complete a group project such as a presentation, a composition, or an art project. Members receive individual grades based on the evaluation of the group product.

4. *Cooperative/Individualized.* Students work alone on a particular assignment or project but their progress contributes to a group grade. They may help each other so that each can achieve the best possible results.

5. *Cooperative Interaction.* Students work as a unit to learn. However, there is no group grade received. Each member of the group is graded individually even though completion of the unit (e.g., a lab experiment, a panel discussion, a dramatic presentation) requires a cooperative effort.

Although the above suggestions are mainly for long-term projects, some very simple applications of cooperative learning can be incorporated in short-term activities at any level for which the specific content is appropriate. Following are some examples:

1. In a version of the activity commonly known as "numbered heads together," the class is divided into several groups of four or five and each student is given a

number within the group. Each student (depending upon the number assigned) does one small portion of the group's work. For example, if a class in adult basic education is studying cultures, the teacher might give the groups several short passages, each describing an important custom in the United States. The person who is assigned the number four in each group could be responsible for reading the passage about how late one can be to a dinner party without being considered rude. The same person is then responsible for sharing this information with the others. The person assigned to number three could do the same for a passage describing who is expected to pay when one is asked to go to a movie, and so forth. Any number of topics can be handled in this manner.

2. The members of each group can study together for a test or work together to complete an assignment.

3. The group can complete a short-term group project such as a brief skit, a description of a scene, a collage, or a small-group discussion. Each member receives a group grade.

Kagan (1985), in his book *Cooperative Learning: Resources for Teachers*, describes a highly structured cooperative learning system consisting of team building, management techniques, and rewards based on a fairly complex system of points. However, some teachers might prefer to downplay behavioristic goals (points and other extrinsic motivational devices) and concentrate on humanistic goals (personal development and respect for others). In spite of the claims made for cooperative learning in its unadulterated forms, it has been my experience that similar results can be had by focusing on the development of intrinsic motivation through the natural reward of a simple smile or a genuine compliment.[6]

PLANNING LESSONS

At beginning to low-intermediate levels it is important to ensure that the same concepts are reinforced over and over using different activities in different situations. Too often inexperienced teachers present concepts once and then let them drop, never to be returned to again.

In the example on page 261, rhyming words are reinforced through the following jazz chant constructed by the teacher and used as a follow-up:

How does the toad stew feel?
Slimy and sticky?
    Yes!
    Slimy and sticky.
Squishy and icky?
    Yes!

---

[6]Sometimes the less structured versions are referred to in the literature as *collaborative learning* rather than *cooperative learning;* other times the two are used interchangeably.

> Squishy and icky.
> Is that how it feels?
> Is that how it feels?
>> Yes!
> That's how it feels.
> That's how it feels.

Students clap or snap their fingers to the beat.

In another activity, pictures of insects are taped to the walls and the students write a group paragraph, language experience style (see pages 203–206). Much later, students might create simple poetry about insects, using the rhyming words (see Chapter 9).

It is important that teachers remain flexible in planning the content of their units. Some of the best lessons teachers have will be those spontaneous ones that grow out of a special need or interest that presents itself at the moment.

Concerning the structure of lessons, Wong-Fillmore (1985) concludes that teacher lessons that are consistent, are well-organized, and have similar formats with clear beginnings and endings appear to be most effective. Familiar routines provide a sort of "scaffold" for the learning of new materials.[7]

The routine outlined below in Lesson Format 1 is similar to the plan described by Madelyn Hunter and Douglas Russell (1977) for classroom lessons but with an *important difference*.

Lesson Format 1

1. PERSPECTIVE (OPENING)

Address the following questions when appropriate:

> What have you learned to do? (previous activity)
> What concepts have you learned? (previous activity)
> How does it make you feel? Proud of yourself? More confident?

Give a preview of possibilities for the new lesson.

2. STIMULATION

The following are a few options:

> Pose a question to get students thinking about the coming activity and the major concepts involved.

---

[7] Her conclusion is based on a study she did with colleagues at the University of California at Berkeley. They observed the input given in thirty kindergarten through fifth-grade classrooms over a five-year period. In addition, she observed and recorded teachers in another ten classrooms in which there were Limited English Proficient (LEP) students.

Help the students to relate the activity to their lives and to their prior knowledge. Begin with an attention grabber: an anecdote, a little scene acted out by peer teachers or lay assistants (see pages 265–270), a picture, or a song.
Use it as a lead into the activity.

3. INSTRUCTION/PARTICIPATION PHASE (TEACHER/STUDENT CONTRIBUTIONS)

Below are examples:

Read and discuss the story or poem, sing the song or have it sung, do the jazz chant, search for the issues, agree upon expectations, check for understanding, divide into groups, and so on. Encourage student involvement to the largest extent possible, depending on the student's emerging capabilities in the target language.

4. CLOSURE

Address these questions when they are appropriate:

What did you learn?
How did you feel about doing the activities?

Give a preview of the possibilities for future lessons. Get student input.

5. FOLLOW-UP

Use other activities to reinforce the same concepts and introduce new ones.
Give students the opportunity to do independent work in class or as homework.

Whereas the original Hunter-Russell model appeared to be highly teacher-centered and teacher-controlled, this model allows for greater student input and participation.[8] As the students gain competence, they can gradually take on a larger role in choosing the content and even in the structure of the lessons themselves.

Note that some elements of the lessons will be downplayed and others emphasized depending upon the situation and upon the proficiency levels of the students. For instance, a full development of the Perspective would probably not be appropriate for preproduction students because not much of it would be understood unless it were given in the primary language. Nor would it be appropriate for young children. Simple statements such as, "I think you know what watercolors are. It will be fun to see what you do with them," would be sufficient. On the other hand, fully developed, highly comprehensible instructions during the Instruction/Participation Phase would be very appropriate for preproduction students and young children. Furthermore, the teacher should keep in mind that students will probably at first not understand

---

[8] The same type of plan can be used by peer teachers and lay assistants for their work with small groups and individuals.

every word in the lesson. Nor should they expect to understand every word. It takes time and many passes through similar structures and concepts to acquire the target language.

For teachers who prefer to use a type of lesson plan that requires detailed and focused preparation prior to the lesson and that leaves the description of the lesson completely open, the lesson format below presents an alternative. It is one I developed for my students at California State University, Los Angeles. The particular lesson used as an example here was adapted from one given to me by Elsa Ortega, a student.[9]

Lesson Format 2

USING THE FIVE SENSES

Name of Student: _Elsa Ortega_
Age level: _teenagers or adults_

Date: _October, 20_
Proficiency level: _high-beginning to low-intermediate_

Concepts introduced: Concepts introduced by the students themselves as part of the language experience portion of the lesson (for some, the concepts will be new; for others they will be recycled—see next item below); the poetic format demonstrated in the lesson; punctuation and capitalization as it is often (but not always) found in poems.

Concepts recycled: A rather extensive range of emotions: happiness, sadness, loneliness, excitement, pride, anger, peacefulness, jealousy, envy, hatred, etc., and the five senses: sight, sound, taste, smell, and touch.

Behaviors expected as a result of this lesson: Students should be able to demonstrate the understanding of the concepts introduced in the language experience portion of the lesson. They should be able to use with relative ease the poetic format demonstrated, including the way it is usually punctuated, with appropriate elements capitalized.

Materials needed: Several large pictures showing people in situations in which strong emotions are likely to be felt; a white board or chalkboard; a felt-tip pen or chalk; paper (for students), unless they are expected to use their own; thick, medium, and thin felt-tip pens in different colors, and/or brushes, and paints for artwork.

Description of the activity:
1. Review the recycled emotions mentioned above by showing the students the pictures of people in different situations likely to bring about strong emotions (i.e., a teenage girl at the store who can't get the attention of the sales clerk, a child handing his sick dog to a veterinarian, an old man hugging an old woman, etc.)

---

[9]Note that the Hunter/Russell version presented earlier could be easily incorporated in the "Description of the Activity" by those liking its structure.

As students mention various emotions, write them in noun form on the board for all to see.

2. Ask the students if they remember what the five senses are. Write them on the board.
3. Tell students that they are to help you write a poem about an emotion using the following format (found in *Scholastic Action*, September, 1984, p. 23):

Title: Name of the emotion
line 1: What color is the emotion?
line 2: What does it sound like?
line 3: What does it taste like?
line 4: What does it smell like?
line 5: What does it look like?
line 6: How does it make you feel?

4. Choose an emotion that the students are not likely to choose. Using elements of language experience (see pages 203–206), write a poem with the students following the above format.
5. Ask each student to choose an emotion and write a poem using the same format (write the format on the board if you have not already done so). They may work with a partner if they so choose.

Strategies used to check for understanding: Can the students talk about the various emotions? Do they show a clear understanding of them in their poems? Do they show an understanding of the format and why they are or are not following it exactly (some may choose to vary the format)? Do they demonstrate in their own poems that they understand appropriate use of punctuation and capitalization, even though they may deviate from it for a logical reason (poetry allows for deviation more than other genres)?

Follow-up lesson(s):
1. Ask each student to complete pieces of art work to accompany their poems. If they choose instead, they may cut pictures out of old magazines to accompany their poems.
2. Have them share their poems in small groups. Later ask volunteers to share their poems with the whole class.

Self-evaluation of the lesson:

Below are a few poems written by Elsa's students as a result of this lesson.

Pride

Pride is the brightest red.
It sounds like 1,000,000 trumpets playing.
Pride tastes like turkey,
And smells like the prettiest rose.
Pride looks like a person holding his head up high.

Greg Barela

Happiness

Happiness is a colorful rainbow in the sky.
It sounds like people cheering.
It tastes like soft, sugary cotton candy,
And it smells like jasmine blooming at night.
Happiness looks like people dancing.
It makes you feel good.

Heather McBrian

THEME CYCLES

One of the most interesting ways of organizing curriculum that has come to my attention since the first edition of *Making It Happen* is called *theme cycles*. In this approach the traditional "lesson plan" as we know it is virtually obsolete. The lesson plan associated with theme cycles represents a negotiated effort on the part of both the teacher and the students. Of course, students must be proficient enough in the target language to participate in the first place. Theme cycles would probably work best with students operating at intermediate and advanced levels.

Theme cycles present not just a general topic as a label around which isolated lessons in math, science, social studies, etc., and their related skills revolve; instead the topic is a subject for genuine investigation. During this investigation, students use math, science, social studies, and so forth, as knowledge bases from which to draw. The process begins with an investigation that evolves into a negotiated curricular plan. Questions lead to more questions that lead to even more questions and further investigation. Thus the curriculum is constructed in a joint effort between the students and the teacher.

Harste, Short, and Burke (1988) outline procedures for curriculum development using theme cycles. I summarize them below:

1. Both teachers and students make a list of topics that interest them. The two lists are blended by mutual agreement to form the basic curriculum plan.
2. Through negotiation, one topic is selected as a starting point.
3. A web or chart is made identifying "What We Know" and "What We Want to Know" about the topic.

The authors use a web around "plants" as the topic for their example. I will use a chart (see Figure 14.4) to illustrate the same thing using the topic Space.

Topic: Space

What We Know	What We Want To Know
Mars, Venus, and Jupiter are planets in space. Neil Armstrong and Sally Ride are astronauts. The sun is a star. The moon revolves around the earth.	What else is there in space? What is the sun made of? How do you become an astronaut? How is it possible to revolve around another object without falling?

Figure 14.4

4. Students and teachers develop a list of resources: books, people to interview, places to visit, etc.
5. Students choose the questions in the "What We Want to Know" column that are the most pressing.
6. With the help of the teacher, students become involved in whole group, small-group, and individual learning activities to explore the questions selected.
7. New questions are added to the chart as new discoveries are made.
8. At the end of particular segments of study, students present what they have found out to one another.
9. Other charts such as the one above are created. And so the process continues.

The authors stress the importance of building a supportive classroom environment before trying to negotiate curriculum. Throughout the process, the teacher acts as a facilitator to ensure its being carried out successfully.

ADAPTING THE CONTENT

Most of the activities recommended in this book can be adapted to almost any age level. Following is an example of how an affective activity (see Chapter 13) developed for use with adults can be modified for use with children. At both levels the students are grouped into pairs. The responses are timed so all students have a chance to express themselves on each item.

Adapting for Age

Describe how you feel when . . .

> *For adults* (late speech emergence stage)
>   someone gives you a compliment.

you are late for a meeting at which you are the speaker.

your boss asks you to work four extra hours and you are very tired.

you receive an all expenses paid vacation to the Bahamas.

For children (late speech emergence stage)

your friend says you have a nice smile.

your teacher scolds you for coming late to class.

your favorite movie is on TV and your mother tells you to go to bed.

someone offers to treat you to a chocolate sundae.

Some activities can be easily modified for different proficiency levels. For example, in the activity below the students are going on a treasure hunt through the local newspaper. The first group of treasures is for students at beginning levels, the second is for students at intermediate levels. See descriptions of the levels on pages 99–100.

Adapting for Proficiency Level

LOW- TO MID-BEGINNING LEVELS

Directions (should be given orally and demonstrated): *You are going on a treasure hunt. You will use the pictures in a newspaper. See how many pictures of these things you can find. Cut out the pictures.*

Find something . . .

small

soft

made of glass

square

short

narrow

heavy

sticky

longer than a pencil

MID- TO HIGH-INTERMEDIATE LEVELS

Directions (can be given orally, in written form or both): *Go on a treasure hunt in the local newspaper. Find pictures of the items and cut them out. Paste them on a piece of paper. Write the name of the category above each picture. For example, you are asked to find something that looks comfortable. You might cut out the picture of a bed. Paste it on your paper. Write the words "something that looks comfortable" above it.*

Find something . . .

that tastes good.
that has a pleasing smell.
that can be harmful or even dangerous.
that is a good buy.
that is durable.
that is accurate.
that you would like to buy.

Find something that is used . . .

to beautify something.
to control something.
to change something.

In the first version of the activity, the items are very concrete and simple; in the second version they are more abstract. Modifications can also be made in the content depending upon various interests, background, goals, and so forth.

SUMMARY

Developing a methodology for both second- and foreign-language classrooms involves the synthesis of theory and practice into a program that works. It generally means drawing from several methods and activities in order to create an integrated curriculum that will meet the needs of the students and the situation. Integrative and/or instrumental goals, the particular concepts being taught, learning and teaching preferences, cultural factors, and age and competency levels of the students are all important considerations.

For beginners and low-intermediate students in particular, lessons need to be structured in such a way that students will receive optimal exposure to important concepts. The lessons should be well organized and contain familiar routines in order to serve adequately as vehicles for new information. Content needs to be modified to be appropriate for various age and proficiency levels. For intermediate and advanced students, theme cycles that require greater proficiency in the target language may offer the most challenges for both students and their teachers.

Peer teachers and other assistants can be trained to help the teacher provide sufficient amounts of comprehensible input, self-image enhancement, encouragement, motivation, and opportunity for negotiating meaning. At the same time, they can serve as linguistic models to help prevent early fossilization. In addition, the peer teachers and other assistants can help make it possible for students to move from cognitively undemanding tasks to more demanding ones and to integrate the four skill areas as they flow with the students' needs and interests.

Versions of cooperative learning also can serve as effective classroom management tools, particularly in intermediate to advanced second-language classes or in mainstream content-area classes in which ESL students are included. Students can make substantial strides in communicative and academic competence through cooperative efforts.

READINGS, REFLECTION, AND DISCUSSION

Suggested Readings and Reference Materials

Bassano, S. and Christison, M. A. (1995). *Community spirit: A practical guide to collaborative language learning.* San Francisco, C.A.: Alta Book Center. This book highlights practical ideas and strategies for creating student-centered classrooms.

Brinton, D., Snow, M. A., and Wesche, M. (1992). *Content-based second language instruction.* New York: Newbury House. Here the authors explore content-based teaching in its many contexts at the university level. Program models are described in-depth and guidelines are given to those interested in developing content-based language programs.

Hill, S. and Hill, T. (1990). *The collaborative classroom: A guide to co-operative learning.* Portsmouth, N.H.: Heinemann. Offers a comprehensive discussion of collaborative learning and its benefits. It includes suggestions for forming groups, problem solving, assessment options, and many other related issues.

Kessler, C., ed. (1992). *Cooperative language learning: A teacher's resource book.* Englewood Cliffs, N.J.: Prentice Hall Regents. This book describes the theory and research supporting cooperative learning and how it can be used in second-language instruction that is content-based. Sample lessons and activities are presented.

Legutke, M., and Thomas, H. (1991). *Process and experience in the language classroom.* London: Longman. In this book, communicative project-tasks are considered "building bricks" to proficiency in the target language in experiential classrooms. In such classrooms, a teacher has many roles: coordinator and facilitator, manager and organizer, instructor, investigator, and researcher.

McGroarty, M. (1992). Cooperative learning: The benefits for content-area teaching. In P. Richard-Amato and M. A. Snow, eds. *The multicultural classroom: Reading for content-area teachers.* White Plains, N.Y.: Longman, pp. 58–69. Here the author describes and supports with empirical research the linguistic, social, and curricular benefits of cooperative learning. She emphasizes the pedagogical advantages that can be realized once teachers let go of their traditional authority and become facilitators in the learning process.

Nunan, D. (1991). Communicative tasks and the language curriculum. *TESOL Quarterly* 25(2), 279–295. A comprehensive look at task-based instruction including its justification, examples of its implementation, and the research supporting its use.

Richard-Amato, P. (1992). Peer teachers: The neglected resource. In P. Richard-Amato and M. A. Snow, eds. *The multicultural classroom: Readings for content-area teachers.* White

Plains, N.Y.: Longman, pp. 271–284. Presents guidelines for the preparation and use of peer teachers, alternative models, and related research.

Questions for Reflection and Discussion

1. Find or create a lesson that is oriented to a particular age group and adapt it to another age group. Doing the same for proficiency level, modify a lesson intended for one proficiency level (beginning, intermediate, or advanced) to make it appropriate for another. What problems needed to be considered in completing each task?

2. Plan a workshop for a small group of peer teachers and other assistants. What important preparation will you want them to have?

3. Can you think of a few units for which you might want to incorporate some version of cooperative learning? Briefly describe how these units might be organized.

4. Develop a complete unit for a hypothetical or real second-language classroom situation.[10] After considering your students' goals, decide what major concepts you will teach and reinforce throughout. Describe the unit, including a few lessons in which several methods and activities are integrated. Develop fully one of the lessons utilizing a structure similar to one of those outlined on pages 273–278. Try it out with the members of your class. Make sure you state clearly the situation, the proficiency and age levels for which it is intended, and how it fits into your unit. Ask the members of your class for feedback.

---

[10] Situations might be one of the following: An elementary, secondary, or university second- or foreign-language program, an adult basic education program, or a language program for special purposes such as preparing students for specific technical occupations, and so forth.

CHAPTER 15

Tools of the Trade: Textbooks, Computer Programs, and Videos

> *. . . part of the task of selection, then, becomes the selection of segments of real world knowledge and experience . . .*
>
> R. Crymes, 1979

QUESTIONS TO THINK ABOUT

1. Think back on the textbooks you may have used when you were trying to learn another language. Describe them. Upon what did they focus? To what extent were they effective in furthering your own interlanguage development?

2. In what ways do you think computers might be used in a second- or foreign-language classroom? What types of programs would you be most likely to use as a teacher? Why?

3. Do you think videos might have a place in the second- or foreign-language classroom? If so, what types of videos would you use? How would you use them?

Many different kinds of materials have been suggested throughout this book. Most of them have been materials not specifically intended for second-language teaching, such as television programs on videotape; newspapers and periodicals, stories and other pieces of literature; catalogs; games; reference books of several kinds; lyrics to popular songs; maps; pictures; and others. They have included both teacher- and student-made materials. Commercial products especially designed for second-language teaching can be just as useful if chosen carefully.

It is not the purpose of this chapter to advocate specific textbooks, computer programs, or videos. Rather the chapter will emphasize the considerations that must be taken into account in making prudent decisions concerning these teaching tools.

TEXTBOOKS

Some teachers and many publishers long for the days when one set of materials (complete with student texts, cassettes, workbooks, and teacher manuals) was considered to be the answer to language teaching needs. Today, although many still cling to that dream, most realize that much more is needed to build a program. Because of the shift in emphasis to interactional approaches, pressure is being placed on publishers to provide the kinds of materials that are communicative and logically motivated, whether they be large programs with multiple components or materials that teachers themselves have developed, that are supplemental to programs. Moreover, many are insisting that the materials require a larger, more active and creative role on the part of teachers and students, and that they focus on relevant, meaningful content. Some teachers are even turning entrepreneur and publishing their own materials in an attempt to fill the gap. Perhaps at this point, we need to address the question of what kind of input found in textbooks is most likely to promote language acquisition. In answer to this question, Oller (1983a) offers the Episode Hypothesis.

The Episode Hypothesis

This hypothesis states that *"text (i.e., discourse in any form) will be easier to reproduce, understand, and recall, to the extent that it is motivated and structured episodically"* (1983a, p. 12). Episodic organization requires both motivation created by conflict and the logical sequencing that is necessary to good storytelling and consistent with experience. Thus a text may be structured temporally but not necessarily episodically.

As mentioned earlier, Schank and Abelson (1977) relate episodic structure to memory itself. It is their view that humans both acquire and store information in episodic form.

Oller agrees and goes one step further by applying this theory to the classroom:

Language programs that employ fully contextualized and maximally meaningful language necessarily optimize the learner's ability to use previously
acquired expectancies to help discover the pragmatic mappings of utterances
in the new language into extralinguistic contexts. Hence they would seem to
be superior to programs that expect learners to acquire the ability to use a
language on the basis of disconnected lists of sentences (1979, pp. 31–32).

Yet many ESL and foreign-language texts written over the years have contained disconnected lists of sentences or, at best, sentences that were related but
were not part of any motivated or logical interaction.

Consider the following example from a typical ESL text. It consists of a
group of items related only in that each illustrates the same grammatical form.

Example 1

1. We're *having* a grammar test today.
2. Bob *is having* a party tomorrow.
3. The Smiths *are having* a good time in Paris.
4. My sister *is having* a baby in June.

(Pollock, 1982, p. 7)

Or read the next typical passage, which is temporally structured but lacks
sufficient motivation or conflict as well as logical sequencing.

Example 2

Tomás is visiting Ralph and Lucy.

RALPH: How long can you stay, Tomás?
TOMÁS: I'm going to leave tomorrow afternoon. I'm taking the bus.
LUCY: I like taking the bus, but Ralph doesn't.
RALPH: What do you want to do tomorrow, Tomás? Do you want to sleep late?
TOMÁS: No, I like to get up early. Let's go to the park. Do you like playing tennis?
RALPH: I don't like to play, but Lucy likes tennis. She plays every day.
LUCY: Ralph likes jogging. Let's go to the park early tomorrow morning. Tomás and
I can play tennis, and you can go jogging. Ralph . . .

(Sutherland. 1981, p. 11)

Compare the first two examples with the following example.

Example 3

DARLENE: I think I'll call Bettina's mother. It's almost five and Chrissy isn't home yet.
MEG: I thought Bettina had the chicken pox.
DARLENE: Oh, that's right. I forgot. Chrissy didn't go to Bettina's today. Where is she?
MEG: She's probably with Gary. He has Little League practice until five.
DARLENE: I hear the front door. Maybe that's Gary and Chrissy.
GARY: Hi.

DARLENE: Where's Chrissy? Isn't she with you?

GARY: With me? Why with me? I saw her at two after school, but then I went to Little League practice. I think she left with her friend.

DARLENE: Which one?

GARY: The one next door . . . the one she walks to school with every day.

DARLENE: Oh, you mean Timmy. She's probably with him.

GARY: Yeah, she probably is.

DARLENE: I'm going next door to check.

(Brinton and Neuman, 1982, p. 33)

Which of these three examples of input would have the best chance for becoming internalized? Of course, the answer would have to be Example 3. It captivates our interest through its episodic organization.

Below are posed a few questions concerning the three examples to reinforce the importance of episodically meaningful text.

Questions for Example 1

1. Who is having a good time in Paris?
2. Who is having a party tomorrow?

These questions are impossible to answer without referring back to the text. Why? In looking back at the words themselves, we realize that the *Smiths* are having a good time in Paris and that *Bob* is having a party tomorrow. But these people are not important to us in that they do not connect meaningfully to our experience, nor do they connect in any meaningful way to each other. They are not part of any conflict and thus they remain unmotivated. They have made little impression and are not easily remembered.

Questions for Example 2

1. Who is visiting?
2. What does the visitor plan to do?
3. Who likes to ride on buses?
4. What does Lucy like to do?
5. Who likes jogging?

The above questions, even though the sentences to which they refer are temporally related and perhaps slightly motivated, are just as difficult to answer as those for Example 1. Why? They are not logical according to our experience. Their only reason for existence seems to be to expose the student to the present progressive tense and to gerunds and to teach the comparative structure "I like taking the bus, but Ralph doesn't" or "I don't like to play, but Lucy likes tennis." People in normal conversation do not speak in this fashion; there is no reason for doing so considering that in natural discourse we are not concerned with exposing others to specific grammatical forms.

In addition to there being no justification for the discourse other than a grammatical one, there is little logic in the flow of the conversation. When Tomás says, "I'm going to leave tomorrow afternoon, I'm taking the bus," one would expect either Lucy or Ralph to say something like "Oh, you're leaving so soon" or at least comment on the leaving. Instead, Lucy says, "I like taking the bus, but Ralph doesn't." Thus our sense of expectancy is violated. Grice (1975) relates this sense of expectancy to the maxim of relation that is essential in normal discourse.

Questions for Example 3

1. Who has disappeared?
2. When was she last seen?
3. Where are they going to look for her?
4. How do the characters feel about her disappearance?

Here we are more apt to remember the details. Why? The structuring is consistent with our own experience, and the dialogue is motivated and logical. Because these requirements are met, we automatically become involved with the language at a subconscious as well as conscious level. We experience a heightened awareness. We become concerned with the little girl's disappearance just as the people in the story are concerned.

Although the Episode Hypothesis is universal in that it is based on the logic of experience, that experience will reflect the culture of which it is a part. The frames of experience in a particular selected text may, in some cases, be unfamiliar. For example, a certain dialogue may not occur in a given culture. Some human concerns will be different. Deciding upon the best nursing home in which to place an elderly parent may be unheard of in a culture in which extended families are the norm. Culturally determined schemata is one important reason to use prereading activities in the second- or foreign-language classroom. (See also Chapters 4 and 12.)

Selection Considerations

Below are some good questions to ask when examining textbooks, supplemental or otherwise. It is assumed here that the main goal is to learn and communicate in the target language.

1. Is the target language generally considered the *means for learning and communicating* about some topic of interest, or is the language itself predominantly the *content* to be studied and analyzed? If the language *is* the main content, then you might want to look for something more motivating and more comprehensible, especially at beginning to intermediate levels.

2. Are the grammatical structures allowed to exist naturally as a result of the content or is the content determined by which grammatical structure is being studied?

3. To what extent are the students encouraged to relate the content to their own lives and to their prior knowledge?

4. Are the materials appropriate to the language needs, age, and interests of the students with whom they are to be used? Consider content, illustrations, activities, formality of the language, and so on.

5. Is the discourse motivated and logical according to human experience?

6. Is the input comprehensible? Consider here the proficiency levels of the students with whom the materials will be used. Does the input gradually become more complex?

7. Are concepts recycled several times or are they introduced and quickly forgotten?

8. Do the materials foster reduced anxiety and a positive self-image?

   a. Are students allowed to develop their interlanguage normally (through the use of indirect correction) or are they expected to produce correct language right from the beginning? This is particularly important for activities involving oral production.

   b. Are the directions clearly presented to prevent needless frustration?

   c. Will the activities enhance self-concepts and boost confidence?

   d. Do the materials promote positive attitudes toward the various cultures, including the target language culture?

   e. Are the materials relatively free of sexual bias?

9. Do the activities encourage use of creative language and negotiated meaning in a variety of situations?

10. Are the skill areas integrated to a large extent or do they seem to be approached as separate entities? (See Chapter 14.)

11. Do the activities involve a wide variety of tasks appropriate to the objectives of the students?

12. Do the questions intended for high beginning to advanced students call for thinking and reflection or are they usually probes for factual, often irrelevant detail?

13. Do the materials intended for intermediate to advanced students become increasingly more challenging academically?

Sometimes the titles of textbooks are misleading and can lure one into believing that the content is generally communicative in nature. Catchy titles, those that imply a cast of characters, and those containing the words "communicative" or "communication" are not always what they appear to be. Often these books are grammar- or function-based texts disguised to look communicative. It pays to scrutinize them carefully before ordering them for student use.

COMPUTER PROGRAMS

Much of the software used in computer-assisted language learning (CALL) programs has been of the drill and test variety. The computer plays the role of the "teacher" and imparts information. The students generally apply the information (often a rule) and then are tested. Those who fail to make the right choices on the test are cycled back for further instruction and application. The teacher may wish to use an authoring system, which makes it possible to set up similar lessons by learning special commands for that purpose. The teacher may choose to use the already established content or may opt for making additions or other modifications by selecting items from a series of possible choices. He or she also may have the option of creating new content for the program.

Although discrete point programs may be appropriate at times, they can simply become one more means for perpetuating the dreariness of discrete point exercises, confining the student to endless branching menus of boredom. Papert (1980), Jamieson and Chapelle (1984), Canale and Barker (1986), and Chun and Brandl (1992) are among those who stress the importance of using computer programs that instead have a highly integrative rather than discrete point focus. For example, there are simulation programs in which students can take fantasy trips and choose, from among many options, where to go, what to eat, and so forth. There are interfacing programs in which students can hear prerecorded messages and interact with the computer by pressing particular keys or touching certain areas of the screen. There are programs in which the students are asked questions to clarify their thinking about essays that are in the planning stages. There are programs in which the students can create and illustrate stories by using graphics. There are programs that enable students to write poetry, sometimes with line-by-line assistance for special patterns (rhymes, limericks, haiku, etc.). And there are programs featuring test-taking and problem-solving strategies.

Canale and Barker suggest that by incorporating integrative programs, the computers can serve many of the same purposes for which language itself is used. Such programs can be used as tools for thought (self-directed language), tools for social interaction (other-directed language), and tools for play and art in which the emphasis is on self-expression. They are convinced that the activities should be intrinsically motivating, provide for the autonomy of the language student, and involve problem solving in many different situations.

Perhaps the most readily available integrative programs on the market today involve word processors, computer networks, games, and programming/problem-solving tools.

Word Processors

Writing on a word processor is sometimes frustrating, often exhilarating, and always challenging to the second-language student. The language used is fully contextualized and creative. Perhaps the best time for the students to begin is at late beginner/early intermediate levels. At that point they have acquired a repertoire (however limited) of language structures and vocabulary. Children, too, provided they can handle the experience cognitively, are able to work on word processors, especially if the programs are designed with them in mind. Some programs use extra large characters on the screen and the menu choices are pictorial in order that they be more easily comprehended.

Students seem to learn best when they are eased into the process gradually with the aid of the teacher, peer teachers, other assistants, or other students. One way to begin, especially for a student who has never been introduced to a computer before, is to type something on the keyboard about the student that he or she can comprehend. The student's name might be used in the message. The student can then respond verbally while the teacher or aide types the words as they are said. The student can eventually proceed from the comprehending and writing of very short messages to fully developed text. The necessary commands can be learned gradually over a period of time.

Some programs, usually called "writing aids," are specifically designed to guide the writer through the preliminary stages of writing. For example, a few programs ask a series of questions to aid the students in targeting the purpose for a specific composition. Other programs enable students to exchange information and react to one another's ideas through a networking system called "electronic mail" (e-mail). Caution should be taken, however, with programs that give general reactions to student efforts such as "How interesting!" or "Nice job!" regardless of what has actually been written. Other programs to be wary of are those that accuse students of being "wordy" if the sentences are too long or of being "unclear" if the ratio of nouns to verbs is too high. Parkhurst (1984) feels that such programs may focus the student on mechanics at the expense of meaning or may make the student overly concerned with sentence length as opposed to clarity.

In most programs, files can be created in which ideas are stored. In some systems these files can be brought into full view on one part of the screen while the students are composing on the remaining area.

Being able to delete material, move whole passages to other parts of a document, select and change formats at will, write and send messages, and perform numerous other functions does much to facilitate the writing process.

Computer Networks

Computer networks can provide an important means for communicating with fellow students in the target language. Nancy Sullivan (1993) describes her two-year experience working in the computer-assisted writing laboratory at the University of Texas at Austin with both native and nonnative speakers of English. She reports that

> ESL students are often hesitant to speak out in class because of shyness, inse-
> curity about being understood, or cultural reasons. . . . In this setting, how-
> ever, students who needed more time to form responses were able to present
> their opinions and to interact more easily. In short, in our electronic discus-
> sions, all the students were able to participate actively (p. 34).

It was her feeling that her students were less threatened in this situation than they would have been had they been expected to speak out loud in front of peers and teachers. Their electronic discussions allowed them to initiate and/or extend their discussions about whatever it was that they happened to be studying or doing as a result of assigned work. For example, students may discuss a poem that each of them had just read or a paper they were working on. Each comment they offered or question asked was transmitted, along with each person's name, on the computer screens of all the students in each small group of four or five. Students often collaborated while responding to and cri-tiquing each other's papers and they negotiated meaning during problem-solving activities.

Many of the same kinds of activities are included in Soh Bee-Lay and Soon Yee-Ping's description of a networking exchange between ESL and EFL stu-dents in Singapore and Quebec (1991). Using CALL, electronic mail, tele-phones, and fax machines, the students exchanged opinions on self-selected topics. They shared cultural stories and other pieces of literature and created an abundance of written work related to what they were reading. The two educa-tors concluded that the exchanges were highly motivating and helped the stu-dents gain insights into a world vastly different from their own.

Games

Computer games, although not usually meant for second-language teaching *per se*, are one means for providing the language learners with challenges in the target language. They can present simulations that call for the students to make decisions and they can require interaction with others involved in the game. Computer games are currently available in many areas: math, science, language arts, and so forth. For example, one company puts out a math pro-gram that introduces children to the concepts number lines, number pairs, and graph plotting. The students are asked to plot their own designs. Another pro-gram takes students on a simulated safari journey through a grid-like envi-ronment where they decipher clues in order to find the hiding place of a "mystery" animal. In the process they get practice in making inferences, creat-ing tactics, and collecting and organizing clues. Other kinds of computer games include chess, word games, memory games, teasers with missing num-bers, and many more.

Programming/Problem-Solving Tools

Some programs immerse the learner in a wide variety of problem-solving strategies. Some even have features that allow the student to "teach the computer" to complete a task. For example, there is the still popular "turtle graphics" using Logo, a computer language first developed as a means by which children could discover concepts, especially in math and geometry. The tasks involve programming the behavior of a small triangle (the "turtle"). The turtle can be taught to draw different shapes and objects through a series of simple commands. Students are stimulated to interact as they discuss, write out, and modify their plans.

Canale and Barker see today's Logo programs mainly as prototypes of the more intelligent systems to come. Among the drawbacks of many of the versions of Logo currently available are a limited working memory, lack of a help-menu feature, difficult error messages, and low operating speed. However, they feel that even with the limitations, the programs are well suited to the needs of second-language learners.

VIDEOS

Videos, too, can be a valuable tool for language acquisition and in the case of interactive video, it can combine both computer and video benefits. Interactive video requires a videodisc player and a computer setup that includes a monitor, a keyboard for giving input, and a microcomputer. In addition, an interface is needed to connect the videodisc player to the computer.

Among its more meaningful uses is its ability to show real people in compelling scenarios like soap operas that enable the learner to have input. For example, a married couple on the screen may be engrossed in an argument about whether or not their teenaged daughter should take a trip to Lake Tahoe with a girlfriend. Arguments fly back and forth. Finally, one of the characters turns to the student and asks for help in forming a solution. Several choices are flashed on the monitor, and the student has to press the button representing his or her choice. One character then comments on the advice and the scenario continues. If all else fails, the character may even seek advice from the "expert tutor" who is part of the computer program.

Another use of interactive video is to teach the listening skills necessary for academic success. A videodisc lecture is presented on some topic of interest. The student presses a key whenever he or she hears what appears to be a main idea. At the end of the lecture, all the main ideas are printed on the monitor and the student is asked to form questions using the ideas. As soon as a question is formed, the program returns to the speaker, who answers the question. Of course, one problem that seems apparent is the matching of questions to answers. There is a strong possibility that the student will want to ask questions for which the speaker has no answers.

Finally, a video disk can also be used as a dictionary. All the student needs to do is type a word onto the keyboard. The computer first checks for spelling and perhaps presents the student with alternative words from which to choose if there has been an error. On the videodisc, a speaker then demonstrates the use of the word in a context. In addition, the word is printed on the screen in a sample sentence.

These are only a few of the possible uses of interactive video. Many programs are just now being developed for second-language students and should be on the market soon.

Video without the computer can work as well as text in the second-language acquisition process. Lessons can be planned around it just as one might plan lessons around a piece of literature (see especially Chapter 12). The text could be a drama such as a Hollywood movie, a television soap opera, or a situation comedy.

Other kinds of lessons could be built around music videos, nonfiction documentaries, television talk shows, sports highlights, or television commercials (see in particular Stempleski and Tomlin, 1990).

SUMMARY

The Episode Hypothesis argues that text that is motivated and structured episodically will be more easily incorporated into our linguistic repertoires than other kinds of text.

Many second-language textbooks, however, are written mainly to teach specific grammar points or structures without much thought given to what constitutes meaningful prose. This is not to say that "grammar" books as such should not be written, particularly if they are supplemental in nature. There is a place for such books (see especially pages 48–51). However, it seems reasonable that if textbooks are to capitalize maximally on our ability to acquire language, then they must engage our emotions as well as our intellects.

The selection of textbooks, computer programs, and videos is not a task that should be treated lightly. In order for these tools to be maximally useful, their substance and the activities they promote must reflect the basic philosophy of the teacher and the goals of the students. If the students' main goals are to communicate effectively and to learn subject matter in the target language, then tools must be chosen that are consistent with those objectives. This means that the materials must allow for active participation on the part of the learner and that the tasks must involve the use of natural language in meaningful contexts.

READINGS, REFLECTION, AND DISCUSSION

Suggested Readings and Reference Materials

The best from Sunburst. Pleasantville, N.Y.: Sunburst Communications. This is a catalog containing award-winning educational courseware for many kinds of computers. Strategies in problem solving seem to be the main thrust of its programs, which are oriented toward the following subject areas: math, social and natural sciences, language arts, and many more. The programs are in English only and are intended for preschool through adult levels.

Dunkel, P. (1991). *Computer-assisted language learning and testing: Research issues and practice*. New York: Newbury House. Research on the effectiveness of CALL, validity issues in research, social factors to consider, the effects of networking, and feedback strategies are just a few of the many topics covered in this book. Carol Chapelle, Joan Jamieson, Donna Johnson, Martha Pennington, Gail Robinson, Joyce Neu, Robin Scarcella, Grant Henning, and Marianne Phinney are among the many authors whose works are represented.

Jones, C., and Fortescue, S. (1987). *Using computers in the language classroom*. London: Longman. This guide is designed for language teachers who wish to incorporate computer use into their curriculum, but who are a bit hesitant due to a lack of experience with computers in general. It discusses the array of programs to choose from and includes the hardware and software commonly available.

Gessler: The foreign language experts. New York: Gessler Educational Software. Language teaching software in French, Spanish, German, Italian, Latin, and English is made available through this catalog. Games, simulations, crossword puzzles, and the more traditional grammar-focused programs are included.

Kenning, M. (1990). Computer assisted language learning. *Language Teaching*, 23(2), 67–76. This comprehensive article summarizes the literature and related research on computer-assisted language learning.

Oller, J., Jr. (1983b). Story writing principles and ESL teaching. *TESOL Quarterly*, 17(1), 39–53. This paper considers four hypotheses: the input hypothesis, the textuality hypothesis, the expectancy hypothesis, and the episode hypothesis. Their relationships are explored and practical applications are offered.

Schank, R., and Abelson, R. (1977). *Scripts, plans, goals, and understanding*. Hillsdale, N.J.: Lawrence Erlbaum. A highly theoretical inquiry into human cognitive structures as they relate to artificial intelligence. The authors in this seminal work examine such areas as memory, causal chains, and motivation.

Stempleski, S., and Tomalin, B. (1990). *Video in action: Recipes for using video in language teaching*. New York: Prentice Hall Regents. This book, the winner of the Duke of Edinburgh English Language Competition for 1990, presents how and when to use video effectively in language teaching. Also included are specific ideas for using video in the language classroom.

Questions for Reflection and Discussion

1. Locate at least three second-language or foreign-language textbooks and/or supplementary materials. Analyze them using appropriate criteria from the list presented toward the beginning of this chapter. Which materials would you select for use in a hypothetical or real teaching situation (see footnote on page 282)? Justify your choices.

2. Discuss how the following considerations might affect the teacher's choice of textbooks and other materials.

   a. the culture in which the materials are to be used
   b. size of the class
   c. experience of the teacher in teaching a second or foreign language
   d. proficiency level of the teacher in the target language

3. How might you incorporate the types of materials listed below into the classroom? Several suggestions for use have been mentioned throughout this book. You can probably think of many additional means for incorporation. Give specific examples.

   a. teacher-made materials
   b. student-made materials
   c. magazines and newspapers
   d. catalogs
   e. pictures and photographs
   f. television shows on video

4. Set up some criteria for rating examples from textbooks in terms of their episodic organization. Include additional aspects that you feel might heighten the awareness of the reader or listener. You might consider aspects of character development, dialogue, or literary devices of various kinds.

   Example:

	Yes or No
	(check one)
Are the characters believable?	_____ _____
Is the dialogue logical?	_____ _____
Is foreshadowing present?	_____ _____

   You might want to refine the ratings by giving numerical value to such categories as "usually," "sometimes," "never," and so on.

5. Using the language texts and other supplemental reading materials that are available to you, choose passages that can be looked at in terms of episodic structure. By rating them according to the criteria you've set up, determine which ones fare best.

6. How might a knowledge of the Episode Hypothesis help you other than in choosing texts and other reading materials? Consider the applicability of such knowledge to other situations used to create an acquisition-rich environment for your students.

7. If you have access to computers and computer software, select four programs for preview (they need not have been created specifically for language teaching). Which of the four would you select to use with your students? Justify your choices and explain how each might fit into your program, hypothetical or real.

CHAPTER **16**

Teaching through the Content Areas

The immersion programs have provided us with ample evidence that it is possible to develop academic and second language skills simultaneously. . . .

L. Wong-Fillmore, 1985

QUESTIONS TO THINK ABOUT

1. What does it mean to "teach through the content areas"? How important do you think it is to do so? Consider differences between second- and foreign-language teaching situations.

2. How might you go about incorporating subject-matter content into your own second- or foreign-language classes?

3. What problems do you think language minority students might have in mainstream classes such as history or science? If you were their second-language teacher, how would you help to prepare them for the transition to mainstream courses?

Cognitive Academic Language Proficiency (CALP) and Basic Interpersonal Communication Skills (BICS) (see Related Reading 4) are both important to the second-language student if he or she is to succeed in an academic environment. Doing well in academic or social settings in which students interact with and are accepted by educated people requires effective communication about a variety of subjects. The student must eventually have a command of the new language as it pertains to abstract thinking and problem solving. Whether the related skills are taught in self-contained classrooms in which a variety of subject areas are covered or in classrooms set up for the purpose of teaching specific subject matter, the lessons must be increasingly challenging academically and the environment must foster high self-esteem to be maximally effective.

Teachers of ESL and foreign languages can teach the target language through basic academic content, drawing from many of the methods and activities described in previous chapters. For example, elements of the total physical response might be used to teach math skills (Draw an octagon. Divide it in half with a vertical line) or to teach the commands associated with physical education (Line up. Count off by fours). The natural approach and its extensions can be used to demonstrate how to prepare a specific food for a meal or how to blend various colored paints for an art project. Jazz chants can be written about famous people in history or about concepts related to various sports. Here again the activities must make greater and greater cognitive demands upon the students in order that they may gain academic competence.

Once students are ready for higher levels within the content areas, they can be introduced to more difficult concepts through concrete approaches and can later progress to more abstract ones. For example, students might first be required to comprehend the intricacies involved in a science experiment by watching the teacher demonstrate and explain it. Following the demonstration, the students can be given specific oral directions (reminiscent of the total physical response) and do the experiment themselves. At an intermediate stage, students might be asked to perform experiments by using only written directions. Much later the students may be required to visualize similar experiments and write about what the results might be under various conditions.

It must be noted, before proceeding, that foreign-language classes are usually independent of the other subject areas in the public school or university and are limited to specific time slots unless, of course, they are part of immersion programs. On the other hand, English as a Second Language classes are often taught in conjunction with one or more content-area programs: a submersion program; an immersion program consisting of sheltered content-area classes; and/or a bilingual program.

SUBMERSION

Students whose first language is different from that of the school and community are often "submerged" in content-area classes in which they are a minority among native speakers. In submersion classrooms they find themselves at a disadvantage in not being given the comprehensible input they need, and they are often treated as intellectual inferiors. The teachers generally do not understand their languages and know very little about their cultures. A first language may be regarded as a hindrance (subtractive)[1] to a mastery of the second. The students may or may not have the opportunity to be tutored individually. Sometimes the students who have the option of being tutored are placed in what are known as "pull-out" programs[2] that frequently put them at an even greater disadvantage. They may miss concepts simply because they were not in class when the concepts were introduced. Submersion programs as a whole can be dangerous, especially for children, whose overall cognitive development may suffer as a result.

Mainstreaming for ESL students is a form of submersion but with a difference. Students are first placed in an ESL class. Once they become more socially and academically proficient in the target language, gradual transition is made to the regular content-area classes. Before they are mainstreamed into a regular class, the students are usually considered ready for entry by the ESL teacher and the content-area teacher into whose class they will be mainstreamed. They should have been introduced to the basic concepts involved and should have the skills necessary to function in the new environment. At first they may be placed in such classes as physical education, art, music, and math and later in the natural and social sciences. The subject matter for beginners during initial stages of transitioning is generally cognitively undemanding, the materials are context embedded, the content-area teacher is aware of the students' need for comprehensible input, and the atmosphere is one of acceptance rather than rejection.

Sometimes a mainstream class is paired with an *adjunct* course for non-English speakers (see especially Saint Michael's College International Center described on pages 314–320). In an adjunct course, students receive assistance with language and content learning from a language teacher who works in conjunction with the mainstream course instructor. So far, adjunct courses have only been attempted at the college/university levels, probably because schedules are generally less flexible in secondary schools.

---

[1] Lambert (1974) identifies two treatments of primary languages within a second language environment: subtractive and additive. A language is said to be *subtractive* when it is considered detrimental to the learning of the second language and *additive* when it is thought a beneficial adjunct.

[2] A pull-out program is one in which the students are taken out of their regular classes for certain portions of the day in order to receive special help with the target language.

IMMERSION

All immersion programs have at least one thing in common. The students are at *similar levels of proficiency* in their new language, meaning that they generally receive input specially tailored to their needs. There are two kinds of immersion programs: foreign-language programs and second-language programs (see also definitions on pages 255–256).

Foreign-Language Immersion

In foreign-language immersion programs, most (if not all) of the students are from the language majority population and are part of the dominant cultural group. They are placed in content-area classes in which a foreign language is the medium for communication. Usually the first language is added gradually later on for some of the subject-area content. An example would be the Thunder Bay French immersion program described on pages 360–364. In this program, all of the students are from English-speaking homes. In foreign-language immersion programs, the new language is additive and generally has the support of the parents and the community. Usually the parents have requested the program for their children and were often instrumental in setting up the program in the first place. The teacher is, in most cases, familiar with the students' first language and knows (and is often part of) their culture. All of these factors contribute to the high self-esteem often found in the students involved in such programs. These factors alone make foreign-language immersion programs for children much different from submersion programs in which children are at a disadvantage (they are often looked down upon because they are members of nondominant groups in the community; their teacher usually doesn't understand their language and often knows little about their culture). Affective advantages coupled with the cognitive benefit of modified input probably account for the significant difference in the results of both programs. Children thrive in foreign-language immersion programs (see studies in Chapter 2); in submersion programs they do not (see especially Cummins, 1981).

Second-Language Immersion

Second-language immersion is found in sheltered and adjunct classes. In these classes, the input is still adjusted to the students' needs, but their first languages and cultures are often very different (unlike foreign-language immersion). The students are considered part of the nondominant groups in the community even though their numbers may be greater than those of the dominant group. Their teacher may or may not be familiar with their first language and culture. However, the teacher is usually prepared in current language and content teaching methodology and often has some knowledge of the various language and cultural backgrounds of the students. ESL itself is an example of second-language immersion.

One of the problems that may occur as a result of an immersion program of any type is the fossilization of interlanguage forms due to a lack of sufficient contact with native or near-native speakers of the target language. However, the continued exposure to peer teachers (see pages 265–270), adult assistants, and peers from outside the classroom who are fluent in the target language will do much to prevent early fossilization from becoming a major problem.

BILINGUAL EDUCATION

Bilingual education can be used in conjunction with any of the above kinds of programs (see Related Reading 4). Bilingual education involves teaching the students in some combination of their first and second languages.

One bilingual education program that is receiving much attention recently is the two-way or dual program found in the San Diego City Schools, where Spanish and English are being learned. Two types of students are involved: Spanish-speaking children who begin their schooling in Spanish and who will eventually learn English, and English-speaking children who also begin their schooling in Spanish (similar to a foreign-language immersion program) and will eventually develop their English skills as well. The subject matter content is taught only in Spanish in grades 1–3. In grades 4–6, half of the content is taught in Spanish and the other half in English. However, English reading is begun in the second grade. It should be noted that the Spanish-speaking children are the majority in the program and so far, test results have focused only on them. Herbert (1987) compared the students who had been in the two-way bilingual program with students who had received ESL without bilingual education. Controlling for the factors ethnicity, sex, socioeconomic status, grade level, and the differences in pretest scores, Herbert found that the children in the two-way bilingual program did significantly better at all levels tested, grades 4–6, on the CTBS math and reading tests. Moreover, they were reclassified one year earlier on the average than their ESL-only counterparts.

An important factor to consider here may be not only that the Spanish-speaking children were able to begin with the language with which they were most comfortable (Spanish), but that they served as Spanish "models" for the English-speaking students, thereby helping to raise their self-esteem. Self-esteem is a critical factor that should not be overlooked when examining program effectiveness (see Chapter 5).

There are basically three types of bilingual education programs: transitional, maintenance, and enrichment. In *transitional* programs, students learn most of the subject matter in L1 until it is determined that they are ready (e.g., after considerable time spent in the ESL component of the program) to be gradually transitioned to all-English classes. In *maintenance* programs, students continue throughout their schooling to learn a portion of the subject matter in their

L1 in order to continue improving their L1 skills. *Enrichment* programs are foreign-language programs in which a portion of the subject matter is taught in L2, not for the purpose of immediate survival, but to broaden cultural horizons or in anticipation of some future move or visit to another culture.

Unfortunately, most of the bilingual education in the United States today is transitional. In other words, once the students have acquired a sufficient amount of the target language to survive, the bilingual component of their schooling is dropped. This is troublesome for two reasons: (1) the students often are not ready for academic mainstreaming, since their academic skills are not yet highly developed in the target language and (2) they will not be able to function with maximal effectiveness in our multicultural society, a society that *needs* people who are highly literate in more than one language.

Language maintenance programs (as opposed to transitional ones) would enable us to take advantage of our tremendous language resource. Ironically, we as a nation spend much time and energy improving and expanding our enrichment language programs so that our citizens will be "cultured," and yet we almost daily discourage the natural resource that many of our students already possess but need to develop—their first languages.

According to Cummins, an important goal of any second-language program should be to develop proficient bilinguals (see the Threshold Hypothesis[3]). He reports:

> . . . studies were carried out with language minority children whose L1 was gradually being replaced by a more dominant and prestigious L2. Under these conditions, these children developed relatively low levels of academic proficiency in both languages. In contrast, the majority of studies that have reported cognitive advantages associated with bilingualism have involved students whose L1 proficiency has continued to develop while L2 is being acquired. Consequently, these students have been characterized by relatively high levels of proficiency in both languages (1981, p. 38).

Cummins further says that one of the major successes of bilingual programs in elementary schools in particular is that they encourage students to take pride in their native languages and cultures, a necessity if the students are to have positive attitudes not only toward themselves but toward the target language and the people who speak it.

One of the problems facing maintenance bilingual education associated with ESL programs in particular is that there may be only one or two students speaking any given language within a particular school. Most school districts require

---

[3] The Threshold Hypothesis argues that being proficient in one language facilitates being proficient in another. There are really two thresholds involved: (1) a higher threshold dividing the *proficient bilingual* (one who has obtained high levels of proficiency in both languages) from the *partial bilingual* (one who is proficient in one of the languages) and (2) the lower threshold dividing the partial bilingual from the *limited bilingual* (one who has only low-level skills in both languages).

that there be a minimum number of students in order to make the hiring of a bilingual teacher feasible. Yet another problem is finding qualified teachers, especially in the languages for which there are fewer speakers. For most of the languages it is possible to hire classroom tutors who are fluent, but unfortunately these people often cannot do much more than aid in transitional bilingual situations. For some teachers the only option available is to encourage students to maintain their first languages by not discouraging their use and by emphasizing the advantages and opportunities for those who become proficient bilinguals.

AN OPTIMAL PROGRAM FOR ESL STUDENTS

Perhaps the optimal program for ESL students would be one in which ESL is combined with mainstreaming, sheltered classes, and maintenance bilingual education. I especially like the one outlined in Table 16.1, adapted from Krashen, 1984.

TABLE 16.1. PROGRAM FOR ESL STUDENTS (ADAPTED FROM KRASHEN, 1984)

Level	Mainstream	Sheltered	First Language
beginning	art, music, physical education	ESL	all core subjects
intermediate	art, music, physical education	ESL, math	social and natural sciences
advanced	art, music, physical education, math	ESL social and natural sciences	enrichment
mainstream	all subjects	—	enrichment

Students at *beginning* levels would be mainstreamed into subject areas in which the concepts are generally concrete and less demanding cognitively. For some students (especially those in high school), home economics and industrial arts might be added as additional mainstream electives. Students would study all the core subjects in the first language. During *intermediate* levels, the same students might add typing to their mainstream course selections. Sheltered mathematics would be offered. The remainder of the core subjects would be taught in the first language. At *advanced* levels, students would be mainstreamed in most subjects except the social and natural sciences, which would be taught in sheltered environments. The first language would be used mainly for enrichment.[4]

---

[4] The term "enrichment" may imply a sort of token treatment of L1. The importance given to it will depend upon those operating the program. It is hoped that L1 will be used for academic as well as social communication in situations that really matter. Program directors might want to consider using L1 for a portion of the subject matter teaching provided that adequate teaching staff and materials are available.

Notice that ESL would be taken throughout the program until the students were completely mainstreamed. The amount of time spent in ESL at each level would depend on the particular needs of each student. If teaching the core subjects in the first language were not possible through the intermediate levels, then these subjects would be taught in the second language within sheltered classes beginning at intermediate levels.

Teachers of mainstream, sheltered, and adjunct classes in the various content areas can do much to lower the cognitive and affective burdens of the students. They can modify their teaching to meet three basic objectives: (1) to integrate the student (in the case of mainstream classes), (2) to communicate effectively with the student, and (3) to teach language and the subject matter in a manner conducive to acquisition. Below are some suggestions to help the content-area teachers meet these goals. Although the majority of ideas can be adapted to almost any situation, there may be a few that are not relevant. Their relevance will usually depend on the age levels, proficiency levels, and cognitive development of the students with whom they are to be used.

For Mainstream Teachers

1. *Provide a warm environment in which help is readily available to the student.* One way to do this is to set up a "buddy" system in which native English-speaking students are paired with ESL students. Another useful technique is peer teaching, in which a native English speaker teaches one or more ESL students. Group work, in general, increases the chances that the student will receive the necessary help. In addition, it increases the amount of interaction and comprehensible input received (see sections on peer teachers and lay assistants and on cooperative learning in Chapter 14).

2. *If possible, use a "satisfactory/unsatisfactory" grade option until the ESL student is able to compete successfully with native speakers.* Students may be ready sooner than expected, since many of them adapt very rapidly. It is important to remember that often the students, particularly those who are older, will already have a high level of academic understanding in the first language and may even surpass native speakers once they have proficiency in the new language.

3. *Record your lectures or talks on tape.* Students need to be able to listen to them as many times as necessary for understanding.

4. *Ask some of your native or near-native speaking students to simplify the textbook by rewriting the chapters.* The job can be made as easy as possible by giving each native-speaking student just a few pages to simplify. The simplified materials not only aid ESL students but other students who may find the regular text too difficult. The students who do the rewriting benefit also in that the task serves as a review for them.

5. *Choose native or near-native speaking students who take effective, comprehensible*

notes to duplicate them for ESL students. By this means, the latter can be provided with study aids.

For Mainstream, Sheltered-Class, and Adjunct Teachers

1. *Plan lessons that are related to the students' lives, utilize a lot of visuals, and provide for "hands on" kinds of involvement.* For example, drawing, coloring, and labeling maps in geography and pinpointing where the students came from is far more valuable than simply listening to a talk about maps.
2. *Communicate individually with the ESL students as much as time permits.* Avoid using complicated words or complex sentences. Speak slowly but keep the volume and intonation as normal as possible. Use few idioms. Incorporate a lot of body language. These strategies will be used subconsciously, for the most part, by those whose main goal is to communicate.
3. *Avoid forcing students to speak.* Allow them to speak when they are ready, in other words, when they volunteer. Students' right to a "silent period" (see Chapter 3) needs to be respected, especially when they are being introduced to new concepts.
4. *Reassure the students that their own languages are acceptable and important.* If other students from the same language group are present, do not insist that they use only English in class. No matter how good the intentions of the teacher, refusing to allow students to speak in their first languages is in essence saying that their languages are not good enough. Of course, students may need to be reminded that first language should not be used to exclude others from discussion.
5. *Make all corrections indirectly by repeating what the students have said in correct form.* For example, suppose an ESL student says, "My book home"; the teacher can repeat, "I see. Your book is at home." It must be remembered, that simplified (ungrammatical) forms are to be regarded as normal while the student is progressing toward more complete competence in English. When the student is ready to move to another level, the indirect correction will probably be picked up and internalized after it is heard several times in a variety of situations. In written production, a few suggestions can be made for improvement as long as they are balanced with positive comments. Keep suggestions simple and offer only what you think each student can handle at his or her proficiency level.
6. *Try to answer all questions that the students ask but avoid overly detailed explanation.* Simple answers that get right to the point will be understood best. If possible, point to objects and pictures, or demonstrate actions to help get the meaning across.
7. *If you are in a situation in which lectures are appropriate, try to make them as comprehensible as possible.* Emphasize key words and phrases through

intonation and repetition. Write them on the chalkboard or on an overhead transparency as you are talking. Give concrete examples. Use pictures and charts, map out ideas, use gestures, acting out, simplifications, expansion of ideas, or whatever is necessary to ensure understanding. Definitions, comparisons, and the like can be incorporated in the lectures to clarify new words and concepts. For example, in a history lesson you might say, "The government's funds were depleted. It was almost out of money." Thus the phrase "funds were depleted" is made more comprehensible.

8. *Check to see that what you are saying is understood.* Frequently ask questions such as, "Do you understand?" or "Do you have any questions?" and be very aware of the feedback you are getting. Students may even nod their heads but still not understand. However, blank stares or puzzled looks are sure signs that you are not being understood. Often it is better to ask more specific questions directly related to the preceding utterance. For example, after saying, "In Arizona rainfall is minimal during most of the year," you might check for understanding by asking, "Does it rain much in Arizona?" Asking a question such as this to confirm interpretation is yet another means by which students can be exposed to new words and concepts without losing the meaning of the message.

9. *Give students sufficient wait-time before expecting answers.* Students need time to formulate their ideas. Often teachers try to avoid silence and move too quickly to another student for an answer or answer the questions themselves. If after a sufficient time you still do not receive a response, you might want to rephrase the questions and/or answer it yourself. The question/answer process helps students to acquire the appropriate language associated with taking turns.

10. *Encourage students to use their bilingual dictionaries when necessary or to ask questions when they don't understand important concepts.* Help them to guess at meanings first by using the context. Assure them that they do not have to understand every word to comprehend the main idea.

11. *Reinforce key concepts over and over in a variety of situations and activities.* Hearing about the concepts once or twice is not enough. Students need to be exposed to them several times through a wide range of experiences in order for internalization to take place.

12. *Whenever possible, utilize tutors who speak the native languages of the students.* Such help is especially important to students operating at beginning to intermediate levels.

13. *Request that appropriate content-area books be ordered for the library in the students' native languages.* These can be particularly useful to students in comprehending the concepts while the second language is being mastered. They also provide the students with a means for maintaining and developing skills in the native language.

14. *Become informed as much as possible on the various cultures represented by your students.* Knowing how particular students might react to classroom events and being able to interpret nonverbal symbols could help prevent misunderstanding and confusion.

15. *Acknowledge and incorporate the students' cultures whenever possible.* For instance, differing number systems can be introduced in math, customs and traditions in social science, various medicines in natural science, native dances and games in physical education, songs in music, ethnic calendars in art, haiku in literature, and so on. In addition, holidays can be celebrated, languages can be demonstrated for appreciation, and literature with translations can be shared.

16. *Prepare the students for your lessons and reading assignments.* You might ask them what they already know about the subject. Encourage them to look for main ideas by giving them a framework or outline beforehand. Ask them to predict outcomes and then to verify their predictions.

17. *Increase possibilities for success.* Alternating difficult activities with easier ones allows the ESL students to experience early successes. For example, in natural science one activity might be to create a diary that Neil Armstrong might have kept on his trip to the moon; the next assignment might be to make a list of the personal items including food that he might have taken with him. Of course, the tasks as a whole should gradually become more academically challenging as the students become more proficient.

AN OPTIMAL PROGRAM FOR FOREIGN-LANGUAGE STUDENTS

Immersion appears to be an optimal program for foreign-language students. Here we cannot ignore the successes of the French immersion programs in Canada and the Spanish immersion program in Culver City, California (see Chapter 2). Immersion programs are usually combined with maintenance bilingual education to ensure that students are developing skills in their first language even though it is also being fostered at home and in the community. Through immersion, students of approximately the same proficiency and age levels are given comprehensible input in the various subject areas (see the description of an early immersion program in Chapter 18).

Unfortunately, most foreign-language programs involve students in the target language for only a small portion of each day. Because the classroom will probably be the only source of input for the student, it is *vitally* important that the class time be spent mainly on meaningful comunication through interaction (see the high school foreign-language program in Chapter 18). However, because the students may not receive a sufficient amount of input, even though the focus is on interaction, they will probably need some formal instruction in order to facilitate the acquisition process, especially those students who are cognitively able to use rule application.

SUMMARY

If we are to succeed in producing individuals who can function with maximum effectiveness in a pluralistic society, we must be concerned not only with their development of interpersonal skills but with their academic language skills as well. There are three basic approaches to content-area teaching: submersion, immersion, and bilingual education. Often these approaches are mixed. The optimal ESL program combines ESL with mainstreaming (a positive type of submersion), sheltered classes (a kind of immersion), adjunct courses, and maintenance bilingual education.

Immersion programs have proven to be optimal for foreign-language teaching as long as there are enough native-speaking or near-native-speaking linguistic models present to help prevent early fossilization of interlanguage forms. However, most foreign-language programs consist of brief daily time slots set aside for the teaching of the target language, making meaningful interaction in class even more important.

READINGS, REFLECTION, AND DISCUSSION

Suggested Readings and Reference Materials

Krashen, S., and Biber, D. (1988). *On course: Bilingual education's success in California*. Sacramento, Calif.: California Association for Bilingual Education. Several highly acclaimed California bilingual programs are presented along with the related research. Programs found in the following districts and schools are included: Baldwin Park Unified School District, Eastman Avenue School, San Jose Unified School District, Fremont Unified School District, San Diego City Schools, Rockwood Elementary School, and the Carpinteria Preschool.

Nissani, H. (1990). Early childhood programs for language minority children. *Focus*, 2. Washington, D.C.: National Clearinghouse for Bilingual Education. The importance of developing appropriate environments for early childhood development, parental involvement, and equal access are all emphasized in this informative booklet.

Perez, B., and Torres-Guzman, M. (1992). *Learning in two worlds: An integrated Spanish/English biliteracy approach*. White Plains, N.Y.: Longman. Ways to create an appropriate learning environment for the simultaneous development of Spanish and English literacy skills are presented in this book.

Richard-Amato, P., and Snow, A. (1992). *The multicultural classroom: Readings for content-area teachers*. White Plains, N.Y.: Addison-Wesley. A sourcebook for teachers in multicultural classrooms (K–12). It focuses on the needs of language minority students and presents selections from the works of experienced teachers and researchers such as Jim Cummins, H. Douglas Brown, Shirley Brice Heath, James Banks, Mary McGroarty, Robin Scarcella, Anna Chamot, and Michael O'Malley.

Rigg, P., and Allen, V., eds. (1989). *When they don't all speak English: Integrating the ESL student into the regular classroom*. Urbana, Ill.: National Council of Teachers of English. Several topics of interest are presented in this book: using literature in the classroom, understanding the visual and written works of second-language children, looking at language variation, and many others. Among the many authors represented are Jean Handsombe, Carole Urzua, Judith Lindfors, David Freeman, Yvonne Freeman, and Sarah Hudelson.

Violand-Sanchez, E., Sutton, C., and Ware, H., (1991). *Fostering home-school cooperation: Involving language minority families as partners in education*. NCBE 6. Washington, D.C.: National Clearinghouse for Bilingual Education. This booklet stresses the importance of parental involvement, offers a framework for involving language minority families in the local schools, and presents ways to implement a participatory model.

Questions for Reflection and Discussion

1. What might be the ideal time for introducing students to a second language? Consider submersion and immersion differences and how they might affect children in the lower grades. Discuss other factors that would be relevant.

2. Find out as much as possible about the cultures that might be represented in a hypothetical or real classroom for which you might be responsible (see footnote on page 282). How can the various cultures be incorporated in some of your lessons? What specific problems might your students have with the subject matter due to cultural factors (see also Chapter 5)? What will you do to help them overcome these difficulties?

3. One of the suggestions for mainstream, sheltered-class, and adjunct teachers is to keep success within each student's reach by alternating difficult activities with easy ones, all the while increasing the academic challenges as the student grows in the new language. Plan a series of activities for one or two lessons of your choice in which you would increase chances for success by this means.

4. Choose additional ideas from the suggestions for mainstream, sheltered-class, and adjunct teachers in this chapter and apply them to a specific situation in which academic skills are taught. To a group of class members, demonstrate the use of one or more of your applications. Ask the group for feedback.

PART **IV**

Programs in Action

Reading about a variety of programs can give teachers a wealth of ideas about how to create and implement methods, activities, and methodologies (including decisions about content, how and when to correct, how to incorporate a silent period, and so forth). Seeing the ways in which vital questions are answered by others and being exposed to the direct application of various methods and activities can give real insights into what might work in certain situations, with specific groups of learners.

The programs here have been divided into ESL programs (Chapter 17) and foreign-language programs (Chapter 18). Several different levels are represented—elementary through university, including adult basic education. Some are districtwide programs, others take place in a single school setting. An immersion foreign-language program; a bicultural institute for children, adolescents, and adults; a sheltered English program; a life-skills program using community resources; a college center for international programs; and a university support program are only a few of the many presented here.

PART IV

Programs in Action

CHAPTER 17

ESL Programs

As was stated in Chapter 16, an optimal program for ESL students (K–12) might be one in which ESL is combined with mainstreaming, sheltered classes, and maintenance bilingual education. Adjunct courses might be added to make the program optimal for college and university levels. Although none of the programs described in this chapter claims to be optimal, all have features at which we may want to take a closer look. The programs include a college center for international programs (Saint Michael's College in Colchester, Vermont), a university support program (California State University, Los Angeles), a life-skills adult basic education program (the North Hollywood Adult Learning Center in Hollywood, California), a secondary sheltered English model (Artesia High School in Artesia, California), a high school academic program (Thomas Jefferson High School in Los Angeles), an elementary district-wide program (Alhambra School District in Alhambra, California), and a kindergarten ESL program within a Spanish bilingual school (Loma Vista Elementary in Maywood, California).

Some of the descriptions focus on the overall design of the programs, others on specific elements within them. Although the programs have been developed for specific age groups and purposes, the basic designs and activities need not be used exclusively in these situations. An imaginative teacher can probably see many ways in which most can be adapted for other educational settings (see Chapter 14).

A COLLEGE CENTER FOR INTERNATIONAL PROGRAMS[1]

The Center for International Programs, established in 1954, at Saint Michael's College in Colchester, Vermont, is one of the oldest centers of its kind in the United States, and it is one of the first (if not the first) to incorporate sheltered and adjunct courses into its curriculum. Over the years, four major programs have evolved: The Intensive English Program, the University Academic Program, Special English Programs,[2] and the Master of Arts in Teaching English as a Second Language (MATESL) Program. For the purpose of this chapter, only two of these programs will be described: the Intensive English Program (IEP), and the University Academic Program (UAP).

The Intensive English Program

The IEP, which serves approximately 60–80 students each semester, is not restricted to students with academic interests only; thus it is varied in its approach and in its offerings. The program is available to students all year round with openings every four weeks. The students generally remain in the program for anywhere from 12–16 weeks, depending upon their needs and interests.

Because the program serves a wide spectrum of students, its goals are both survival and academic. It offers five levels of instruction, all the way from low beginning to advanced. Once students have completed the Institutional TOEFL, a writing sample, and an oral diagnostic test, they are placed at the appropriate level. Students operating at the lowest levels focus on oral activities in the morning, which are complemented by reading and writing activities in the afternoon.

Students operating at higher levels have a somewhat different schedule. They take a reading lab in the morning followed by what is known as "The Core" which consists of reading, writing, and grammar. Additional help with grammar is available in the individualized grammar lab. In the afternoon they take a listening lab, a listening/speaking class, and an elective. See Figure 17.1.

---

[1] I am very grateful to Sally Cummings, Carolyn Duffy, and their colleagues at the Center for International Programs at Saint Michael's College for describing their program to me and for giving me permission to summarize it in this edition.

[2] These programs are specially designed for groups from other countries who want short-term language and cultural programs tailored to their needs (e.g., a group of Colombian high school students wanting to improve their academic English skills while learning about culture in the United States).

8:30 - 9:00	READING LAB
9:10 - 11:00	CORE — Reading / Writing / Grammar
11:00 - 11:30	INDIVIDUALIZED GRAMMAR LAB
1:00 - 1:30	LISTENING LAB
1:40 - 3:30 (T/Th)	LISTENING/SPEAKING LAB
1:40 - 3:30 (M/W/F)	ELECTIVE

Figure 17.1. A Typical IEP Schedule

The Reading Lab

The Reading Lab immerses students in content in specific topic areas (e.g., the history of Vermont, business issues, etc.). Often the selections are on cassettes so that the students can hear them read aloud. The work is individualized and learner-centered in that students plan what they will work on with their instructor as a guide. Students select books for independent reading (again under the guidance of the instructor) from the Center's library. They respond to what they are reading either by writing in their journals or by giving oral and/or written reports.

The Core

The Core Curriculum uses an integrated skills approach. Each unit has a theme around which reading, writing, and grammar revolve. The required texts are supplemented with films, guest speakers, field trips, and authentic related readings. For example, in the reading component, a unit on education and learning styles is supplemented by an article about student test scores from *The New York Times*; in the writing component, letters requesting information on alternative schools in the area are written; in the listening/speaking component, phone interviews are completed, and a field trip is taken to an alternative school. A culmination of the work accomplished up to this point is provided by viewing the movie *Stand and Deliver*. The in-depth discussion and writing activities that follow allow the students to synthesize what they have learned.

The Listening Lab

The Listening Lab has a dual function: (1) it supplements, extends, and enriches what students are learning in the listening/speaking class and (2) it provides an opportunity to practice aural skills through materials that students themselves have chosen. Students can focus on activities to improve general comprehension;

on specific items such as numbers, prepositions, reduced forms; or on academic skills such as note taking.

The Listening/Speaking Class

This class, which is usually coordinated with the Listening Lab, includes work with both academic and conversational oral and aural skills. Activities typical of this class include listening to academic lectures, conducting interviews, listening and responding to guest speakers, participating in role plays, creating videos, or having debates.

The Elective Classes

Examples of elective classes from which students make choices are as follows:

(1) Current Events—high-intermediate and advanced students read and discuss human interest articles from *The New York Times*.

(2) Games and Puzzles—students at all levels select games consonant with their proficiency levels. Popular choices are Jeopardy and Clue. Word games of various sorts and number puzzles are among the many possibilities available.

(3) English through TV—students view news items, commercials, and clips from programs such as "The People's Court." By this means, they acquire new vocabulary and improve their listening skills. In addition, the lively discussions generated by the TV shows enable students to practice communication skills.

The University Academic Program

The UAP serves as a bridge to academic coursework. The UAP involves intensive English study to prepare students for the academic courses typically found at American colleges and universities. It evolved out of a need to provide a transition to the campus mainstream. Before the program was established in 1972, students often found themselves floundering for up to a year or more in courses for which they were not adequately prepared, culturally or linguistically. Drawing on Cummins's distinction[3] between the context-rich learning environments (as represented by the ESL classes) and the context-reduced learning environments (as represented by undergraduate mainstream classes), a rationale was developed for the establishment of the UAP.

The program's courses are credit-bearing, and students who successfully complete them can transfer the credits to their undergraduate degree programs either at Saint Michael's College or at other institutions. The courses integrate both content-based and language-based teaching procedures and are taken over a two-semester time period. Students may enter the program either directly

---

[3] See discussion on page 431 of this book.

from the IEP or by applying to the program. Acceptance is based on scores from the TOEFL, and/or from the MTELP. In addition, students take a test in academic skills prepared by the Center. This test includes an authentic academic lecture and reading followed by a multiple-choice/essay task. Teacher recommendations and prior academic performance are part of the data used to determine appropriate placement within the program. All students entering the UAP are first required to take a course which focuses on academic readings, lectures, and note taking.

Within the UAP itself there are two levels: Level 1 and Level 2. Level 1 is oriented to intermediate students. During the first semester, these students take a sheltered course in college writing and a cooperative course. The latter course has evolved over the years to include an adjunct model. It features mainstream academic content, taught by regular undergraduate faculty, and a language component, taught by a language teacher from the Center. Level 2, on the other hand, is oriented to advanced students who take sheltered courses in literature and advanced college writing and two mainstream undergraduate courses. See Figure 17.2 below.

LEVEL 1		LEVEL 2	
Cooperative Course (adjunct)	(3/4 credit)	Intro to Literature (sheltered)	(3 credits)
College Writing (sheltered)	(3 credits)	Advanced College Writing (sheltered)	(3 credits)
		Two undergraduate courses (mainstream)	(6 credits)

Figure 17.2. UAP Courses and Credits

The Cooperative Course (Adjunct)

The first cooperative course offered at the UAP was a sheltered course in chemistry, taught by a mainstream undergraduate professor and a language instructor from the Center. The course was sheltered in that the students taking it were all international students and the input was modified for their comprehension.

Soon it became apparent that it might be better to have international students mixed with native speakers to give them the skills needed to function in mainstream situations in which the input was not modified for their benefit. Changes were made. The course soon lost the characteristics inherent in a sheltered model and began to resemble instead an adjunct model. The language instructor from the Center now attended all lecture and discussion sessions, took notes, and recorded all classroom events on cassettes. The language instructor then conducted an adjunct language class for the international students in which the concepts and academic language requirements of the cooperative course were integrated. Below were the goals of the adjunct class.

The development and integration of:

cognitive academic language proficiency
a solid knowledge base in the content
discussion/interaction skills
academic grammatical competence
library research skills
study skills
computer literacy

The cooperative course became so successful that it was offered in several content areas: biology, human genetics, nutrition, business, economics, political science, mass communication, religious studies, and philosophy. Sally Cummings and Carolyn Duffy, both instructors in the Center, report significant benefits of the course based on their discussions with undergraduate faculty, the international students themselves, and the native speakers in the cooperative courses.

1. Benefits to members of the undergraduate faculty:
   a. The cooperative teaching approach caused many of them to reexamine their own teaching styles.
   b. They gained a better understanding of the tasks that face international students in an academic course.
   c. Their courses improved due to the new and necessary viewpoint contributed by the international students.
2. Benefits to the international students:
   a. Their opportunities for interaction with native speakers increased substantially even after the course ended.
   b. They were more confident and more active class participants in all their classes, once they had taken the cooperative course.
3. Benefits to native-speaking students in the cooperative courses:
   a. They had gained a new awareness of international students through the sharing of cultural values and experiences.
   b. They had learned other points of view.

College Writing (Sheltered)

The second course in Level 1 is the sheltered course in college writing. This course integrates academic reading, writing, listening, problem areas of grammar, and other academic skills. However, its central focus is on writing for academic purposes. It is coordinated with the cooperative course described above and allows for even more language work and additional reinforcement.

Introduction to Literature (Sheltered)

Students in Level 2 take a sheltered course in Introduction to Literature, which includes selections from both American and international literature. They read, discuss, and write about the novels, short stories, poetry, and plays they are reading. One special feature of this course is that sometimes the plays they read are the same plays being produced by the theater department. The students are often invited to attend rehearsals.

Advanced College Writing (Sheltered)

The second course in Level 2 is a course in sheltered advanced college writing. Here students further develop their writing competence by exploring rhetorical modes of academic discourse. It is here that they become aware of their own developing styles. In addition to reading and writing essays in various rhetorical modes, they complete a library research paper. Importance is placed on peer and student/teacher conferences throughout the revision process.

Mainstream Undergraduate Courses

In addition to the courses mentioned, Level 2 students will take two mainstream courses of their choice at the undergraduate level. Before making their selections, these students will have been advised by the Director of International Student Affairs. Once they are in the mainstream, they are invited to return to their teachers in the Center, particularly to their composition teachers. They also are encouraged to use the university writing center, which is staffed to support international students. At times they seek tutorial help from MATESL practicum students.

Support Services

Student assistants organize and execute the international student orientation program and serve as Big Brothers/Big Sisters for international students during their first week on campus. The student assistants meet the international students at the airport, take them to a local bank, serve as English language conversation partners, and in many other ways assist them and serve as their support group.

The Director of International Student Affairs conducts campus and community orientation sessions and provides ongoing support for all international students. In addition, this person serves as a liaison between the Center and student affairs offices such as housing and health services. The Assistant Director of International Student Affairs plans evening and weekend trips off campus, and publishes a weekly bulletin highlighting upcoming events of interest, cultural information, and language related quizzes and puzzles.

The Center itself attempts to maximize the interaction and integration of the international students with their English-speaking peers. The Assistant Director of International Student Affairs also organizes additional activities and involves the international students in volunteer work such as serving dinner at the local soup kitchen for the homeless, planting and harvesting a garden for the food shelf, or assisting at Special Olympic events.

The Center also sponsors weekly afternoon coffee hours during which the international students are integrated with mainstream students on campus who are studying foreign languages. The coffee hours offer at least two benefits for all the students who attend. First, the coffee hours increase the opportunities for the students to interact in the languages that they are trying to learn. And second, the students have a chance to gain increased knowledge of the various cultures represented and to make new friends.

Yet another service provided by the Center is the individual study program which utilizes a computer-assisted instructional component for grammar, a self-study reading lab, and a writing center. The latter is staffed by students in the Master of Arts in Teaching English as a Second Language program who set up individual conferences with the international students about their writing. Participation in the writing center is also of benefit to the M.A. students themselves. It gives them the opportunity to work with international students and obtain the advantages that such authentic experiences give.

Future Directions

One might wonder what the Center would need to better provide for the needs of international students. A major strength of the center is that it is flexible and that it does change in response to the needs of its students and in the light of current theory and research in the field of second-language acquisition and second-language teaching. Because of the success of its cooperative courses, it plans to add more of them and make them available to students at both levels in the UAP. Because of increased student interest in theme-based content as found in upper levels of the IEP, it is extending this method of organization to the lower levels as well. The Center has found that themes such as tourism and global issues (e.g., environment and peace education) are highly motivating for students and are a good way to integrate language development and content. Moreover, themes such as these encourage analysis, synthesis, and the critical evaluation of information.

UNIVERSITY SUPPORT PROGRAM: PROJECT LEAP[4]

Overview of the Project

Project LEAP (Learning English-for-Academic-Purposes), a three-year project at California State University, Los Angeles, was funded by the U.S. Department of

---

[4]I want to thank Ann Snow and Janet Tricamo, Codirectors of Project LEAP, for making their materials and program available to me.

Education Fund for the Improvement Of Postsecondary Education. Its main goal is to make the undergraduate general education curriculum more accessible to the University's language minority student population, by enhancing an eleven-year-old support system that was developed by the Educational Opportunity Program (EOP).

The students included in Project LEAP were the same students in the already existing EOP, whose program was aimed at bilingual, low income, first generation college students, both immigrant and native English-speaking. Thirty-three percent of the students in EOP had been admitted to the university on special admission status because their SAT scores and high school grade point averages did not qualify them for regular admission.

The EOP Study Group Program

The students in EOP Study Group Program were advised by counselors to select certain sections among the general education courses required of all incoming freshmen. These sections were paired with one-credit study group courses[5] taught by trained peer leaders. Each study group met for three hours each week with its peer leader, who had attended the same lectures and had completed the same course readings as the students. From the peer leader, the students received assistance in comprehending course content, preparing for exams, developing individual study skills, and practicing group study techniques. Each peer leader was considered to be a facilitator of the many activities planned for the group.

The peer leaders (who were generally recommended by faculty members) were either upper division or graduate students. They had themselves received at least a "B" in the courses with which their study groups were paired. They were required to complete an initial eighteen-hour training program and be closely observed and evaluated weekly during their first quarter of employment as peer leaders. In addition they attended biweekly staff training meetings.

Project LEAP

The following were the four major goals of Project LEAP:

1. to improve and expand the existing EOP study group courses
2. to provide faculty development training for the professors teaching the regular general education courses
3. to effect curriculum modification to institutionalize language-sensitive instruction

---

[5] The study group courses in the already existing program and in Project LEAP were similar in concept to the adjunct courses described in Chapter 16 and to the adjunct courses associated with the Center at Saint Michael's College in Colchester, Vermont (see previous program).

4. to gain project continuity and dissemination to train future instructors and peer leaders of the study group courses

To meet these goals, Project LEAP prepared peer leaders to more effectively address the academic *language* (as well as content) needs of the students to whom they had been assigned; instructed content-area faculty teaching the general education courses in strategies for teaching academic literacy; developed a language- and content-based curriculum that could be used in all of the group study courses on campus, even after the project was completed; and created and/or adapted materials for the targeted general education courses.

During the first year of the project, three general education courses were targeted: biology, history, and introductory psychology. Attached to each of these courses was a LEAP study group course, which was led by a peer and a professional language specialist. This course aimed to integrate content instruction and related academic language skills. The time frame for the study group course was extended from three hours to four hours per week and two credits were earned instead of just one. During the second year of the project, political science, sociology, and speech were targeted and during the third year, anthropology, health science, and a laboratory biology course.

Academic Content/Language-Teaching Strategies

LEAP Group Study Courses
In addition to work with academic content and language, the LEAP study group courses taught the students self-sufficiency and interpersonal communication skills in order that they might become more active participants in the groups to which they had been assigned. A question-answer format was used by group leaders who initially prepared the pertinent questions (both knowledge-based and inferential) from the lectures and readings. Once students gained experience in answering questions, they brought in more and more of their own questions as they began to take on greater responsibility for the group's effectiveness. Study skills presentations were made at least three times each quarter by the peer leader or a study skills specialist from the University's Learning Resource Center. Actual course material was used in the presentations. Practice quizzes were given often by the peer leaders to emphasize the content of the readings or to help the students prepare for exams.

Below are questions from the peer leader self-evaluation form.

Discussion Leading

1. Did everyone participate in the discussion?
2. Did you give the students enough time to respond, and wait until they were through?
3. Did you give reinforcement for correct and for partially correct answers?

4. Did you make sure that all the words used in the discussion were clear to the students?
5. Did you redirect the questions asked to you back to the group?
6. Did you test the students even though they said they understood the material?
7. Did the students do more talking than you did?
8. Was the level of difficulty of questions or materials appropriate?

Study Skills

1. Did you explain the study skill clearly?
2. Did you give the students ample opportunity to implement the skill?
3. Did you explain how they can benefit by using this skill?
4. Did you relate it to your subject area?
5. Did you explain how it can be applied to other areas?
6. Will you remember to refer to this skill again throughout the quarter?

Quizzes and Tests

1. Was it short enough for the students to complete in the allotted time period?
2. Was the level of difficulty appropriate?
3. Did you review the quiz immediately after the students completed it?
4. Did you ask the students to explain how they got their answers?
5. Do the students who missed a question know why they missed it and where to find the correct answer?
6. Did you make notes of the questions that were frequently missed, so that you can test the students again later?

The General Education Courses

The strategies presented here were designed by the LEAP study group leaders, language specialists, and course instructors for use in one or more of the three general education courses: biology, history, and introductory psychology. However, because they were originally intended for the general education courses did not preclude their being used in the study group courses if they were appropriate. All the strategies were aimed to assist the students in learning the content and in improving their academic language regardless of language background. They included the following:

1. Letting students submit assignments in phases (especially longer papers) instead of the previous "one-shot" term paper assignment
2. Making expectations more clear on the course syllabus
3. Accommodating diverse learning styles in the classroom through a variety of instructional techniques (e.g., increased wait time, avoiding "spotlighting" students, group work)

4. Making explicit the critical thinking or analytical requirements of assignments by setting up guidelines
5. Encouraging more interaction between faculty and students (e.g., making one visit to the professor during office hours a course requirement)
6. Making students more accountable for keeping up with reading assignments (e.g., pop quizzes, assigning chapter study guides)
7. Improving lectures by reviewing key concepts from the previous lecture, writing an agenda on the board for each class session; explicitly defining general academic vocabulary, referring less frequently to cultural, generational, or class-based references that might not be part of the students' background experiences

Below are samples from some of the activities used in the general education courses. Although each sample is intended for a specific course, with some modification, it could perhaps be adapted for other courses.

List-Making Exercise

RECONSTRUCTION

To answer a complicated question, you first need to compile all of the relevant information. Eventually you will be able to answer the question: Was the Civil War and Reconstruction Era a watershed in the South? Why or why not?

1. List all of the evidence that shows change. List all of the evidence that shows continuity.

	Change		Continuity
a.			
b.			
c.			

Contributed by Carole Srole.

Model Textbook Survey

(to accompany *Elements of Psychology*, by R. S. Feldman, 1992, McGraw-Hill)

Understanding how your textbook is organized will help familiarize you with the basic content and organization of the text. In this way, reading for academic purposes will be easier because you will understand the purpose that each of the different sections in the chapters serve.

I. *Instructions:* Working in small groups, fill in the blanks below.

Name of course: _
Title of textbook: _
Author(s) : _
Author(s') qualifications (e.g., university degree, professional affiliation, etc.):
_ _
Copyright date: _
Has the book been revised? _

II. *Instructions:* Working in groups, survey your textbook and decide which of the following features it contains. Place a check in the appropriate column. Then, by analyzing each of the sections, determine the purpose that each serves. Be ready to share your ideas with the entire class.

	Yes	No
Table of contents		
Bibliography		
Name Index		
Subject Index		
Preface		
Glossary		
etc.		

III. *Instructions:* Using your textbook and working in small groups, answer the following questions or locate the following information. Be prepared to explain how you found the information to the rest of the class.

1. What were the author's goals in writing the book? Where did you find the information?

   _
   _

2. Look at the table of contents. Is the organization of topics easy to follow?

_____
_____

3. On what page(s) will you find a discussion of *stereotyping*?

_____

4. How did you find the page number?

_____
_____

5. How does the author explain *stereotyping*?

_____
_____

6. If you wanted to read all of the article quoted on page 382, where could you
find the complete reference?

_____
_____

Contributed by Gloria Romero, Carolina Espinoza, and Lia Kamhi-Stein.

Grammar Exercise: Error Analysis

I. *Instructions:* The following sentences were taken from student papers. Working in pairs
or small groups, analyze the structural or grammatical problems and discuss ways to rewrite the sentences.

1. The incentive was to have people buy American products instead of foreign
   trade.
2. Industrialization led to a transformation from an agrarian to an industrial economy, which caused much more social problems and a social class system.
3. Also government supported the business by passing vagrancy law. These laws
   made business profitable. By using blacks to work in there company.
4. In 1914 congress passed the Clayton act prohibited unfair trading practices.
5. An example of this was the Sugar treaty. The sugar treaty was good for the business because they saved money in two way's and they were that they paid low
   wages, and did not have to pay tariff's to the Hawaiian government.
etc.

Contributed by Nick Zonen.

Identifying Cause and Effect

I. *Instructions:* Identifying the cause and effect of events and movements is a critical part
of any study of history. Sometimes students don't make a clear differentiation between the
cause and its results, or even mistake one for the other. Identify the causes and effects in
the following statements.

Example:
The owl and the pussycat went to sea in a beautiful pea green boat. They felt the need to get away.

Cause: They felt the need to get away.
Effect: The owl and the pussy cat went to sea in a beautiful pea green boat.

1. The Emancipation Proclamation and the freeing of the slaves did not produce a society with complete equality for African-Americans, and their condition remained desperate.

Cause:
Effect:

2. Because of the development of birth control, women could delay having children or avoid having them altogether; consequently, women had the opportunity to acquire an education or pursue a career.

Cause:
Effect:

etc.

Contributed by Nick Zonen.

Research

Dr. Desdemona Cardoza, an administrator and professor at California State University, who had previously served as an evaluator for numerous programs for language minority students both at the University and at UCLA, looked at the effectiveness of the LEAP Study Group Courses in improving performance in the three general education courses during the first year. She compared the academic performance of the LEAP students, all of whom had taken *both* the general education course taught by a faculty member who had been prepared in language teaching strategies and its accompanying study group course with the non-LEAP students, all of whom had taken the same general education course as the LEAP students, but *not* the study group course.

She found that the LEAP students performed as well as or better than the control group in the following areas: grade point average, persistence in completing the course, and number of "D" and "F" grades received. Moreover, a greater proportion of LEAP students earned a grade of "B" in the general education course in which they were enrolled.

Concerning the institutionalization of Project LEAP strategies, there was evidence that the participating faculty who were prepared in LEAP techniques were actually using these techniques in their other teaching assignments. Moreover, non-LEAP peer group leaders were experimenting with LEAP techniques in their regular EOP study group courses.

Data on students who participated in Project LEAP the second year revealed that in the three general education courses targeted, half of the students earned "A" and "B" grades. Their overall grade point average was a 2.6 compared to their non-LEAP peers who earned a 2.9 overall. When the LEAP students were tracked from one academic year to the next, it was found that they returned to the university at the same rate as their peers. Data on students who participated in the third year is not yet available.

Ann Snow and Janet Tricamo, Codirectors of Project LEAP, report that they are very encouraged by the findings so far. In addition, they have noted that the faculty members involved in the project are seeing positive results both in content learning and in the written performance of their students. Most, in fact, have altered the way they teach now that they are more aware of their students' language needs. Because of the project's effectiveness, new funding has been provided to extend the faculty in-service component.

A LIFE-SKILLS ADULT BASIC EDUCATION PROGRAM[6]

In attempting to meet the needs of adults who are struggling not only with a new language but with providing a living for themselves and their families, the North Hollywood Adult Learning Center has made the community its classroom.

The 500 students who are enrolled in the program represent many different cultural groups from around the world: Hispanic (70%), Asian (12%), Middle Eastern (9%), and European (4%). The remaining 5 percent are native English speakers who are taking courses outside of the basic ESL program. The curriculum itself consists of six levels of ESL, running from beginning to advanced; a reading lab for students with special problems in reading; a language skills lab which emphasizes writing, spelling, and grammar; and a high school lab for those desiring a GED Certificate or a high school diploma. In the latter three, the ESL and native-speaking students are mixed.

Incorporating Community Resources

Every month the activities are built around specific life-skills topics such as the following:

Community Resources	*Mental and Physical Health*
the community and its members	medical care
autobiographical data	nutrition
cultural-social integration	personal hygiene

[6] I would like to thank the program's coordinator Sandra Brown, who provided much information upon which this summary was based. Appreciation also goes to Harriet Fisher, Rheta Goldman, Roberto Martinez, Ethel Schwartz, Katie Treibach, and the many others I talked with during my observation.

Community Resources (continued)

the world around us
police-fire-paramedic services
   the telephone
   the post office
leisure-time activities
   athletic activities
   entertainment activities
   recreational activities
educational services
   schools
   libraries

Occupational Knowledge

vocational training/counseling
   job searches
   the interview
   on-the-job skills

Mental and Physical Health

dental care
safety and home

Government and the Law

vehicles and the law
law and legal services
taxes
current issues

Consumer Economics

individual/family economy
   physical concerns
   financial services
consumer rights
insurance
consumerism
   general shopping skills
   food shopping
   meals
   clothing shopping
   housing

These topics and the information related to them serve as an important part of the content through which the structures, vocabulary, and pronunciation of English are taught. Integral to these units are the trips that the students at all levels take to city government offices, occupational centers, markets, commercial businesses, factories, music/arts centers, libraries, museums, parks, hospitals, and many other places in and around the city.

On one such trip to the Farmers' Market, Rheta Goldman, a teacher of intermediate ESL, asked her students to search out the answers to the following questions:

What animals are in the window of the pet shop?
Find the post office. What shops are next to the post office?
What's the name of a store where you can get shoes repaired?
Go to the Farmers' Market newspaper stand. Can you buy a newspaper in your native language?
How much does it cost?

What kind of food can you buy at the shop *next* to Gill's Ice Cream Shop?
Find the glassblower. Write the names of four glass animals you can buy
    there.
How much does a fresh-baked pie cost from Du-Bar's Bakery?
What kinds of pies do they have today? Name three.

In addition to the trips and related activities, the students are exposed to
films, real-life materials, and a stream of representatives from the community:
an immigration attorney to give advice on becoming citizens; a speaker from
the Red Cross to help the students be better prepared in the event of a major
earthquake; a representative from the Department of Consumer Affairs to
inform them of their rights as consumers; police officers to make them aware of
strategies to use in protecting themselves from crime, to name a few. Also in
connection with the units, the students participate in activities in their classes
such as role play, dialogues, conversations, discussions, and writing activities
commensurate with their proficiency levels.

To aid other teachers in setting up similar programs, the coordinator and
teachers at North Hollywood have compiled extensive lists of ideas in several
areas: community services, consumer education, cultural awareness, employment, family life, government/citizenship/law, health, and recreation. Below is
an example.

Community Services

Real-life materials/transparencies:

1. *Post office* forms

2. *Bank* forms, statements, checks, travelers' checks

3. *Telephone* directory pages of zip code maps; emergency telephone numbers; emergency number stickers for the telephone; telephone bills

4. *Telegram* form

5. *Driver's license* application form, test, change of address form

6. *Traffic* signs; parking/traffic citation forms; bus, train, airline schedules;
   bus maps from local bus company; road maps (from oil company, local
   Chamber of Commerce)

7. *School* (elementary, secondary, adult) enrollment forms; school report
   card; announcement of school activity

8. *Library* card applications

Brochures:
Police Department (home protection, self-defense, drugs, and so on); *Fire Department* (fire prevention); *automobile club and National Safety Council* (traffic safety); Department of Motor Vehicles (driver manual); *library; Building and Safety Department* (earthquake safety); *adult school* (schedule of classes); *city councilman, state assemblyman* (booklets on local agencies and services)

Audiovisuals:
Recorded tapes of telephone conversations (tell students prior to hearing the tapes that they are only simulations) with police and fire departments, telephone operators, directory assistance; Western Union; bus, train, taxi, and airline personnel; *taped conversations in the community*, at the post office, bank, with child's teacher, and so on; *taped telephone recordings* of weather, time, telephone numbers, disconnected telephones, and so on; *Teletrainers*—actual telephones with a control unit (on loan from telephone company)/free films

Speakers:
Police officer (home protection or self-defense, with film and demonstration); *fireman* (with film on fire safety and exit procedures); *paramedics* with demonstration of life-saving equipment and techniques; *AAA and National Safety Council representatives* with films on traffic safety; *library aide; elementary, secondary and/or adult school principal; telephone company representative* with film on use of telephone; *city councilman* on community services; *United Way representative*

Trips:
Fire station; police department; post office; bank (before it opens); library; telephone company; local elementary school; airport

Subjects for Discussion, Dialogue, Role-Playing, and Other Activities:
At the post office: sending, insuring, picking up packages; buying stamps, airletters, money orders; correctly addressing letters, and so on

At the bank: savings/checking; deposit/withdrawal; travelers' checks, safe deposit boxes, and so on

Emergency services: the role of police—home and self-protection; fire prevention; reporting a fire, a prowler, a break-in, an auto accident, calling the paramedics; what to do in case of a fire, earthquake, break-in, rape attempt; experiences with and attitudes toward police

Telephone: emergency calls; long distance calls; directory assistance; wrong number; out of order; telegrams; taking messages; weather report; using the telephone directory; social and business calls

Transportation: car, taxi, bus, train, airline schedules; map reading activities; locating local services; geography of local areas; traffic safety; dangers of hitchhiking; obtaining a driver's license; at the gas station, garage; asking directions

Education: registering child/self in school; conference with child's teacher, counselor, principal, nurse; participation in child's school activities; report cards; education in the United States compared with education in other countries; levels and types of education; special education; private schools; new approaches to education; admission requirements to colleges and universities

Library: card application; Dewey Decimal System; overdue books; reserving books; foreign-language books; using children's books

Philanthropic organizations: becoming involved in volunteer activities; charities; charity drives; animal protection agencies

Community Volunteers

One of the most interesting aspects of the program is its utilization of volunteers from the community. Eighteen community workers arrive every week to assist the teachers in classrooms, to tutor students, or to help out wherever they are needed. They come primarily from the ranks of housewives and retirees. Although they receive no monetary rewards for their time, they do receive numerous rewards of a different kind. Their individual birthdays are celebrated, articles in school papers are written to honor their accomplishments, and special days are set aside to recognize the work they do. Ranging in age from 26 to 82, they form a dependable resource. Some are there only one or two hours a week; others are there 15 to 20. The volunteers determine, in advance, their own schedules and sign contracts confirming the agreement (see the sample contract, Figure 17.3).

Once officially accepted as part of the staff, the volunteers are given mailboxes and their names are added to the check-in sheets. Then they receive an orientation and off they go to their assigned classrooms, where they are trained by the teacher with whom they will be working. In addition to the orientation and training, the volunteers are given suggestions in writing concerning general strategies to use when working with students (see pages 266–267 for a similar list intended for peer teacher and lay assistant training). They also receive self-evaluation checklists containing items about cooperation with others, following the teacher's directions, being friendly and encouraging, and so forth.

North Hollywood Adult Learning Center
Volunteer Job Description

POSITION TITLE: Adult Basic Education Tutor

PLACE: _____ Reading Lab   _____ High School Lab

          _____ Language Skills Lab   _____ English as a Second
                                               Language

PROGRAM OBJECTIVES: To assist students who want to learn to improve their basic
                            skills in English as a Second Language or to earn a GED
                            certificate or a high school diploma.

TIME COMMITMENT: Days _____ Hours _____

                            _____ _____

RESPONSIBILITIES:
- To work under the guidance and supervision of the teacher to whom you have been assigned
- To work with either individuals or groups according to the needs of the teacher and students
- To follow the teacher's plans for each session
- To assist the teacher in any way the teacher feels will be of benefit to the students
- To be reliable and on time on regularly scheduled days
- To sign in and out on the sign-in sheet
- To inform the office or teacher if you must be absent (The volunteer does not: diagnose student needs, prescribe instruction, select materials, evaluate student progress, or counsel students.)

QUALIFICATIONS:
- A positive attitude, interest and enthusiasm in working with adult basic education students
- Ability to work cooperatively with school personnel and other volunteers
- Adequate communication skills
- Dedication to fulfill all of the obligations of the position

TRAINING: BY THE TEACHER TO WHOM YOU ARE ASSIGNED

I have read and understand the above and agree to conscientiously carry out the responsibilites as described.

                         X _____

Figure 17.3

A SECONDARY SHELTERED ENGLISH MODEL[7]

We learned in Chapter 16 that a sheltered class is a kind of immersion situation in that the students are at similar levels of proficiency in the target language. We also learned that the teacher may be familiar with their first languages and usually has a knowledge of their cultures. A sheltered class can provide the comprehensible input necessary for the student to acquire the target language through content based instruction. At the same time, it can serve as a surrogate family of sorts or a temporary buffer between the student and the mainstream.

Artesia High School in Artesia, California, is one of the schools in the ABC Unified School District that has a highly developed network of sheltered classes. The school offers 36 sections of ESL and sheltered classes to approximately 350 Limited English Proficient (LEP) students who represent 21 different languages. All the students in what is called the "Diverse Language Program" (ESL only) are eligible to take the special courses. Pam Branch, the school's program coordinator, reports:

> What immersion has taught us is that comprehensible subject matter teaching *is* language teaching; students can profit a great deal from subject matter classes in which the conscious focus is on the topic and not on language. Classes are taught in English, but native speakers are excluded in order to make the teacher's input more understandable for limited-English students.

Students in this program begin with two periods of ESL and three sheltered classes in specific subject-matter areas (see Figure 17.4). Later they are able to add other sheltered classes (see Figure 17.5). Gradually they are fully mainstreamed, first in those areas that require less command of English and later in all subjects. Bilingual aides provide primary language support for the students.

Identification and Evaluation

A home language survey and supplementary questionnaire is used first to identify LEP students in the school district. Once the student is so identified, he or she receives the Language Assessment Scale (LAS) test and, when appropriate, a battery of other tests, including subtests of the Comprehensive Test of Basic Skills (CTBS) and an informal writing sample. Each student is then rated on an oral language observation matrix that is similar to the ACTFL (American Council on the Teaching of Foreign Languages, 1982) proficiency levels 1–5. On the basis of these measures, students are placed in either Level I, II, or III.

---

[7] I wish to thank Pam Branch, Lilia Stapleton, Marie Takagaki, Ted Marquez, and many others with the ABC Unified School District who made it possible for me to observe their sheltered class program and include it in this chapter.

Description of Each Level

Level I (akin to the beginning stages described on page 99) includes two periods of ESL: Skills I and Conversation I. At this level, the students can also choose from among several sheltered courses (see Figure 17.4).

Skills I focuses on survival skills such as telling time, using the telephone, filling out application forms, and so forth. *Conversation I* emphasizes various topics of interest such as those recommended by Krashen and Terrell (see Chapter 8). In both classes the total physical response and the natural approach are relied upon to foster low anxiety and provide sufficient comprehensible input. The sheltered classes at this level require tasks that are cognitively undemanding and heavily context embedded. For example in *Art* the students are given a wide variety of art experiences in which they can express themselves freely while they study composition and color as these are used in drawing, painting, and making three-dimensional objects. *Geography* also relies on concrete concepts for which pictures, maps, and globes can be used. Drawing maps or making papier-mâché ones in relief can provide a great deal of hands-on activity. *Horticulture* finds students planting and caring for a garden after diagramming and labeling the plants in a basic plan. The course not only helps students acquire the language through here and now tasks but may even open up some possible jobs for the future. *Piano* offers individualized instruction on the use of electric keyboards with headsets. If the students wish, they may elect to continue Piano into the next level. Students are placed in *Math* (in Levels I and II) according to math ability rather than level of proficiency in English. Problems are worked out on the chalkboard, and vocabulary banks are used to help students remember words already learned and to add new words for future work. Because word problems remain a continuing difficulty, the teacher helps students to break down the problems into various steps, making the tasks more manageable.

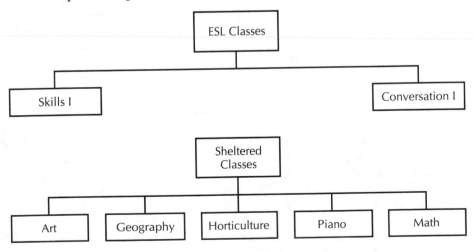

Figure 17.4. Level I

Level II (akin to the intermediate stages described on page 100) includes two periods of ESL: Skills II and Conversation II. At this level, the students have even more choices from among sheltered classes (see Figure 17.5).

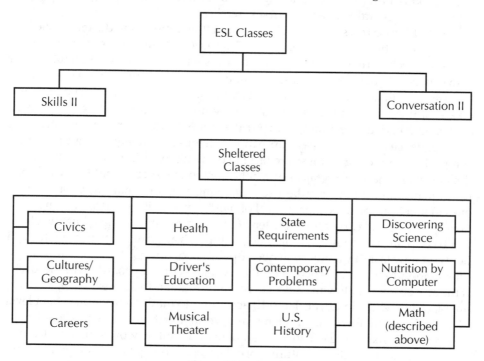

Figure 17.5. Level II

Skills II and Conversation II, like their counterparts at Level I, extend survival skills through a topical organization, adding vocabulary appropriate to the students' needs. At this level the tasks are more cognitively demanding but are still highly context embedded. *Careers* looks at various vocational post possibilities and helps the students to discover their own strengths and weaknesses. It makes an effort to find what kinds of jobs are best suited to each individual. The students receive practice in interview technique by role-playing (see Chapter 10). *Cultures/Geography* helps students to gain an appreciation of many different cultures in relation to their geographical advantages and constraints. *Civics* takes a historical approach to the American governmental system, its organization, and the ramifications of its tenets. *Driver's Education* gives the students an opportunity to prepare for the written portion of the driver's exam and presents a reading task for which the students are already highly motivated (later they can enroll in the driver's training course, which teaches them how to actually drive a car). *Health* covers the human body and emphasizes the prevention and control of common diseases. *Musical Theater* presents American culture as depicted through Hollywood's version of Broadway musicals. *State Requirements* includes a variety of units mandated by the state of California: mental health, first aid (students receive a certificate upon completion of the unit), and fire and accident prevention. *Contemporary Problems* is also a sort of catchall course highlighting issues on consumerism and interpersonal relations. Topics covered include money management, credit, insurance, self-awareness, alternative lifestyles, sexuality, and parenting. *U.S. History* is taught through frequent dramatizations of events, bringing the past alive and making it meaningful to the students. *Discovering Science* includes experiments and a lot of realia to explain physical phenomena. *Nutrition by Computer* exposes students to the benefits of a balanced diet and at the same time introduces them to computers, a rather unusual but effective combination. Students chart daily food intake, categorize foods into groups, and plan well-balanced meals.

Mainstream classes are gradually added beginning at Level II. Students are required to take mainstream physical education and can elect to take other mainstream courses such as typing or home economics.

Level III (akin to the advanced stages described on page 100) is tailored for advanced students who are into a full schedule of mainstream courses except for regular English. Literature is at the core of the program, and the basic skills (listening, speaking, reading, writing) are integrated into the activities evolving out of it. Students are eventually reclassified from Level III ESL once they demonstrate through a variety of means (similar to the initial battery of tests) that they are ready to move on to more challenging activities.

Staff Development

One reason for the apparent success of Artesia's program in helping students to acquire English is the emphasis the school places on staff development. In fact, this was one of the qualities cited when Artesia High School was given national recognition as an Exemplary School in 1983–1984 by the Department of Education. All seventeen of the ESL/content-area teachers have received special training in giving effective comprehensible input and in correcting through modeling and expansion. This special training is part of a series of after-school inservices provided by the district's ESL resource teachers. In addition, Krashen has consulted with the district on several occasions, offering its teachers practical applications of his theories.

Alfredo Schifini and other language arts and reading consultants from the Los Angeles County Office of Education have conducted inservices in writing/reading activities. Schifini stresses that introducing the main points of a lesson increases the use of contextual clues for comprehension of the material. Recapping the major points on the chalkboard or an overhead also increases the possibility of acquisition. He feels that lectures ladened with jargon are inappropriate in a sheltered class. Instead, oral interaction should be used extensively. Students can be engaged in small group tasks such as science experiments, mapmaking, creating murals, preparing skits, and similar activities. It is the teacher's job to demonstrate or model the task for the students to then carry out. He advises teachers, when choosing textbooks, to consider the readability, print size, paragraph length, and types of illustrations used. He recommends mapping or other kinds of graphic organization as useful techniques for helping students obtain meaning from the materials. About sheltered classes, he reminds the teachers:

> Sheltered English classrooms do not involve any magical approach to teaching. Certainly there is no "quick fix". . . . The potential exists with the sheltered model to provide truly meaningful instruction for a wide range of LEP students. It is important to restate that sheltered English should not be viewed as a substitute for bilingual education, but rather as a component in a carefully planned out developmental program designed to facilitate academic success.[8]

In addition to the inservicing provided by the ABC Unified School District, several of the staff members at Artesia are in the master's degree program in teaching second languages offered through a joint effort between the district and California State University, Los Angeles. All the courses in the program are taught locally to make them even more attractive to the teachers.

Staff members working in the program have come to the conclusion that the sheltered class model is an effective means for teaching the target language to diverse primary language groups for whom bilingual education is not currently considered a possibility.

A HIGH SCHOOL ESL ACADEMIC PROGRAM: HUMANITAS[9]

Description of the Program

Thomas Jefferson High School in the Los Angeles Unified School District was one of the first sites to become part of the Humanitas project.

The project was an interdisciplinary program designed to synthesize various disciplines such as social science, biology, history, language arts, and so forth, and break down the artificial boundaries between them. The project,

---

[8] Here it should be noted that the school discontinued its bilingual program in Spanish, some think to its detriment (see Chapter 16), when it began the sheltered model program.

[9] I want to express my appreciation to Eva Wegrzecka-Monkiewicz, a teacher at Thomas Jefferson High School in Los Angeles, California, for sharing with me her numerous writings and research on Humanitas. Because of her work, I was able to summarize the program for inclusion in this edition.

funded by a grant from the Rockefeller Foundation, has now been expanded to over thirty schools in the district. The program, developed by Cleveland teacher Neil Anstead, was an attempt to integrate academic competence and language communication skills.

The ESL section of Humanitas, begun in 1990 at Thomas Jefferson High School, involved students in the following coordinated classes: ESL, biology, and U.S. history. Its goals were to develop academic literacy and oral skills through a writing-based curriculum. The three classes were integrated through the same themes each semester and through coordinated assignments. In the ESL class (somewhat reminiscent of adjunct courses found at the post-secondary level), students read, wrote, and had discussions about the content being studied in biology and U.S. history.

The ESL students in Humanitas at Thomas Jefferson were all Latin American and were operating at intermediate levels of proficiency (see page 100). Every day they met in a four-hour block (two hours of ESL, one hour of biology, and one hour of U.S. history).

The main theme for the two-semester program was human relations. The subthemes are listed below:

Fall Semester

Culture and human behavior

Identity and self-awareness

The Protestant ethic and the spirit of capitalism

Spring Semester

Immigration and racial prejudice

Individual and group power

Atomic age—conflicts and resolutions

Theme integration was the goal of the wide variety of assignments given. For example, during the first unit on culture and human behavior, in ESL the students presented a visual-oral self-awareness project in which they looked at their own Indian-Hispanic cultural roots; in biology they focused on biological adaptation of humans to new environments through hypothetical situations created by the students; in U.S. history they focused on the cultural heritage of Latino populations, both Indian and European, and took a historical view of cultural differences between the United States and Latin America.

Because the teachers were a team, they were able to coordinate assignments right from the beginning of the school year. Students could pursue a single assignment throughout the school day, continuing to develop it as they moved from class to class.

The products of their assignments often reflected the differences in opinion they might encounter as they discussed the content with teachers and classmates. Thus, the environment was often highly stimulating and motivating as students sought to discover information that might shed light on the issues being studied. Over time, they began to think critically, ask questions, seek answers through reading and discussion, and form their own judgments which then became part of products they produced.

Resources

In order to make Humanitas work, certain resources were necessary. Teachers needed time to plan together, to develop teaching materials, to attend workshops, to coordinate field trips and cultural events, and to adapt materials to accommodate the students' emerging language skills. Moreover, they needed access to adequate photocopying facilities, particularly since many of the materials were created by the teachers themselves using a large number of resources.

Research Findings

One of the results of research done by the Center for the Study of Evaluation at UCLA (Aschbacher, 1991) revealed that Humanitas students in general (not only ESL students) demonstrated significant improvement in their writing and conceptual understanding over the two semesters. A second study, reported by Wegrzecka-Monkiewicz (1992), found (among other things) that the ESL Humanitas group made greater gains in reading scores than did the control group consisting of regular ESL students (see Figure 17.6). Pretest and posttest scores on the Gates-MacGinitie Reading Test were used in the comparison.

Wegrzecka-Monkiewicz attributed her results partially to the ESL Humanitas students' greater exposure to more cognitively demanding reading in their course work. She concluded also that the integration of language and content provided an immediate and meaningful context for the language use. She recommended that ESL students be exposed to integrated academic content and that the academic content be linked to language development early on in the language acquisition process.

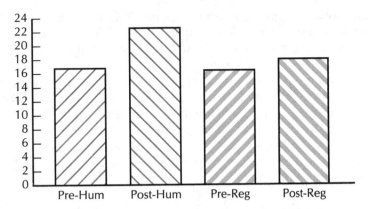

Figure 17.6. Mean Scores on the Gates-MacGinitie Reading Test

AN ELEMENTARY DISTRICT-WIDE PROGRAM[10]

To meet the needs of its ESL students, grades K–3, the Alhambra School District in Alhambra, California has developed a multifaceted program and a thematic curriculum that it is now trying to extend to the higher grades. The program itself integrates features of several of the methods and activities discussed in Part II of this book: the total physical response, the natural approach, jazz chants, storytelling, drama, and many more.

Demographics

The district, which currently serves 13 elementary schools, has a total of 3,583 ESL students, representing about 30 languages. Based on the information gained from the home language surveys required of each student, the most common languages represented include Spanish, Vietnamese, Cantonese, Mandarin, and

---

[10] I wish to thank Linda Sasser at the Alhambra School District in Alhambra, California for making available the information upon which this summary is based. Appreciation goes also to the other people in the Alhambra School District who contributed, either directly or indirectly, to the development of the thematic curriculum: Lilia Sarmiento, Mary Ellen De Santos, Lourdes Brito, Marie Ibsen, Linda Naccarato, Sharon Oliver, Gina Tesner, Virginia Torres-Lopez, Cathy Tyson, and Florence Wong.

Cambodian. However, languages less common to ESL classrooms are also found in this diverse student population: Punjabi (India), Urdu (Pakistan), Illocano (northwestern Luzon, part of the Republic of the Philippines), and Tongan (Tonga, an island group in the South Pacific).

Although many of the language minority children arriving from other countries come from large urban population centers, there are many who come from the isolated rural regions of China and Latin America. In spite of the fact that most of the parents state that their goal for their children is a postsecondary degree, only a few of these parents have themselves obtained such a degree; however, many of them do have some formal education beyond the secondary level.

Assessment and Placement

If a language other than English is spoken in the home, the student is tested at the district's Elementary Orientation and Assessment Center. All elementary students are assessed in the primary language and in English, using a short form of the appropriate Language Assessment Scales (LAS).

The district has recently developed and is using on a trial basis Chinese and Vietnamese tests, drawing from the English and Spanish LAS format. When appropriate (for children in grades 3 and above), the district also assesses performance in mathematics, and English reading, and obtains an English writing sample.

The students who are classified by the district as Limited English proficient (LEP) generally are operating from low-beginning to intermediate proficiency levels (see pages 99–100). Generally they are placed in one of three types of classrooms: a bilingual classroom, a language development classroom, or a language development cluster classroom. In all three types of classrooms, a bilingual paraprofessional is provided whenever possible to assist in the instruction.

A Bilingual Classroom

Bilingual classes are offered K–6 in Spanish, Cantonese, and Vietnamese where there is a teacher available speaking the necessary language. The teacher must have been given Bilingual authorization by the state of California. In addition, the number of students must warrant having a bilingual class.

A Language Development Classroom

This is an intensive English environment for students operating from low-beginning to low-intermediate proficiency levels. It is taught by a state authorized Bilingual or Language Development teacher.

A Language Development Cluster Classroom

This is a transitional classroom that includes ESL students operating at intermediate to advanced levels, native English speakers, and language minority students who are designated as English-fluent. The ESL students are usually placed in this classroom after they have been in the Language Development Classroom for a sufficient amount of time to obtain the necessary skills. The teacher must be a state authorized Bilingual or Language Development teacher.

Staff Development

In an attempt to better meet the needs of language minority students, all of the K–3 teachers in the district participated in staff development sessions. Grouped by grade level, the teachers were given information about the language acquisition process, conditions conducive to learning, and instruction in the recommended methodology. Teachers had a chance to try out various activities and strategies on each other and receive peer feedback. From time to time, they were asked to reflect upon what they had learned and upon their own growth as developing teachers. Linda Sasser, an ESL program specialist for the school district, reported that the teachers' comments on the staff development sessions were generally very positive and that she and the district were encouraged by the enthusiasm.

The Thematic Curriculum

The thematic curriculum that has been developed for K–3 is incorporated into all three classroom designs described on page 342. It is based on the premise that learning is most likely to occur when ideas and activities are integrated and interrelated in the classroom as they are in life. The thematic units link several disciplines (literature, social science, art, and so forth) around a central idea or theme. The district felt that such an organization would encourage the following:

> An emphasis on processes for constructing meaning, solving problems, and discovering relationships
> Greater teacher/student involvement in planning and implementing the curriculum
> Increased individual work appropriate to each student's developmental level and interests
> More effective and productive use of instructional time
> Greater student involvement in dynamic, experiential learning through the myriad of resources provided

Below are graphic representations of the themes developed by the district (with teacher input) and used at level K–3 (see Figures 17.7, 17.8, 17.9, 17.10). Literature, appropriate to the proficiency and age levels of the students, was selected by the teachers to accompany each theme.

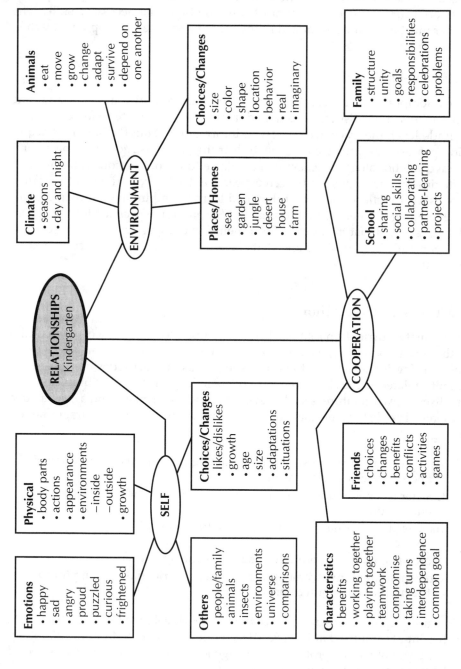

Figure 17.7. Theme: Relationships, Alhambra School District

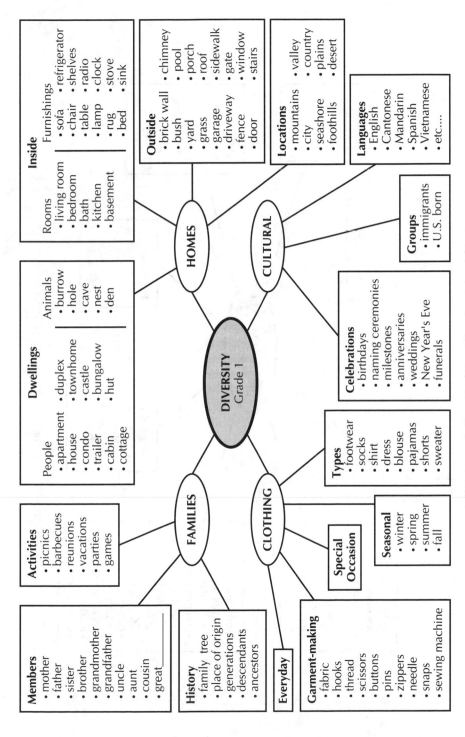

Figure 17.8. Theme: Diversity, Alhambra School District

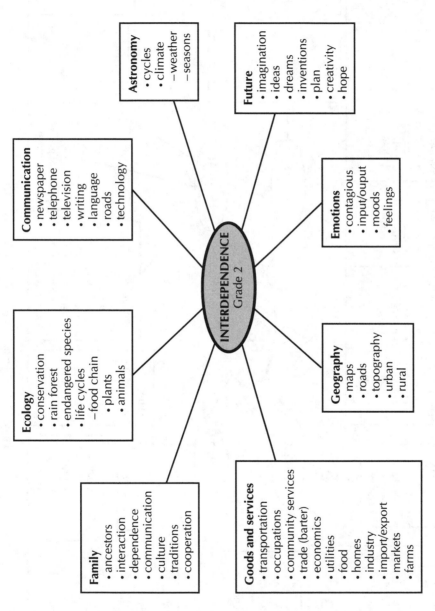

Figure 17.9. Theme: Interdependence, Alhambra School District

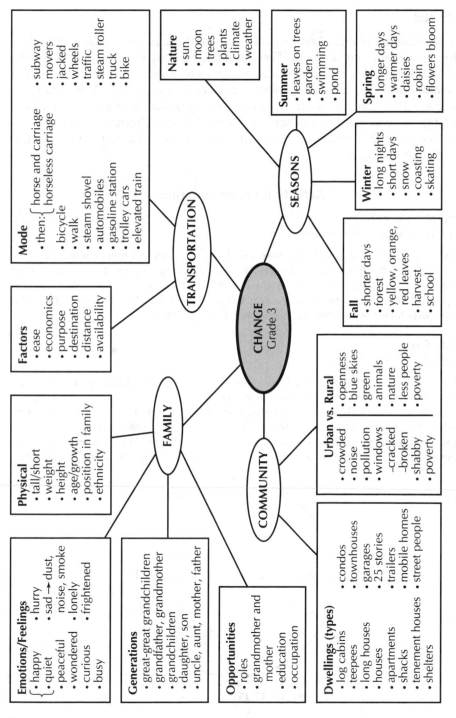

Figure 17.10. Theme: Change, Alhambra School District

Activities

The activities mentioned here are only a few of those recommended to teachers using a thematic organization. The activities, most of which are both flexible and adaptable, can be used at virtually any elementary grade level and in any thematic unit. They include clustering devices (see page 210), Venn diagrams (see page 217), concrete poetry (see page 166), graphic devices (see page 209), the language experience approach (see pages 203-206), alternative types of journals (see page 222), and many more. In addition, the following are included in the recommendations:

Activity Recommendations

Dramatic Corner
Level: Low- to high-intermediate

Set aside a place in the classroom where the children can go and role play real-life situations related to the theme being studied (buying a coat, taking a pet to the veterinarian, selling shoes, etc.). The scenery is designed by the children and all of the necessary props are provided by the children or made available by the teacher. This activity enables children to experiment with language in relatively risk-free environments.

Circle Story
Level: Mid- to high-beginning

The children create a circle divided like a pie (see figure 17.11 below). In each section of the pie, they make a drawing to represent an event in the story. The first event is given the number 1, the second the number 2, and so forth. The children may then cut the segments apart, eliminate the numbers, and give the pieces to a partner to reassemble. They may tell the story by looking at the pictures and/or paste their reassembled circles on construction paper and bind them together to create a class booklet for the future telling of the stories.

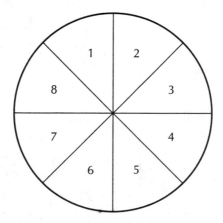

Figure 17.11. Circle Story

Draw and Remember
Level: Low- to mid-beginning

Using strategies from the total physical response, the children are asked to fold a sheet of paper into a predetermined number of sections and number each section. Using crayons, the children are to draw according to the teacher's directions. The pictures should be relevant to the theme's content.

> Pick up your red crayon.
> In box number 1, draw a ball.
> Put your red crayon down.
> Pick up your green crayon.
> In box number 4, draw a chair.

After the children have drawn in all of the boxes, the teacher asks questions such as these: What's in number 2? What color is the ball? What two objects are the same color? Did you draw something orange? What was it? (See Chapter 7 for similar ideas).

Echo Chants
Level: Mid- to high-beginning.

In an echo chant, the children repeat a line or a portion of a line after the teacher or another student has read it aloud first. The district feels that the chant provides a "soft focus" on intonation, inflection, and pronunciation. A simple poem or a teacher-written chant can be easily converted to an echo chant by looking for the repetitive phrases or refrains. See the example[11] below:

POEM ——— conversion ———->	ECHO CHANT	
Snow on the cars.	T:	Snow on the cars.
Snow on the bus.	Ss:	On the cars.
Snow on the vans.	T:	Snow on the bus.
Snow on us!	Ss:	On the bus.
Snow in the puddles.	T:	Snow on the vans.
Snow in the street.	Ss:	on the vans.
Snow in the gutters.	T:	Snow on us!
Snow on my feet!	Ss:	Snow on us!
	T.	Snow in the puddles.
	Ss:	In the puddles.
	T:	Snow in the street.
	Ss:	In the street.
	T:	Snow in the gutters.
	Ss:	In the gutters.
	T:	Snow on my feet!
	Ss:	Snow on my feet!

Within the theme curriculum, teachers are encouraged to use whole-group activities (chanting, role-playing, creating graphic representations discussing, etc.) and

---

[11] The source for this poem is unknown.

small-group instruction (using the Magnetic Way[12] to learn concepts related to the theme, reviewing with a partner, sharing homework). In addition, the following centers are set up where students can go during various times of the day. Examples of activities taking place in each center are in parenthesis.

Book Corner (share a big book with a friend; choose a book to read)

The Art Corner (explore color by mixing any two colors; draw pictures for a collaborative story)

Manipulative Area (sequence four pictures; cut pictures of kitchen items out of magazines)

Discovery Corner (investigate water evaporation; experiment with the effects of the sun on a planted seed)

Listening Area (follow directions on a cassette tape; listen to a story on a cassette tape)

Homework related to the theme being explored is expected of each student. They may be asked to share stories, rhymes, or chants with someone at home and come back with the responses; count the number of chairs or lamps in the house; interview adults to discover their opinions, and so forth.

Teachers are encouraged by the district to adhere to the following practices that are consonant with the philosophies supporting the total physical response and the natural approach (see Chapters 7 and 8): maintaining a low-stress environment, allowing for a silent period, generally focusing on content rather than form, adjusting input to accommodate the student, using an appropriate rate, checking for understanding, and giving timely feedback on student performance.

A KINDERGARTEN ESL PROGRAM WITHIN A SPANISH BILINGUAL SCHOOL

At Loma Vista Elementary School in the heart of Maywood, California, a Spanish-speaking community, every class has two components: ESL and Spanish bilingual education.[13] The kindergarten is no exception.

Beverly McNeilly, a teacher of the ESL component of the kindergarten program, takes a holistic approach to teaching English to her thirty-one students. In her class, English is the vehicle by which the students are exposed to stories films, songs, games, and other items of interest. Structured ESL lessons represent only a small portion of the program; they are the first to go if any spontaneous opportunity presents itself. For example, one day the class abandoned a lesson

---

[12] The Magnetic Way, made available by Creative Edge, Inc. (Steck-Vaughn), consists of a large magnetic board with pieces (people representing multicultural family groups, houses, streets, buildings of various sorts, furniture, etc.) that stick to the board. Overlay pieces (clothing, interchangeable store fronts, etc.) can be placed on top.

[13] Loma Vista Elementary School is in the Los Angeles Unified School District.

to watch the tree trimmers as they sawed off the limbs of an old tree outside the window.

The Subject Matter, Activities, and Classroom Management

The subject matter itself is integrated into a variety of skill areas. Target vocabulary words are generally presented in an introductory lesson and then used again and again throughout the day, whether in math, science, art, physical education, or music. The words will be reinforced naturally in the course of events. For example, in a unit on ocean life the children, as part of an art project, create starfish and coral for a mural. In math they choose which of several drawings are "true octopi" (the ones with eight legs). Music finds the children dancing to aquatic sounds on a recording as they imagine how a shark, a crab, a whale, or a dolphin might move. The reading lesson for the day consists of a game in which the children use magnets to "catch" fish on which letters of the alphabet have been written. A science display (see display area in Figure 17.12) features shells and sand for the children to explore. The entire room environment reflects the topic in other ways with pictures, bulletin boards created by the children, and books on the theme.

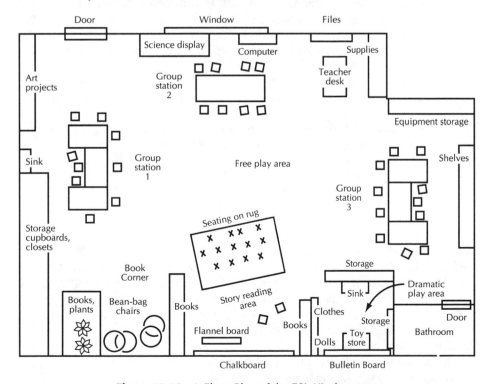

Figure 17.12. A Floor Plan of the ESL Kindergarten

The teacher and her assistants, including one or two peer teachers from the fifth grade, manage a variety of activities for small-group participation. Group size varies from six to nine members depending on the task at hand and on the number of assistants available. Instead of rigidly defined groups and timetables, fluid grouping is used. Several centers are set up each day which focus on related concepts. For example, one day during the study of mathematics, the children were divided into groups to participate in some of the activities from the still popular *Mathematics Their Way* by Lorton (1976). One group found how many designs they could make with only three Tinkertoys. Another group explored the different ways of separating six cubes into two piles. Other groups made geometric shapes with rubber bands and sequential patterns with rocks and shells. The amount of time needed to complete a task depended on each individual. Ongoing informal evaluation and the periodic pretesting and posttesting of key objectives provided evidence that children were mastering the concepts.

For the above lessons, the groups were formed based on a placement test that accompanies the Lorton book. However, usually the small-group activities are not sequentially organized and the children are allowed to select their own groups. Because they are allowed the freedom of choice, interest and curiosity remain at high levels. There are times when the group into which a student wants to go is full (all the chairs are taken). In that case, the student has two choices. He or she either can move to another activity or can participate in free or dramatic play in the areas designated for those purposes (see Figure 17.12). It is in these areas that the child can reinforce concepts just learned or pursue other goals of immediate interest.

The teacher claims that she is often heartened to see the themes with which they have been working reflected in their choices of play activity. She reported:

> When we discussed transportation, block play produced trains and rocket ships. When we were concentrating on body parts, the table in the dramatic play area was an operating table, as amateur doctors came out with appropriate original language. To me, having a child produce "I'm a doctor. What's the problem? Let me see your leg"—a combination of words that had never been taught her—is so much more rewarding than having little parrots.

Total physical response (Chapter 7) is combined with drama (Chapter 10) and songs and poetry (Chapter 9) to reinforce concepts. Props and pictures are used to aid understanding. For example, a skit about a firefighter's day includes the following song, which is sung to the tune of "Frère Jacques." The children act out the words as they sing the song.

Are you sleeping? Are you sleeping?
Firefighters, firefighters.
Alarm bells are ringing, alarm bells are ringing.
Ring, ring, ring . . . ring, ring, ring.

Because the lyrics are accompanied by action, even rank beginners can respond to the cues after observing their more advanced classmates. Children who are in the early speech production stage begin to sing along with the words. Thus, children at all levels are accommodated in this activity.

The teacher frequently reads aloud stories related to the units. Some of the children "read" the stories to each other later in the book corner (see Figure 17.12), prompted only by the pictures. One of McNeilly's favorite stories to read to the children is Esphyr Slobodkina's *Caps for Sale* (1984) during a unit on clothing. She generally simplifies the story to ensure understanding. She reports that because she often repeats the same story several times in a row, she is not surprised to hear expressions from it used by the children in other situations. For instance, "Hats for sale! Does anybody want to buy a hat?" the next day became "Pencils for sale!" when one of the students was handing out the pencils.

Nursery rhymes also are used. One day she exposed the children to "Baa, baa, black sheep," and the next day she asked if they could remember it. In unison they said, "Baa, baa, black sheep, you have any wool?" This made more sense to them than the original syntax, indicating that they were focused more on meaning than on form. Other nursery rhymes such as "Pat-a-cake" and "Pease porridge hot" are introduced as they relate to the topics at hand. The rhymes are memorized by the children and seem to serve a function similar to jazz chants (Chapter 9), appealing to the senses through their rhythmic and other poetic qualities.

McNeilly's attitude toward error correction is that "only global errors that impede communication" should be corrected. She accepts most surface form errors and primary language responses, which she considers to be perfectly healthy and normal. She feels that if the children are not overly corrected, they will be able to develop the self-confidence they need to acquire the language naturally.

To build self-esteem, the children also are given responsibilities to make the classroom function successfully. Even the rituals that begin the class each day are handled almost entirely by children, including the flag salute and attendance procedures. Children are given center stage whenever possible. On some occasions they hold the book from which the teacher is reading aloud; on other days they steady the flannel graph so it won't fall over while others are sticking figures to it, illustrating a story that is being read. In addition, the children's own drawings are mimeographed and made into booklets for the book corner.

The following is one of the integrated units the teacher likes to use.

Topic: Food

Whole Class Activities

Introduce vocabulary with real objects.
Use a grab bag of fruits and vegetables.

Have a fruit-tasting party.

Play the song "Alice's Restaurant" (See H. Palmer in references. Children are asked to hold pictures of food and respond to the verbal cues.).

Make vegetable soup from items brought from home.

Small Group Follow-up Activities

Make macaroni collages.

Use cookie cutters in dough made of clay.

Put illustrated cookbooks in the book corner.

Make collages, gluing pictures of food onto paper plates.

Fingerpaint in chocolate pudding.

Practice writing in thin layers of Jell-O crystals placed in trays.

String popcorn.

Bake cookies.

Set up a supermarket in the play area with food boxes, cans, and so forth; have the children "go shopping."

A Typical Day

11:25–11:45 A.M.

1. Greeting. The teacher greets the students and they greet her back.
2. Calendar coloring takes place. Today's numeral on a large calendar at the front of the room is colored in by a child volunteer. The teacher and students sing the song "What is the day to be happy?" which cues the answer to the question "What day is it today?"
3. Attendance. Children are learning to respond to visual cues. The teacher holds up flash cards and asks, "Is the person with this last name here today?"
4. Quick review of this week's concepts through the use of a picture dictionary.
5. Large-group ESL lesson. With use of posters and other realia, the Chinese New Year, which is coming soon, is discussed. Comparisons between the Chinese New Year and holidays that the children celebrate with their families are drawn.

11:45–12:25 P.M.

Small-group activities. Children choose one or more of the following:

Make paper firecrackers for the Chinese New Year.

Play a game involving guessing how many pennies are in "red packets" (made previously in preparation for the Chinese New Year).

Listen to *The Story about Ping* by Marjorie Flack as it is being read in the book corner.

Decorate paper plates with water colors; plates will later be assembled
into a giant dragon for the Chinese New Year parade.
Dramatic free play.

12:25–12:35 P.M.

Cleanup and nursery rhymes. All the children participate in the cleanup.
Then the children retire to the rug (see Figure 17.12). The "teacher of the
day" (a child volunteer) leads in a chanting of some of the nursery
rhymes the children have learned to date.

12:35–12:55 P.M.

Recess. Outdoor free play with sand toys, balance beams, and climbing
apparatus for psychomotor and large muscle development. At this time
the children are transitioned to the Spanish component of the program.
The Spanish bilingual teacher is also on the playground with her group of
children. When recess is over, the teachers return to their respective
rooms, each with a different group.

CHAPTER 18

Foreign-Language Programs

Many foreign-language students are finding that they can indeed acquire a second language in the classroom, particularly if interactional strategies are employed. The five programs selected for illustration in this chapter were chosen because they contain combinations of features that may be of special interest to foreign-language teachers.

The first program to be described is the Instituto Cultural Argentino Norteamericano (ICANA) in Buenos Aires, Argentina. Its approach to English as a foreign language is making it one of the fastest-growing binational centers in South America. Next is an early immersion program in four elementary schools in Thunder Bay, Ontario, Canada, where children are acquiring French through exposure to the various subject-matter areas. The third is a middle school Spanish language program at Millikan Junior High School in Los Angeles, California. Students at this school begin with an exploratory course in the seventh grade that prepares and motivates them for the two years of Spanish to follow. Then comes the Spanish program at Artesia High School in Artesia, California. There students are acquiring the target language mainly through classroom interaction, but in the traditional one-period-a-day mode. And last is Jefferson County's approach to teaching foreign languages in Lakewood, Colorado. Here, in the largest school district in Colorado, students are supplementing their classroom experiences with foreign-language camps and a district-wide "springfest internationale."

In this chapter, as in the previous one, the descriptions focus on the more salient characteristics of each program, sometimes on the overall organization and other times on specific activities and strategies. Although the programs are designed for particular age groups and specific purposes, it must again be kept in mind that most of the ideas can be readily adapted to other age levels and other kinds of programs.

A BICULTURAL INSTITUTE FOR CHILDREN, ADOLESCENTS, AND ADULTS[1]

The Instituto Cultural Argentina Norteamericano (ICANA), a private, nonprofit organization, was founded in 1927 in Buenos Aires. Its main goal was to link the education and cultural communities of Argentina and the United States. Since 1982, its enrollment has grown from 800 students to 12,000 students today, according to its director, Blanca Arazi. She reports that the Institute's popularity in recent years is due mainly to the communicative methodologies that have emerged in its courses. She credits the natural approach (see Chapter 8) for serving as the main impetus for this radical departure from a past reliance on grammatical approaches as the basis for language development. She is convinced that communicative approaches serve as ". . .the central most important means for gaining linguistic skills."

Students

The student population at the Institute is quite heterogeneous and includes students of all ages and proficiency levels. The students represent diverse cultural and economic backgrounds. But, in spite of all their differences, they have one thing in common: their desire to communicate in English, both in oral and written forms. Their goals at each level are mainly instrumental. At the adult level, goals include preparing themselves for travel to English-speaking countries, being promoted in jobs for which fluency in English is an important asset, and bettering themselves personally as well as professionally. At the adolescent level, goals include preparing for the job market, attending school or traveling in English-speaking countries, understanding English lyrics, communicating through the use of computers, and enriching their personal lives. For children, the goals include understanding English songs, working with computers, playing American games, and understanding cartoons written in English.

Teachers

The Institute's teachers, most of whom have college degrees from local universities, number 210. But not all have college degrees. Some of them come from the ranks of public translators; others are about to graduate from teacher education programs. No matter what their background and preparation, all of them are required to attend the ongoing in-service programs offered by the Institute. Stress is placed on keeping them informed about current happenings in the field and on giving them the opportunity to share ideas and discuss problems. At in-service sessions, the teachers are taught strategies on how to provide

---

[1] Appreciation goes to Blanca Arazi, the director of ICANA, for sharing this information with me.

comprehensible input and how to facilitate the language acquisition process without interfering with it, without imposing their own ideas and values upon those expressing opinions, or without spoon-feeding the language to their students. In addition, teachers are asked to reflect upon their own experiences in learning a foreign language. What seemed to facilitate the process for them? What problems did they face? Each in-service program has a specific focus and stated goals. Participating also in the in-service programs are teachers, not only from all over Argentina, but from neighboring countries. Thus the in-service program experience is very rich and stimulating.

Classes

At ICANA the classes are divided according to age level. Some classes are for children; others for adolescents; yet others for adults. All of the classes will be appropriate for one of three proficiency levels: beginning, intermediate, and advanced (see pages 99–100). Students may select from among the four month long courses offered. Some of them meet twice a week; others meet three or four times a week. Some meet for two hours each session; others meet for two and one-half hours. Classes for adults operating at advanced levels generally are longer in duration then those intended for adults operating at lower levels, adolescents, and children. Intensive courses meet during the summer for three hours per session.

Students at all levels generally pay tuition; however, there are free conversation sessions with native speakers of English, interactive labs where students practice their listening skills, and video sessions during which students watch five-minute video segments and participate in prepared activities relating to the segments.

The classes revolve around main topics of interest such as the environment, health care and nutrition, exercising, sports, science, education, travel, and sociology. No matter what the topic, it is connected to every day life as much as possible. All of the activities, including oral and written activities, grow out of the main topics. Grammar and pronunciation are dealt with in a nontraditional way within the lessons themselves and only when needed. Most students at the Institute appear to internalize message and form simultaneously without formal instruction.

Within the classes, students work in pairs and other small groups in which they actively participate in activities designed to help them move quickly in the interlanguage development process. They frequently are involved in "mixers", which are activities involving interaction with the whole class and the facilitator/teacher. Through such activities it is felt that the students will internalize the skills through active and constant participation and by correcting their own mistakes, sometimes with the help of peers. These activities are described below.

Small-Group Work

Working in pairs and other small groups is particularly stimulating for the students and seems to maximize their effectiveness in the new language. If the issue being discussed is somewhat controversial, then a spokesperson from each group tries to convince the other groups that his or her group is right. If the other groups are not easily convinced, then a vote settles the matter and the groups accept its results. However, that doesn't mean that minds have been changed. The students know that it is all right to disagree with one another. In small groups, the facilitator/teacher circulates among the groups and does not interfere, but rather encourages students to talk and become actively involved.

Mixers

From time to time, all the students are asked to stand up and interact with one another within a time limit set by the facilitator/teacher. Generally a question or problem is posed and students have to actively answer the question or see if they can solve the problem. The teacher and the students often alternate roles as they become facilitators and guides, resource people, managers, and so forth. It is not easy to just sit back as either a teacher or a student and let others do all the work.

Other Kinds of Activities

Affective/humanistic activities are called "field study" activities at the Institute. Through them the teachers and students get to know each others' interests, likes, dislikes, weekend activities, favorite foods, and so on. By this means, barriers between them seem to be lowered and a highly supportive environment results.

Games focusing on discussion, action, group competition, problem solving, or guessing provide strong motivation to learn English. At the same time games serve as a review of structure and vocabulary from previous lessons.

Preparatory activities such as prelistening and prereading activities are used to give contextualization to the content of the courses. It is felt that they increase the relevancy of whatever is going to happen during the ensuing classroom events, and they give students a chance to think about and mentally plan a course of action.

Other activities include the use of maps, charts, graphs of comparison, radio or newspaper stories, giving and receiving directions, open dialogues, debates, discussions, role plays, and improvisations. Whatever the activity the facilitator/teacher engages his or her students in, it must be appropriate to their age and proficiency levels, and it must appeal to their interests. The facilitator/teacher is asked to first provide a model of what it is that the students are supposed to do. It is emphasized that students need to know what is expected of them in order that they not become too frustrated.

Language Assessment

In order to place students in the appropriate courses, they are given a battery of tests in all four skill areas. These tests, created by the Institute, include an oral interview and a written multiple-choice test. Children complete only the oral interview portion of the test unless they already have developed some literacy in their first language and in English.

Once students are placed in the appropriate classes, they are evaluated on an ongoing basis through the use of specially designed oral and written testing activities given twice to students at each proficiency level. They are also given the opportunity to measure their proficiency when it is appropriate by the use of a standardized test such as the CELT and the SLEP. Some opt to take the University of Michigan's Examination for the Certificate of Proficiency in English (ECPE), which is recognized worldwide.

Texts

In addition to some of the standard texts on the market in English as a foreign language, the programs rely heavily on what they call "real-life" materials. Such materials include articles and advertisements from newspapers and magazines, songs, television shows (including soap operas), and of course, the work that the students themselves have done. At the levels intended for children, books about the "Sesame Street" characters, Big Bird, Cookie Monster, and so forth, are used daily. At all levels, importance is placed on involvement and the lowered anxiety and inhibitions that can result from high participation.

A FRENCH IMMERSION MODEL FOR ELEMENTARY STUDENTS[2]

Background

Two out of three English-speaking Canadians want their children to learn French to "improve their career options and broaden their horizons."[3] Hence it is not surprising that a group of Thunder Bay, Ontario, parents (of mainly Finnish or Italian origin) approached the Lakehead Board of Education to request a French *immersion* program for their children. Why did they choose an

---

[2] I wish to thank the following for sharing information about their programs with me and for allowing me to observe French immersion classes in their respective schools: Ken Cressman, Nicole Gaudet, George Rendall, Lise Bagdon, Colette Aubry, John Brusset, Carol Nabarra, Glenn Coriveau, and Roy Fossum. My thanks also to Wendy Hansen for providing transportation and lodging.

[3] From "Making Choices Campaign" (1986). In *Canadian Parents for French, 24,* 8. The statistics are based on the results of a Gallup Poll taken for the Canadian Parents for French organization.

immersion program over one of the more traditional ones? They believed, as do many parents in Canada, that immersion does in fact produce bilinguals. Their views were compatible with those of the Ontario Ministry of Education, which concluded that immersion is an optimal means for achieving a high level of competency in French. Immersion programs (see Chapter 16) involve a far more extensive and meaningful experience with French than can be provided by the more traditional *core* programs, in which students study French for one period each day, or the more recently developed *extended* programs in which at least one content-area class is taught in French in addition to the core.

While their children are learning the subject matter in French, the parents feel assured that the skills in the first language will not be adversely affected. According to Lapkin and Swain (1984), any fears that may be present concerning this issue have no basis in reality. This is at least partially due to the fact that the children belong to the majority culture (in the case of Thunder Bay, only 3 percent of the households claim French as the home language) and that English dominates their lives outside of the school environment. Lapkin and Swain report:

> The English achievement results for students in the early total-immersion program indicate that, although initially behind students in unilingual English programs in literacy skills, within a year of the introduction of an English Language Arts component into the curriculum, the immersion students perform equivalently on standardized tests of English achievement to students in the English-only program (1984, p. 50).

They claim that this is true even for students who are not introduced to English until grade 3 or 4. They point out, too, that after grade 4, French immersion students sometimes outperform their English-only peers in some aspects of English language skills. Their achievement in the subject areas (math, science, social studies, etc.) is also comparable to that of their English-only peers (see Krashen, 1984).

In addition, parents are convinced that their children do not need particularly high IQs to be successful in French immersion programs (see also Related Reading 4). On this issue, Lapkin and Swain assert that IQ is not any more predictive of success in French immersion programs than it is in regular English-only programs. Students of below-average intelligence are not at a greater disadvantage in immersion programs. In fact, being bilingual may boost their confidence and have other positive results affectively.

In general, most students can expect to reach nativelike levels in French intake skills (listening and reading) by the time they finish elementary school. However, in the output skills (speaking and writing), they are often less nativelike until they have had considerable contact with native French speakers or Francophones. The only children found by the organization of Canadian Parents of French to be less than adequate candidates for immersion programs are those who exhibit a lack of ability in auditory discrimination or auditory memory. Problems in these areas are usually detected in the first year of kindergarten and the students having them can be steered early on into English-only programs.

Because of the efforts of those first parent advocates of French immersion in Thunder Bay and those parents, teachers, and other educators who were to follow, the program has mushroomed. It began with 36 students in one elementary school and now boasts of having 647 students in four elementary schools, one of which has a program extending from the second year of kindergarten (for five-year-olds) all the way through grade 8. The programs, which are allowed to grow with the students, increase by one grade level at a time as the students become older, until all the programs extend at least through grade 8. However, the school board is currently considering the incorporation of French immersion into the secondary curriculum beginning with grade 9. Future plans also include the establishment of a French Immersion Center (where the regular English-only program would be dropped) at Redwood Public School, should the current enrollments continue. For the past two years, 16 to 17 percent of all second-year kindergarten children have been enrolled in French immersion programs throughout the district.

Enrollment and Transportation

Enrollment is on a first come, first served basis, and transfers from other immersion programs are accepted provided there is room. Transportation is generally available for those accepted into the program, making it possible for a larger number of students to be involved. The students within the urban area are bused from designated neighborhood pickup points to the schools, and for those in the rural areas transportation arrangements can be made at a reasonable cost.

Support Services

Every school in which a French immersion program is located attempts to maintain an ever-expanding collection of books and reference materials in French. The teachers are now looking for materials oriented to the needs of immersion students in particular. In addition, audiovisual resources appear to be in ample supply and new ones are ordered yearly.

Assistance is available for enrichment or remediation from a bilingual resource teacher or a qualified special education resource teacher. Parents of children with severe problems will be counseled and recommendations will be given depending upon the type of problem and upon the resources available at each school.

The home itself can be considered a "support service." Nicole Gaudet, an education officer for the district, reports, "Because the parents have made a decision about the education of their children to be in French immersion programs, they are more involved in their children's education." Parents seem more than happy to read stories in English to their children at home, work with teachers to provide experiences with Francophones whenever possible, take their children to French cultural events, and volunteer to aid in classroom ventures.

Program Description

In the first two years of the program, the language for instruction is 100 percent French (except in emergency situations). In addition, all communication within the classroom is in French. In the second, third, fourth, and fifth grades, English is added but is limited to 75 minutes per day of English Language Arts. French is the language for instruction 75 percent of the time, English 25 percent of the time. During grades 6, 7, and 8, 50 percent of the instruction is in French and 50 percent in English. By the end of the eighth grade the students will have studied history, geography, math, science, and other subjects in both languages. The subjects cover a wide range of content areas at each level (see Table 18.1).

The concepts to which the students are exposed in the French immersion program are comparable to those to which they are exposed in the regular English-only classroom.[4] In listening, the goals include helping children to listen with interest and selectivity at appropriate levels in a variety of experiences. They are taught to judge validity, make comparisons, make inferences, draw conclusions, generalize, and understand intent. During speaking, children learn to articulate their ideas and feelings confidently in a supportive environment, extend and synthesize various speaking skills (drama, role-playing, conversation, discussion, oral reading, and others), and develop opinions through interaction with the teacher and peers. They learn to tell stories, interpret pictures, name and describe objects, explain events, evaluate, and question using verbal as well as nonverbal clues. Reading skills and processes involve exposing students to a variety of reading materials (legends, myths, folktales, poems, plays, cartoons, novels, biographies, magazine articles, recipes, directions, newspapers), enabling them to respond to print within the environment (e.g., names, labels, signs, initials), comprehend and respond to ideas, relate pictures to print, recall details, sequence events, recognize plot, understand relationships, follow directions, make judgments, distinguish fact from fantasy and fact from opinion, check for bias, predict outcomes, and so forth. Writing involves being able to label components on maps and diagrams; record personal experiences in their own words; adapt style to intended purpose; write from dictation; and create stories, poetry, diaries, letters, sets of directions, expositions, and reports. Even by the end of kindergarten, children have acquired a fairly extensive vocabulary in French; they are able to follow instructions and to comprehend simple stories.

---

[4] The concepts listed here are paraphrased from the *Core Language Guide* made available by the Lakehead Board of Education. No attempt is made to list all of the goals set down by the board. A few of the more typical ones have been selected for inclusion.

They can answer questions appropriately, participate effectively in drama, and sing a number of songs.

TABLE 18.1. FRENCH IMMERSION CURRICULUM

Grade	K	1	2	3	4	5	6	7	8
French	X	X	X	X	X	X	X	X	X
Math	X	X	X	X	X	X	*	X *	
Environmental Studies	X	X	X	X	X	X	X		
Science							*		X
Music	X	X	X	X	X	X	*X	*X	*X
Physical Education	X	X	X	X	X	X	*X	*X	*X
Art	X	X	X	X	X	X	*X	*X	*X
History								X	*
Geography								*	X
English			*	*	*	*	*	*	*

Code: * subjects taught in English
     X subjects taught in French

Adapted from *Programme d'Immersion Précoce*, The Lakehead Board of Education, 1985.

Because the immersion classes focus on the subject matter rather than on the target language itself, it is important that the teachers have an adequate knowledge of the subject areas they teach and that they be native speakers of French or have nativelike fluency. It is also important for the students to associate specific teachers with French and others with English. For this reason, the school district always assigns teachers to classes taught in the same language. This is especially important when there is a possibility that the same students will be present in more than one class taught by the same teacher.

Strengths and Weaknesses of the Program

Ken Cressman, the principal of Redwood Public School, feels that the French immersion program in his school has benefited the entire student body. When French cultural events are arranged, they are planned not only for the French immersion students but for everyone. It is his feeling that any cultural activity, even one in another language, can be enriching for all the students, be it singing, mime, or drama. In addition, he has observed that the French immersion students have improved the ambiance of the school in general in that they tend to be more tolerant of other cultures and differences among people. When asked if one segment of the school has benefited more than others from the immersion program, he targeted the core French program as having perhaps received the most advantages. Although the students in this program take French for only one period a day, they profit from exposure to French immersion students with whom they can sometimes converse in a limited fashion and from whom they can often receive help with their homework.

Nicole Gaudet also is convinced that French immersion has been a real boon to the environments of all the schools of which it is a part. Because of the increased parental support and interest of the parents of these children, the schools' parent associations thrive and the atmospheres of the schools are becoming more positive.

However, both Cressman and Gaudet agree that improvements can be made. Lack of materials appropriate to French immersion was one of the problems mentioned. Currently, most of the materials come from Francophone programs and are intended for native French speakers. However, teachers are busy creating their own materials and translating the ones intended for the English-only programs. Another problem mentioned was recruiting enough teachers with expertise and fluency to meet the growing needs. In addition, developing a long-range plan for inservicing was felt to be necessary means for helping the teachers to keep current once they have been hired.

Because these weaknesses are not inherent in the immersion programs themselves, both administrators are of the opinion that they can be overcome with additional funds and further effort on the part of everyone involved with the programs.

A MIDDLE SCHOOL SPANISH LANGUAGE PROGRAM[5]

Background

Millikan Junior High School is in the Los Angeles Unified School District, and, like many schools in that district, it serves a very large language minority population: Latin (30 %), Asian (30%), Anglo (30%), Black (5%). The remaining 5% of the students represent various ethnic backgrounds.

The Foreign Language Department opens its courses in Spanish and French to all who want them, including students in its Special Education programs. The department's faculty is firmly committed to the idea that the foreign-language experience is for all who seek a liberal education, and that through this experience, increased understanding and personal growth will result, regardless of ethnic background or other circumstances.

The students' motivation for studying a foreign language is generally instrumental—to fulfill academic requirements. However, many of the students are interested in developing basic interpersonal communication skills.

---

[5] I want to thank Brandon Zaslow, the Chair of the Foreign Language Department at Millikan Junior High School, for providing me with the information upon which this summary is based.

The Goals of the Foreign Language Department

The Department has adopted the following goals set down by the California Foreign Language Framework to develop individuals who can:

a. communicate accurately and appropriately with representatives of other languages and cultures
b. understand themselves as individuals shaped by a given culture
c. function appropriately in at least one other culture
d. exhibit sensitivity to cultural differences in general

It is the feeling of the Department that these goals can be achieved when programs stress communication over the learning of grammar rules and the memorization of vocabulary items. The governing principle of the Department's programs is, and I quote, "To learn content and culture through language and to learn language through content and culture."

More specifically, the Department expects that students will be able to function in informal environments, understand simple face-to-face conversation, and deal with relevant academic and survival topics. In addition, it is expected that they will be able to determine overall meaning from written discourse, create meaning through writing, and transfer learned material to new situations.

Although some may consider the Department's more general goals to be somewhat lofty, it is difficult to argue with them, particularly in view of the fact that in the Spanish Foreign Language Program, students scored 80 percent above the norm in California in speaking proficiency, 13 percent above in listening proficiency; and 12 percent in writing proficiency, according to the 1989 report put out by the California Foreign Language Competency Project.

Description of the Spanish as a Foreign Language Program

The Department offers two programs in Spanish: Spanish as a Foreign Language and Spanish for Spanish Speakers. For the purpose of this chapter, only the Spanish as a Foreign Language Program—Level 1 will be described in depth. Its two-year program (Levels 1 and 2) serves approximately 200 students each year, and seeks to bring eighth- and ninth-graders to intermediate levels in Spanish (see page 100) by the end of the second year. A ten-week exploratory Spanish module is offered to seventh-graders to introduce them to basic concepts and give them an overview of what to expect. Often these students become group leaders in the Level 1 classes and sometimes serve as resources for the other students.

The following practices are a few of those developed by the Department and adhered to by the teachers (one full-time and two part-time) in the Spanish as a Foreign Language Program.

Instruction is appropriate to the learners' levels of proficiency in each of the skill areas.

Students perform in a wide range of culturally valid situations.

Lessons challenge students to interact with increasingly demanding academic content.

Students perform a wide range of communicative tasks (emphasis on higher-level thinking skills).

Teachers use paralinguistic clues (visuals, objects, etc.) and modify their speech to make input comprehensible (simplification, expansion, restatement, slower speed, use of cognates, etc.).

Teachers frequently confirm and clarify responses and check for comprehension.

Guided practice is both meaningful and personalized.

Teachers provide opportunities for paired and small-group interactions and use strategies that provide for various learning styles.

Below is an overview of Level 1 and a description of sample activities.

An Overview

UNIT 1: FIRST ENCOUNTERS

Introducing oneself/saying where you are from

Understanding and spelling names and places

Greeting and leave taking/saying how you feel/being polite

Understanding prices/giving and receiving phone numbers

Asking and telling times and dates

Discussing the weather/seasons/temperature

Role-playing in the target culture and U.S. contexts

UNIT 2: ACTIVE LIVES

Describing daily activities in and out of school

Asking questions about activities

Expressing what one desires/hopes/needs to do

Expressing what one likes/dislikes doing

Role-playing in target culture and U.S. contexts

UNIT 3: FRIENDS AND FAMILY

Identifying others (friends and family)

Describing self and others

Talking about feelings

Talking about activities related to friends and family

Talking about sports
Talking about pets
Talking about living space at home
Talking about routine care of the home
Role-playing in target culture and U.S. contexts

UNIT 4: DAILY LIFE

Talking about daily routines (discussing similarities and differences)
Focus on weekdays and weekends
Talking about clothes (colors/combinations)
Learning about healthful living/the body/medical care
Talking about food (marketing/restaurants/invitations for meals)
Talking about school/physical layout/activities in more detail
Role-playing in target culture and U.S. contexts

UNIT 5: COMMUNITY LIFE

Identifying places in various communities (maps/directions)
Talking about community/cultural activities
Talking about community resources
Talking about travel
Role-playing in target culture and U.S. contexts

UNIT 6: THE WORKING WORLD

Identifying abilities
Discussing career preferences
Identifying professional opportunities
Making plans for the future

Sample Activities

THE LOW-BEGINNING LEVEL

The first samples come from the unit El Cuerpo (the body) that has been developed for students in the Spanish as a Foreign Language Program who are operating at the low-beginning level (see page 99). Its major goal is to help students develop listening comprehension and a large receptive vocabulary. Speech will be encouraged but not expected at this point.

The unit draws from the total physical response and the audio motor unit (Chapter 7) and story experience (Chapter 10).

1. Using aspects of the total physical response, students are asked to touch specific body parts: head, chest, stomach, back, arms, hands, fingers, legs, knees, and

feet. However, not all items are introduced at once. First, two items are introduced, followed by a check for understanding. Then, a third item is added, followed by a check understanding. Then, a fourth is added, and so forth.

2. Students are divided into groups. Each group is given a life-size doll made of construction paper. Aspects of the story experience are then used to tell the story of a terrible accident involving the doll which represents a real person. The students are "doctors" and have each been given a number (they were taught numbers previously). They are instructed by the teacher to place the bandages (they have sticking putty on their backs) on the various injured body parts. Below is the story. The students will probably only understand the body parts, the word "bandage," the command "put" and some of the words made clear through visual aids.

   The teacher says in Spanish, "Carlos has had a terrible accident (the instructor points to the picture of a person with mild injuries). He was hit by a car. Doctors, doctors, what should we do?" (The teacher holds up a card with a huge question mark on it and shrugs his or her shoulders as if puzzled.) "Put a bandage on his head, Doctor 1." (Doctor 1 in each group puts the bandage on the doll's head.) The teacher repeats the question and asks the students to put bandages on other parts, until all the targeted body parts have been recycled. Then the teacher says, "Carlos is well now" (shows a picture of the same person obviously recovered). "Take the bandage off his/her head, Doctor 2", and so forth until all the bandages have been removed.

3. For further reinforcement, students cut out pictures of the various body parts from discarded magazines, and paste them on a blank sheet of paper to form bodies of their own creation. Then they are asked to label the parts.

THE HIGH-BEGINNING LEVEL

Next are sample activities from a unit entitled Bienvenidos (welcome). This unit has been developed for students who are operating at the high-beginning level (see page 99). The unit focuses on encouraging positive attitudes toward Mexico and on specific communicative demands such as being able to greet others, talk about time, make appointments, plan schedules, order food in a restaurant, buy necessary items for survival, etc. It centers around a story line in which the students pretend to be participating in a year-abroad program in Mexico. They arrive at their respective Spanish-speaking homes where they need to be able to get things done with language. Below are just a few activities from the unit, which is designed to last about six weeks. It should be noted that the new concepts and structures encountered will be recycled many times in a variety of circumstances.

1. Students make simulated telephone calls to their hosting peers. They give their names and spell them and they ask many questions about what to pack for their stay, etc.
2. Students write down the addresses of their hosts. Then they each write to their host, indicating their feelings about visiting the host's country.
3. Once in the host's village or city, students change their watches to reflect the time in the time zone they have entered, if it is different from their own time zone.

4. Students take the roles of hosts or guests as they introduce themselves and tell where they are from. Consideration is given to appropriate forms: first name basis using *tú* or title plus last name basis using *Ud*. Versions of this activity are repeated as needed.

5. Each student chooses favorite activities from a list provided by the host. The lists include events such as soccer games, concerts, dining out, shopping, etc. They then talk about the dates and starting times of the activities in which they will be participating.

6. Students are given calendars upon which they can write down the events in which they will participate. What is the event? Where is it? When does is start? Will someone pick them up? If so, at what time? Must they meet a person somewhere? If so, where and at what time? Students can also enter other events such as birthdays of the host family members, holidays, etc.

Strengths/Problems

One of the strengths of the program is its exploratory module for seventh-graders, giving them insight into what it might be like to learn another language. However, according to Brandon Zaslow, the Chair of the Foreign Language Department, its main strength is its focus on relevant content and culture. But this is also where its chief problem lies. The high schools into which it feeds often adhere to traditional, structure-based programs, making transitions difficult, and sometimes painful, for the students who matriculate with high expectations for continued relevant study. In spite of this problem, most of the students are able to adjust and do very well in their new settings as long as they have at least some opportunity to express themselves creatively in Spanish.

A HIGH SCHOOL SPANISH PROGRAM[6]

Although working against odds common to many high school foreign-language programs, Christina Rivera uses natural methods as much as possible in her Levels I and II (first and second year) Spanish classes at Artesia High School in Artesia, California. One of the constraints under which she works is that she must cover a certain amount of formal grammar so that the students will be ready for what is expected at subsequent levels. A second constraint is that she is able to meet with her students only one period a day, five days a week. Yet a third constraint is that, as in other California schools, the students are in foreign-languages classes not always by choice. Often they are there to satisfy graduation or college entrance requirements. Thus, many of her students bring to her classes less than positive attitudes.

Nevertheless, it is her hope that by the end of the program the students will be able to communicate effectively and appropriately in the target language. It

---

[6] Artesia High School is part of the ABC Unified School District.

is also her hope that students will become more sensitive to cultural differences. Activities in her classes, for the most part, center around her students' world: their objectives, their personal attempts to deal with uncertainties, and their efforts to comprehend and speak another language.

Level I

Before beginning the instruction in Spanish, Rivera takes time to educate the students in the theories upon which her methods are predicated. She feels that as a result of her doing so, the students are less apt to find her methods "strange" and are more apt to try.

Using an outline similar to what Krashen and Terrell suggest (see pages 129–132), she works on receptive skills first with Level I students. Body language, gestures, facial expressions, and tone of voice are all important in the initial stages. Through total physical response (see Chapter 7), students learn colors by manipulating pieces of colored paper. They learn about the objects in their immediate environment, food, clothing, and many other relevant concepts by manipulation of various items. Pictures and props are used to act out scenes. Familiar stories are told as visuals are shown. And because it does not require students to respond orally, bingo is played, reinforcing concepts related to the topics covered. Simple treasure hunts (see also Chapter 11) are designed requiring students to find objects of certain colors or that have other specific characteristics.

The following activities combining the natural approach and total physical response are typical:

1. Describe a picture from a current magazine and follow up by making statements or giving commands.
   Example: *This is a picture of some skirts. Notice the colors. This one* (points to a skirt) *is green. Jane* (a student in class) *is wearing a skirt. Her skirt is green. This one* (points to another skirt) *is pink. Point to the pink skirt, etc.*
   Follow-up: (Thumbs up means "yes"; thumbs down means "no.") *This skirt* (points to a pink skirt) *is green* (thumbs should be pointed down). *This skirt* (points again to the pink skirt) *is pink* (thumbs should be pointed up), and so forth.
2. Ask students to draw or cut out pictures of items in a category (food, clothing, kitchen utensils, etc.). Ask them to hold up pictures of specific items. Have them take specific pictures to various places around the room.
3. Using pictures, facial expressions, and gestures, introduce the students to some of the more common emotions: happy, sad, angry, bored, fearful, etc. Hold up cue cards on which the names of the different emotions have been written. Have the students point to the picture that clearly expresses the specific emotion indicated.
4. Using numbered pictures, ask the students to say the number of the picture described by the teacher.

5. Have the students make "self" collages with items that they feel best express themselves. Later in the year they will be discussing these with class members in the target language.

As the students progress to early speech production, mass media are relied upon because of their relevance and contextuality. Rivera finds commercials particularly effective. Students act out the commercials with props as the teacher gives commands. Much later, students will be writing and acting out their own commercials. Other activities she feels are appropriate to this stage are described below:

1. Using a real suitcase and real clothing and other items for travel, students prepare for an imaginary trip. The teacher asks the students to place the items in the suitcase that they would take to Acapulco, Aspen, etc.
2. The students are shown a picture from a magazine. They are asked to name what they see. A list of the items mentioned is written on the chalkboard.
3. Students make a chart consisting of several of their names, the clothes they are wearing, and the color of each item (see a similar activity in Chapter 8).
4. Matrices such as the following are used as starters for scenarios:

¿Cuánto cuesta el _____?
Está de venta. Le cuesta_____?
¡Qué bueno! (¡Que malo!)
Necesito un _____.
Por qué no vas a_____?
¿Cuánto cuesta?
Cuesta_____ mas o menos.

5. Students write in a journal each day using the target language. The teacher guides them at first. They begin by writing down their favorite colors and favorite items of clothing. At later stages the writing becomes freer as students write their feelings and thoughts.

The study of culture also is included as the students progress. Discussions are conducted entirely in the target language aided by props, maps, and a lot of visuals. Cultural information is frequently woven into other activities such as listening to music and game playing.

Grammar is introduced at early stages. However, the concepts are those that are generally easily learned and applied. Many of the grammar activities are assigned as homework.

Level II

Level II students (those in their second year of language study) are usually somewhere in the early production stage. Rivera feels that many of them regress over the summer since they have had almost no exposure to the target language then. However, after spending a few weeks doing activities similar to those described above, the students will soon move into speech emergence. Students at this level are expected to listen to Spanish-language broadcasts during a part of each day for several days in sequence.[7] They may hear traffic reports, time/temperature/weather reports, commercials, horoscope readings, song dedications, listener call-ins, interviews, sports reports, the news, or lyrics to music. They are encouraged to tape the broadcasts for repeated listening experiences. They are asked to write down what items they understand from each report. As they listen to the same reports from time to time, they are pleased to find that they understand more and more of the broadcasts. Through this process students are exposed to native speakers using contemporary, idiomatic speech. They learn to take advantage of cognates, intonation, and other clues to meaning.

Affective activities (see Chapter 13) are favorites among Rivera's students at this level. It must be kept in mind that the students have spent some time preparing for humanistic activities all along. At earlier stages, emotions were identified through the natural approach and total physical response. The journals allowed students to express their likes and dislikes and their attitudes in general. In addition, the collages contributed to their willingness to reveal themselves in low-risk situations.

Below are a few of the activities used:

1. To reinforce the terminology describing human emotions, the teacher reads a soap opera melodramatically. The cue cards (mentioned on page 183) with the names of various emotions can be held up by the teacher or an assistant as the story is being read. The students as a group can act out the emotion that is being displayed.
2. Students are asked in the target language to draw a happy baby, a mad father, and so forth. Then they are instructed to draw the following:
   a. a father who has just heard that his teenager has smashed the family car
   b. a mother seeing an "A" on her child's report card
   c. a girl seeing her boyfriend with her best friend
   d. a cheerleader after falling off the human "pyramid"
3. Students hold up small cue cards with the names of emotions written on them. Each card is held up in response to statements in the target language made by the teacher. Below are some examples.
   a. When someone is mean to me, I feel. . .
   b. At a party I feel. . .
   c. Before a test, I feel. . .
   d. With my family I feel. . .
   e. At the doctor's office I feel. . .
4. Students are asked to name songs that make them feel happy, sad, like dancing, etc.
5. Students draw and label pictures about their favorite activities. They then interview each other about the activities depicted.

---

[7] Credit for this idea is given to Lynne La Fleur.

Eventually the students are able to discuss problems, goals, and everyday matters in the target language. Although they may not be able to converse in perfect Spanish by the end of the second year, they seem to communicate with a minimum of anxiety.

Rivera insists that her main goal throughout the stages is to create as natural a learning environment as possible. She feels that she still has a long way to go to create an optimal classroom. However, she admits modestly that she is coming closer to her vision with each passing year.

ONE DISTRICT'S APPROACH TO FOREIGN-LANGUAGE TEACHING[8]

Lorenzo Trujillo, Coordinator of Second Language Education for the Jefferson County Public Schools in Lakewood, Colorado, is calling the renewed interest in foreign-language study within his school district a "renaissance." At the high school level alone, the enrollment in foreign-language classes has grown 12 percent in the last four years. Over 21,000 students, K–12 (approximately 26 percent of the total school population), have signed up for one of the district's many foreign-language classes, including French, German, Latin, Russian, and Spanish. The classroom teachers are strongly encouraged to emphasize oral skills (except in Latin) through a variety of activities including role play, games, singing, dancing, ethnic food preparation, interacting with native-speaking guests, field trips, and so forth. In addition to recommending these kinds of activities for the classes themselves, the district feels that the apparent revitalization has been due, at least in part, to a few innovations that have become integral aspects of the program. It is these innovations that will be the focus here.

Language Camps

The camps began in 1970 when a group of high school Russian teachers transformed a mountain ranch complex owned by the school district into the "ancient Russian village" of Sosnovka. Russian menus, typical Russian activities, traditional costumes, Russian-language signs, make-believe passports, and radio-broadcast tapes were prepared for the events, which were scheduled to last through the weekend. The students, who arrived by bus, were first stopped for an inspection at a roadblock (the local police cooperated in this activity). The visitors were asked by pretend Russian border guards, dressed in rented

---

[8] Thanks to the Jefferson County Public Schools for giving me permission to summarize their foreign-language program and related activities. Special thanks go to the people who helped supply the details upon which this summary is based: Lorenzo Trujillo, Patsy Jaynes, Martha Quiat, Xavier Valenzuela, and Jennie Green (the former Coordinator of Second Language Education).

costumes, to show their passports and open all their luggage for inspection. Only Russian was spoken. After several good-natured hassles over the luggage and paperwork, the students were officially welcomed to Sosnovka by the newly appointed commissar, who gave a rather lengthy and dramatic speech.

Today similar procedures are used to welcome newcomers to El Pinar (Spanish), Tannenbaum (German), and Val-les-Pins (French), in addition to Sosnovka. Each camp is visited by approximately 150 students, 20 to 30 teachers, and 10 to 20 native speakers. The native speakers usually play the largest roles (commissary mayors, or police chiefs) and the teachers sometimes are the gendarmes, priests, or other village personalities.

A typical day at the camp might include rap sessions with group leaders or activities such as dancing, singing, watching skits, movies, and other programs. Each visitor is given plenty of time to soak up the ambiance and browse through the many colorful shops featuring perfumes, arts and crafts (made by the schools' language clubs), and souvenirs (usually imported). Play currency is created and an exchange rate established to provide the students with the experience of dealing with foreign money. Cafés sell pastries, espresso, piroshki, alouette sans tête, paella, auschnit, and other foreign delicacies. At any given moment there may be seven to fifteen different activities to choose from, all being carried out in the target language. For example, there may be lessons in macramé, lectures on various subjects of "local" interest, games, Ukrainian Easter egg painting, weaving, baking, candle dipping, or silk-screen painting, to name a few. The village of Val-les-Pins even has an artist-in-residence who does caricatures. In some of the village's night spots, a piano player is often on hand with foreign-language song sheets for those who wish to sing along.

For the participants, the cost of the weekend is minimal, usually running about thirty dollars. Participation is voluntary. Anyone, regardless of proficiency level, who is in a foreign-language class in one of the district's secondary schools is eligible to attend.

Concerning the effectiveness of the program, one of the students sums it up best, "I really want to go to Spain now that I have tried El Pinar."

A Springfest Internationale

An event with features similar to those of the language camps is the Springfest Internationale, which occurs every three years. All foreign-language and English as a Second Language students K–12 are involved in the one-day celebration of multiple languages. The day begins with much pomp and circumstance. A parade of about 50 units, representing the various schools in the county, marches through the city. Included are international flags and banners, floats, Roman chariots, children attired in traditional ethnic costumes, and other entries of interest. Even the members of the Board of Education and other school/community groups and individuals participate in the parade. Ribbons and medals are given to what are judged to be the outstanding units entered in the competition.

After the parade arrives at the location for the day's activities, faculty members give welcoming speeches in six languages. Then there is the lighting of the Springfest Internationale flame, reminiscent of the Olympics. The children dressed in ethnic costumes place flowers into a bouquet of many colors, signifying the coming together of nations and languages. Balloons are released as the throngs of people enter the many language villages to begin the day's cultural and competitive activities.

Competitions include trivia bowls, speeches, skits, and many other events in all the target languages. Athletic games include relays, tugs-of-war, volleyball, soccer, and many others.

The buildings at the chosen site are all decorated in streamers, posters, and other paraphernalia to represent the different villages. Each building has its share of booths, cafes, game areas, stages for presentations, and display sections to simulate each country's culture. In order to play the games and buy food items and souvenirs, the students exchange their money for "quichees" (the common currency) at the International Bank. Profits are used to pay the expenses of the fest, and whatever is left over is divided among the schools to help purchase supplementary materials for the language classes.

Foreign Languages in the Elementary Schools (FLES)

The district's FLES program began as a grassroots movement sponsored by several local parent, teacher, and student groups. The sponsors were motivated by the notion that children gain many advantages by becoming bilingual at an early age. The parents thought that their children would perhaps experience a higher degree of creativity and cognitive flexibility due to the additional challenge that acquiring a second language brings. In addition, they felt that learning a second language would be fun.

The children (K–6) now meet every day either before or after school to learn Spanish, German, French, Latin, Modern Greek, or Russian. The teachers, who have been hired by a parent group, must be fluent in the target language, work well with children, have a communicative philosophy, and be able to maintain a high level of excitement in the classroom. However, it is not required that they be certified as teachers. Once hired, they must be trained in natural methods at workshops provided by the school district. It is interesting to note that many parents also participate in the workshops to learn ways in which they can encourage and provide assistance to their children at home.

The four-year-old program already encompasses 48 elementary schools in the district and it is still expanding. About 3,000 of the district's elementary students are enrolled. Each school has from 1 to 4 FLES teachers, who are paid according to the number of students registered. In order to allow for meaningful interaction, only 10 to 15 students are allowed in a class. The cost of participation is approximately fifty dollars per child for each semester; this pays for materials and the teacher's salary. The school district and the FLES Committee, consisting mainly of parents elected from 48 schools, aid in the entire process. They survey community needs, assist new schools where parents want programs, and make recommendations concerning hiring procedures and other organizational decisions. However, each school designs and is in charge of its own program. A volunteer parent in each school serves as the program's coordinator and acts as a liaison between the school and the community.

Conclusion

There is a solid theoretical foundation for an interactional approach to second-language teaching with far-reaching implications for the classroom. Programs that involve the students in real communication about interesting, relevant subject matter in low-anxiety environments appear to be the most effective avenues to acquisition in the classroom.

This does not mean that there is never any value in grammar exercises, drills of various sorts, translating, or other such activities. On the contrary, all of these may have a place depending upon the objectives, age and proficiency levels, and cognitive development of the learner. However, it is when such relatively noncommunicative activities become the focus of the curriculum that they can be detrimental to the progression of second-language students in programs in which communication is a goal.

Organizing interactional activities related to content, providing for a silent period, and allowing for the natural development of interlanguage require creativity, flexibility, and patience on the part of teachers. For those willing to accept the challenge, the feelings of satisfaction are great once they find their students growing in the target language, whatever that language may be.

PART V

Related Readings

This section presents a vintage collection of edited readings from four people in fields related directly or indirectly to second-language teaching: Chomsky, Ellis, Vygotsky, and Cummins.

The Related Readings, which are referred to in the book, are intended mainly for those desiring supplemental materials. This section may be particularly useful in the teaching of theory or methods courses at the graduate level, in which the readings might be assigned in preparation for subsequent class discussions (see also the questions that end each chapter in Parts I, II, and III).

It must be noted that only a few readings could be presented here. The ones selected seemed to be most appropriate in that they expanded the book's implications and provided additional areas for reflection, discussion, and research.

RELATED READING 1
HOW LANGUAGE IS SHAPED: An Interview
Noam Chomsky (interviewed by J. Gliedman)

In 1953 a rickety old tub that had been sunk by the Germans and later salvaged was plodding its way across the Atlantic on the first voyage of its new life. Aboard that listing ship, a seasick young Philadelphian hit on an idea that would make him an internationally known scholar and would radically alter the way linguists view language.

"I remember exactly the moment when I finally felt convinced," Noam Chomsky recalls of the crossing. Sure of himself, he set about emphasizing the role of the mind, outlining the unconscious mechanisms that make human speech possible and insisting that a genetically programmed "language organ" in the brain primed the human infant to master the intricacies of his mother tongue. This language organ allows for the gift of speech that sets humans apart from the other animals. But it also defines and delimits the characteristics of all human languages, from Urdu to Navajo.

Before Chomsky's breakthrough in the mid-Fifties, American linguists did not believe that brain structure played any significant role in shaping language. They viewed the young child's mind as a blank slate, capable of learning virtually *any* conceivable kind of language. They had no concept then that certain languages might exist almost beyond human comprehension, just as X rays and ultraviolet radiation are invisible to the naked human eye.

Many of these linguists were searching for purely mechanical procedures—"discovery procedures"—that would objectively describe the structure of any human language. Chomsky himself started out as a structural linguist and published a technical paper on discovery procedures while he was a junior fellow at Harvard, in the early Fifties. He considered this work to be real linguistics, although he was exploring alternative ideas.

But by the time he set out on that fateful ocean voyage, he was ready to concede that "several years of intense effort devoted to improving discovery procedures had come to naught." His other efforts, carried out in almost complete isolation, were yielding consistently interesting results. This was Chomsky's pioneering research in generative grammars and explanatory theory. Chomsky

From "Interview (with Noam Chomsky)," *Omni*, 6 (2): November, 1983.

expanded the definition of *grammar* to include all the elements and rules of each language that the child assimilates as he learns to speak and understand what is said to him, as well as the linguist's theory of what goes on in the speaker's/hearer's brain.

Chomsky believes that language, along with most other human abilities, depends upon genetically programmed mental structures. In other words, language learning during childhood is part of the body's preprogrammed pattern of growth. Just as heredity endows each infant with a heart and lungs that continue to develop after birth, it provides each newborn with a highly complex language organ. The accidents of evolution have shaped this language organ so that it is capable of learning only those languages within a relatively narrow range of logical structures. Other languages, no less suitable for intelligent communication but lacking these human hallmarks, would be virtually unlearnable, even for the most gifted linguist. Chomsky foresees the day when scientists will have constructed a kind of linguistic analogue to Mendeleyev's periodic table—a list of the linguistic "atoms" and their permissible combinations that defines *every possible* human language. . .

Chomsky once said that "anybody who teaches at age fifty what he was teaching at age twenty-five had better find another profession." Over the last 25 years, his own linguistic theory has passed through four main stages, each differing in major ways from its predecessor. Chomsky is unique among contemporary scientists in that most of his opponents defend theories he either originated or profoundly influenced. Today he is a professor in the department of linguistics and philosophy at the Massachusetts Institute of Technology.

Psychologist and science journalist John Gliedman, who studied Chomsky's theories in the late Sixties at MIT, discussed ideas about language and mind in the linguist's austere campus office.

OMNI: Why do you believe that language behavior critically depends on the existence of a genetically preprogrammed language organ in the brain?

CHOMSKY: There's a lot of linguistic evidence to support this contention. But even in advance of detailed linguistic research, we should expect heredity to play a major role in language because there is really no other way to account for the fact that children learn to speak in the first place.

OMNI: What do you mean?

CHOMSKY: Consider something that everyone agrees is due to heredity—the fact that humans develop arms rather than wings. Why do we believe this? Well, since nothing in the fetal environments of the human or bird embryo can account for the differences between birds and men, we assume that heredity must be responsible. In fact, if someone came along and said that a bird embryo is somehow "trained" to grow wings, people would just laugh, even though embryologists lack anything like detailed understanding of how genes regulate embryological development.

OMNI: Is the role of heredity as important for language as it is for embryology?

CHOMSKY: I think so. You have to laugh at claims that heredity plays no significant role in language learning, because exactly the same kinds of genetic arguments hold for language learning as hold for embryological development.

I'm very much interested in embryology, but I've got just a layman's knowledge of it. I think that recent work, primarily in molecular biology, however, is seeking to discover the ways that genes regulate embryological development. The gene-control problem is conceptually similar to the problem of accounting for language *growth*. In fact, language development really ought to be called language growth, because the language organ grows like any other body organ.

OMNI: Is there a special place in the brain and a particular kind of neurological structure that comprises the language organ?

CHOMSKY: Little enough is known about cognitive systems and their neurological basis, so caution is necessary in making any direct claims. But it does seem that the representation and use of language involve specific neural structures, though their nature is not well understood.

OMNI: But clearly, environment plays *some* role in language development. What's the relationship between heredity and environment for human language?

CHOMSKY: The language organ interacts with early experience and matures into the grammar of the language that the child speaks. If a human being with this fixed endowment grows up in Philadelphia, as I did, his brain will encode knowledge of the Philadelphia dialect of English. If that brain had grown up in Tokyo, it would have encoded the Tokyo dialect of Japanese. The brain's different linguistic experience—English versus Japanese—would modify the language organ's structure.

Roughly the same thing goes on in animal experiments showing that different kinds of early visual experience can modify the part of the brain that processes visual information. As you may know, cats, monkeys, and humans have hierarchically organized brain-cell networks connected to the retina in such a way that certain cells fire only when there is a horizontal line in the visual field; other hierarchies respond only to vertical lines. But early experience can apparently change the relative numbers of horizontal- and vertical-line detectors. MIT psychologists Richard Held and Alan Hein showed some time ago, for example, that a kitten raised in a cage with walls covered by bold, black vertical lines will display good sensitivity to vertical lines as an adult but poor horizontal-line sensitivity. Lack of stimulation apparently causes the horizontal-line detectors to atrophy.

An even closer analogy exists between language growth and the growth that occurs in human beings *after* birth—for example, the onset of puberty. If someone came along and said, "Kids are trained to undergo puberty because they see other people," once again everybody would laugh. Would we laugh because we know in great detail the gene mechanisms that determine puberty? As far as I can tell, no one knows much of anything about that. Yet we all assume that puberty is genetically determined.

OMNI: Still, as your own example shows, environmental factors do play a major role in physiological growth.

CHOMSKY: And it goes without saying that the onset of puberty may well vary over quite a range depending on childhood diet and all kinds of other environmental influences. Nonetheless, everyone takes for granted that the fundamental processes controlling puberty are genetically programmed. This is probably true of death as well. You may be genetically programmed to die at roughly a certain point; it's a reasonable theory.

Look, all through an organism's existence, from birth to death, it passes through a series of genetically programmed changes. Plainly language growth is simply one of these predetermined changes. Language depends upon a genetic endowment that's on a par with the ones that specify the structure of our visual or circulatory systems, or determine that we have arms instead of wings.

OMNI: What about the linguistic evidence? What have you learned from studying human languages to corroborate your biological viewpoint?

CHOMSKY: The best evidence involves those aspects of a language's grammar that are so obvious, so intuitively self-evident to everyone, that they are quite rightly never mentioned in traditional grammars.

OMNI: You mean that school grammars fill in the gaps left by heredity? They teach everything about French or Russian, for example, that can't be taken for granted by virtue of the fact that you're a human?

CHOMSKY: That's right. It is precisely what seems self-evident that is most likely to be part of our hereditary baggage. Some of the oddities of English pronoun behavior illustrate what I mean. Take the sentence, "John believes he is intelligent." Okay, we all know that *he* can refer either to John or to someone else, so the sentence is ambiguous. It can mean either that John thinks he, John, is intelligent, or that someone else is intelligent. In contrast, consider the sentence, "John believes him to be intelligent." Here the pronoun *him* can't refer to John; it can refer only to someone else.

Now, did anyone teach us this peculiarity about English pronouns when we were children? It would be hard to even imagine a training procedure that would convey such information to a person. Nevertheless, everybody knows it—knows it without experience, without training, and at quite an early age. There are any number of other examples that show that we humans have explicit and highly articulate linguistic knowledge that simply has no basis in linguistic experience.

OMNI: There's just no way that children can pick up this kind of information by listening to the grown-ups around them?

CHOMSKY: Precisely. But let me give you another example. English contains grammatical constructions that are called parasitic gaps. In these constructions, you can drop a pronoun and still understand the sentence in the same way as when the sentence contains a pronoun. Consider the sentence, "Which article did you file without reading it?" Notice that you can drop the pronoun it without changing meaning or grammaticality. You can say, "Which article did you file without reading?" But you can't say, "John was killed by a rock falling on," when you mean, "John was killed by a rock falling on him." This time omitting the pronoun destroys both meaning and grammaticality.

Constructions of this type—where you can or cannot drop the pronoun—are very rare. In fact, they are so rare that it is quite likely that during the period a child masters his native language (the first five or six years of life), he never hears any of these constructions, or he hears them very sporadically. Nonetheless, every native speaker of English knows flawlessly when you can and can't drop pronouns in these kinds of sentences.

OMNI: So we're faced with a mystery. How could anyone possibly learn enough about the English language to possess the rich and exotic grammatical knowledge that we all seem to possess by the time we are five or six years old?

CHOMSKY: There's an obvious answer to that: The knowledge is built in. You and I can learn English, as well as any other language, with all its richness because we are designed to learn languages based upon a common set of principles, which we may call universal grammar.

OMNI: What is universal grammar?

CHOMSKY: It is the sum total of all the immutable principles that heredity builds into the language organ. These principles cover grammar, speech sounds, and meaning. Put differently, universal grammar is the inherited genetic endowment that makes it possible for us to speak and learn human languages.

OMNI: Suppose that somewhere else in the universe intelligent life has evolved. Could we, with our specialized language organ, learn the aliens' language if we made contact with them?

CHOMSKY: Not if their language violated the principles of our universal grammar, which, given the myriad ways that languages can be organized, strikes me as highly likely.

OMNI: Maybe we shouldn't call it *universal*, then. But please explain what you mean.

CHOMSKY: The same structures that make it possible to learn a human language make it impossible for us to learn a language that violates the principles of universal grammar. If a Martian landed from outer space and spoke a language that violated universal grammar, we simply would not be able to learn that language the way that we learn a human language like English or Swahili. We would have to approach the alien's language slowly and laboriously—the way that scientists study physics, where it takes generation after generation of labor to gain new understanding and to make significant progress. We're designed by nature for English, Chinese, and every other possible human language, but we're not designed to learn perfectly usable languages that violate universal grammar. These languages would simply *not* be within our range of abilities.

OMNI: How would you assess current research about universal grammar?

CHOMSKY: In the last three or four years there's been a major conceptual change in the underlying theory. We now assume that universal grammar consists of a collection of preprogrammed subsystems that include, for example, one responsible for meaning, another responsible for stringing together phrases in a sentence, a third one that deals, among other things, with the kinds of relationships between nouns and pronouns that I discussed earlier. And there are a number of others.

These subsystems are not genetically preprogrammed down to the last detail. If they were, there would be only one human language. But heredity does set rather narrow limits on the possible ways that the rules governing each subsystem's function can vary. Languages like English and Italian, for example, differ in their choice of genetically permitted variations that exist as options in the universal grammar. You can think of these options as a kind of linguistic menu containing mutually exclusive grammatical possibilities.

For example, languages like Italian have chosen the "null subject" option from the universal-grammar menu. In Italian you can say *left* when you mean "He left" or "She left." English and French have passed up this option and chosen instead a rule that requires explicit mention of the subject.

OMNI: What are some other grammatical options on the universal grammar menu?

CHOMSKY: In English the most important element in every major grammatical category comes first in its phrase. In simple sentences, for example, we say *John hit Bill*, not *John Bill hit*. With adjectives we say *proud of John*, not *John of proud*; with nouns we say *habit of drinking wine*, not *drinking wine of habit*, and with prepositions we say *to John*, not *John to*. Because heads of grammatical categories always come first, English is what is called a head-initial language.

Japanese is a head-final language. In Japanese you say *John Bill hit*. And instead of prepositions, there are postpositions that follow nouns: *John to*, rather than *to John*. So here's another parameter the child's got to learn from experience: Is the language head-initial or head-final?

These grammatical parameters are interconnected. You can't pick them any more freely than, say, a wine fanatic who insists on white wine with fish and red wine with meat is free to choose any main dish once he's decided on his wine. But grammars are even more sensitive than this culinary example might suggest. A slight change in just one of the universal grammar's parameters can have enormous repercussions throughout the language. It can produce an entirely different language.

Again, there's a close parallel to embryology, where a slight shift in the gene mechanisms regulating growth may be all that separates a fertilized egg from developing into a lion rather than a whale.

OMNI: So what exactly would you say is the grammar of English?

CHOMSKY: The grammar of English is the collection of choices—head-initial rather than head-final, and null subject forbidden, for example—that define one of a limited number of genetically permitted selections from the universal-grammar menu of grammatical options. And of course there are all the lexical facts. You just have to learn your language's vocabulary. The universal grammar doesn't tell you that *tree* means "tree" in English.

But once you've learned the vocabulary items and fixed the grammatical parameters for English, the whole system is in place. And the general principles genetically programmed into the language organ just churn away to yield all the particular facts about English grammar.

OMNI: It sounds as if your present research goal is to reach the point where you can define every human language's grammar simply by specifying its choices from the universal grammar's menu of options.

CHOMSKY: That's the kind of work you would hope would soon be done: to take a theory of universal grammar, fix the parameters one way or another, and then deduce from these parameters the grammar of a real human language— Japanese, Swahili, English, or whatnot.

This goal is not on the horizon. But I think that it is within our conceptual grasp. Undoubtedly the principles of universal grammar that we currently theorize are wrong. It would be a miracle if we were right this early along. But the principles *are* of the right type, and we can now begin to test our present system with complex examples to see what is wrong and to make changes that will improve our theory . . .

OMNI: Moving on to another controversial area in the behavioral sciences, how do you think your views differ from B. F. Skinner's behaviorist theory of language, learning, and mind?

CHOMSKY: Skinner used to take a relatively extreme position. At one point he held that, apart from the most rudimentary functions, essentially nothing of importance was genetically programmed in the human brain. Skinner agreed that humans were genetically programmed to see and hear, but that's about all. Accordingly he argued that all human behavior was simply a reflection of training and experience. This view can't possibly be correct. And, in fact, Skinner's approach has led absolutely nowhere in this area. It has yielded no theoretical knowledge, no nontrivial principles as far as I am aware—thus far, at any rate.

OMNI: Why is that?

CHOMSKY: Because Skinnerian behaviorism is off the wall. It's as hopeless a project as trying to explain that the onset of puberty results from social training. But I really don't know whether Skinner still maintains this extreme position. *[He has since modified it.—Ed.]*

OMNI: What about the late Jean Piaget? Where do you stand on his theories of the child's mental development?

CHOMSKY: Piaget's position is different; it's more complex than Skinner's. Piaget held that the child passes through cognitive states. According to my understanding of the Piagetian literature, Piaget and his supporters were never really clear about what produced a new stage of cognitive development. What they could have said—though they seemed to shy away from it—is that cognitive development is a genetically determined maturational process like puberty, for example. That's what the Piagetians *ought* to say. They don't like this formulation, but it seems right to me.

OMNI: In other words, Piagetians place much more emphasis on the role of experience in cognitive development than you do. Are there other differences as well?

CHOMSKY: Yes. Piagetians maintain that the mind develops as a whole rather than as a modular structure with specific capacities developing in their own ways. This is a possible hypothesis, but in fact it seems to be extremely wrong.

OMNI: How do you mean?

CHOMSKY: Well, consider the properties that determine the reference of pronouns that we talked about earlier. Once you ferret out these rules of pronouns, they seem to have nothing in common with the logical operations that Piagetians single out as being typical of the early stages of the child's mental development.

OMNI: In other words, a four-year-old who may not realize that the amount of water stays the same when you pour the contents of a low, wide glass into a tall, thin container nevertheless displays sophisticated logical abilities in his grasp of the complex rules of English grammar?

CHOMSKY: Yes. And these abilities are independent of the logical capacities measured by tests. There's just no resemblance between what a child does with blocks and the kind of knowledge that he displays of English grammar at the same age. In fact, I think it's sort of quixotic to expect tight interconnections between language development and growth in other mental domains. By and large, body systems develop in their own ways at their own rates. They interact, but the circulatory system doesn't wait until the visual system reaches a certain stage of organization before proceeding to imitate the visual system's organizational complexity. Cognitive growth shouldn't be different in this respect either. As far as we know, it isn't. . . .

Related Reading 2
THEORIES OF SECOND LANGUAGE ACQUISITION
Rod Ellis

INTRODUCTION

There has been no shortage of theorizing about second language acquisition (SLA). The research literature abounds in approaches, theories, models, laws, and principles. It is arguable that there has been a superfluity of theorizing. Schouten (1979, p. 4), for instance, claims:

> . . . in second language learning, too many models have been built and taken for granted too soon, and this has stifled relevant research.

He believes that theorizing should only follow extensive and rigorous empirical research. However, it might also be argued that theorizing should precede and, therefore, inform empirical study, guiding the specific hypotheses it seeks to examine. Irrespective of these methodological issues, SLA research has gone ahead and spawned a plethora of theories.

The main aim of this reading is to review a number of theories of SLA. The ones that have been selected for discussion have assumed a central place in SLA research. They reflect the variety of perspectives evident in SLA studies. They are:

1. The Acculturation Model (and closely associated with it, the Nativization Model)
2. Accommodation Theory
3. Discourse Theory
4. The Monitor Model[1]
5. The Variable Competence Model
6. The Universal Hypothesis
7. A Neurofunctional Theory

The discussion of each theory will take the form of an account of its central premises, followed by a critical evaluation.

Rod Ellis, "Theories of Second Language Acquisition," from *Understanding Second Language Acquisition* (Oxford: Oxford University Press, 1986), pp. 248–276.

THE ROLE OF THEORY IN SLA RESEARCH

What is the role of theory in SLA research? Hakuta (1981, p. 1) sees the main goal of SLA research as follows:

> The game of language acquisition research can be described as the search for an appropriate level of description for the learner's system of rules.

In other words, the main goal of a theory of SLA is *description*—the characterization of the nature of the linguistic categories which constitute the learner's interlanguage at any point in development. However, most other researchers have aimed at more than just description. They have tried to discover why the learner develops the particular linguistic categories that he does. As Rutherford (1982, p. 85) puts it:

> We wish to know *what* it is that is acquired, how it is acquired and *when* it is acquired. But were we to have the answers even to these questions, we would still want to know *why* . . .

In other words, theory building is concerned with explanation as well as with description.

But the term 'explanation' is ambiguous. Firstly, it can refer to the way in which the learner works on samples of the input data, converting them into intake and then using his knowledge to produce output. Explanation in this sense covers the acquisition sequence and order and the processes responsible for it. Secondly, the term 'explanation' can also refer to what motivates the learner to learn and what causes him to cease learning (i.e., fossilize). Schumann (1976) distinguishes these two types of explanation, which he refers to respectively as 'cognitive processes' responsible for *how* SLA takes place and 'initiating factors' responsible for *why* SLA takes place. Ellis (1984a) refers to the two types as 'assembly mechanisms' and 'power mechanisms'. The distinction is an important one where SLA theorizing is concerned, because, as will be shown, whereas some theories focus on the *how*, others focus on the *why*. The kind of explanation they offer, therefore, is of a different order. A comprehensive theory of SLA will need to explain both assembly and power mechanism.

How do researchers set about building an explanation of how and why SLA takes place? Long (1983a), drawing on the work of Reynolds (1971), distinguishes two approaches to theory building: the *theory-then-research* approach and the *research-then-theory* approach. These will be discussed briefly.

The theory-then-research approach involves five stages:

1. Develop an explicit theory.
2. Derive a testable prediction from the theory.
3. Conduct research to test the prediction.

4. Modify (or abandon) the theory if the prediction is disconfirmed.
5. Test a new prediction if the first prediction is confirmed.

The starting point of this approach is to invent a theory using hunches and relevant research. The theory constitutes what Popper (1976) calls 'dogmatic thinking'. It is important that the theory is presented in such a way that it is falsifiable. That is, the researcher must not be able to interpret any conceivable event as verification of the theory, or, as Popper puts it, it must exclude some 'immunizations'. The strength of the theory rests both in its ability to 'cover' what is already known about the phenomenon under investigation and also to predict what will be observed in future. The prediction is a test of the theory. The process of testing and amending the theory is a continuous one that, in Popper's view, never ends. Thus it is possible to talk about a comprehensive theory which accounts for all the available facts, but it is not possible to talk about a true theory, as any theory must remain open to modification.

The research-then-theory approach has four stages:

1. Select a phenomenon for investigation.
2. Measure its characteristics.
3. Collect data and look for systematic patterns.
4. Formalize significant patterns as rules describing natural events.

The starting point of this approach is not a theory but a 'research question'—an area of interest into which the researcher wants to enquire. This area is likely to have been decided on as a result of hunches or reading the relevant research, but the research question is not formulated in such a way as to provide a testable prediction. The research-then-theory approach need never lead to a comprehensive theory—it can produce a 'bits-and-pieces' view of SLA, a series of insights into what motivates behaviour.

The study of SLA has involved both approaches. The experimental studies of the effects of motivation and attitudes undertaken by Canadian researchers (e.g., Gardner & Lambert, 1972) are examples of a theory-then-research approach. In contrast, many longitudinal studies of individual L2 learners follow a research-then-theory approach. Their aim is not so much to build a comprehensive theory as to examine specific aspects of SLA in detail.

As Long points out, both approaches have their strengths and weaknesses. The theory-then-research approach provides an approximate answer and a basis for systematically testing aspects of the overall theory. But researchers are not always prepared to abandon a theory even in the face of substantial disconfirmatory evidence. The research-then-theory approach means that the researcher is less likely to be 'wrong' at any time and can provide valuable insights into selected aspects of the whole process being investigated. But the claims that derive from this approach are necessarily limited, and it is not always clear how one claim relates to another.

Long argues that the theory-then-research approach leads to more efficient research because:

> ... the theory governing the research at any point in time tells the investigator what the relevant data are, which is the crucial experiment to run. (1983a, p. 22)

The study of SLA, however, needs both approaches. First, there is no agreed initial theory to motivate an experimental hypothesis-testing approach, and it is doubtful whether there will be in the near future. The insights provided by a research-then-theory approach provide a basis for theory building. Second, there is a recognized need to construct theories in order to provide a general explanation of SLA. The fact that different researchers have used different approaches may, as Long suggests, be a reflection of their different personalities, but it probably also reflects the recognition that the field of SLA requires different research perspectives.

The subsequent sections of this reading review a number of theories of SLA. They differ in what they seek to explain—the 'assembly mechanisms' that govern how SLA takes place or the 'power mechanisms' that explain why it takes place, or both. They also differ in how they have been arrived at. Some are the result of a theory-then-research approach, while others owe more to a research-then-theory approach. The reader who seeks a tidy and exhaustive account of SLA is likely to be disappointed. The theories offer 'complementary alternatives', as Selinker and Lamendella (1978b, p. 168) put it; 'each perspective has advantages others lack, while at the same time embodying disadvantages'.

SEVEN THEORIES OF SLA

1. The Acculturation Model

Acculturation is defined by [H. D.] Brown (1980, p. 129) as 'the process of becoming adapted to a new culture'. It is seen as an important aspect of SLA, because language is one of the most observable expressions of culture and because in second (as opposed to foreign) language settings the acquisition of a new language is seen as tied to the way in which the learner's community and the target language community view each other. One view of how acculturation affects SLA has already been described. The account that follows is based on the work of John Schumann (see Schumann, 1978a, 1978b, 1978c). In addition, an elaborated version of Schumann's model—the Nativization Model—is discussed, with reference to Andersen (1980, 1981, 1983).

The central premise of the Acculturation Model is:

> ... second language acquisition is just one aspect of acculturation and the degree to which a learner acculturates to the target language group will control the degree to which he acquires the second language. (Schumann, 1978a, p. 34)

Acculturation, and hence SLA, is determined by the degree of *social* and *psychological distance* between the learner and the target language culture. Social distance is the result of a number of factors which affect the learner as a member of a social group in contact with the target language group. Psychological distance is the result of various affective factors which concern the learner as an individual. The social factors are primary. The psychological factors come into play in cases where the social distance is indeterminant (i.e. where social factors constitute neither a clearly positive nor a clearly negative influence on acculturation), although they can also modify the modal level of learning associated with a particular social situation.

Schumann (1978c) lists the various factors which determine social and psychological distance. The social variables govern whether the overall learning situation is 'good' or 'bad'. An example of a 'good' learning situation is when (1) the target language and L2 groups view each other as socially equal; (2) the target language and L2 groups are both desirous that the L2 group will assimilate; (3) both the target language and L2 groups expect the L2 group to share social facilities with the target language group (i.e. there is low enclosure); (4) the L2 group is small and not very cohesive; (5) the L2 group's culture is congruent with that of the target language group; (6) both groups have positive attitudes to each other; and (7) the L2 group envisages staying in the target language area for an extended period. An example of a 'bad' learning situation is when the conditions are opposite to the ones described above.[2] It is, of course, possible to have varying degrees of social distance.

The psychological factors are affective in nature. They include (1) language shock (i.e. the learner experiences doubt and possible confusion when using the L2); (2) culture shock (i.e. the learner experiences disorientation, stress, fear, etc. as a result of differences between his or her own culture and that of the target language community); (3) motivation; and (4) ego boundaries.

Social and psychological distance influence SLA by determining the amount of contact with the target language that the learner experiences, and also the degree to which the learner is open to that input which is available. Thus in 'bad' learning situations the learner will receive very little L2 input. Also, when the psychological distance is great, the learner will fail to convert available input into intake.

Schumann also describes the kind of learning which takes place. He suggests that the early stages of SLA are characterized by the same processes that are responsible for the formation of pidgin languages. When social and/or psychological distances are great, the learner fails to progress beyond the early stages, with the result that his language is pidginized. Schumann refers to this account of SLA as the *pidginization hypothesis*. He documents in detail the pidginization that characterizes one adult Spanish speaker's acquisition of L2 English in the United States. The learner, Alberto, was subject to a high degree of social distance and failed to progress very far in learning English. His English was characterized by many of the forms observed in pidgins, e.g. 'no + V' negatives, uninvested interrogatives, the absence of possessive and plural inflections, and a restricted verb morphology. Schumann suggests 'pidginization may characterize all early second language acquisition and . . . under conditions of social and psychological distance it persists' (1978b, p. 110). When pidginization persists, the learner fossilizes. That is, he no longer revises his interlanguage system in the direction of the target language. Thus early fossilization and pidginization are identical processes.[3]

Thus continued pidginization is the result of social and psychological distance. The degree of acculturation leads to pidgin-like language in two ways. First, as suggested above, it controls the level of input that the learner receives. Second, it reflects the function which the learner wishes to use the L2 for. Following [D.] Smith (1972), Schumann distinguishes three broad functions of language: (1) the communicative function, which concerns the transmission of purely referential, denotative information; (2) the integrative function, which involves the use of language to mark the speaker as a member of a particular social group; and (3) the expressive function, which consists of the use of language to display linguistic virtuosity (e.g. in literary uses). Initially L2 learners will seek to use the L2 for the communicative function. Pidgins and interlanguages which fossilize in the early stages of development remain restricted to the communicative function. Native speakers of the target language use it for both the communicative and integrative functions, as will those L2 learners who do not fossilize early on, but many native speakers and L2 learners will never aspire to master the expressive uses of language.

The Nativization Model

Andersen builds on Schumann's Acculturation Model, in particular by providing a cognitive dimension which Schumann does not consider. For Schumann, SLA can be explained simply in terms of input and the general function the learner wants to use the L2 for. He is not concerned with the learner's internal processing mechanisms. Andersen, to a much greater extent, is concerned with learning processes.

Andersen sees SLA as the result of two general forces, which he labels *nativization and denativization*. Nativization consists of assimilation; the learner makes the input conform to his own internalized view of what constitutes the L2 system. In terms of the typology of learner strategies, the learner simplifies the learning task by building hypotheses based on the knowledge he already possesses (e.g. knowledge of his first language; knowledge of the world). In this sense, then, he attends to an 'internal norm'. Nativization is apparent in pidginization and the early stages of both first and second language acquisition. Denativization involves accommodation (in the Piagetian sense); the learner adjusts his internalized system to make it fit the input. The learner makes use of inferencing strategies which enable him to remodel his interlanguage system in accordance with the 'external norm' (i.e. the linguistic features represented in the input language). Denativization is apparent in depidginization (i.e. the elaboration of a pidgin language which occurs through the gradual incorporation of forms from an external language source) and also in later first and second language acquisition. Figure 1 summarizes Andersen's Nativization Model.

Evaluation

The Acculturation and Nativist models focus on the power mechanisms of SLA. They provide explanations of why L2 learners, unlike first language learners, often fail to achieve a native-like competence. L2 learners may be cut off from the necessary input as a result of social distance, or they may fail to attend to it as a result of psychological distance. These models also indicate that SLA involves processes of a very general kind, which are also found in the formation and elaboration of pidgin languages. The notions of 'internal' and 'external norms' are elegant devices for explaining why early and late interlanguage systems are so very different. Characterizing SLA as the gradual transition of attention from an internal to an external norm explains the developmental sequence which has been observed in SLA, and the switch that learners make from reliance on simplifying to reliance on inferencing strategies.

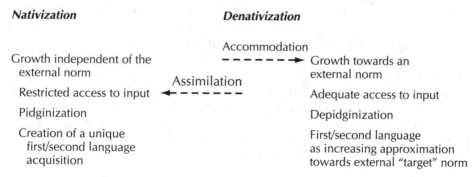

Nativization   **Denativization**

                                                 Accommodation

Growth independent of the   – – – – – – ➤ Growth towards an
external norm   external norm
                                 Assimilation

Restricted access to input   ◄ – – – – – –   Adequate access to input

Pidginization   Depidginization

Creation of a unique   First/second language
first/second language   as increasing approximation
acquisition   towards external "target" norm

Figure 1. Andersen's Nativization Model (slightly simplified from Andersen, 1983, p. 11)

Neither model sheds light on how L2 knowledge is internalized and used. In other words, there is no specification of the learner's assembly mechanisms. This is quite evident in the Acculturation model. It is also true of the Nativization model. Although this model does consider internal factors (in the form of the assimilation/accommodation distinction), there is no discussion of how these operate. The relationship between primary linguistic data and internal processing is an intricate one, requiring a detailed account of how learner strategies operate on input and produce output. Thus, while accepting that in the final analysis SLA is dependent on input and on a preparedness of the learner to convert input into intake, a comprehensive theory of SLA will also need to consider *how* input becomes intake and *how* this is integrated into the existing interlanguage system. In particular it will need to consider whether intake is controlled by the way the input is shaped in interaction involving the learner and other speakers or whether it is controlled by the structure of the internal processing mechanisms themselves—the differential contribution of environment and 'black box'. Andersen's 'internal' and 'external norms' suggest that the internal mechanisms play a crucial part, but this is not elaborated upon. And neither Andersen nor Schumann pays attention to the potentially facilitating effects of input/interaction, as described by Hatch and Long. In short, what is missing from these models is an account of the role of the interaction between situation and learner.

The Acculturation and Nativization Models address naturalistic SLA, where the L2 learner has contact with the target language community. It is not clear whether the models are also applicable to classroom SLA (i.e. foreign language instruction), where no such contact is possible. Presumably the factors responsible for social distance are not relevant in foreign language learning, although those responsible for psychological distance may be.[4]

2. Accommodation Theory

Accommodation Theory derives from the research of Giles and associates into the intergroup uses of language in multilingual communities such as Britain. Giles operates within a socio-psychological framework, drawing on the work of Lambert and Gardner in the Canadian context. His primary concern is to investigate how intergroup uses of language reflect basic social and psychological attitudes in inter-ethnic communication. As an offshoot of this, he has also considered SLA from an intergroup stance (see Giles & Byrne, 1982) and it is the resulting view of SLA which has become known as Accommodation Theory.

The Accommodation Theory shares certain premises with the Acculturation Model, but it also differs from it in a number of significant ways. Like Schumann, Giles is concerned to account for successful language acquisition. Both seek the answer in the relationships that hold between the learner's social group (termed the 'ingroup') and the target language community (termed the 'outgroup'). However, whereas Schumann explains these relationships in terms of variables that create *actual* social distance, Giles does so in terms of *perceived* social distanced.[5] Giles argues that it is how the ingroup defines itself in relationship to the outgroup that is important for SLA. Also, where Schumann appears to treat social and psychological distance as absolute phenomena that determine the level of interaction between the learner and native speakers, Giles sees intergroup relationships as subject to constant negotiation during the course of each interaction. Thus, whereas for Schumann social and psychological distance are static (or at least change only slowly over time), for Giles intergroup relationships are dynamic and fluctuate in accordance with the shifting views of identity held by each group *vis-á-vis* the other. As will be discussed later, this enables Accommodation Theory to take account of the variability inherent in language-learner language and, also, the native speaker's input.

Giles agrees with Gardner (1979) that motivation is the primary determinant of L2 proficiency. He considers the level of motivation to be a reflex of how individual learners define themselves in ethnic terms. This, in turn, is governed by a number of key variables:

1. Identification of the individual learner with his ethnic ingroup: the extent to which the learner sees himself as a member of a specific ingroup, separate from the outgroup.
2. Inter-ethnic comparison: whether the learner makes favourable or unfavourable comparisons between his own ingroup and the outgroup. This will be influenced by the learner's awareness of 'cognitive alternatives' regarding the status of his own group's position, for instance when he perceives the intergroup situation as unfair.
3. Perception of ethno-linguistic vitality: whether the learner sees his ingroup as holding a low or high status and as sharing or excluded from institutional power.
4. Perception of ingroup boundaries: whether the learner sees his ingroup as culturally and linguistically separate from the outgroup (= hard boundaries) or as culturally and linguistically related (= soft boundaries).
5. Identification with other ingroup social categories: whether the learner identifies with few or several other ingroup social categories (e.g. occupational, religious, gender) and as a consequence whether he holds adequate or inadequate status within his ingroup.

Column A in Table 1 shows when the individual learner is likely to be highly motivated to learn the L2 and hence acquire a high level of proficiency. Conversely, column B shows when he is likely to be unmotivated and so achieve only a low level of proficiency. Where the motivation is high as a result of favourable socio-psychological attitudes (as described in column A in Table 1), the learner will not only benefit from formal instruction in the L2, but is also likely to avail himself of the opportunities for informal acquisition (in Seliger's (1977) terms, high input generators in the classroom are likely to also obtain a high level of exposure outside). In contrast, when motivation is low as a consequence of unfavourable socio-psychological attitudes (as described in column B of Table 1), whether the learner succeeds in formal language contexts will depend instead on intelligence and aptitude, because he is less likely to take advantage of informal acquisition contexts.

TABLE 1. DETERMINANTS OF SUCCESSFUL AND UNSUCCESSFUL LEARNING ACCORDING TO ACCOMMODATION THEORY

Key variables	A high motivation, high level of proficiency	B low motivation, low level of proficiency
1. Identification with ingroup	weak identification	strong identification
2. Inter-ethnic comparison	makes favourable or no comparison, i.e. ingroup not seen as inferior	makes negative comparison, i.e. ingroup seen as inferior
3. Perception of ethno-linguistic vitality	low perception	high perception
4. Perception of ingroup boundaries	soft and open	hard and closed
5. Identification with other social categories	strong identification—satisfactory ingroup status	weak identification—inadequate group status

In addition to determining the overall level of proficiency achieved in SLA, Accommodation Theory also accounts for the learner's variable linguistic output. Giles, Bourhis, and Taylor (1977) write:

> . . . people are continually modifying their speech with others so as to reduce or accentuate the linguistic (and hence) social differences between them depending on their perceptions of the interactive situation.

Giles (1979) distinguishes two types of change which occur in the L2 speaker's use of 'ethnic speech markers' (i.e. linguistic features which mark the ingroup membership of the speaker).[6] *Upward convergence* involves the attenuation of ingroup speech markers. It occurs when the learner is positively motivated towards the outgroup community (i.e. when his socio-psychological set is favourable). *Downward divergence* involves the accentuation of ethnic speech markers. It occurs when the learner is not positively motivated towards the outgroup (i.e. when his socio-psychological set is unfavourable). In language *use* the occurrence of upward convergence or downward divergence can fluctuate as a result of the L2 speaker's ongoing assessment of himself *vis-à-vis* his own group and the outgroup community. It follows, therefore, that the learner possesses a stylistic repertoire from which he selects in accordance with his shifting socio-psychological set, and that in any one situation the learner may employ different linguistic forms according to the extent to which he chooses to mark his speech as that of the ingroup. In language *acquisition*, progress takes place when the overall predisposition of the learner is towards upward convergence, although this need not be evident in every instance of use. Conversely, fossilization occurs when the overall predisposition of the learner is towards downward divergence.

Evaluation

Accommodation Theory, like the Acculturation Model, does not explain assembly mechanisms. It does not account for the developmental sequence. It is another 'black box' model in this respect. The strength of Accommodation Theory is that it encompasses language acquisition and language use within a single framework. It also relates the acquisition of a new dialect or accent to the acquisition of a L2, as both are seen as a reflection of the learner's perception of himself with regard to his own social group and the target language/dialect group.

Accommodation Theory provides an explanation of language-learner language variability. Variable language use is the result of conflicting socio-psychological attitudes in different situations. Variability of use is related to acquisition, in the sense that the same set of factors is responsible for both. Tarone accounts for variability in terms of varying degrees of attention to form, but she does not address what motivates this. Attention to form can be seen as a consequence of the kind of factors that Giles considers. That is, the learner's perception of himself *vis-à-vis* the target-language community in face-to-face interaction governs when he attends to form. Upward convergence will be characterized by attention to form and to the use of the careful style. Downward divergence will be characterized by an absence of attention to form and a reliance on the vernacular style, through which the learner displays his ingroup membership. Thus diverging or converging may represent aspects of style-shifting involving the vernacular-careful style continuum. However, it is doubtful whether Accommodation Theory can be applied to foreign language learning, when intergroup relationships are not an obvious issue. Foreign language learners also style-shift. This suggests that although ethnic identity is an important aspect of variability in SLA, it does not account for total variability.

3. Discourse Theory

It follows from a theory of language use, in which communication is treated as the matrix of linguistic knowledge (as proposed for instance in Hymes's description of communicative competence), that language development should be considered in terms of how the learner discovers the meaning potential of language by participating in communication. This is how Halliday (1975) views first language acquisition. In a study of how his own child acquired language, Halliday shows that the development of the formal linguistic devices for realizing basic language function grows out of the interpersonal uses to which language is put. Because the structure of language is itself a reflection of the functions it serves, it can be learnt through learning to communicate. As [L.] Cherry (1979, p. 122) puts it:

> Through communicating with other people, children accomplish actions in
> the world and develop the rules of language structure and use.

It is because the L2 learner is similarly motivated to 'accomplish actions' (at least in informal SLA) that a parallel can be drawn between first and second language acquisition. In SLA this view of how development takes place has become known as the Discourse Theory.

Only the main principles of Discourse Theory, proposed by Hatch (1978b, 1978c), are considered here:

1. SLA follows a 'natural' route in syntactical development.
2. Native speakers adjust their speech in order to negotiate meaning with non-native speakers.
3. The conversational strategies used to negotiate meaning, and the resulting adjusted input, influence the rate and route of SLA in a number of ways:
   a. the learner learns the grammar of the L2 in the same order as the frequency order of the various features in the input;
   b. the learner acquires commonly occurring formulas and then later analyses these into their component parts;
   c. the learner is helped to construct sentences vertically; vertical structures are the precursors of horizontal structures.
4. Thus, the 'natural' route is the result of learning how to hold conversations.

Evaluation

Whereas Schumann and Giles are interested in explaining the rate of SLA and the level of proficiency achieved, Hatch is interested in explaining how SLA takes place. As Hatch says:

> The basic question that second language acquisition research addresses is: how can we describe the *process* of second language acquisition. (1980, p. 177—my [Ellis's] italics)

Hatch tries to provide an answer to this question by qualitative analyses of face-to-face interactions involving L2 learners. The route of development is explained in terms of the properties of these interactions. The strength of Hatch's approach lies in the detailed insights it provides into how the process of constructing discourse contributes to the process of building an interlanguage.

It is arguable, however, that notwithstanding these insights, Hatch has not been able to demonstrate conclusively that negotiation of input is the necessary and sufficient condition of SLA. Hatch herself notes:

> We have not been able (nor have we tried) to show how, or if, making messages simpler or more transparent promotes language learning. (1980, p. 181)

Hatch is only too aware of the huge leap that is made from 'low-inference descriptions' to 'high-inference explanations'. The relationship between negotiated input and SLA is, therefore, likely but not substantiated. SLA research still needs to carry out the kind of empirical studies which have taken place in first language acquisition research and which demonstrate that where rate of development is concerned, at least some discourse features are facilitative (e.g. Cross, 1978; Ellis & Wells, 1980). Moreover, the Discourse Theory needs to accommodate the fact that, as Larsen-Freeman (1983a) has observed, successful SLA can take place even when there is no negotiated input (e.g. in self-study).

The Discourse Theory, like the two preceding theories, does not address the nature of the learner strategies responsible for SLA. When Hatch talks of *processes,* she means external processes—those which can be observed in face-to-face interaction—not internal processes, those that can only be inferred by observing how learners perform. Hatch does not look at the cognitive processes that control how the learner (and native speaker) construct discourse, or how data made available through discourse are sifted and internalized. There is no specification of the relationship between external and internal processing. In fairness, though, it should be noted that Hatch does not intend to dismiss the cognitive side of SLA. Hatch writes:

> While social interaction may give the learner the 'best' data to work with, the brain in turn must work out a fitting and relevant model of that input. (1983, p. 186)

The Discourse Theory, however, is not concerned with what this model consists of.

4. The Monitor Model

Krashen's Monitor Model has enjoyed considerable prominence in SLA research. In so far as it is probably the most comprehensive of existing theories, this is justified. However, as I shall attempt to show later, the theory is seriously flawed in a number of respects, in particular in its treatment of language-learner variability.

The Monitor Model consists of five central hypotheses. In addition, it makes reference to a number of other factors which influence SLA and which relate to the central hypotheses. Each hypothesis is briefly summarized below. Krashen's views on the different causative variables of SLA are also considered. A full account of the Monitor Model is available in Krashen (1981b, 1982), and in Krashen and Terrell (1983).

The Five Hypotheses
1. The Acquisition Learning Hypothesis. The 'acquisition-learning' distinction lies at the heart of Krashen's theory. It is applicable to the process of internalizing new L2 knowledge, to storing this knowledge, and also to using it in actual performance. 'Acquisition' occurs subconsciously as a result of participating in natural communication where the focus is on meaning. 'Learning' occurs as a

result of conscious study of the formal properties of the language. In storage, 'acquired' knowledge is located in the left hemisphere of the brain (in most users) in the language areas; it is available for automatic processing. 'Learnt' knowledge is metalinguistic in nature. It is also stored in the left hemisphere, but not necessarily in the language areas; it is available only for controlled processing. Thus, 'acquired' and 'learnt' knowledge are stored separately. In performance, 'acquired' knowledge serves as the major source of initiating both the comprehension and production of utterances. 'Learnt' knowledge is available for use only by the Monitor (see Hypothesis 3 below).

2. The Natural Order Hypothesis. The natural order hypothesis draws on the SLA research literature that indicates that learners may follow a more or less invariant order in the acquisition of formal grammatical features. The hypothesis affirms that grammatical structures are 'acquired' in a predictable order. Thus when the learner is engaged in natural communication tasks, he will manifest the standard order. But when he is engaged in tasks that require or permit the use of metalinguistic knowledge, a different order will emerge.

3. The Monitor Hypothesis. The Monitor is the device that learners use to edit their language performance. It utilizes 'learnt' knowledge by acting upon and modifying utterances generated from 'acquired' knowledge. This can occur either before the utterance is uttered or after (see Figure 2). In either case its use is optional. Krashen argues that Monitoring has an extremely limited function in language performance, even where adults are concerned. He gives three conditions for its use: (1) there must be sufficient time; (2) the focus must be on form and not meaning; and (3) the user must know the rule. Krashen recognizes that editing can also take place using 'acquired' competence. He refers to this as editing by 'feel'. However, this aspect of L2 performance is not developed. Figure 2, for instance, does not show how editing by 'feel' takes place.

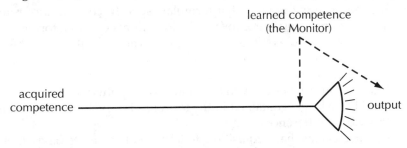

Figure 2. A Model of Adult Second Language Performance
(Krashen & Terrell, 1983, p. 30)

4. The Input Hypothesis. This states that 'acquisition' takes place as a result of the learner having understood input that is a little beyond the current level of his competence (i.e. the $i + 1$ level). Input that is comprehensible to the learner will automatically be at the right level.

5. The Affective Filter Hypothesis. This deals with how affective factors relate to SLA, and covers the ground of the Acculturation Model. Krashen incorporates the notion of the Affective Filter as proposed by Dulay and Burt (1977). The filter controls how much input the learner comes into contact with, and how much input is converted into intake. It is 'affective' because the factors which determine its strength have to do with the learner's motivation, self-confidence, or anxiety state. Learners with high motivation and self-confidence and with low anxiety have low filters and so obtain and let in plenty of input. Learners with low motivation, little self-confidence, and high anxiety have high filters and so receive little input and allow even less in. The Affective Filter influences the rate of development, but it does not affect the route.

Causative Variables Taken into Account in the Monitor Model

Krashen also discusses a number of other factors, each of which figures conspicuously in the SLA research literature.

1. Aptitude

   Krashen argues that aptitude only relates to 'learning'. That is, the learner's aptitude predicts how well he will perform on grammar-type tests that provide the right conditions for the operation of the Monitor. In contrast, attitude is related to 'acquisition' (see Hypothesis 5 above).

2. Role of the first language

   Krashen rejects the view that the first language interferes with SLA. Rather, he sees the use of the first language as a performance strategy. The learner falls back on his first language when he lacks a rule in the L2. He initiates an utterance using his first language (instead of 'acquired' L2 knowledge) and then substitutes L2 lexical items, also making small repairs to the resulting string by means of the Monitor.

3. Routines and patterns

   Krashen rejects the view that formulaic speech (consisting of routines and patterns) contributes to 'acquisition'. In his opinion, formulas play a performance role only by helping the learner to 'outperform his competence'. They are not broken down, and their separate parts are not, therefore, incorporated into the learner's creative rule system. Rather 'acquisition' catches up with the routines and patterns; that is, the structural knowledge contained in the formulas is developed separately.

4. Individual differences

   Krashen claims that 'acquisition' follows a natural route (Hypothesis 2). Thus there is no individual variation in the acquisition process itself. However, there is variation in the rate and the extent of acquisition as a result of the amount of comprehensible input received, and the strength of the Affective Filter. There is also variation in performance, brought about by the extent of the learner's reliance on 'learnt' knowledge. Krashen indicates three types of Monitor Users: (1) over-users,

(2) under-users, and (3) optimal users (i.e. those who apply conscious knowledge when it is appropriate).
5. Age
   Age influences SLA in a number of ways. It affects the amount of comprehensible input that is obtained; younger learners may get more than older learners. Age also affects 'learning'; older learners are better suited to study language form and also to use 'learnt' knowledge in monitoring. Finally, age influences the affective state of the learner; after puberty the Affective Filter is likely to increase in strength.

Evaluation

Perhaps as a result of its prominence in SLA research, the Monitor Model has also attracted a lot of criticism. I shall select three central issues for detailed consideration. These are the 'acquisition-learning' distinction, the Monitor, and Krashen's treatment of variability.

THE 'ACQUISITION-LEARNING' DISTINCTION. The 'acquisition-learning' distinction has been called 'theological', in that it has been formulated in order to confirm a specific goal, namely that successful SLA is the result of 'acquisition' ([J.] James, 1980). McLaughlin (1978) argues that the Monitor Model is unreliable, because the 'acquisition-learning' distinction is defined in terms of 'subconscious' and 'conscious' processes, which are not open to inspection. The first criticism, then, is a methodological one. The 'acquisition-learning' hypothesis is not acceptable, because it cannot be tested in empirical investigation.

A further objection concerns Krashen's claims that 'acquisition' and 'learning' are entirely separate, and that 'acquired' knowledge cannot turn into 'learnt' knowledge. Krashen refers to this as the *non-interface position*. McLaughlin (1978), Rivers (1980), Stevick (1980), Sharwood-Smith (1981), and Gregg (1984) have all challenged this position on the basis that when 'learnt' knowledge is automatized through practice it becomes 'acquired' i.e. available for use in spontaneous conversation.

Irrespective of whether the 'acquisition-learning' distinction is valid or not, it can also be criticized on the grounds that Krashen does not really explicate the cognitive processes that are responsible either for 'acquisition' or 'learning'. As Larsen-Freeman (1983b) observes, Krashen does not explain what the learner does with input. If the 'acquisition-learning' distinction is to have any power, it is surely necessary to specify in what way the processes responsible for each knowledge type are different from each other. This Krashen does not do. Thus, despite its comprehensiveness, the Monitor Model is still a 'black box' theory.

MONITORING. There are several difficulties with Krashen's account of Monitoring. One of these is again methodological. The only evidence for Monitoring lies in the language user's own account of trying to apply explicit rules (e.g. Cohen & Robbins, 1976). But both McLaughlin (1978) and Rivers (1980) point to the difficulty of distinguishing introspectively 'rule' application (as in Monitoring) and 'feel' (the implicit use of 'acquired' knowledge to judge or modify an utterance). Editing by 'feel' (or 'monitoring' with a small 'm') subsumes Monitoring (with a big 'M'). Both can be seen as aspects of what Morrison and Low (1983) refer to as the 'critical faculty'. This enables us to become critically aware of what we have created and hence allows us to control it. We are able to attend to the form of our utterances without using conscious rules, and without being able to make explicit how modifications in the initial output have been effected. This happens all the time in writing when we seek to conform to the conventions of the written medium, and it also happens in speech.

Morrison and Low offer a number of other criticisms of Monitoring. They point out that Monitoring does not account for the reception of utterances (i.e. as explained by Krashen, it refers only to production). They also note that Monitoring is limited to syntax, but in fact learners and users have the ability to edit their pronunciation, lexis, and, perhaps most important of all, their discourse. Krashen does not give any consideration to Monitoring as a collaborative activity involving both the learner and his interlocutor. To this list, I would also draw attention to the fact that Krashen tends to conflate Monitoring and 'learning', although the former refers to performance and the latter to rule internalization. As commented on above, there is no detailed discussion of how 'learning' takes place.

VARIABILITY. The Monitor Model is a 'dual competence' theory of SLA. That is, it proposes that the learner's knowledge of the L2, which is reflected in variable performance, is best characterized in terms of two separate competences, which Krashen labels 'acquisition' and 'learning'. The alternative position is to build a variable competence model (see next section), in which the learner's variable performance is seen as a reflection of a stylistic continuum. Which model—the Monitor Model or a variable competence model—best fits the known facts about SLA?

The available evidence indicates that learners produce utterances which are formally different even when it is evident that they are focused on meaning. Consider two utterances from Ellis (1984b) produced by one classroom learner within seconds of each other, each performing the same communicative function:

No look my card.   (instruction to another pupil during a word
Don't look at my card.   bingo game)

Data such as these, which are common in SLA research literature (see the case studies in Hatch, 1978a, for instance), demonstrate that even what Krashen calls 'acquired' knowledge is not homogeneous. But once claims about the homogeneity or 'acquired' knowledge are seen to be ill-founded, it makes little sense to maintain a dual competence explanation. The kinds of performance that result from focusing on meaning and on form are best treated as aspects of a single but variable competence which contains alternative rules for realizing the same meanings, in much the same way as does the native speaker's competence.

In summary, despite the comprehensiveness of the Monitor Model, it poses serious theoretical problems regarding the validity of the 'acquisition-learning' distinction, the operation of Monitoring, and the explanation of variability in language-learner language. Also the input hypothesis does not account for the fact that acquisition can take place without two-way negotiation of meaning, nor does it recognize that output also plays an important role.

5. The Variable Competence Model

Here I shall summarize the Variable Competence theory proposed by Ellis (1984a). This draws on and extends the work of Tarone (1982, 1983), Widdowson (1979b, 1984), and Bialystok (1982).

The Model is based on two distinctions—one of which refers to the process of language use, and the other to the product. The theory also proposes to account for SLA within a framework of language use. In other words, it claims that the way a language is learnt is a reflection of the way it is used.

The *product* of language use comprises a continuum of discourse types ranged from entirely unplanned to entirely planned. To summarize briefly, unplanned discourse is discourse that lacks forethought and preparation. It is associated with spontaneous communication, e.g. everyday conversation or brainstorming in writing. Planned discourse is discourse that is thought out prior to expression. It requires conscious thought and the opportunity to work out content and expression. Examples are a prepared lecture or careful writing.

The *process* of language use is to be understood in terms of the distinction between linguistic knowledge (or *rules*) and the ability to make use of this knowledge (*procedures*). Widdowson (1984) refers to a knowledge of rules as *competence* and to a knowledge of the procedures involved in using rules to construct discourse as *capacity*. Widdowson points out that the narrow concept of linguistic competence has been widened to include appropriate use as well as correct use (i.e. communicative competence). But he argues that even this broader view of competence does not account for the language user's ability 'to create meanings by exploiting the potential inherent in the language for continual modification . . . ' (Widdowson, 1984, p. 8). It is for this reason that he adds the term *capacity*. The language user possesses procedures for realizing the meaning potential of rules in context. In other words, the language user makes his knowledge of linguistic rules work by exploiting them in relationship to both the situational and linguistic context. He actualizes his abstract knowledge of sentences to create utterances in discourse.

It follows from this view of the process of language use that the product (i.e. the different types of discourse) is the result of either or both of the following:

1. a variable competence, i.e. the user possesses a heterogeneous rule system;

2. variable application of procedures for actualizing knowledge in discourse.

The Variable Competence Model of SLA claims that both (1) and (2) occur. Furthermore, it claims that they are related.

The variability of the learner's rule system is described with reference to Bialystok's (1982) dual distinction between automatic/non-automatic and analytic/unanalytic. The first distinction concerns the relative access that the learner has to L2 knowledge. Knowledge that can be retrieved easily and quickly is automatic. Knowledge that takes time and effort to retrieve is non automatic. The second distinction concerns the extent to which the learner possesses a 'propositional mental representation which makes clear the structure of the knowledge and its relationship to other aspects of knowledge' (op. cit., 183). Bialystok points out that unanalysed knowledge is the general form in which we know most things, in that we are usually not aware of the way in which our knowledge is structured. Both the automatic/non-automatic and the analysed/unanalysed distinctions represent continua rather than dichotomies. There are degrees of automatic and analysed knowledge.

Procedures for actualizing knowledge are of two types, which Ellis (1984a) refers to as primary and secondary processes.[7] Each set of processes has an external and internal representation, referred to as discourse and cognitive processes respectively. Primary processes are responsible for engaging in unplanned discourse. They draw on knowledge that is relatively unanalysed and automatic. Secondary processes come into play in planned discourse and draw on knowledge towards the analysed end of the continuum. An example of a primary process is *semantic simplification* (i.e. the omission of elements from a proposition in production). An example of a secondary process is *monitoring* (i.e. the editing of language performance). As an example of what is meant by discourse and cognitive processes, semantic simplification can be accounted for as follows:

Discourse process:

Simplify the semantic structure of a message by omitting meaning elements that are communicatively redundant or that can be realized by a non-verbal device (e.g. mime).

Cognitive process:

a. Construct an underlying conceptual structure of a message.
b. Compare this structure with the frame of reference shared with an interlocutor.
c. Eliminate redundant elements and elements for which no lexical item is available.

Primary and secondary processes account for how L2 learners actualize their linguistic knowledge in discourse. They account for the variability of language-learner language by positing that both different types of knowledge and different procedures are involved in the construction of different discourse types. They also account for acquisition. To explain how, it is necessary to return to what Widdowson has to say about rules and procedures.

Widdowson argues that through using procedures, not only does the language user utilize his existing linguistic knowledge but he also, potentially at least, creates new linguistic rules. As Widdowson (1979b, p. 62) puts it:

> We draw upon our knowledge of rules to *make sense*. We do not simply measure discourse up against our knowledge of pre-existing rules, we create discourse and commonly bring new rules into existence by so doing. All competence is transitional in this sense.

In other words, language acquisition is the result of our capacity to make sense. New rules are created when we endeavour to use existing knowledge in relation to the linguistic and situational context in order to create shared frames of reference. A theory of language use is the matrix of a theory of language acquisition.

Ellis (1984a) goes one step further and suggests that SLA follows the sequence that it does because the processes that the learner calls on to participate in discourse are themselves developmental. That is, their prominence in SLA coincides with different stages of development. Thus, for instance, early SLA is characterized by the heavy use of semantic simplification, because this is a procedure that requires little L2 knowledge. Later procedures, such as those used to reduce reliance on shared knowledge and non-verbal devices, by making explicit the relationship between one proposition and another and between each proposition and its situational context (see Widdowson (1984, pp. 67ff)), are characteristic of later SLA. Also knowledge that to begin with is available only for use via secondary processes (because it exists only in analysed form) can eventually be accessed by means of primary processes and so used in unplanned as well as planned discourse.

To summarize, the Variable Competence Model proposes:

1. There is a single knowledge store containing variable interlanguage rules according to how automatic and how analysed the rules are.
2. The learner possesses a capacity for language use which consists of primary and secondary discourse and cognitive processes.
3. L2 performance is variable as a result of whether primary processes employing unanalysed L2 rules are utilized in unplanned discourse, or secondary processes employing analysed L2 rules are utilized in planned discourse.
4. Development occurs as a result of
   a. acquisition of new L2 rules through participation in various types of

discourse (i.e. new rules originate in the application of procedural knowledge),

   b. activation of L2 rules which initially exist in either a non-automatic unanalysed form or in an analysed form so they can be used in unplanned discourse.

These proposals are shown in Figure 3.

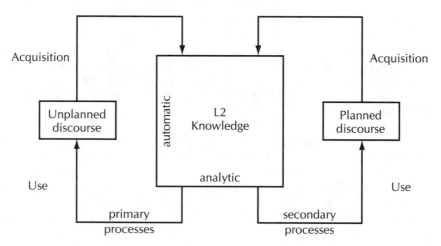

Figure 3. Variable Competence Model of SLA

Evaluation

The Variable Competence Model of SLA attempts to account for (1) the variability of language-learner language, and (2) the external and internal processes responsible for SLA. It incorporates within the same framework a theory of language use and a theory of SLA. As it stands at the moment, the Model is in need of development in two directions. First it needs to provide a more detailed analysis of the primary and secondary processes responsible for use and acquisition. Second, it needs to incorporate the role of input into the overall framework. Learners do not construct discourse in isolation (at least not in face-to-face interaction), so how input is negotiated must be considered. SLA is the result of the exchange of linguistic information which occurs in the process of discourse construction involving both the learner and an interlocutor.

6. The Universal Hypothesis

The Universal Hypothesis states that there are linguistic universals which determine the course of SLA as follows.

   1. Linguistic universals impose constraints on the form that interlanguages can take.

2. Learners find it easier to acquire patterns that conform to linguistic universals than those that do not. The linguistic markedness of L2 rules explains the developmental route.
3. Where the L1 manifests linguistic universals, it is likely to assist inter-language development through transfer.

Linguistic universals have been investigated by the in-depth study of a single language. Those working in this tradition argue that there is a Universal Grammar that constrains the kind of hypotheses that the learner can form and that is innate. An alternative approach to investigating linguistic universals is to study a large number of languages from different language families in order to discover typological universals.[8] A number of possible explanations for universals are entertained by those working in this tradition, including pragmatic explanations.

In both L1 and L2 acquisition the effect of linguistic universals has been investigated primarily in terms of markedness theory. This states that some rules are unmarked or weakly marked and others marked or more strongly marked. Various criteria have been proposed for determining the markedness of a rule. Chomsky proposes that an unmarked rule is one that requires no or minimal 'triggering' from the environment. A typological universal or a strong universal tendency can also be considered as unmarked. There is some evidence to suggest that language acquisition proceeds by mastering the easier unmarked properties before the more difficult marked ones. In SLA there is also some evidence to suggest that when the L2 rule is marked, the learner will turn to his L1, particularly if this has an equivalent unmarked rule.

Evaluation

The Universal Hypothesis provides an interesting account of how the linguistic properties of the target language and the learner's first language may influence the course of development. It constitutes an attempt to explain SLA in terms of an independent language faculty, rather than in more general cognitive terms. One advantage of this is that it brings SLA studies into line with current linguistic research that follows the Chomskyan tradition. It also avoids the quagmire of explanations based on learner strategies.

The value of the Universal Hypothesis for SLA theory is twofold: (1) it focuses attention on the nature of the target language itself, lending support to Wode's (1980, pp. 136–137) claim that 'the linguistic devices used in a given language are the major variable(s) determining . . . linguistic sequences'; and (2) it provides a subtle and persuasive reconsideration of transfer as an important factor in SLA.

One of the major problems of the Universal Hypothesis lies in the difficulty in defining the markedness construct. Various criteria have been used to explicate it—core vs peripheral grammar, complexity and explicitness. Moreover, it is not clear whether markedness is to be seen as just a linguistic construct or whether it has psycholinguistic validity.

Even if linguistic markedness is a major determinant of SLA (and this is not yet proven, as it is possible that many of the facts explained in terms of markedness theory might also be explained by other factors, such as the frequency of occurrence of different structures in the input), it is unlikely that it will be able to explain the complexity of SLA by itself. In addition, the Universal Hypothesis operates on the assumption that linguistic knowledge is homogeneous, and, therefore, ignores variability.

7. A Neurofunctional Theory

Whereas all the previous models discussed have attempted to explain SLA in linguistic or *psycholinguistic* terms, the theory considered in this section draws on *neurolinguistic* research. It constitutes, therefore, a different type of explanation. Lamendella (1979, pp. 5–6) defines the scope of a neurofunctional approach as follows:

> A neurofunctional perspective on language attempts to characterize the neurolinguistic information processing systems responsible for the development and use of language.

The account of a neurofunctional theory of SLA that follows draws primarily on the work of Lamendella (1977, 1979; Selinker & Lamendella, 1978b).

The basic premise of a neurofunctional view of SLA is that there is a connection between language function and the neural anatomy. It is important, however, to recognize that, as Hatch (1983, p. 213) puts it, 'there is no single "black box" for language in the brain'. It is not possible to identify precisely which areas of the brain are associated with language functioning. Therefore it is better to speak of 'the relative contribution of some areas more than others under certain conditions' (Seliger, 1982, p. 309). The adult's brain never entirely loses the plasticity of the new-born baby's brain, with the result that in cases of damage to specific areas of neural tissue (as in aphasia), the functions associated with those areas need not be completely lost, but transferred to other areas.

Neurofunctional accounts of SLA have considered the contribution of two areas of the brain: (1) the right (as opposed to the left) hemisphere, and (2) the areas of the left hemisphere (in particular those known as Wernicke's and Broca's areas), which clinical studies have shown to be closely associated with the comprehension and production of language. Neurofunctional accounts have also tended to focus on specific aspects of SLA: (1) age differences, (2) formulaic speech, (3) fossilization, and (4) pattern practice in classroom SLA. The relationship between the maturation of neural mechanisms and SLA has already been considered and so will not be dealt with again here. The other issues are considered briefly below in a discussion of the two areas of the brain that research has focused on.

Right Hemisphere Functioning

Right hemisphere functioning is generally associated with holistic processing, as opposed to serial or analytic processing, which occurs in the left hemisphere. Not surprisingly, therefore, it has been suggested (e.g. by Obler, 1981; Krashen, 1981b) that the right hemisphere is responsible for the storing and processing of formulaic speech. The routines and patterns which comprise formulaic speech are unanalysed wholes and as such belong to the 'gestalt' perception of the right hemisphere. It has also been suggested that right hemisphere involvement in L2 processing will be more evident in the early, non-proficient stages than in later, more advanced stages of SLA. This hypothesis is compatible with the link between the right hemisphere and formulaic speech, as the early stages of SLA are more likely to be characterized by heavy use of formulaic speech. However, Genesee (1982), reviewing this hypothesis, found conflicting evidence. Out of the thirteen studies he examined, three provided positive support, six found comparable patterns of left hemisphere involvement, and four were opposed to the stage hypothesis. Genesee concluded that the stage hypothesis has received insufficient support. He found greater support for another hypothesis concerning right hemisphere involvement, namely that it is associated to a greater extent with informal than formal language acquisition. This hypothesis is also compatible with the right hemisphere connection with formulaic speech, which is generally considered to be more prominent in settings where natural language use is common. It seems, therefore, that there is considerable evidence to associate the acquisition and use of formulaic speech with the right hemisphere.

The right hemisphere may also be involved in pattern practice in class room SLA. Seliger (1982) suggests that the right hemisphere may act as an initial staging mechanism for handling patterns which can then be re-examined later in left hemisphere functioning. Pattern practice and minimal pair drills may utilize right hemisphere abilities in the adult learner and so contribute to what Seliger calls 'primitive hypotheses'. If subsequent analysis by the left hemisphere does not take place, the learner will not be able to utilize the language forms that have been drilled in the construction of spontaneous, creative speech. This offers an interesting neurolinguistic explanation of why formal language practice does not appear to facilitate natural language use immediately.

Left Hemisphere Functioning

Where the left hemisphere is concerned, there is less clarity regarding the location of specific language functions. In general the left hemisphere is associated with creative language use, including syntactic and semantic processing and the motor operations involved in speaking and writing. However, the extent to which these different functions can be localized is not clear (see

Hatch, 1983, for a detailed review of this issue). Walsh and Diller (1981) distinguish two broad types of functioning: (1) lower order functioning and (2) higher order functioning. The former, associated with Wernicke's and Broca's areas, involves basic grammatical processing, together with the motor operations. The latter, associated with a different area of the cerebral cortex, involves semantic processing and verbal cognition. Walsh and Diller suggest that lower-order processing is a function of early maturing, while higher-order processing depends on late developing neural circuitry. Thus whereas younger learners rely primarily on lower-order processing, older learners make use of higher-order processing. There have also been suggestions that different levels of language processing (e.g. pronunciation vs. syntax) are linked to different neural mechanisms. The fact that different aspects of language fossilize at different times (e.g. learners with native-like syntax but non-native pronunciation are not uncommon) is evidence of this. Seliger (1978) develops an interesting argument based on neurolinguistic evidence to support a differential fossilization hypothesis. In general, though, claims about localized functions need to be treated circumspectly.

These various observations do not amount to a theory of SLA. However, Lamendella has attempted to formulate a neurofunctional theory of SLA. This is described below.

Lamendella's Neurofunctional Theory

Lamendella distinguishes two basic types of language acquisition: (1) Primary Language Acquisition and (2) Secondary Language Acquisition. (1) is found in the child's acquisition of one or more languages from 2 to 5 years. (2) is subdivided into (a) foreign language learning (i.e. the formal classroom learning of a L2), and (b) second language acquisition (i.e. the natural acquisition of a L2 after the age of five).

Linked to these two types of language acquisition are different neurofunctional systems, each of which consists of a hierarchy of functions. Each system has a different overall role in information processing. Lamendella pinpoints two systems as particularly important for language functioning:

1. The communication hierarchy: this has responsibility for language and other forms of interpersonal communication.
2. The cognitive hierarchy: this controls a variety of cognitive information processing activities that are also part of language use.

Primary language acquisition and also second language acquisition (i.e. (2b)) are marked by the use of the communication hierarchy, whereas foreign language acquisition, i.e. (2a), is marked by the use of the cognitive hierarchy. Pattern practice drills are likely to involve the cognitive hierarchy and hence material learnt in this way is not available in language behaviour that draws on the communicative hierarchy. As Lamendella puts it:

> . . . the executive functions of the communication hierarchy do not seem to
> have the capacity to call up automated subroutines whose construction was
> directed by the cognitive hierarchy. (1979, p. 17)

Thus the theory posits a different neurolinguistic base for the kind of acquisition and language use typically found in natural SLA and tutored SLA. The distinction between the communicative and cognitive hierarchies seems to parallel
the psycholinguistic distinction between 'acquisition' and 'learning' in the
Monitor Model.

Each neurofunctional system is composed of different levels, ranged from
higher to lower order, and each associated with different levels of neural organization (which Lamendella does not specify). The different levels can be interconnected, but they can also be disassociated. Thus, for instance, it is possible to
engage what Lamendella calls 'copying circuits' in order to repeat what someone
has said, without engaging other circuits that are responsible for language comprehension or formulation (e.g. a typist can type out a letter without bothering to
understand its content). Furthermore, L2 forms acquired by means of higher-
level systems can be stored as automatic sub-routines at lower levels of the communication hierarchy. In language performance, lower-level sub-routines can be
accessed without calling upon higher levels within the same hierarchy.

Lamendella sums up the task facing the language learner:

> When first confronted with the need to acquire new information structures
> . . . a learner must identify the functional hierarchy best suited to this learn-
> ing, then establish the appropriate level and subsystems within the hierarchy
> with which to begin the learning process. (1979, p. 15)

In other words, Lamendella claims that SLA can be explained neurofunctionally
with reference to (1) which neurofunctional system is used—the communication
or the cognitive—and (2) which level within the chosen neurofunctional system
is engaged.

Evaluation

Neurofunctional explanations of SLA are based on the premise that it is possible to trace the neurolinguistic correlates of specific language functions. However, there is still considerable uncertainty regarding the identification of
specific neurofunctions and their neurolinguistic correlates. The evidence from
clinical studies (see Genesee, 1982) is conflicting. Also it is not clear to what
extent studies of language *processing* based on tests where linguistic stimuli are
presented separately to the left and right ear (i.e. dichotic listening tests) or
studies of aphasia, which together serve as the major sources of information
about neurofunctioning, provide reliable insights into the neurolinguistic bases
of language *acquisition*.

Lamendella's neurofunctional theory offers an interesting account of a
number of facts about SLA (e.g. the inutility of material learnt through pattern

practice in spontaneous communication). But there are many facts which it does not explain (or even seek to). In particular it is not clear how it can account for the natural sequence of development. Also the distinction between foreign and second language learning is a simplification. It is not so much the type of setting which is important, as the type of interaction which occurs in these settings. Thus natural communication in a L2 is quite possible in a foreign language classroom.

Neurolinguistic and neurofunctional explanations are perhaps best treated as affording additional understanding about SLA, rather than an explanation of it. However, in the long run it will be useful if psycholinguistic constructs used to explain SLA can be matched up with neurofunctional mechanisms. . . .

A FRAMEWORK FOR INVESTIGATING SLA

A number of components of SLA need to be considered. These are (1) situational factors, (2) the linguistic input, (3) learner differences, (4) learner processes, and (5) linguistic output. Figure 4 shows the interrelationship between these components. Situational factors influence input (e.g. input in a classroom setting is likely to differ from that in a natural setting) and also the use of learner processes (e.g. communication strategies). Learner differences on such variables as motivation and personality help to determine the quantity and quality of the input and also affect the operation of learner strategies (e.g. the use of metalingual strategies). Input comprises (1) the inherent properties of the target language system, and (2) the formally and interactionally adjusted features found in foreigner and teacher talk. Input constitutes the data upon which the

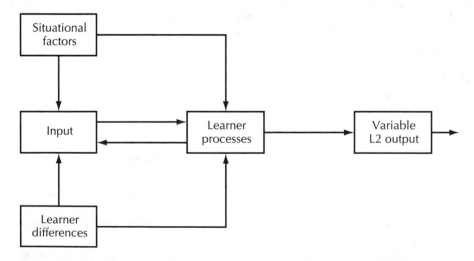

Figure 4. A Framework for Examining the Components of SLA

learner strategies work, but also the input is itself in part determined by the learner's use of communication strategies. Thus the relationship between input and learner processes is an interactive one. The learner's strategies (composed of learning, production, and communication strategies) produce a variable L2 output. This in turn is part of the input. Thus the framework is cyclical. . . .

NOTES

[1] Krashen's Monitor Model and Dulay and Burt's Creative Construction Theory are closely related, sharing many premises. The former is considered in this reading, as a recognition of the considerable interest it has aroused in SLA research.

[2] More than one type of 'bad' learning situation is possible, as many of the variables permit three-way alternatives. For instance, a 'bad' situation arises when the target language group sees itself as either dominant *or* subordinate.

[3] Schumann's (1978b) study of Alberto lasted ten months. This is perhaps too short a period to conclude that fossilization has taken place. Ellis (1984a) observed little syntactical development in three classroom learners over a similar period, but another twelve months showed evidence of considerable development.

[4] To the best of my knowledge, neither Schumann nor Andersen has discussed the application of their theories to classroom SLA. The psychological factors which Schumann considers are likely to be relevant to the classroom, as Gardner and Lambert's (1972) work on motivation and attitude has shown.

[5] H. D. Brown (1980) has in fact criticized Schumann's theory on the grounds that there is no objective means of measuring actual social distance. He points out that it is how the learner views his own culture in relation to the culture of the target language community that affects SLA.

[6] Giles also identifies a third type of speech marker—*upward divergence*—which occurs when an outgroup speaker accentuates speech markers that distinguish him from the ingroup speaker. In so doing the outgroup speaker may deviate from the standard forms of his language. Thus the L2 learner may find the prestige dialect 'an ever-moving target' (Giles & Byrne, 1982, p. 22).

[7] The terms 'primary' and 'secondary processes' are chosen to reflect the primacy of unplanned discourse. It is not intended to suggest that 'primary processes' are more important than 'secondary processes', only that they are responsible for the style associated with spontaneous face-to-face communication.

[8] In order to carry out a cross-linguistic comparison it is, of course, necessary to work on hypothetical assumptions about what the universal categories will be.

RELATED READING 3
INTERACTION BETWEEN LEARNING AND DEVELOPMENT
Lev S. Vygotsky

The problems encountered in the psychological analysis of teaching cannot be correctly resolved or even formulated without addressing the relation between learning and development in school-age children. Yet it is the most unclear of all the basic issues on which the application of child development theories to educational processes depends. Needless to say, the lack of theoretical clarity does not mean that the issue is removed altogether from current research efforts into learning; not one study can avoid this central theoretical issue. But the relation between learning and development remains methodologically unclear because concrete research studies have embodied theoretically vague, critically unevaluated, and sometimes internally contradictory postulates, premises, and peculiar solutions to the problem of this fundamental relationship; and these, of course, result in a variety of errors.

Essentially, all current conceptions of the relation between development and learning in children can be reduced to three major theoretical positions.

The first centers on the assumption that processes of child development are independent of learning. Learning is considered a purely external process that is not actively involved in development. It merely utilizes the achievements of development rather than providing an impetus for modifying its course.

In experimental investigations of the development of thinking in school children, it has been assumed that processes such as deduction and understanding, evolution of notions about the world, interpretation of physical causality, and mastery of logical forms of thought and abstract logic all occur by themselves, without any influence from school learning. An example of such a theory is Piaget's extremely complex and interesting theoretical principles, which also shape the experimental methodology he employs. The questions Piaget [1955] uses in the course of his "clinical conversations" with children clearly illustrate his approach. When a five-year-old is asked "why doesn't the sun fall?" it is assumed that the child has neither a ready answer for such a question nor the general capabilities for generating one. The point of asking questions that are so far beyond the reach of the child's intellectual skills is to eliminate the influence of previous experience and knowledge. The experimenter seeks to obtain the tendencies of children's thinking in "pure" form, entirely independent of learning.

Similarly, the classics of psychological literature, such as the works by Binet and others, assume that development is always a prerequisite for learning and

From L. S. Vygotsky, *Mind in Society: Development of Higher Psychological Processes,* edited by M. Cole, S. Scribner, V. John-Steiner, and E. Souberman. (Cambridge, MA: Harvard University Press, 1978), pp. 79–91.

that if a child's mental functions (intellectual operations) have not matured to the extent that he is capable of learning a particular subject, then no instruction will prove useful. They especially feared premature instruction, the teaching of a subject before the child was ready for it. All effort was concentrated on finding the lower threshold of learning ability, the age at which a particular kind of learning first becomes possible.

Because this approach is based on the premise that learning trails behind development, that development always outruns learning, it precludes the notion that learning may play a role in the course of the development or maturation of those functions activated in the course of learning. Development or maturation is viewed as a precondition of learning but never the result of it. To summarize this position: Learning forms a superstructure over development, leaving the latter essentially unaltered.

The second major theoretical position is that learning *is* development. This identity is the essence of a group of theories that are quite diverse in origin.

One such theory is based on the concept of reflex, an essentially old notion that has been extensively revived recently. Whether reading, writing, or arithmetic is being considered, development is viewed as the mastery of conditioned reflexes; that is, the process of learning is completely and inseparably blended with the process of development. This notion was elaborated by James, who reduced the learning process to habit formation and identified the learning process with development.

Reflex theories have at least one thing in common with theories such as Piaget's: in both, development is conceived of as the elaboration and substitution of innate responses. As [W.] James expressed it, "Education, in short, cannot be better described than by calling it the organization of acquired habits of conduct and tendencies to behavior" [1958, pp. 36–37]. Development itself is reduced primarily to the accumulation of all possible responses. Any acquired response is considered either a more complex form of or a substitute for the innate response.

But despite the similarity between the first and second theoretical positions, there is a major difference in their assumptions about the temporal relationship between learning and developmental processes. Theorists who hold the first view assert that developmental cycles precede learning cycles; maturation precedes learning and instruction must lag behind mental growth. For the second group of theorists, both processes occur simultaneously; learning and development coincide at all points in the same way that two identical geometrical figures coincide when superimposed.

The third theoretical position on the relation between learning and development attempts to overcome the extremes of the other two by simply combining them. A clear example of this approach is Koffka's theory [1924], in which development is based on two inherently different but related processes, each of which influences the other. On the one hand is maturation, which depends directly on the development of the nervous system; on the other hand is learning, which itself is also a developmental process.

Three aspects of this theory are new. First, as we already noted, is the combination of two seemingly opposite viewpoints, each of which has been encountered separately in the history of science. The very fact that these two viewpoints can be combined into one theory indicates that they are not opposing and mutually exclusive but have something essential in common. Also new is the idea that the two processes that make up development are mutually dependent and interactive. Of course, the nature of the interaction is left virtually unexplored in Koffka's work, which is limited solely to very general remarks regarding the relation between these two processes. It is clear that for Koffka the process of maturation prepares and makes possible a specific process of learning. The learning process then stimulates and pushes forward the maturation process. The third and most important new aspect of this theory is the expanded role it ascribes to learning in child development. This emphasis leads us directly to an old pedagogical problem, that of formal discipline and the problem of transfer.

Pedagogical movements that have emphasized formal discipline and urged the teaching of classical languages, ancient civilizations, and mathematics have assumed that regardless of the irrelevance of these particular subjects for daily living, they were of the greatest value for the pupil's mental development. A variety of studies have called into question the soundness of this idea. It has been shown that learning in one area has very little influence on overall development. For example, reflex theorists Woodworth and Thorndike found that adults who, after special exercises, had achieved considerable success in determining the length of short lines, had made virtually no progress in their ability to determine the length of long lines. These same adults were successfully trained to estimate the size of a given two-dimensional figure, but this training did not make them successful in estimating the size of a series of other two-dimensional figures of various sizes and shapes.

According to Thorndike [1914], theoreticians in psychology and education believe that every particular response acquisition directly enhances overall ability in equal measure: Teachers believed and acted on the basis of the theory that the mind is a complex of abilities—powers of observation, attention, memory, thinking, and so forth—and that any improvement in any specific ability results in a general improvement in all abilities. According to this theory, if the student increased the attention he paid to Latin grammar, he would increase his abilities to focus attention on any task. The words "accuracy," "quick-wittedness," "ability to reason," "memory," "power of observation," "attention," "concentration," and so forth are said to denote actual fundamental capabilities that vary in accordance with the material with which they operate; these basic abilities are substantially modified by studying particular subjects, and they retain these modifications when they turn to other areas. Therefore, if someone learns to do any single thing well, he will also be able to do other entirely unrelated things well as a result of some secret connection. It is assumed that mental capabilities function independently of the material with which they operate, and that the development of one ability entails the development of others.

Thorndike himself opposed this point of view. Through a variety of studies he showed that particular forms of activity, such as spelling, are dependent on the mastery of specific skills and material necessary for the performance of that particular task. The development of one particular capability seldom means the development of others. Thorndike argued that specialization of abilities is even greater than superficial observation may indicate. For example, if, out of a hundred individuals we choose ten who display the ability to detect spelling errors or to measure lengths, it is unlikely that these ten will display better abilities regarding, for example, the estimation of the weight of objects. In the same way, speed and accuracy in adding numbers are entirely unrelated to speed and accuracy in being able to think up antonyms.

This research shows that the mind is not a complex network of *general* capabilities such as observation, attention, memory, judgment, and so forth, but a set of specific capabilities, each of which is, to some extent, independent of the others and is developed independently. Learning is more than the acquisition of the ability to think; it is the acquisition of many specialized abilities for thinking about a variety of things. Learning does not alter our overall ability to focus attention but rather develops various abilities to focus attention on a variety of things. According to this view, special training affects overall development only when its elements, material, and processes are similar across specific domains; habit governs us. This leads to the conclusion that because each activity depends on the material with which it operates, the development of consciousness is the development of a set of particular, independent capabilities or of a set of particular habits. Improvement of one function of consciousness or one aspect of its activity can affect the development of another only to the extent that there are elements common to both functions or activities.

Developmental theorists such as Koffka and the Gestalt School—who hold to the third theoretical position outlined earlier—oppose Thorndike's point of view. They assert that the influence of learning is never specific. From their study of structural principles, they argue that the learning process can never be reduced simply to the formation of skills but embodies an intellectual order that makes it possible to transfer general principles discovered in solving one task to a variety of other tasks. From this point of view, the child, while learning a particular operation, acquires the ability to create structures of a certain type, regardless of the diverse materials with which she is working and regardless of the particular elements involved. Thus, Koffka does not conceive of learning as limited to a process of habit and skill acquisition. The relationship he posits between learning and development is not that of an identity but of a more complex relationship. According to Thorndike, learning and development coincide at all points, but for Koffka, development is always a larger set than learning. Schematically, the relationship between the two processes could be depicted by two concentric circles, the smaller symbolizing the learning process and the larger the developmental process evoked by learning.

Once a child has learned to perform an operation, he thus assimilates some structural principle whose sphere of application is other than just the operations of the type on whose basis the principle was assimilated. Consequently, in making one step in learning, a child makes two steps in development, that is, learning and development do not coincide. This concept is the essential aspect of the third group of theories we have discussed.

ZONE OF PROXIMAL DEVELOPMENT: A NEW APPROACH

Although we reject all three theoretical positions discussed above, analyzing them leads us to a more adequate view of the relation between learning and development. The question to be framed in arriving at a solution to this problem is complex. It consists of two separate issues: first, the general relation between learning and development; and second, the specific features of this relationship when children reach school age.

That children's learning begins long before they attend school is the starting point of this discussion. Any learning a child encounters in school always has a previous history. For example, children begin to study arithmetic in school, but long beforehand they have had some experience with quantity—they have had to deal with operations of division, addition, subtraction, and determination of size. Consequently, children have their own preschool arithmetic, which only myopic psychologists could ignore.

It goes without saying that learning as it occurs in the preschool years differs markedly from school learning, which is concerned with the assimilation of the fundamentals of scientific knowledge. But even when, in the period of her first questions, a child assimilates the names of objects in her environment, she is learning. Indeed, can it be doubted that children learn speech from adults; or that, through asking questions and giving answers, children acquire a variety of information; or that, through imitating adults and through being instructed about how to act, children develop an entire repository of skills? Learning and development are interrelated from the child's very first day of life.

Koffka, attempting to clarify the laws of child learning and their relation to mental development, concentrates his attention on the simplest learning processes, those that occur in the preschool years. His error is that, while seeing a similarity between preschool and school learning, he fails to discern the difference—he does not see the specifically new elements that school learning introduces. He and others assume that the difference between preschool and school learning consists of nonsystematic learning in one case and systematic learning in the other. But "systematicness" is not the only issue; there is also the fact that school learning introduces something fundamentally new into the child's development. In order to elaborate the dimensions of school learning, we will describe a new and exceptionally important concept without which the issue cannot be resolved: the zone of proximal development.

A well known and empirically established fact is that learning should be matched in some manner with the child's developmental level. For example, it has been established that the teaching of reading, writing, and arithmetic should be initiated at a specific age level. Only recently, however, has attention been directed to the fact that we cannot limit ourselves merely to determining developmental levels if we wish to discover the actual relations of the developmental process to learning capabilities. We must determine at least two developmental levels.

The first level can be called the *actual developmental level*, that is, the level of development of a child's mental functions that has been established as a result of certain already *completed* developmental cycles. When we determine a child's mental age by using tests, we are almost always dealing with the actual developmental level. In studies of children's mental development it is generally assumed that only those things that children can do on their own are indicative of mental abilities. We give children a battery of tests or a variety of tasks of varying degrees of difficulty, and we judge the extent of their mental development on the basis of how they solve them and at what level of difficulty. On the other hand, if we offer leading questions or show how the problem is to be solved and the child then solves it, or if the teacher initiates the solution and the child completes it or solves it in collaboration with other children—in short, if the child barely misses an independent solution of the problem—the solution is not regarded as indicative of his mental development. This "truth" was familiar and reinforced by common sense. Over a decade even the profoundest thinkers never questioned the assumption; they never entertained the notion that what children can do with the assistance of others might be in some sense even more indicative of their mental development than what they can do alone.

Let us take a simple example. Suppose I investigate two children upon entrance into school, both of whom are ten years old chronologically and eight years old in terms of mental development. Can I say that they are the same age mentally? Of course. What does this mean? It means that they can independently deal with tasks up to the degree of difficulty that has been standardized for the eight-year-old level. If I stop at this point, people would imagine that the subsequent course of mental development and of school learning for these children will be the same, because it depends on their intellect. Of course, there may be other factors, for example, if one child was sick for half a year while the other was never absent from school; but generally speaking, the fate of these children should be the same. Now imagine that I do not terminate my study at this point, but only begin it. These children seem to be capable of handling problems up to an eight-year-old's level, but not beyond that. Suppose that I show them various ways of dealing with the problem. Different experimenters might employ different modes of demonstration in different cases: some might run through an entire demonstration and ask the children to repeat it, others might initiate the solution and ask the child to finish it, or offer leading questions. In short, in some way or another I propose that the children solve the problem with my assistance. Under these circumstances it turns out that the first child can deal with problems up to a twelve-year-old's level, the second up to a nine-year-old's. Now, are these children mentally the same?

When it was first shown that the capability of children with equal levels of mental development to learn under a teacher's guidance varied to a high degree, it became apparent that those children were not mentally the same age and that the subsequent course of their learning would obviously be different. This difference between twelve and eight, or between nine and eight, is what we call *the zone of proximal development. It is the distance between the actual developmental level as determined by independent problem solving and the level of potential development as determined through problem solving under adult guidance or in collaboration with more capable peers.*

If we naively ask what the actual developmental level is, or, to put it more simply, what more independent problem solving reveals, the most common answer would be that a child's actual developmental level defines functions that have already matured, that is, the end products of development. If a child can do such-and-such independently, it means that the functions for such-and-such have matured in her. What, then, is defined by the zone of proximal development, as determined through problems that children cannot solve independently but only with assistance? The zone of proximal development defines those functions that have not yet matured but are in the process of maturation, functions that will mature tomorrow but are currently in an embryonic state. These functions could be termed the "buds" or "flowers" of development rather than the "fruits" of development. The actual developmental level characterizes mental development retrospectively, while the zone of proximal development characterizes mental development prospectively.

The zone of proximal development furnishes psychologists and educators with a tool through which the internal course of development can be understood. By using this method we can take account of not only the cycles and maturation processes that have already been completed but also those processes that are currently in a state of formation, that are just beginning to mature and develop. Thus, the zone of proximal development permits us to delineate the child's immediate future and his dynamic developmental state, allowing not only for what already has been achieved developmentally but also for what is in the course of maturing. The two children in our example displayed the same mental age from the viewpoint of developmental cycles already completed, but the developmental dynamics of the two were entirely different. The state of a child's mental development can be determined only by clarifying its two levels: the actual developmental level and the zone of proximal development.

I will discuss one study of preschool children to demonstrate that what is in the zone of proximal development today will be the actual developmental level tomorrow—that is, what a child can do with assistance today she will be able to do by herself tomorrow.

The American researcher Dorothea McCarthy [1930] showed that among children between the ages of three and five there are two groups of functions: those the children already possess, and those they can perform under guidance, in groups, and in collaboration with one another but which they have not mastered independently. McCarthy's study demonstrated that this second group of functions is at the actual developmental level of five-to-seven-year-olds. What her subjects could do only under guidance, in collaboration, and in groups at the age of three-to-five years they could do independently when they reached the age of five-to-seven years. Thus, if we were to determine only mental age—that is, only functions that have matured—we would have but a summary of completed development, while if we determine the maturing functions, we can predict what will happen to these children between five and seven, provided the same developmental conditions are maintained. The zone of proximal development can become a powerful concept in developmental research, one that can markedly enhance the effectiveness and utility of the application of diagnostics of mental development to educational problems.

A full understanding of the concept of the zone of proximal development must result in reevaluation of the role of imitation in learning. An unshakable tenet of classical psychology is that only the independent activity of children, not their imitative activity, indicates their level of mental development. This view is expressed in all current testing systems. In evaluating mental development, consideration is given to only those solutions to test problems which the child reaches without the assistance of others, without demonstrations, and without leading questions. Imitation and learning are thought of as purely mechanical processes. But recently psychologists have shown that a person can imitate only that which is within her developmental level. For example, if a child is having difficulty with a problem in arithmetic and the teacher solves it on the blackboard, the child may grasp the solution in an instant. But if the teacher were to solve a problem in higher mathematics, the child would not be able to understand the solution no matter how many times she imitated it.

Animal psychologists, and in particular Köhler [1925], have dealt with this question of imitation quite well. Köhler's experiments sought to determine whether primates are capable of graphic thought. The principal question was whether primates solved problems independently or whether they merely imitated solutions they had seen performed earlier, for example, watching other animals or humans use sticks and other tools and then imitating them. Köhler's special experiments, designed to determine what primates could imitate, reveal that primates can use imitation to solve only those problems that are of the same degree of difficulty as those they can solve alone. However, Köhler failed to take account of an important fact, namely, that primates cannot be taught (in the human sense of the word) through imitation, nor can their intellect be developed, because they have no zone of proximal development. A primate can learn a great deal through training by using its mechanical and mental skills, but it cannot be made more intelligent, that is, it cannot be taught to solve a variety of more advanced problems independently. For this reason animals are incapable of learning in the human sense of the term; *human learning presupposes a specific social nature and a process by which children grow into the intellectual life of those around them.*

Children can imitate a variety of actions that go well beyond the limits of their own capabilities. Using imitation, children are capable of doing much more in collective activity or under the guidance of adults. This fact, which seems to be of little significance in itself, is of fundamental importance in that it demands a radical alteration of the entire doctrine concerning the relation between learning and development in children. One direct consequence is a change in conclusions that may be drawn from diagnostic tests of development.

Formerly, it was believed that by using tests, we determine the mental development level with which education should reckon and whose limits it should not exceed. This procedure oriented learning toward yesterday's development, toward developmental stages already completed. The error of this view was discovered earlier in practice than in theory. It is demonstrated most clearly in the teaching of mentally retarded children. Studies have established that mentally retarded children are not very capable of abstract thinking. From this the pedagogy of the special school drew the seemingly correct conclusion that all teaching of such children should be based on the use of concrete, look-and-do methods. And yet a considerable amount of experience with this method resulted in profound disillusionment. It turned out that a teaching system based solely on concreteness—one that eliminated from teaching everything associated with abstract thinking—not only failed to help retarded children overcome their innate handicaps but also reinforced their handicaps by accustoming children exclusively to concrete thinking and thus suppressing the rudiments of any abstract thought that such children still have. Precisely because retarded children, when left to themselves, will never achieve well-elaborated forms of abstract thought, the school should make every effort to push them in that direction and to develop in them what is intrinsically lacking in their own development. In the current practices of special schools for retarded children, we can observe a beneficial shift away from this concept of concreteness, one that restores look-and-do methods to their proper role. Concreteness is now seen as necessary and unavoidable only as a stepping stone for developing abstract thinking—as a means, not as an end in itself.

Similarly, in normal children, learning which is oriented toward developmental levels that have already been reached is ineffective from the viewpoint of a child's overall development. It does not aim for a new stage of the developmental process but rather lags behind this process. Thus, the notion of a zone of proximal development enables us to propound a new formula, namely that the only "good learning" is that which is in advance of development.

The acquisition of language can provide a paradigm for the entire problem of the relation between learning and development. Language arises initially as a means of communication between the child and the people in his environment. Only subsequently, upon conversion to internal speech, does it come to organize the child's thought, that is, become an internal mental function. Piaget and others have shown that reasoning occurs in a children's group as an argument intended to prove one's own point of view before it occurs as an internal activity whose distinctive feature is that the child begins to perceive and check the basis of his thoughts. Such observations prompted Piaget [1955] to conclude that communication produces the need for checking and confirming thoughts, a process that is characteristic of adult thought. In the same way that internal speech and reflective thought arise from the interactions between the child and persons in her environment, these interactions provide the source of development of a child's voluntary behavior. Piaget has shown that cooperation provides the basis for the development of a child's moral judgment. Earlier research established that a child first becomes able to subordinate her behavior to rules in group play and only later does voluntary self-regulation of behavior arise as an internal function.

These individual examples illustrate a general developmental law for the higher mental functions that we feel can be applied in its entirety to children's learning processes. We propose that an essential feature of learning is that it creates the zone of proximal development; that is, learning awakens a variety of internal developmental processes that are able to operate only when the child is interacting with people in his environment and in cooperation with his peers. Once these processes are internalized, they become part of the child's independent developmental achievement.

From this point of view, learning is not development; however, properly organized learning results in mental development and sets in motion a variety of developmental processes that would be impossible apart from learning. Thus, learning is a necessary and universal aspect of the process of developing culturally organized, specifically human, psychological functions.

To summarize, the most essential feature of our hypothesis is the notion that developmental processes do not coincide with learning processes. Rather, the developmental process lags behind the learning process; this sequence then results in zones of proximal development. Our analysis alters the traditional view that at the moment a child assimilates the meaning of a word, or masters an operation such as addition or written language, her developmental processes are basically completed. In fact, they have only just begun at that moment. The major consequence of analyzing the educational process in this manner is to show that the initial mastery of, for example, the four arithmetic operations provides the basis for the subsequent development of a variety of highly complex internal processes in children's thinking.

Our hypothesis establishes the unity but not the identity of learning processes and internal developmental processes. It presupposes that the one is converted into the other. Therefore, it becomes an important concern of psychological research to show how external knowledge and abilities in children become internalized.

Any investigation explores some sphere of reality. An aim of the psychological analysis of development is to describe the internal relations of the intellectual processes awakened by school learning. In this respect, such analysis will be directed inward and is analogous to the use of x-rays. If successful, it should reveal to the teacher how developmental processes stimulated by the course of school learning are carried through inside the head of each individual child. The revelation of this internal, subterranean developmental network of school subjects is a task of primary importance for psychological and educational analysis.

A second essential feature of our hypothesis is the notion that, although learning is directly related to the course of child development, the two are never accomplished in equal measure or in parallel. Development in children never follows school learning the way a shadow follows the object that casts it. In actuality, there are highly complex dynamic relations between developmental and learning processes that cannot be encompassed by an unchanging hypothetical formulation.

Each school subject has its own specific relation to the course of child development, a relation that varies as the child goes from one stage to another. This leads us directly to a reexamination of the problem of formal discipline, that is, to the significance of each particular subject from the viewpoint of overall mental development. Clearly, the problem cannot be solved by using any one formula; extensive and highly diverse concrete research based on the concept of the zone of proximal development is necessary to resolve the issue.

RELATED READING 4
LANGUAGE PROFICIENCY, BILINGUALISM AND ACADEMIC ACHIEVEMENT
Jim Cummins

EVOLUTION OF A THEORETICAL FRAMEWORK FOR CONCEPTUALIZING LANGUAGE PROFICIENCY

Skutnabb-Kangas & Toukomaa (1976) initially drew attention to the distinction between "surface fluency" in a language and academically-related aspects of language proficiency. They noted that Finnish immigrant students who were either born in Sweden or who immigrated at a relatively young (i.e. pre-school) age appeared to converse in peer-appropriate ways in everyday face-to-face situations (in both L1 and L2), despite literacy skills that were very much below age-appropriate levels in both languages. Following Skutnabb-Kangas and Toukomaa (1976), a distinction was introduced between "surface fluency" and "conceptual-linguistic knowledge" (Cummins, 1979b) and was later (Cummins, 1979a, 1980) formalized in terms of basic interpersonal communicative skills (BICS) and cognitive/academic language proficiency (CALP). The former was defined in terms of "the manifestation of language proficiency in everyday communicative contexts" whereas CALP was conceptualized in terms of the manipulation of language in decontextualized academic situations.

This distinction was applied to a broad range of theoretical and educational situations: for example, it was used to dispute Oller's (1979) theoretical claim that one global dimension could account for all individual differences in "language proficiency" as well as to emphasize the consequences of extrapolating from L2 BICS to L2 CALP in psychological assessment and bilingual education situations.

The distinction between BICS and CALP was expressed in terms of the "iceberg" metaphor adapted from Roger Shuy (1978, 1981). Shuy used the iceberg metaphor to highlight the distinction between the "visible", quantifiable, formal aspects of language (e.g. pronunciation, basic vocabulary, grammar) and the less visible and less easily measured aspects dealing with semantic and functional meaning ("pragmatic" aspects of proficiency in Oller's (1979) terms). He pointed out that most language teaching (whether L1 or L2) attempted to develop functional or communicative proficiency by focusing on the surface forms despite the fact that the direction of language acquisition was from deeper communicative functions of language to the surface forms.

From Jim Cummins, *Bilingualism and Special Education: Issues in Assessment and Pedagogy* (San Diego, CA: College-Hill, 1984), pp. 136–151.

Shuy's (1978, 1981) analysis can be seen as elaborating some of the linguistic realizations of the BICS/CALP distinction. Chamot (1981) and Skinner (1981) have suggested that the cognitive aspects can be elaborated in terms of Bloom's taxonomy of educational objectives (Bloom & Krathwohl, 1977). Specifically, the surface level would involve Knowledge (remembering something previously encountered or learned), Comprehension (grasp of basic meaning, without necessarily relating it to other material), Application (use of abstractions in particular and concrete situations), while the deeper levels of cognitive/academic processing would involve Analysis (breaking down a whole into its parts so that the organization of elements is clear), Synthesis (putting elements into a coherent whole) and Evaluation (judging the adequacy of ideas or material for a given purpose.

The conceptualization of language proficiency to which these notions gave rise is depicted in Figure 1. Clearly what is suggested here is not a precise model of proficiency but rather a series of parallel distinctions that are generally consistent with research evidence and appear to have important heuristic value. The major points embodied in the BICS/CALP distinction are that some heretofore neglected aspects of language proficiency are considerably more relevant for students' cognitive and academic progress than are the surface manifestations of proficiency frequently focused on by educators, and that educators' failure to appreciate these differences can have particularly unfortunate consequences for minority students.

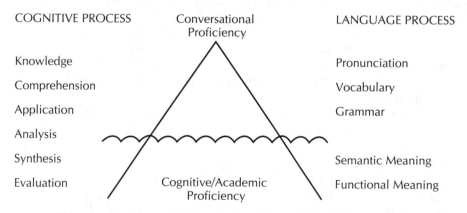

Figure 1. Surface and Deeper Levels of Language Proficiency

However, any dichotomy inevitably oversimplifies the reality and it became clear that the terms "BICS" and "CALP" had the potential to be misinterpreted (see e.g. Edelsky, Hudelson, Flores, Barkin, Altweger, & Jilbert, 1983; Rivera, 1984). Consequently, the theoretical framework was elaborated in terms of the contextual and cognitive dimensions underlying language performance while still maintaining the essential aspects of the BICS/CALP distinction.

The framework in Figure 2 proposes that "language proficiency" can be conceptualized along two continuums. First is a continuum relating to the range of contextual support available for expressing or receiving meaning. The extremes of this continuum are described in terms of "context-embedded" versus "context-reduced" communication. They are distinguished by the fact that in context-embedded communication the participants can actively negotiate meaning (e.g. by providing feedback that the message has not been understood) and the language is supported by a wide range of meaningful paralinguistic and situational cues; context-reduced communication, on the other hand relies primarily (or at the extreme of the continuum, exclusively) on linguistic cues to meaning and thus successful interpretation of the message depends heavily on knowledge of the language itself. In general, context-embedded communication is more typical of the everyday world outside the classroom, whereas many of the linguistic demands of the classroom (e.g. manipulating text) reflect communicative activities which are closer to the context-reduced end of the continuum.

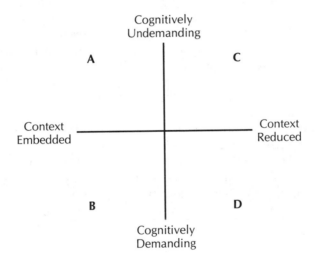

Figure 2. Range of Contextual Support and Degree of Cognitive Involvement in Communicative Activities

The upper parts of the vertical continuum consist of communicative tasks and activities in which the linguistic tools have become largely automatized (mastered) and thus require little active cognitive involvement for appropriate performance. At the lower end of the continuum are tasks and activities in which the communicative tools have not become automatized and thus require active cognitive involvement. Persuading another individual that your point of view is correct and writing an essay are examples of quadrant B and D skills respectively.

The framework is compatible with several other theoretical distinctions elaborated to elucidate aspects of the relationships between language proficiency and academic development; for example, Bruner's (1975) distinction between communicative and analytic competence, Olson's (1977) distinction between utterance and text, Donaldson's (1978) embedded and disembedded thought and language and Bereiter and Scardamelia's (1981) distinction between conversation and composition (see Cummins, 1981, 1983b). The current framework owes most to Donaldson's distinction and thus it is briefly considered here.

Embedded and Disembedded Thought and Language

Donaldson (1978) distinguishes between embedded and disembedded cognitive processes from a developmental perspective and is especially concerned with the implications for children's adjustment to formal schooling. She points out that young children's early thought processes and use of language develop within a "flow of meaningful context" in which the logic of words is subjugated to perception of the speaker's intentions and salient features of the situation. Thus, children's (and adults') normal productive speech is embedded within a context of fairly immediate goals, intentions, and familiar patterns of events. However, thinking and language that move beyond the bounds of meaningful interpersonal context make entirely different demands on the individual, in that it is necessary to focus on the linguistic forms themselves for meaning rather than on intentions.

Donaldson offers a reinterpretation of Piaget's theory of cognitive development from this perspective and reviews a large body of research which supports the distinction between embedded and disembedded thought and language. Her description of pre-school children's comprehension and production of language in embedded contexts is especially relevant to current practices in assessment of language proficiency in bilingual programmes. She points out that

> the ease with which pre-school children often seem to understand what is said to them is misleading if we take it as an indication of skill with language *per se*. Certainly they commonly understand us, but surely it is not our words alone that they are understanding—for they may be shown to be relying heavily on cues of other kinds (1978, p. 72).

She goes on to argue that children's facility in producing language that is meaningful and appropriate in interpersonal contexts can also give a misleading impression of overall language proficiency:

> When you produce language, you are in control, you need only talk about what you choose to talk about. . . The child is never required, when he is himself producing language, to go counter to his own preferred reading of the

situation—to the way in which he himself spontaneously sees it. But this is no longer necessarily true when he becomes the listener. And it is frequently not true when he is the listener in the formal situation of a psychological experiment or indeed when he becomes a learner at school (1978, pp. 73–74).

The relevance of this observation to the tendency of psychologists and teachers to overestimate the extent to which ESL students have overcome difficulties with English is obvious.

Donaldson provides compelling evidence that children are able to manifest much higher levels of cognitive performance when the task is presented in an embedded context, or one that makes "human sense". She goes on to argue that the unnecessary "disembedding" of early instruction in reading and other academic tasks from students' out-of-school experiences contributes significantly to educational difficulties.

Application of the Theoretical Framework

How does the framework elaborated in Figure 2 clarify the conceptual confusions that have been considered above? The framework has been applied to a variety of issues which will be only briefly noted here.

First, the context-embedded/context-reduced distinction suggests reasons why ESL students acquire peer-appropriate L2 conversational proficiency sooner than peer-appropriate academic proficiency, specifically the fact that there are considerably more cues to meaning in face-to-face context-embedded situations than in typical context-reduced academic tasks. The implications for psychological assessment and exit from bilingual programmes have already been noted.

A *second* application of the framework relates to language pedagogy. A major aim of schooling is to develop students' ability to manipulate and interpret cognitively-demanding context-reduced text. The more initial reading and writing instruction can be embedded in a meaningful communicative context (i.e. related to the child's previous experience), the more successful it is likely to be. The same principle holds for L2 instruction. The more context embedded the initial L2 input, the more comprehensible it is likely to be, and paradoxically, the more successful in ultimately developing L2 skills in context-reduced situations. A central reason why minority students have often failed to develop high levels of L2 academic skills is because their initial instruction has emphasized context-reduced communication insofar as instruction has been through English and unrelated to their prior out-of-school experience.

A *third* application concerns the nature of the academic difficulties experienced by most children characterized as "learning disabled" or "language disordered". These students' language and academic problems are usually confined to context-reduced cognitively-demanding situations (see e.g. Cummins & Das, 1977; Das & Cummins, 1982). For example, children with "language learning disabilities" (Stark & Wallach, 1980) have extreme difficulty acquiring French in typical French-as-a-second language classes where the language is taught as a subject, yet acquire fluency in French in context-embedded French immersion programmes (Bruck, 1984). This suggests that it may be especially important for these children to experience instruction that is embedded in a meaningful context. The framework is also relevant to theories of communicative competence (see e.g. Oller, 1983a), in that it provides a means for carrying out a task analysis of proficiency measures and predicting relationships among them. For example, it is immediately apparent why the issue of the relationship between "oral" language and reading is so confused. Measures of "oral" language can be located in any one of the four quadrants and consequently they often have very low correlations with each other (compare, for example, the WISC-R vocabulary subtest with a measure of conversational fluency).

In conclusion, the framework proposed above has the advantage of allowing the academic difficulties of both minority students and students characterized as "learning disabled" to be conceptualized in terms of more general relationships between language proficiency and academic achievement. The context-embedded/context-reduced and cognitively-undemanding/cognitively-demanding continuums are clearly not the only dimensions that would require consideration in a theoretical framework designed to incorporate all aspects of language proficiency or communicative competence. However, it is suggested that these dimensions are directly relevant to the relationships between language proficiency and educational achievement and that they facilitate the interpretation of research data on the linguistic and academic progress of minority students. In the next section, the cross-lingual dimensions of language proficiency are considered.

CONCEPTUALIZING BILINGUAL PROFICIENCY

On the basis of the fact that in bilingual programme evaluations little relationship has been found between amount of instructional time through the majority language and academic achievement in that language, it has been suggested that first and second language academic skills are interdependent, i.e. manifestations of a common underlying proficiency. The interdependence principle has been stated formally as follows (Cummins, 1981, p. 29):

> To the extent that instruction in Lx is effective in promoting proficiency in Lx, transfer of this proficiency to Ly will occur provided there is adequate exposure to Ly (either in school or environment) and adequate motivation to learn Ly.

In concrete terms what this principle means is that in a Spanish-English bilingual programme, Spanish instruction that develops first language reading skills for Spanish-speaking students is not just developing Spanish skills, it is also developing a deeper conceptual and linguistic proficiency that is strongly related to the development of English literacy and general academic skills. In other words, although the surface aspects (e.g. pronunciation, fluency) of, for example, Spanish and English or Chinese and English are clearly separate, there is an underlying cognitive/academic proficiency which is common across languages. This "common underlying proficiency" makes possible the transfer of cognitive/academic or literacy-related skills across languages. Transfer is much more likely to occur from minority to majority language because of the greater exposure to literacy in the majority language and the strong social pressure to learn it.

Continuing with the "iceberg" metaphor, bilingual proficiency is represented in Figure 3 as a "dual-iceberg" in which common cross-lingual proficiencies underlie the obviously different surface manifestations of each language. The interdependence or common underlying proficiency principle implies that experience with *either* language can promote development of the proficiency underlying both languages, given adequate motivation and exposure to both either in school or in the wider environment.

What are some of the literacy-related skills involved in the common underlying proficiency? Conceptual knowledge is perhaps the most obvious example. An immigrant child who arrives in North America at, for example, age 15, understanding the concept of "honesty" in his or her L1 only has to acquire a new *label* in L2 for an already-existing concept. A child, on the other hand, who does not understand the meaning of this term in his or her L1 has a very different, and more difficult, task to acquire the *concept* in L2. By the same token, subject matter knowledge, higher-order thinking skills, reading strategies, writing composition skills etc. developed through the medium of L1 transfer or become available to L2 given sufficient exposure and motivation.

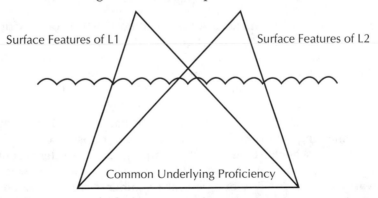

Figure 3. The "Dual Iceberg" Representation of Bilingual Proficiency

Common experience also indicates the existence of some form of common underlying proficiency. For example, as John Macnamara (1970) has pointed out, if L1 and L2 proficiencies were separate (i.e. if there were *not* a common underlying proficiency) this would leave the bilingual in a curious predicament in that "he would have great difficulty in 'communicating' with himself. Whenever he switched languages he would have difficulty in explaining in L2 what he had heard or said in L1" (1970, pp. 25–26).[1]

Comprehensive reviews of the extremely large amount of data supporting the common underlying proficiency principle have been carried out. The supporting evidence is derived from (1) results of bilingual education programmes (see Baker & de Kanter, 1981; Cummins, 1983a), (2) studies relating both age on arrival and L1 literacy development to immigrant students' L2 acquisition (see Cummins, 1983b), (3) studies relating bilingual language use in the home to academic achievement, (4) studies of the relationships of L1 and L2 cognitive/academic proficiency (Cummins, 1979a), and (5) experimental studies of bilingual information processing (Katsaiti, 1983).

Three bilingual education programme evaluations that are of particular interest are reviewed in the next section in order to illustrate the process of L1-L2 transfer and the potency of the interdependence principle to predict the academic outcomes of bilingual programmes. The first example carries important implications with respect to the appropriacy of bilingual programmes for students of low academic ability while the latter two point to the potential academic benefits of strong L1 promotion for minority students who are academically at risk.

ILLUSTRATIVE BILINGUAL PROGRAMME EVALUATIONS

Malherbe's Afrikaans-English Bilingual Education Study

In 1938 E. G. Malherbe conducted a survey of almost 19,000 South African students from Afrikaans and English backgrounds in different types of school programmes. The results were published in 1946 in his book entitled *The Bilingual School*. The aim of the study was to compare the effects of having children from each language background in bilingual as compared to monolingual schools. In the bilingual schools children generally received their instruction in the early grades through L1 and thereafter through both languages. Both intelligence level and home language were kept constant in comparisons of the effects of these two types of school. At the time of the survey, 32% of students spoke only English at home, 25% only Afrikaans and 43% were from homes that were bilingual in varying degrees. Fifty-one percent of students received English-only instruction, 28% only Afrikaans, and 21% were in bilingual schools receiving instruction through both English and Afrikaans.

Some of the major findings of the study were as follows (see Malherbe, 1946, 1969, 1978):

1. South African students gained considerably in their L2 when it was used as a medium of instruction and not merely taught as a school subject.
2. The proficiency of students in their L1 was not adversely affected either by having the two languages represented in the same school or by using the L2 as a medium of instruction. In other words, as in French immersion programmes, instructional time through the medium of L2 did not entail any loss in L1 academic skills.
3. Again as in French immersion programmes, an initial lag in mastery of subjects taught through L2 was experienced by children from monolingual home backgrounds: however, this lag became progressively less and tended to disappear by the end of elementary school (grade 6).
4. In order to test the hypothesis that bilingual instruction might be appropriate for bright students but be too "challenging" for those who are less bright, Malherbe compared the performance of children at different IQ levels in bilingual and monolingual schools. It is worth quoting Malherbe (1969) in some detail on this point in view of the assumption of some teachers and special educators that bilingual instruction will add to the difficulties of students who are academically at risk.

Not only the bright children but also the children with below normal intelligence do better school work all round in the bilingual school than in the unilingual school. What is most significant is that the greatest gain for the bilingual school was registered in the second language by the lower intelligence groups. Not only do they more than hold their own in the first language [in comparison to equivalent IQ children in monolingual schools], but in their second language their gain was nearly twice as big as that registered by the higher intelligence groups (1969, p. 48)

In other words, low ability children are especially disadvantaged when taught the second language in a traditional (context-reduced) programme; however, they appear to fare well in acquiring L2 in a bilingual programme where the L2 is used as a meaningful medium of communication. This result parallels the findings of French immersion programmes.

In short, Malherbe's massive and well-controlled study illustrates the transfer of academic skills across languages and also suggests that bilingual programmes are appropriate for students with potential learning difficulties.

The San Diego Spanish-English Language "Immersion" Programme[2]

This demonstration project, implemented in 1975 in the San Diego City Schools, involved approximately 60% Spanish L1 and 40% English L1 students. Instruction was predominantly in Spanish from pre-school through grade 3 after which half the time was spent through the medium of each language. Twenty minutes of English instruction was included at the preschool level, 30 minutes at grades K–1, and 60 minutes at grades 2–3. Originally implemented in just one school, the project has now spread to several others. The original project was located in a lower-middle class area and, although participation was (and is) voluntary, the Spanish-background students appear typical of most limited-English proficient students in regular bilingual programmes.

The project evaluation shows that although students lag somewhat behind grade norms in both Spanish and English reading skills until near the end of elementary school, by grade 6 they were performing above grade norms in both languages. Math achievement also tended to be above grade norms. The evaluation results for both groups of students are summarized as follows:

> Native-English-speaking project students—because they do not receive instruction in English reading as early as do students in the district's regular elementary level program—begin to develop English reading skills some-what later than regular-program students. However, project students make rapid and sustained progress in English reading once it is introduced and, as has been noted, ultimately meet or exceed English language norms for their grade levels. Also, though native-Spanish-speaking project students are not exposed to English reading and writing as early as they would be in the regular English-only instructional program, they eventually acquire English language skills which are above the norm for students in regular, English-only instructional programs and, in addition, develop their native-language skills (San Diego City Schools, 1982, p. 183).

Although clearly these demonstration project results must be treated with caution, confidence in their potential generalizability is increased by the fact that they are entirely predictable from the interdependence hypothesis and consistent with data from similar programmes involving minority franco-phones in the Canadian context (Carey & Cummins, 1983; Hebert *et al.*, 1976). The results strongly support the feasibility of bilingual programmes designed to promote additive bilingualism among minority children who are academi-cally at risk. This conclusion is also supported by the findings of the Carpinte-ria evaluation examined in the next section.

The Carpinteria Spanish-Language Pre-school Program

The proposal to implement an intensive Spanish-only pre-school programme in the Carpinteria School District near Santa Barbara, California, derived from dis-trict findings showing that a large majority of the Spanish-speaking students entering kindergarten each year lacked adequate skills to succeed in the kinder-garten programme. On the *School Readiness Inventory*, a district-wide screening measure administered to all incoming kindergarten students, Spanish-speaking students tended to average about eight points lower than English-speaking students despite the fact that the test was administered in students' dominant language (approximately 14.5 compared to 23.0, averaged over four years from 1979 to 1982). A score of 20 or better was viewed by the district as predicting a successful kindergarten year for the child. Prior to the implementation of the experimental programme, the Spanish-background children attended a bilingual pre-school programme (operated either by Head Start or the Community Day Care Center) in which both English and Spanish were used concurrently, but with strong emphasis on the development of English skills. According to the district kindergarten teachers, children who had attended these programmes often mixed English and Spanish into a "Spanglish".

The major goal of the experimental Spanish-only pre-school programme was to bring Spanish-dominant children entering kindergarten up to a level of readiness for school similar to that attained by English-speaking children in the community. The project also sought to make parents of the programme participants aware of their role as the child's "first teacher" and to encourage them to provide specific types of experiences for their children in the home.

The pre-school programme itself involved the integration of language with a large variety of concrete and literacy-related experiences. As summarized in the evaluation report:

> The development of language skills in Spanish was foremost in the planning and attention given to every facet of the pre-school day. Language was used constantly for conversing, learning new ideas, concepts and vocabulary, thinking creatively, and problem-solving to give the children the opportunity to develop their language skills in Spanish to as high a degree as possible within the structure of the pre-school day (Carpinteria Unified School District 1982, p. 25).

Participation in the programme was on a voluntary basis and students were screened only for age and Spanish-language dominance. Family characteristics of students in the experimental programme were typical of other Spanish-speaking families in the community. More than 90% were of low socio-economic status, and the majority worked in agriculture and had an average educational level of about sixth grade.

The programme proved to be highly successful in developing students' readiness skills as evidenced by the average score of 21.6 obtained by the 1982/83 incoming kindergarten students who had been in the programme compared to the score of 23.2 obtained by English-speaking students. A score of 14.6 was obtained by Spanish-speaking students who experienced the regular bilingual pre-school programme.

Of special interest is the performance of the experimental programme students on the English and Spanish versions of the Bilingual Syntax Measure

(BSM) (Hernandez-Chavez, Burt, & Dulay, 1976), a test of oral syntactic development. Despite the fact that they experienced an exclusively Spanish preschool programme, they outperformed the other Spanish-speaking students in both English and Spanish. Eighty-one percent of the 1982 programme students scored at the fluent speaker level (i.e. 5 on a five-point scale) on the Spanish version compared to only 53% of the other Spanish-speaking students; in English, 76% of the programme students scored 3 or higher compared to 35% of the other Spanish-speaking students. It appears likely that the highly effective language promotion that was going on in the experimental pre-school allowed children to acquire more of the English to which they were exposed in the environment.

Educational programmes *can* succeed in preventing the academic failure experienced by many minority students. Among the students who did not experience the experimental pre-school programme, the typical pattern of low levels of academic readiness and limited proficiency in both languages was observed. These are the students who are likely to be referred for psychological assessment early in their school careers. By contrast, students who experienced a pre-school programme in which meaningful use of language was integrated into every aspect of daily activities developed high levels of conceptual and linguistic skills in both languages. The reinforcement of children's cultural identity in the programme and the involvement of parents are also likely to have positively influenced outcomes.

The findings clearly suggest that for minority students who are academically at risk, strong promotion of first language conceptual skills may be more effective than either a half-hearted bilingual approach or a monolingual English "immersion" approach.

CONCLUSION

In this reading, research findings on how long it takes minority language students to acquire "English proficiency" were reviewed and interpreted within a theoretical framework concerned with the nature of language proficiency and its cross-lingual dimensions. The fact that immigrant students require, on the average, 5–7 years to approach grade norms in L2 academic skills, yet show peer-appropriate L2 conversational skills within about two years of arrival, suggests that conversational and academic aspects of language proficiency need to be distinguished. It is apparent that, as a result of failure to take account of these two dimensions of language proficiency, many of the psychological assessments underestimated children's academic potential by assessing students whose academic functioning still reflected insufficient time to attain age appropriate levels of English proficiency.

Some of the reasons why minority children acquire L2 conversational skills more rapidly than age-appropriate L2 academic skills are apparent from the dimensions hypothesized to underlie the relationships between language proficiency and academic development. Considerably less knowledge of the L2 itself is required to function appropriately in conversational settings than in academic settings as a result of the greater contextual support available for communicating and receiving meaning.

A large amount of data suggests that L1 and L2 context-reduced cognitively-demanding proficiencies are interdependent or manifestations of a common underlying proficiency. This theoretical principle accounts for the fact that instruction through the medium of a minority language does not result in lower levels of academic performance in the majority language.

Thus, there is little justification for the frequent scepticism expressed by educators about the value of bilingual or heritage language programmed especially for students with potential language or learning difficulties. As the Carpinteria and South African findings suggest, it is this type of student who appears to need and to benefit most from the promotion of L1 literacy skills and the development of an additive form of bilingualism.

These same findings also suggest how ill-advised it is for educators to encourage parents of bilingual children with learning difficulties to switch to English in the home. This is not only unnecessary in view of the common underlying proficiency principle but it will often have damaging emotional and cognitive effects as a result of the lower quality and quantity of interaction that parents are likely to provide in their weaker language.

Finally, it is clear on the basis of the data supporting the common underlying proficiency principle that policy in regard to the education of minority students is not as bereft of research evidence as most educators and policy-makers appear to believe. Although the causes of minority students' under-achievement are not yet fully understood, we do have a partial theoretical basis for policy in that we can predict with confidence the academic outcomes of bilingual programmes implemented in a variety of societal contexts; specifically, we can predict that students instructed through a minority language for all or a part of the school day will perform in majority language academic skills as well as or better than equivalent students instructed entirely through the majority language. For minority students academically at risk there is evidence that strong promotion of L1 proficiency represents an effective way of developing a conceptual and academic foundation for acquiring English literacy.

NOTES

[1]Research data (Cummins, Swain, Nakajima, Handscombe, Green, & Tran, 1984) suggest that some aspects of context-embedded language skills are also interdependent across languages. Specifically it was found that Japanese immigrant students in Canada manifested similar interactional styles in both Japanese and English and that these styles in L1 and L2 were related to personality variables. On the basis of these results, Cummins *et al.* suggest a distinction between "attribute-based" and "input-based" aspects of language proficiency: the former are cross-lingual in nature and reflect stable attributes of the individual (e.g. cognitive skills, personality) while the latter are largely a function of quality and quantity of exposure to the language in the environment.

[2]By definition the San Diego Spanish-English Language "Immersion" Program is considered a bilingual program today, although it is "immersion" for the English L1 students.

References

Allen, J., and VanBuren, P. (1971). *Chomsky: Selected readings.* London: Oxford University.

Allwright, R. (1978). Abdication and responsibility in teaching. Paper presented at the Berne Colloquium on Applied Linguistics.

Allwright, R. (1979). Language learning through communication practice. In Brumfit and Johnson, pp. 167-182.

Atwerger, B. and Resta, V. (1986). Comparing standardized test scores and miscues. Paper presented at the annual convention of International Reading Association, Philadelphia, PA.

Andersen, R. (1980). The role of creolization in Schumann's Pidginization Hypothesis for second-language acquisition. In R. Scarcella and S. Krashen, eds. *Research in second language acquisition.* Rowley, Mass.: Newbury House.

Andersen, R. (1981). *New dimensions in second language acquisition research.* Rowley, Mass.: Newbury House.

Andersen, R. (1983). Introduction: A language acquisition interpretation of pidginization and creolization. In R. Andersen, ed. *Pidginization and creolization as language acquisition.* Rowley, Mass.: Newbury House.

Anthony, E. (1963). Approach, method and technique. *English Language Teaching, 17,* 63–67.

Armstrong, B., Johnson, D. W., and Balow, B. (1981). Effects of cooperative versus individualistic learning experiences on interpersonal attraction between learning-disabled and normal-progress elementary school students. *Contemporary Educational Psychology, 6,* 102–109.

Arthur, B., Weiner, R., Culver, M., Young, J., and Thomas, D. (1980). The register of impersonal discourse to foreigners: Verbal adjustments to foreign accent. In D. Larsen-Freeman, ed. *Discourse analysis in second language research* (pp. 111–124). Rowley, Mass.: Newbury House.

Aschbacher, P. (1991). Humanitas: A thematic curriculum. *Educational Leadership, 49(2),* 17–19.

Asher, J. (1972). Children's first language as a model for second-language learning. *Modern Language Journal, 56,* 133–139.

Asher, J. (1982). *Learning another language through actions: The complete teachers' guidebook.* Los Gatos, Calif.: Sky Oaks.

Asher, J. (1983). Motivating children and adults to acquire a second language. In Oller and Richard-Amato, pp. 329–336. Also in *SPEAQ Journal* (1979), *3,* 87–99.

Asher, J. (1993). *The total physical response.* Presentation at the California Education Association, San Francisco, Calif., January 14.

Asher, J., Kusudo, J., and de la Torre, R. (1974). Learning a second language through commands: The second field test. *Modern Language Journal, 58,* 24-32.

Atwell, N. (1987). *In the middle: Writing, reading, and learning with adolescents.* Portsmouth, N.H.: Heinemann.

Austin, J. (1962). *How to do things with words.* Oxford: Clarendon.

Ausubel, D. (1968). *Educational psychology: A cognitive view.* New York: Holt, Rinehart, and Winston.

Bailey, K. (1983). Competitiveness and anxiety in adult second-language learning: Looking at and through the diary studies. In Seliger and Long, pp. 67–103.

Bailey, K. (1986, Spring). Class lecture, Monterey Institute of International Studies.

Bailey, N., Madden, C., and Krashen, S. (1974). Is there a "natural sequence" in adult second-language learning? *Language Learning, 21,* 235–243.

Baker, K., and de Kanter, A. (1981). *Effectiveness of bilingual education: A review of the literature.* Washington, D.C.: Office of Planning and Budget, U.S. Department of Education.

Baltra, Armando (1992). On breaking with tradition: The significance of Terrell's natural approach. *The Canadian Modern Language Review, 48*(3), 564–593.

Banks, J. (1988). *Multiethnic education: Theory and practice* (second edition). Boston, Mass.: Allyn & Bacon.

Banks, J. (1990). The stages of ethnicity. In P. Richard-Amato and M. A. Snow, *The multicultural classroom: Readings for content-area teachers.* White Plains, N.Y.: Addison-Wesley, pp. 93–101.

Bassano, S., and Christison, M. (1983). *Drawing out.* Englewood Cliffs, N.J.: Prentice Hall.

Bassano, S., and Christison, M. A. (1995). *Community spirit: A practical guide to collaborative language learning.* San Francisco, C.A.: Alta Book Center.

Beebe, L. (1983). Risk-taking and the language learner. In Seliger and Long, pp. 39–66.

Bereiter, C., and Scardamelia, M. (1981). From conversation to composition: The role of instruction in a developmental process. In R. Glaser, ed. *Advances in instructional psychology* (Vol. 2). Hillsdale, N.J.: Erlbaum.

The best from Sunburst. Pleasantville, N.Y.: Sunburst Communications.

Beyond language: Social and cultural factors in schooling language minority students. (1986). Office of Bilingual Bicultural Education, California State Department of Education, Sacramento. Los Angeles: Evaluation, Dissemination and Assessment Center, California State University.

Bialystok, E. (1982). On the relationship between knowing and using forms. *Applied Linguistics, 3,* 181–206.

Bialystok, E., and Fröhlich, M. (1977). Aspects of second-language learning in classroom settings. *Working Papers on Bilingualism, 13,* 2–26.

Bialystok, E., and Fröhlich, M. (1978). Variables of classroom achievement in second-language learning. *Modern Language Association Journal, 62,* 327–336.

Bloom, B., and Krathwohl, D. (1977). *Taxonomy of educational objectives: Handbook I: Cognitive domain.* White Plains, N.Y.: Longman.

Bodinger-de Vriarte, C. (1991). The rise of hate crime on school campuses. *Research Bulletin, Phi Delta Kappa,* Number 10.

Bonne, R. (1973). (Pam Adams, Illus.). *There was an old lady who swallowed a fly.* Purton Wilts, England: Child's Play (International).

Breen, M., and Candlin, C. (1979). Essentials of a communicative curriculum. *Applied Linguistics, 1*(2), 90–112.

Brinton, D., and Neuman, R. (1982). *Getting along (book 2),* p. 33. Englewood Cliffs, N. J.: Prentice Hall.

Brinton, D., Snow, M. A., and Wesche, M. (1989). *Content-based language instruction.* New York: Newbury House.

Brown, H. D. (1987). *Principles of language learning and teaching.* Englewood Cliffs, N. J.: Prentice Hall.

Brown, H. D. (1994). *Teaching by principles: An interactive approach to language pedagogy.* Englewood Cliffs, N.J.: Prentice Hall.

Brown, H. D., Yorio, C., and Crymes, R., eds. (1977). *On TESOL '77.* Washington, D.C.: Teachers of English to Speakers of Other Languages.

Brown, R. (1973). *A first language: The early stages.* Cambridge, Mass.: Harvard University.

Brown, R. (1977). Introduction. In C. Snow and C. Ferguson, eds. *Talking to children* (pp. 1–30). Cambridge: Cambridge University.

Brown, R., Cazden, C., and Bellugi, U. (1973). The child's grammar from I to III. In C. Ferguson and D. Slobin, eds. *Studies of child language development,* pp. 295–333. New York: Holt, Rinehart, and Winston.

Brown, S. (1979). Life situations: Incorporating community resources into the adult ESL curriculum. *CATESOL Occasional Papers,* No. 5, pp. 48–65.

Brown, S., and Dubin, F. (1975). Adapting human relations training techniques for ESL classes. In Burt and Dulay, pp. 204–209.

Bruck, M. (1984). The feasibility of an additive bilingual program for language-impaired children. In M. Paradis and Y. Lebrun, eds. *Early bilingualism and child development.* Amsterdam: Swets and Zeitlinger.

Brumfit, C. J., and Johnson, K., eds. (1979). *The communicative approach to language teaching.* Oxford: Oxford University.

Bruner, J. (1975). Language as an instrument of thought. In A. Davies, ed. *Problems of language and learning.* London: Heinemann.

Bruner, J. (1978a). From communication to language: A psychological perspective. In I. Markova ed. *The social context of language,* pp. 17–48. New York: Wiley.

Bruner, J. (1978b). The role of dialogue in language acquisition. In A. Sinclair, R. Javella, and W. Levelt, eds. *The child's conception of language,* pp. 241–256. New York: Springer-Verlag.

Burt, M., and Dulay, H., eds. (1975). *New directions in second language learning, teaching, and bilingual education.* Washington, D.C.: Teachers of English to Speakers of Other Languages.

Burt, M., and Dulay, H. (1983). Optimal language learning environments. In Oller and Richard-Amato, pp. 38–48. Also in J. E. Alatis, H. Altman, and P. Alatis, eds. (1981), *The second language classroom* (pp. 177–192). New York: Oxford University Press.

Burt, M., Dulay, H., and Finocchiaro, M., eds. (1977). *Viewpoints on ESL,* pp. 172–184. New York: Regents.

Burt, M., Dulay, H., and Hernandez-Chavez, E. (1975). *Bilingual syntax measure: Technical handbook*. New York: Harcourt Brace Jovanovich.

Busch, D. (1982). Introversion-extraversion and the EFL proficiency of Japanese students. *Language Learning, 32*, 109–132.

Butterworth, G., and Hatch, E. (1978). *A Spanish-speaking adolescent's acquisition of English syntax*. In Hatch (1978a), pp. 231–245.

Byrne, D. (1967). *Progressive picture compositions*. New York: Longman.

Campbell, C., and Ortiz, J. (1991). Helping students overcome foreign language anxiety. In E. Horwitz and D. Young, eds. *Language anxiety: From theory and research to classroom implication*, pp. 153–168. Englewood Cliffs, N.J.: Prentice Hall.

Canale, M., and Barker, G. (1986). How creative language teachers are using microcomputers. *TESOL Newsletter 20*(1), Supplement (3), 1–3.

Canale, M. and Swain, M. (1980). Theoretical bases of communicative approaches to second language teaching and testing. *Applied Linguistics, 1*(1), 1–47.

Carey, S., and Cummins, J. (1983). Achievement, behavioral correlates and teachers' perceptions of Francophone and Anglophone immersion students. *Alberta Journal of Educational Research, 29*, 159–167.

Carpinteria Unified School District. (1982). Title VII evaluation report 1981–82. Unpublished report.

Carrell, P. (1983). Some issues in studying the role of schemata, or background knowledge, in second-language comprehension. *Reading in a Foreign Language, 1*(2), 81–92.

Carrell, P. (1984). Evidence of a formal schema in second-language comprehension. *Language Learning, 34*(2), 87–112.

Carrell, P. (1985). Facilitating ESL reading by teaching text structure. *TESOL Quarterly, 19*(4), 727–752.

Carrell, P., Devine, J., and Eskey, D. (1988). *Interactive approaches to second language reading*. New York: Cambridge University Press.

Carroll, J. (1960). Wanted: A research basis for educational policy on foreign language teaching. *Harvard Educational Review, 30*, 128–140.

Carroll, J. (1961). Fundamental considerations in testing for English proficiency of foreign students. In *Testing the English proficiency of foreign students* (pp. 31–40). Washington, D.C.: Center for Applied Linguistics.

Carroll, J. (1963). The prediction of success in intensive foreign language training. In R. Glazer, ed. *Training, research, and education*. Pittsburgh: University of Pittsburgh.

Carroll, J. (1967). Foreign language proficiency levels attained by language majors near graduation from college. *Foreign Language Annals, 1*(2), 131–151.

Carroll, S., and Swain, M. (1993). Explicit and Implicit negative feedback: An empirical study of the learning of linguistic generalizations. *Studies in Second Language Acquisition, 15*(3), 357–386.

Carson, J. G., and Leki, I., eds. (1993). *Reading in the composition classsroom: Second language perspectives*. Boston, Mass.: Heinle and Heinle.

Cathcart, R. (1972). *Report on a group of Anglo children after one year of immersion in Spanish*. Unpublished master's thesis, UCLA.

Cazden, C. (1972). *Child language and education*. New York: Holt, Rinehart and Winston.

Celce-Murcia, M. (1991). Grammar pedagogy in second and foreign language teaching. *TESOL Quarterly, 25*(3), 459–480.

Chamot, A. (1981). Applications of second language acquisition research to the bilingual classroom. *Focus, 8*.

Chamot, A. (1990). Cognitive instruction second language classroom: The role of learning strategies. In J. Alatis, ed. *Georgetown University Round Table on Languages and Linguistics 1990: Linguistics language teaching and language acquisition: The importance of theory, practice and research*. Georgetown: Georgetown University, pp. 497–513.

Chastain, K. (1975). Affective and ability factors in second language learning. *Language Learning, 25*, 153–161.

Chaudron, C. (1985). A method for examining the input/intake distinction. In Gass and Madden, pp. 285–302.

Chaudron, C. (1991). What counts as formal languagge instruction? Problems in observation and analysis of classroom teaching. In J. Alatis, ed. *Georgetown University Round Table on Languages and Linguistics 1991: Linguistics and language pedagogy: The state of the Art*. Georgetown: Georgetown University, pp. 56–64.

Cherry, C. (1957). *On human communication*. Cambridge, Mass.: M.I.T.

Cherry, L. (1979). A sociolinguistic approach to language development and its implications for education. In O. Garnica and M. King, eds. *Language, children, and society*. Oxford: Pergamon.

Chomsky, N. (1959). Review of B.F. Skinner, "Verbal Behavior." *Language, 35*, 26–58.

Chomsky, N. (1971). *Problems of knowledge and freedom*. New York: Pantheon.

Chomsky, N. (1975). *Reflections on language*. New York: Pantheon.

Chomsky, N. (1980). *Rules and representations*. New York: Columbia University.

Christison, M. (1982). *English through poetry*. Hayward, Calif.: Prentice Hall.

Christison, M., and Bassano, S. (1981). *Look who's talking*. Englewood Cliffs, N. J.: Prentice Hall.

Chun, D., and Brandl, K. (1992). Beyond form-based drill and practice: Meaning-enhancing CALL on the Macintosh. *Foreign Language Annals, 25*(3), 255–261.

Clark, H., and Clark, E. (1977). *Psychology and language*. New York: Harcourt Brace Jovanovich.

Clark, J., and Clifford, R. (1988). The FSI/ILR/ACTFL proficiency scales and testing techinques: Development, current status, and needed research. *Studies in Second Language Acquisition, 10*(2): 129–148.

Clifford, J., and Clifford, R. (1988). Reliability and validity of language aspects contributing to oral proficiency of prospective teachers of German. In J. Clark, ed. *Direct testing of speaking proficiency: Theory and application*, pp. 191–209. Princeton, N. J.: Educational Testing Service.

Cohen, A. (1974). The Culver City Spanish immersion program: The first two years. *Modern Language Journal, 58*, 95–103.

Cohen, A., and Robbins, M. (1976). Toward assessing interlanguage performance: The relationship between selected errors, learners' characteristics and learners' explanations. *Language Learning, 26*, 45–66.

Condon, C. (1983). Treasure hunts for English practice. In Oller and Richard-Amato, pp. 309–312. Also in *English Language Teaching* (1979), 34(1), 53–55.

Connor, U., and Kaplan, R. (1987). *Writing across languages: Analysis of L2 text*. Reading, Mass.: Addison-Wesley.

Coopersmith, S. (1967). *The antecedents of self-esteem*. San Francisco, Calif.: W. H. Freeman.

Corder, S. P. (1967). The significance of learners' errors. *IRAL, 4*, 161–169.

Crookall, D., and Oxford, R. (1990). *Simulation, gaming, and language learning*. New York: Newbury House.

Crookes, G., and Schmidt, R. (1991). Motivation: Reopening the research agenda. *Language Learning, 41*(4), 469–512.

Cross, T. (1978). Mothers' speech and its association with rate of linguistic development in young children. In N. Waterson and C. Snow, eds. *The development of communication.* New York: Wiley.

Crowley, S. (1989). *A teacher's introduction to deconstruction.* Urbana, Ill.: National Council of Teachers of English.

Crymes, R. 1979. Current trends in ESL instruction. Paper presented at the Indiana TESOL Convention, October. In J. Haskell, ed. *Selected Articles* from the TESOL Newsletter (1966–1983): Washington, D.C.: TESOL.

Cummins, J. (1976). The influence of bilingualism on cognitive growth: A synthesis of research findings and explanatory hypotheses. *Working Papers on Bilingualism, 9,* 1–43.

Cummins, J. (1979a). Cognitive/academic language proficiency, linguistic interdependence, the optimum age question and some other matters. *Working Papers on Bilingualism, 19,* 121–129.

Cummins, J. (1979b). Linguistic interdependence and the educational development of bilingual children. *Review of Educational Research, 49*(2), 222–251.

Cummins, J. (1980). The entry and exit fallacy in bilingual education. *NABE Journal, 4,* 25–60.

Cummins, J. (1981). The role of primary language development in promoting educational success for language minority students. In *Schooling and language minority students: A theoretical framework,* pp. 3–49. Office of Bilingual Bicultural Education, California state Department of Education, Sacramento. Los Angeles: Evaluation, Dissemination and Assessment Center, California State University.

Cummins, J. (1983a). *Heritage language education: A literature review.* Toronto: Ministry of Education, Ontario.

Cummins, J. (1983b). Language proficiency and academic achievement. In J. Oller, Jr., ed. *Issues in language testing research.* Rowley, Mass.: Newbury House.

Cummins, J. (1984). *Bilingualism and special education: Issues in assessment and pedagogy.* San Diego: College-Hill.

Cummins, J., and Das, J. (1977). Cognitive processing and reading difficulties: A framework for research. *Alberta Journal of Educational Research, 23,* 245–256.

Cummins, J., Swain, M., Nakajima, K., Handscombe, J., Green, D., and Tran, C. (1984). Linguistic interdependence among Japanese and Vietnamese immigrant students. In C. Rivera, ed. *Communicative competence approaches to language proficiency assessment: Research and application.* Clevedon, England: Multilingual Matters Ltd.

Curran, C. (1972). *Counseling-learning: A whole-person model for education.* New York: Grune and Stratton.

d'Anglejan, A. (1978). Language learning in and out of classrooms. In Richards, pp. 218–278.

Das, J., and Cummins, J. (1982). Language processing and reading disability. In K. Gadow and I. Bialer, eds. *Advances in learning and behavioral disabilities: A research annual.* Greenwich, Conn.: JAI.

Day, R. (1984). Student participation in the ESL classroom or some imperfections in practice. *Language Learning, 34*(3), 69–102.

Derrida, J. (1976). *Of Grammatology.* Translated by Gayatri Chakravorty Spivak. Baltimore, Md.: Johns Hopkins University.

Derrida, J. (1981). *Dissemination*. Translated by Barbara Johnson. Chicago, Ill.: University of Chicago.

DeVilliers, P., and DeVilliers, J. (1973). A cross-sectional study of the acquisition of grammatical morphemes in child speech. *Journal of Psycholinguistic Research, 2*, 267–278.

de Saussuré, F. (1959). *Course in general linguistics*. New York: Philosophical Library.

Dewey, J. and Bentley, A. F. (1949). *Knowing and the known*. Boston, Mass.: Beacon Press.

Diller, K. (1978). *The language teaching controversy*. Rowley, Mass.: Newbury House.

Di Pietro, R. (1983). Scenarios, discourse, and real-life roles. In Oller and Richard-Amato, pp. 228–238.

Dixon, C., and Nessel, D. (1983). *Language experience approach to reading (and writing)*. Hayward, Calif.: Alemany.

DLM teaching resources comprehensive catalog. Allen, Tex.: DLM Teaching Resources.

Donaldson, M. (1978). *Children's minds*. Glasgow: Collins.

Doughty, C. (1991). Second language instruction does make a difference: Evidence from an empirical study of second language relativization. *Studies in Second Language Acquisition, 13*(4), 431–470.

Dulay, H. and Burt, M. (1974). Natural sequences in child second-language acquisition. *Language Learning 25*(1), 37–53.

Dulay, H., and Burt, M. (1977). Remarks on creativity in language acquisition. In Burt, Dulay, and Finocchiaro, pp. 95–126.

Dunleavy, D. (1992). *The language beat*. Portsmouth, N.H.: Heinemann.

Dvorak, T. (1977). Grammatical practice, communicative practice, and the development of linguistic competence. Ph.D. dissertation, University of Texas at Austin.

Edelsky, C. (1993). Whole language in perspective. *TESOL Quarterly, 27*(3), 548–550.

Edelsky, C., Altwerger, B., and Flores, B. (1991). *Whole language: What's the difference?* Portsmouth, N.H.: Heinemann.

Edelsky, C., Hudelson, S., Flores, B., Barkin, F., Altweger, B., and Jilbert, K. (1983). Semilingualism and language deficit. *Applied Linguistics, 4*, 1–22.

Edwards, H., Wesche, M., Krashen, S., and Krudenier, B. (1984). Second-language acquisition through subject-matter learning: A study of sheltered psychology classes at the University of Ottawa. *Canadian Modern Language Review, 41*, 268–282.

Elbow, P. (1993). Ranking, evaluating, and liking: Sorting out three forms of judgment. *College English, 55*(7), 187–206.

Ellis, R. (1984a). *Classroom second language development*. Oxford: Pergamon.

Ellis, R. (1984b). Sources of variability in interlanguage. Paper presented at the Interlanguage Seminar in Honor of Pit Corder, Edinburgh.

Ellis, R. (1984c). Formulaic speech in early classroom second-language development. In J. Handscombe, R. Orem, and B. Taylor, eds. *On TESOL '83: The question of control*. Washington, D.C.: Teachers of English to Speakers of Other Languages.

Ellis, R. (1985). Teacher-pupil interaction in second-language development. In Gass and Madden, pp. 69–85.

Ellis, R. (1986). *Understanding second language acquisition*. Oxford: Oxford University.

Ellis, R., and Wells, G. (1980). Enabling factors in adult-child discourse. *First Language, 1*, 46–82.

Enright, D. S., and McCloskey, M. L. (1985). Yes, talking! Organizing the classroom to promote second-language acquisition. *TESOL Quarterly, 19*(3), 431–453.

Ervin-Tripp, S. (1973). Some strategies for the first and second years. In A. Dil, ed. *Language acquisition and communicative choice*, pp. 204–238. Stanford, Calif.: Stanford University.

Ervin-Tripp, S. (1974). Is second language learning like the first? *TESOL Quarterly, 8,* 111–127.

Evans, J., and Moore, J. (1979). *Art moves the basics along: Animal units.* Carmel, Calif.: Evan-Moor, 80.

Evans, J., and Moore, J. (1982). *Art moves the basics along: Units about children.* Carmel, Calif.: Evan-Moor, 57.

Fanselow, J. (1992). *Contrasting conversations: Activities for exploring our beliefs and teaching practices.* White Plains, N.Y.: Longman.

Farnette, C., Forte, I., and Loss, B. (1977). *I've got me and I'm glad.* ABC Unified School District, Cerritos, California. Nashville, Tenn.: Incentive Publications.

Feenstra, H. J. (1967). Aptitude, attitude, and motivation in second language acquisition. Unpublished doctoral dissertation, University of Western Ontario, London, Ont.

Felix, S. (1988). UG-generated knowledge in adult second language acquisition. In S. Flynn and W. O'Neil, eds. *Linguistic theory in second language acquisition*, pp. 277–294. Dordrecht, Netherlands: Kluwer Academic.

Fellag, L.R. (1993). *Life, language, and literature.* Boston, Mass.: Heinle and Heinle.

Ferguson, C. (1975). Toward a characterization of English foreigner talk. *Anthropological Linguistics, 17*(1), 1–14.

Flack, M. (1977). *The story about Ping.* New York: Penguin.

Flynn, S. (1987). Contrast and construction in a parameter setting model of L2 acquisition. *Language Learning, 37*(1), 19–62.

Flynn, S. (1990). Theory, practice, and research: Strange or Bliss bedfellows? In J. Alatis ed. *Georgetown University Round Table on Languages and Linguistics 1990: Linguistics, language teaching and language acquisition: The importance of theory, practice and research,* pp. 112–122. Washington, D.C.: Georgetown University

Ford, C., and Silverman, A. (1981). *American cultural encounters.* San Francisco, Calif.: Alemany.

Fotis, S. , and Ellis, R. (1991). Communication about grammar: A task-based approach. *TESOL Quarterly 25*(4), 605–628.

Francois, L. (1983). *English in action.* Southgate, Calif.: Linda Francois.

Freed, B. (1978). Foreigner talk: A study of speech adjustments made by native speakers of English in conversation with non-native speakers. Unpublished doctoral dissertation, University of Pennsylvania, Philadelphia.

Freedman, S. ed. (1989). *The acquisition of written language: Response and revision.* Norwood, N. J.: Ablex.

Freeman, D. (1989). Teacher training, development, and decision making: A model of teaching and related strategies for teacher education. *TESOL Quarterly, 23*(1), 27–46.

Freeman, D. (1991). "Mistaken constructs": Reexamining the nature and assumptions of language teacher education. In *Georgetown University Round Table on Languages and Linguistics 1991. Linguistics and language pedagogy: The state of the art,* pp. 25–39. Georgetown: Georgetown University

Freeman, D. (1992). Language teacher education emerging discourse, and change in classroom practice. In J. Flowerdew, M. Brock, and S. Hsia, eds. *Perspectives in second language teacher education.* Hong Kong: City Polytechnic of Hong Kong, pp. 1–21.

Freire, P. (1970). *Pedagogy of the oppressed.* New York: Seabury.

Freud, S. (1920). *A general introduction to psychoanalysis.* New York: Liveright.

Fries, C. (1945). *Teaching and learning English as a foreign language.* Ann Arbor: University of Michigan.

Fuller, J., and Gundel, J. (1987). Topic prominence in interlanguage. *Language Learning, 37,* 1–18.

Gaies, S. (1977). The nature of linguistic input in formal second language learning: Linguistic and communicative strategies in ESL teachers' classroom language. In Brown, Yorio, and Crymes, pp. 204–212.

Galyean, B. (1976). *Language from within: A handbook of teaching strategies for personal growth and self-reflection in the language classes.* Long Beach, Calif.: Ken Zel.

Galyean, B. (1982). A confluent design for language teaching. In R. Blair, ed. *Innovative approaches to language teaching,* pp. 176–188. Rowley, Mass.: Newbury House.

Gardner, R. (1973). Attitudes and motivation: Their role in second language acquisition. In J. Oller, Jr., and J. Richards, eds. *Focus on the learner: Pragmatic perspectives for the language teacher,* pp. 235–245. Rowley, Mass.: Newbury House.

Gardner, R. (1979). Social psychological aspects of second language acquisition. In H. Giles and R. St. Clair, eds. *Language and social psychology.* Oxford: Basil Blackwell.

Gardner, R., Lalonde, R., and Moorcroft, R. (1985). The role of attitudes and motivation in second language learning: Correlational and experimental considerations. *Language Learning, 35*(2), 207–227.

Gardner, R., and Lambert, W. (1959). Motivational variables in second-language acquisition. *Canadian Journal of Psychology, 13,* 266–272.

Gardner, R., and Lambert, W. (1972). *Attitudes and motivation in second-language learning.* Rowley, Mass.: Newbury House.

Gardner, R., Smythe, P., Clement, R., and Gliksman, L. (1976). Second-language learning: A social-psychological perspective. *Canadian Modern Language Review, 32,* 198–213.

Garvie, E. (1990). *Story as vehicle: Teaching English to young children.* Clevedon, England: Multilingual Matters Ltd.

Gary, J. (1975). Delayed oral practice in initial stages of second-language learning. In Burt and Dulay, pp. 89–95.

Gass, S., and Madden, C., eds. (1985). *Input in second language acquisition.* Rowley, Mass.: Newbury House.

Gass, S., and Varonis, E. (1985). Task variation and nonnative/nonnative negotiation of meaning. In Gass and Madden, pp. 149–161.

Genesee, F. (1982). Experimental neuropsychological research on second-language processing. *TESOL Quarterly, 16,* 315–324.

Gessler: The foreign language experts. New York: Gessler Educational Software.

Giles, H. (1979). Ethnicity markers in speech. In K. Scherer and H. Giles, eds. *Social markers in speech.* Cambridge: Cambridge University.

Giles, H., Bourhis, R., and Taylor, D. (1977). Toward a theory of language in ethnic group relations. In H. Giles, ed. *Language ethnicity and intergroup relations.* New York: Academic.

Giles, H., and Byrne, J. (1982). An intergroup approach to second-language acquisition. *Journal of Multilingual and Multicultural Development, 3,* 17–40.

Gill, M. , and Hartmann, P. (1993). *Get it? Got it!: Listening to others/speaking for ourselves.* Boston, Mass.: Heinle and Heinle.

Gillespie, J. (1993). Buddy book journals: Responding to literature. *English Journal,* October, pp. 64–68.

Gliedman, J. (1983). Interview (with Noam Chomsky). *Omni, 6*(2), 113–118.

Glisan, E. (1993). Total physical response: A technique for teaching all skills in Spanish. In J. Oller, Jr., pp. 30 –39.

Goldstein, L. , and Conrad, S. (1990). Student input and negotiation of meaning in ESL writing conferences. *TESOL Quarterly, 24*(3), 443–461.

Goodman, J., and Tenney, C. (1979). Teaching the total language with readers theater. *CATESOL Occasional Papers*, No. 5, pp. 84–89.

Goodman, K. (1982). Acquiring literacy is natural: Who skilled Cock Robin? In F. Gollasch, ed. *Language and literacy: Selected writings of Kenneth S. Goodman, Volume II.* Boston Mass.: Routledge and Kegan Paul.

Goodman, K. (1986). *What's whole in whole language.* Portsmouth, N.H.:   Heinemann.

Grabe, W. (1991). Current developments in second language reading research. *TESOL Quarterly, 25*(3), 375–406.

Graham, C. (1978). *Jazz chants.* New York: Oxford University Press.

Graham, C. (1978). *Jazz chants for children.* New York: Oxford University Press.

Graham, C. (1986). *Small talk.* New York: Oxford University Press.

Graham, C. R. (1984). Beyond integrative motivation: The development and influence of assimilative motivation. Paper presented at the TESOL Convention, Houston, Texas, March.

Graves, D. (1992). *Explore poetry.* Portsmouth, N.H.: Heinemann.

Gregg, K. (1984). Krashen's monitor and Occam's razor. *Applied Linguistics 5*(2), 79–100.

Grice, H. P. (1975). Logic and conversation. In P. Cole and J. L. Morgan, eds. *Syntax and semantics: Speech acts 3*, pp. 365–372. New York: Seminar Press.

Guiora, A., Acton, W., Erard, R., and Strickland, F. (1980). The effects of benzodiazepine (Valium) on permeability of ego boundaries. *Language Learning, 30*, 351–363.

Guiora, A., Beit-Hallami, B., Brannon, R., Dull, C., and Scovel, T. (1972). The effects of experimentally induced changes in ego states on pronunciation ability in second language: An exploratory study. *Comprehensive Psychiatry, 13*, 421–428.

Guiora, A., Brannon, R., and Dull, C. (1972). Empathy and second language learning. *Language Learning, 22*, 111–130.

Hakuta, K. (1981). Some common goals for second and first language acquisition research. In R. Andersen ed. *Pidginization and creolization as language acquisition.* Rowley, Mass.: Newbury House.

Halliday, M.A.K. (1975). *Learning how to mean.* London: Edward Arnold.

Halliday, M.A.K. (1979). Towards a sociological semantics. In Brumfit and Johnson, pp. 27–46.

Hammond, R. (1988). Accuracy versus communicative competency: The acquisition of grammar in the second-language classroom. *Hispania, 71*, 408–417.

Harste, J., Snort, K., and Burke, C. (1988). *Creating for Authors.* Portsmouth, N.H.: Heinemann.

Hatch, E. ed., (1978a). *Second language acquisition: A book of readings.* Rowley, Mass.: Newbury House.

Hatch, E. ed., (1978b). Discourse analysis and second language acquisition. In Hatch, *Second-language acquisition*, pp. 401–474.

Hatch, E. (1978c). Discourse analysis, speech acts and second language acquisition. In W. Ritchie ed. *Second language acquisition research.* New York: Academic.

Hatch, E. (1979). Apply with caution. *Studies in Second Language Acquisition, 2*, 123–143.

Hatch, E. (1980). Second language acquisition—avoiding the question. In S. Felix, ed. *Second language development.* Tübingen: Gunther Narr.

Hatch, E. (1983). *Psycholinguistics: A second language perspective.* Rowley, Mass.: Newbury House.

Hatch, E., Shapira, R., and Gough, J. (1978). "Foreigner-talk" discourse. *ITL Review of Applied Linguistics, 39–40,* 39–60.

Hébert, R., et al. (1976). *Rendement académique et langue d'enseignement chez les élèves Franco-Manitobains.* Saint-Boniface, Manitoba: Centre de recherches du College Universitaire de Saint-Boniface.

Hedgcock, J., and Lefkowitz, N. (1992). Collaborative oral/aural revision in foreign language writing instruction. *Journal of Second Language Writing, 1(3),* 255–276.

Hendrickson, J. (1976). The effects of error correction treatments upon adequate and accurate communication in written compositions of adult learners of English as a second language. Ph.D. dissertation, Ohio State University.

Hensl, V. (1973). Linguistic register of foreigner language instruction. *Language Learning, 2,* 203–222.

Herbert, C. (1987). *San Diego Title VII two-way bilingual program.* San Diego Unified School District, San Diego, Calif.

Hernandez-Chavez, E., Burt, M., and Dulay, H. (1976). *The bilingual syntax measure.* New York: Psychological Corporation.

Heyde, A. (1977). The relationship between self-esteem and the oral production of a second language. In H.D. Brown, C. Yorio, and R. Crymes, pp. 226–240.

Heyde, A. (1979). The relationship between self-esteem and the oral production of a second language. Unpublished doctoral dissertation, University of Michigan, Ann Arbor.

Higgs, T., and Clifford, R. (1982). The push toward communication. In T. Higgs, ed. *Curriculum, competence, and the foreign language teacher,* pp. 57–79. Skokie, Ill.: A National Textbook.

Hill, S. and Hill, T. (1990). *The collaborative classroom: A guide to co-operative learning.* Portsmouth, N. H.: Heinemann.

Hook, J. N. (1963). *Writing creatively.* Boston Mass.: D.C. Heath.

Hooker, D., and Gallagher, R. (1984). *I am gifted, creative, and talented.* New York: Educational Design.

Horowitz, D. (1986). What professors actually require: Academic tasks for the ESL classroom. *TESOL Quarterly, 20(3),* 445–462.

Horwitz, E., and Young, D. (1991). *Language anxiety: From theory and research to classroom implications.* Englewood Cliffs, N.J.: Prentice Hall.

Hughes, A. (1989). *Testing for language teachers.* Cambridge: Cambridge University.

Hulk, A. (1991). Parameter setting and the acquisition of word order in L2 French. *Second Language Research, 7(1),* 1–34.

Hunter, M., and Russell, D. (1977). How can I plan more effective lessons? *Instructor, 87,* 74–75.

Hymes, D. (1970). On communicative competence. In J. Gumperz, and D. Hymes, eds. *Directions in sociolinguistics,* pp. 35–71. New York: Holt, Rinehart, and Winston.

Ioup, G., Boustagui, E., El Tigi, M., and Moselle, M. (1994). Reexamining the critical period hypethesis: A case study of successful adult SLA in a naturalistic environment. *Studies in Second Language Acquisition, 16,* 73–98.

Jain, M. (1969). Error analysis of an Indian English corpus. Unpublished manuscript, University of Edinburgh.

James, J. (1980). Learner variation: The monitor model and language learning. *Interlanguage Studies Bulletin, 2*, 99–111.

James, W. (1958). *Talks to teachers.* New York: Norton.

Jamieson, J., and Chapelle, C. (1984). Prospects in computer assisted language lessons. *CATESOL Occasional Papers*, No. 10, pp. 17–34.

Jespersen, O. (1904). *How to teach a foreign language.* London: Allen and Unwin.

Johns, A. (1993). Written argumentation for real audiences: Suggestions for teacher research and classroom practice. *TESOL Quarterly 27*(1), 75–90.

Johnson, C. (1979). Choosing materials that do the job. In J. Phillips, ed. *Building on experience-Building for success.* Skokie, Ill.: National Textbook.

Johnson, D. and Roen, D. (1989). *Richness in writing: Empowering ESL students.* White Plains, N.Y.: Longman.

Johnson, J. (1992). Critical period effects in second language acquisition: The effect of written versus auditory materials on the assessment of grammatical competence. *Language Learning, 42*(2), 217–248.

Johnson, K. (1979). Communicative approaches and communicative processes. In Brumfit and Johnson, pp. 192–205.

John-Steiner, V. (1985). The road to competence in an alien land: A Vygotskian perspective on bilingualism. In J. Wertsch, ed. *Culture, communication, and cognition: Vygotsky in perspective.* Cambridge: Cambridge University.

John-Steiner, V., and Souberman, E. (1978). Afterword. In Vygotsky, pp. 121–140.

Jones, L., and von Baeyer, C. (1983). *Functions of American English:Communication activities for the classrooms*, p. 17. New York: Cambridge University Press .

Kachru, B. (1977). The Englishes and old models. *English Language Forum*, July.

Kadia, K. (1988). The effect of formal instruction on monitored and spontaneous naturalistic interlanguage performance, *TESOL Quarterly, 22*(3), 509–519.

Kagan, S. (1986). Cooperative learning and sociocultural factors in schooling. *In Beyond language: Social and cultural factors in schooling language minority students*, pp. 231–298. Los Angeles: Evaluation, Dissemination and Assessment Center, California State University, Los Angeles.

Kagan, S. (1985). *Cooperative learning: Resources for teachers.* Riverside, Calif.: Spencer Kagan, University of California.

Kalivoda, T., Morain, G., and Elkins, R. (1971). The audio-motor unit: A listening comprehension strategy that works. *Foreign Language Annals, 4*, 392–400. Also in Oller and Richard-Amato, pp. 337–347.

Katsaiti, L. (1983). Interlingual transfer of a cognitive skill in bilinguals. Unpublished master's thesis, University of Toronto.

Kenning, M. (1990). Computer assisted language learning. *Language Teaching, 23*(2), 67–76.

Kepner, C. (1991). An experiment in the relationship of types of written feedback to the development of second-language writing skills. *Modern Language Journal, 75*(iii), 305–313.

Kind, U. (1980). *Tune in to English: Learning English through familiar melodies.* New York: Regents.

Kleifgen, J. (1985). Skilled variation in a kindergarten teacher's use of foreigner talk. In Gass and Madden, pp. 59–68.

Kleinman, H. (1977). Avoidance behavior in adult second-language acquisition. *Language Learning, 27*, 93–105.

Koestler, A. (1964). *The act of creation.* New York: Macmillan.

Koffka, K. (1924). *The growth of the mind.* London: Routledge and Kegan Paul.

Köhler, W. (1925). *The mentality of apes.* New York: Harcourt Brace.

Krashen, S. (1973). Lateralization, language learning, and the critical period: Some new evidence. *Language Learning, 23,* 63–74.

Krashen, S. (1977). Some issues relating to the Monitor Model. In H. D. Brown, C. Yorio, and R. Crymes, pp. 144–158.

Krashen, S. (1980). The theoretical and practical relevance of simple codes in second language acquisition. In Scarcella and Krashen, pp. 7–18.

Krashen, S. (1981a). The fundamental pedagogical principle in second language teaching. *Studia Linguistica, 61.*

Krashen, S. (1981b). *Second language acquisition and second language learning.* Oxford: Pergamon.

Krashen, S. (1981c). The case for narrow reading. *TESOL Newsletter,* December, p. 23.

Krashen, S. (1982). *Principles and practice in second language acquisition.* Oxford: Pergamon.

Krashen, S. (1984). Immersion: Why it works and what it has taught us. *Language and Society,* (12), 61–64.

Krashen, S. (1985). *The input hypothesis: Issues and implications.* London: Longman.

Krashen, S. (1995). What is intermediate natural approach. In P. Hashemipour, R. Maldonado, and M. van Naerssen, eds. *Studies in language learning and Spanish linguistics in honor of Tracy D. Terrell.* New York: McGraw-Hill, pp. 92–105.

Krashen, S., and Biber, B. (1988). *On course: Bilingual education's success in California.* Sacramento, Calif.: California Association for Bilingual Education.

Krashen, S. and Pon, P. (1975). An error analysis of an advanced ESL learner. *Working Papers on Bilingualism, 7,* 125–129.

Krashen, S., and Terrell, T. (1983). *The natural approach: Language acquisition in the classroom.* Englewood Cliffs, N.J.: Alemany/Prentice Hall.

Kroll, B. (1991). *Second language writing: Research insights for the classroom.* New York: Cambridge University Press.

Kumaravadivelu, B. (1994). The postmethod condition: (E)merging strategies for second/foreign language teaching. *TESOL Quarterly, 28*(1), 27–48.

Lado, R. (1961). *Language testing.* New York: McGraw-Hill.

Lado, R. (1977). *Lado English series.* New York: Regents.

Ladousse, G. (1987). *Role play.* Oxford: Oxford Press.

Lafayette, R., and Buscaglia, M. (1983). Students learn language via a civilization course—a comparison of second language classroom environments. *Studies in Second Language Acquisition 7,* 323–342.

LaForge, P. (1971). Community language learning: A pilot study. *Language Learning, 20,* 103–108.

Lambert, W. (1972). *Language, psychology, and culture: Essays by Wallace E. Lambert.* Stanford, Calif.: Stanford University.

Lambert, W. (1974). Culture and language as factors in learning and education. Paper presented at the Annual TESOL Convention, Denver, Colo.

Lambert, W., and Tucker, G. (1972). *Bilingual education of children: The St. Lambert experiment.* Rowley, Mass.: Newbury House.

Lamendella, J. (1977). General principles of neurofunctional organization and their manifestations in primary and nonprimary acquisition. *Language Learning, 27,* 155–196.

Lamendella, J. (1979). The neurofunctional basis of pattern practice. *TESOL Quarterly, 13*, 5–20.

Lapkin, S., and Swain, M. (1984). Research update. *Language and Society, (12)*, 48–54.

Larsen, D., and Smalley, W. (1972). *Becoming bilingual: A guide to language learning.* New Canaan, Conn.: Practical Anthropology.

Larsen-Freeman, D. (1978). An explanation for the morpheme accuracy order of learners of English as a second language. In Hatch, *Second Language Acquisition: A Book of Readings,* pp. 371–382.

Larsen-Freeman, D. (1983a). The importance of input in second language acquisition. In R. Andersen ed. *Pidginization and creolization as language acquisition.* Rowley, Mass.: Newbury House.

Larsen-Freeman, D. (1983b). Second language acquisition: Getting the whole picture. In K. Bailey, M. Long, and S. Peck, eds. *Second language acquisition research.* Rowley, Mass.: Newbury House.

Larsen-Freeman, D. (1986). The total physical response method. In D. Larsen-Freeman, *Techniques and principles in language teaching,* pp. 109–122. New York: Oxford University Press.

Larsen-Freeman, D. (1991). Second language acquisition research: Staking out the territory. *TESOL Quarterly, 25*(2), 315–350.

Larsen-Freeman, D., and Long M. (1991). *An introduction to second language acquisition.* London: Longman.

Lawson, J. (1971). Should foreign language be eliminated from the curriculum? *Foreign Language Annals, 4,* 427. Also in J. W. Dodge, ed. *The case of foreign language study.* New York: Northeast Conference on the Teaching of Foreign Languages.

Lee, H. (1960). *To kill a mockingbird.* Philadelphia, Pa.: J. B. Lippincott.

Leki, I. (1990). Potential problems with peer responding in ESL writing classes. *CATESOL Journal, 3,* 5–19.

Leki, I. (1992). *Understanding ESL writers: A guide for teachers.* Portsmouth, N.H.: Boynton/Cook Heinemann.

Legutke, M., and Thomas, H. (1991). *Process and experience in the language classroom.* London: Longman.

Lenneberg, E. (1962). Understanding language without ability to speak: A case report. *Journal of Abnormal and Social Psychology, 65,* 419–425.

Lenneberg, E. (1967). *Biological foundations of language.* New York: Wiley.

Lightbrown, P. (1983). Exploring relationships between developmental and instructional sequences. In H. Seliger and M. Long, eds., pp. 217–243.

Ligon, F., and Tannenbaum, E. (1990). *Picture stories: Language and literacy activities or beginners.* White Plains, N.Y.: Longman.

LoCastro, V. (1994). Learning strategies and learning environments. *TESOL Quarterly 28*(2), 409–414.

Long, M. (1981). Input, interaction, and second language acquisition. In H. Winitz, ed. *Native language and foreign language acquisition: Annals of the New York Academy of Sciences, v. 379,* 259–278.

Long, M. (1983a). Input and second language acquisition theory. Paper presented at the Tenth University of Michigan Conference on Applied Linguistics.

Long, M. (1983b). Linguistic and conversational adjustments to non-native speakers. *Studies in Second Language Acquisition, 5* (2), 177–193.

Long, M. (1983c). Native speaker/nonnative speaker conversation in the second-language classroom. In M. Clarke and J. Handscombe, eds. *On TESOL '82: Pacific perspectives on language learning and teaching.* Washington, D.C.: Teachers of English to Speakers of Other Languages.

Long, M. (1984). Process and product in ESL program evaluation. *TESOL Quarterly, 18*(3), 409–426.

Long, M. (1985). A role for instruction in second language acquisition. In K. Hyltenstam and M. Pienemann, eds. *Modelling and assessing second language acquisition,* pp. 77–99. Clevedon, England: Multilingual Matters Ltd.

Long, M., Adams, L., McLean, M., and Castanos, F. (1976). Doing things with words—verbal interaction in lockstep and small group classroom situations. In J. Fanselow and R. Crymes, eds. *On TESOL '76,* pp. 137–153. Washington, D.C.: Teachers of English to Speakers of Other Languages.

Long, M., and Porter, P. (1984). Group work, interlanguage talk and classroom second language acquisition. Paper presented at TESOL 1984, Houston, Tex.

Long M., and Richards, J., eds. (1987), *Methodology in TESOL: A book of readings.* Rowley, Mass.: Newbury House.

Lorton, M. B. (1976). *Mathematics their way.* Menlo Park, Calif.: Addison-Wesley.

Lozanov, G. (1978). *Suggestology and outlines of suggestopedy.* New York: Gordon and Breach.

Lukmani. Y. (1972). Motivation to learn and language proficiency. *Language Learning, 22,* 261–273.

MacIntyre, P. , and Gardner, R. (1994). The effects of induced anxiety on three stages of cognitive processing in computerized vocabulary learning. *Studies in Second Language Acquisition, 16*(1), 1–17.

Macnamara, J. (1970). Bilingualism and thought. In J. Alatis ed. *Georgetown round table on languages and linguistics.* Washington, D.C.: Georgetown University.

Macnamara, J. (1973). The cognitive strategies of language learning. In Oller and Richards, pp. 57–65.

Macnamara, J. (1983). Nurseries, streets, and classrooms: Some comparisons and deductions. In Oller and Richard-Amato, pp. 259–266. Also in *Modern Language Journal, 57*(5–6) (1981), 250–254.

Madden, C., and Swales, J. (1986). A description of the activities of the English Language Institute: University of Michigan. Unpublished document.

Madrid, A. (1991). Diversity and its discontents. In L. Samovar and R. Porter, eds. *Intercultural communication: A reader,* 6th ed. Belmont, Calif.: Wadsworth.

Magnan, S. (1986). Assessing speaking profiency in the undergraduate curriculum: Data from French. *Foreign Language Annals, 19,* 429–438.

Making choices campaign. (1986). In *Canadian Parents for French, 24,* 8.

Maley, A., and Duff, A. (1983). *Drama techniques in language learning: A resource book of communication activities for language teachers.* Cambridge: Cambridge University.

Malherbe, E. (1946). *The bilingual school.* Johannesburg: Bilingual School Association.

Malherbe, E. (1969). Introductory remarks. In L. G. Kelly, ed. *UX (Description and measurement of bilingualism).* Toronto: Canadian National Commission for UNESCO and University of Toronto.

Malherbe, E. (1978). Bilingual education in the Republic of South Africa. In B. Spolsky, and R. Cooper, eds. *Case studies in bilingual education.* Rowley, Mass.: Newbury House.

Marino, E., Martini, M., Raley, C., and Terrell, T. (1984). *A rainbow collection: A natural approach to teaching English as a Second Language.* Norwalk, Calif.: Santillana.

Martino, L., and Johnson, D. W. (1979). Cooperative and individualistic experiences among disabled and normal children. *Journal of Social Psychology, 107,* 177–183.

Maslow, A. (1970). *Motivation and personality,* 2nd ed. New York: Harper and Row.

McCallum, G. (1980). *101 word games.* Oxford: Oxford University Press.

McCarthy, D. (1930). *The language development of the pre-school child.* Minneapolis: University of Minnesota.

McGroarty, M. (1992). Cooperative learning: The benefits for content-area teaching. In P. Richard-Amato and M. A. Snow, pp. 58–69.

McKay, S. (1993). *Agendas for second language literacy.* New York: Cambridge University Press.

McLaughlin, B. (1978). The Monitor Model: Some methodological considerations. *Language Learning, 28,* 309–332.

McLaughlin, B., Rossman, T., and McLeod, B. (1984). Second language learning: An information-processing perspective. *Language Learning, 33*(2), 135–158.

Mehan, H. (1979). *Learning lessons.* Cambridge, Mass.: Harvard University.

Mendes Figueiredo, M. (1991). Acquisition of second language pronunciation: The critical period. *CTJ Journal, 24,* 41–47.

Milk, R. (1990). Preparing ESL and bilingual teachers for changing roles: Immersion for teachers of LEP children. *TESOL Quarterly, 24*(3), 407–425.

Mohan, B., and Au-Yeung Lo, W. (1985). Academic writing and Chinese students: Transfer and developmental factors. *TESOL Quarterly, 19*(3), 515–534.

Morley, J. (1991). The pronunciation component in teaching English to speakers of other languages. *TESOL Quarterly, 25*(3), 481–520.

Morley, J., Robinett, B. W., Selinker, L., and Woods, D. (1984). ESL theory and the Fries legacy. *JALT Journal, 6*(2), 171–207.

Morrison, D. M., and Low, G. (1983). Monitoring and the second-language learner. In J. Richards and R. Schmidt, eds. *Language and communication.* London: Longman.

Moskowitz, G. (1978). *Caring and sharing in the foreign language class: A source book on humanistic techniques.* Rowley, Mass.: Newbury House.

Moskowitz, G. (1981). Effects of humanistic techniques on attitude, cohesiveness, and self-concept on foreign language students. *Modern Language Journal, 65,* 149–157.

Moustfa, M. (1989). CI plus the LEA: A long term perspective. *The Reading Teacher, 41*(3), 276–287.

Mullen, K. (1980). Rater reliability and oral proficiency evaluations. In J.W. Oller and K. Perkins, eds. *Research in language testing,* pp. 91–101. Rowley, Mass.: Newbury House.

Murphey, T. (1992). The discourse of pop songs. *TESOL Quarterly, 26*(4), 770–774.

Murray, D. (1982). *Learning by teaching: Selected articles on writing and teaching.* Upper Montclair, N.J.: Boynton Cook.

Naiman, N., Frohlich, M., and Stern, H.H. (1978). *The good language learner.* Toronto: Ontario Institute for Studies in Education.

National Center for Educational Statistics. (1982). *Adult learning activities terminology.* Washington, D.C.: U.S. Department of Education.

Nelson, G., and Murphy, J. (1993). Peer response groups: Do L2 writers use peer comments in revising their drafts? *TESOL Quarterly, 27*(1), 135–141.

Nelson, G., and Winters, T. (1980). *ESL operations: Techniques for learning while doing.* Rowley, Mass.: Newbury House.

Nelson, R., and Jakobovits, L. (1970). Motivation in foreign language learning. In J. Tursi, ed. *Foreign languages and the "new" student, reports of the working committees.* New York: Northeast Conference on the Teaching of Foreign Languages.

Nessler, C., ed. (1992). Cooperative language learning: A teacher's resource book. Englewood Cliffs, N.J.: Prentice Hall Regents.

Newmark, L. (1979). How not to interfere with language learning. In Brumfit and Johnson, pp. 160–166. Also in Oller and Richard-Amato (1983), pp. 49–58.

Nieto, S. (1992). *Affirming diversity.* White Plains, N.Y.: Longman.

Nissani, H. (1990). Early childhood programs for language minority children. *Focus 2.* Washington, D.C.: Clearinghouse for Bilingual Education.

Nunan, D. (1989). *Designing tasks for the communicative classroom.* Cambridge: Cambridge University.

Nunan, D. (1991). Communicative tasks and the language curriculum. *TESOL Quarterly, 25(2),* 279–295.

Obler, L. (1981). Right hemisphere participation in second language acquisition. In K. Diller, ed. *Universals in language learning aptitude.* Rowley, Mass.: Newbury House.

Ochs, E., and Schieffelin, B. (1984). Language acquisition and socialization: Three developmental stories and their implications. In R. Shweder and R. Levine, eds. *Culture theory: Essays on mind, self and emotion,* pp. 276–320. New York: Cambridge University Press.

Oller, J., Jr., (1975). Cloze, discourse and approximations to English. In Burt and Dulay, pp. 345–356.

Oller, J., Jr., (1979). *Language tests at school.* London: Longman.

Oller, J., Jr., (1981). Research on the measurements of affective variables: Some remaining questions. In Andersen, pp. 14–27.

Oller, J., Jr., (1983a). Some working ideas for language teaching. In Oller and Richard-Amato, pp. 3–19.

Oller, J., Jr., (1983b). Story writing principles and ESL teaching. *TESOL Quarterly, 17(1),* 39–53.

Oller, J., Jr., (1993). *Methods that work: Ideas for literacy and language teachers.* Boston, Mass.: Heinle and Heinle.

Oller, J., Jr., Baca, L., and Vigil, A. (1977). Attitudes and attained proficiency in ESL: A sociolinguistic study of Mexican-Americans in the southwest. *TESOL Quarterly, 11,* 173–183.

Oller, J., Jr., Hudson, A., and Liu, P. (1977). Attitudes and attained proficiency in ESL: A sociolinguistic study of native speakers of Chinese in the United States. *Language Learning, 27(1),* 1–27.

Oller, J., Jr., and Obrecht, D. (1969). The psycholinguistic principle of informational sequence: An experiment in second-language learning. *International Review of Applied Linguistics in Language Teaching, 7(2),* 117–123.

Oller, J., Jr., and Perkins, K., eds. (1978). *Language in education: Testing and tests.* Rowley, Mass.: Newbury House.

Oller, J., Jr., and Richard-Amato, P., eds. (1983). *Methods that work.* Rowley, Mass.: Newbury House.

Oller, J., Jr., and Richards, J., eds. (1973). *Focus on the learner: Pragmatic perspectives for the language teacher.* Rowley, Mass.: Newbury House.

Olson, D. (1977). From utterance to text: The bias of language in speech and writing. *Harvard Educational Review, 47,* 257–281.

Omaggio, A. (1986). *Teaching language in context: Proficiency-oriented instruction.* Boston, Mass.: Heinle and Heinle.

O'Malley, J., and Chamot, A. (1990). *Learning strategies in second language acquisition.* Cambridge: Cambridge University.

Oxford, R. (1990). *Language learning strategies: What every teacher should know.* New York: Newbury House.

Oxford, R., and Cohen, A. (1992). Language learning strategies: Crucial issues of concept and classification. *Allied Language Learning, 3*(1), 1–35.

Palmer, H. (1971). *Songbook: Learning basic skills through music I.* Freeport, N.J.: Educational Activities.

Palmer, H., and Palmer, D. (1925). *English through actions* (reprinted ed., 1959). London: Longman Green.

Papert, S. (1980). *Mindstorms: Children, computers, and powerful ideas.* New York: Basic Books.

Parkhurst, C. (1984). Using CALL to teach composition. In P. Larson, E. Judd, and D. Messerschmitt, eds. *On TESOL '84: A brave new world for TESOL,* pp. 255–260. Washington, D.C.: Teachers of English to Speakers of Other Languages.

Penfield, W., and Roberts, L. (1959). *Speech and brain-mechanisms.* Princeton, N.J.: Princeton University.

Pennington, M. (1989). *Teaching languages with computers: The state of the art.* La Jolla, Calif.: Athelstan.

Pérez, B., and Torres-Guzman, M. (1992). *Learning in two worlds: An integrated Spanish/English biliteracy approach.* White Plains, N.Y.: Longman.

Peyton, J. K. and Staton, J. (1992). *Dialogue journal writing with non-native English speakers: An instructional packet for teachers and workshop leaders.* Alexandria, Va.: TESOL.

Piaget, J. (1955). *The language and thought of the child.* New York: Meridian Books.

Piaget, J. (1979). *The development of thought.* New York: Viking.

Pica, T. (1983). Adult acquisition of English as a second language under different conditions of exposure. *Language Learning, 33*(4), 465–497.

Pica, T. (1988). Inter-language adjustments as an outcome of NS-NNS negotiated instruction. *Language Learning, 38*(1), 45–73.

Pica, T., and Doughty, C. (1985). Input and interaction in the communicative language classroom: A comparison of teacher-fronted and group activities. In Gass and Madden, pp. 115–132.

Pienemann, M. (1984). Psychological constraints on the teachability of languages. *Studies in Second Language Acquisition, 16*(2), 186–214.

Pienemann, M. (1988). Determining the influence of instruction on L2 speech processing. *AILA Review 5,* 40–72.

Pierce, L. , and O'Malley, J.M. (1992). *Performance and portfolio assessment for language minority students.* Washington, D.C.: National Clearinghouse for Bilingual Education.

Plann, S. (1977). Acquiring a second language in an immersion classroom. In H. D. Brown, C. Yorio, and R. Crymes, pp. 213–225.

Pollock, C. (1982). *Communicate what you mean* (p. 7). Englewood Cliffs, N.J.: Prentice Hall.

Poole, D. (1992). Language Socialization in the second-language classroom. *Language Learning 42*(4), 593–616.

Popper, K. (1976). *Unended quest.* London: Fontana Collins.

Porter, P. (1986). How learners talk to each other: Input and interaction in task-centered discussions. In. R. Day, ed. *Talking to learn: Conversation in Second Language Acquisition.* Rowley, Mass.: Newbury House, pp. 200–222.

Porter, R. (1977). A cross-sectional study of morpheme acquisition in first language learners. *Language Learning, 27,* 47–62.

Postovsky, V. (1974). Effects of delay in oral practice at the beginning of second language learning. *Modern Language Journal, 58,* 5–6.

Postovsky, V. (1977). Why not start speaking later? In Burt, Dulay, and Finocchiaro, pp. 17–26.

Prabhu, N. S. (1990). There is no best method—Why? *TESOL Quarterly, 24*(2), 161–176.

The Random House book of poetry for children. (1983). New York: Random House.

Raths, L., Merrill, H., and Simon, S. (1966). *Values and teaching.* Columbus, Ohio: Charles E. Merrill.

Ravem, R. (1978). Two Norwegian children's acquisition of English syntax. In E. Hatch, ed. 1978a, pp. 148–154.

Readence, J., Bean, T., and Baldwin, R. (1981). *Content area reading: An integrated approach.* Dubuque, Iowa: Kendall/Hunt.

Reid, J. (1992). Helping students write for an academic audience. In Richard-Amato and Snow, pp. 210–221.

Reynolds, P. (1971). *A primer in theory construction.* Indianapolis: Bobbs-Merrill.

Richard-Amato, P. (1983). ESL in Colorado's Jefferson County Schools. In Oller and Richard-Amato, pp. 393–397.

Richard-Amato, P. (1984). Teacher talk in the classroom: Native and foreigner. Unpublished Ph.D. dissertation, University of New Mexico, Albuquerque.

Richard-Amato, P. (1992a). Peer teachers: The neglected resource. In P. Richard-Amato and M. A. Snow, eds. *The multicultural classroom: Readings for content-area teachers.* White Plains, N.Y.: Addison-Wesley, pp. 271–284.

Richard-Amato, P. (1992b). Using reaction dialogues to develop second-language writing skills. Keynote speech at the TESOL Summer Institute, Comenius University, Bratislava, Slovakia, July 15.

Richard-Amato, P. (1993a). An interactive approach to reading in a second language. Presentation at the 27th Annual Convention of TESOL, April 16, Atlanta, Georgia.

Richard-Amato, P. (1993b). *Exploring themes.* Reading, Mass.: Addison-Wesley.

Richard-Amato, P., and Hansen, W. A. (1995). *Worlds together: A journey into multicultural literature,* Reading, Mass.: Addison-Wesley.

Richard-Amato, P., and Lucero, R. (1980). Foreigner talk strategies in the ESL classroom. Course paper written for C. Cazden at the University of New Mexico, TESOL Institute.

Richard-Amato, P., and Snow, A. (1992). *The multicultural classroom: Readings for content-area teachers.* White Plains, N.Y.: Addison-Wesley.

Richards, J. (1970). A psycholinguistic measure of vocabulary selection. *IRAL, 8,* 87–102.

Richards, J. (1975). The context for error analysis. In Burt and Dulay, pp. 70–79.

Richards, J. (1978). *Understanding second and foreign language learning.* Rowley, Mass.: Newbury House.

Richards, J. (1980). Conversation. *TESOL Quarterly, 14*(4), 413–431.

Richards, J. (1989). Beyond training: Approaches to teacher education in language teaching. *Perspectives,* 1–12.

Richards, J. (1991). Content knowledge and instructional practice in second-language teacher education. In *Georgetown University Round Table on Languages and Linguistics 1991: Linguistics and pedagogy: The state of the art*, pp. 76–99. Georgetown: Georgetown University.

Richards, J., and Nunan, D. (1990). *Second language teacher education.* New York: Cambridge University Press.

Richards, J., and Rodgers, T. (1986). *Approaches and methods in language teaching: A description and analysis.* New York: Cambridge University Press.

Rigg, P., and Allen, V., eds. (1989). *When they don't all speak English: Integrating the ESL student into the regular classroom.* Urbana, Ill.: National Council of Teachers of English.

Riggenbach, H. (1993). Discourse analysis and spoken language instruction. Featured speaker at the TESOL Institute in San Bernardino, Calif.

Rivera, C. (1984). *Language proficiency and academic achievement.* Clevedon, England: Multilingual Matters Ltd.

Rivers, W. (1980). Foreign language acquisition: Where the real problems lie. *Applied Linguistics, 1*(1), 48–59.

Rodgers, T. (1978). Strategies for individualized language learning and teaching. In Richards, *Understanding second and foreign language learning*, pp. 251–273.

Rogers, C. (1969). *Freedom to learn.* Columbus, Ohio: Merrill.

Romijn, E., and Seely, C. (1980). *Live action English for foreign students (LAEFFS).* San Francisco: Alemany.

Rose, M. (1983). Remedial writing courses: A critique and a proposal. *College English, 45,* 109–128.

Rosenblatt, L. (1978). *The reader, the text, the poem: The transactional theory of the literary work.* Carbondale, Ill.: Southern Illinois University.

Rosenblatt, L. (1985). Viewpoints: Transaction versus interaction, a terminal rescue operation. *Research in the Teaching of English, 19*(1), 96–107.

Ross, S., and Berwick, R. (1992). The discourse of accommodation in oral proficiency interviews. *Studies in Second Language Acquisition, 14*(2): 157–176.

Rowland, P. (1990). *Happily ever after big book packages.* Reading, Mass.: Addison-Wesley.

Rubin, J. (1975). What the "good language learner" can teach us. *TESOL Quarterly, 9,* 41–51.

Rumelhart, D. E. (1980). Schemata: The building blocks of cognition. In R. Spiro, B., Bruce, and W. Brewer, eds. *Theoretical issues in reading comprehension.* Hillsdale, N.J.: Lawrence Erlbaum.

Rutherford, W. (1982). Markedness in second language acquisition. *Language Learning, 32,* 85–107.

Rutherford, W. (1987). *Second language grammar: Learning and teaching.* White Plains, N.Y.: Longman.

Rutherford, W. and Sharwood Smith, M. (1988). *Grammar and second language teaching.* New York: Newbury House.

Sanaoui, R. and Lapkin, S. (1992). A case study of an FLS senior secondary course integrating computer networking. *The Canadian Modern Language Review, 48*(3), 525–552.

San Diego City Schools. (1982). *An exemplary approach to bilingual education: A comprehensive handbook for implementing an elementary-level Spanish-English language immersion program.* San Diego, Calif.: San Diego City Schools.

Savignon, S. (1983). *Communicative competence: Theory and classroom practice: Texts and contexts in second language learning.* Reading, Mass.: Addison-Wesley.

Saville-Troike, M. (1976). *Foundations for teaching ESL.* Englewood Cliffs, N.J.: Prentice Hall.

Scarcella, R. (1983). Sociodrama for social interaction. In Oller and Richard-Amato, pp. 239–245. Also in *TESOL Quarterly, 12*(1) (1978), 41–46.

Scarcella, R. (1990). *Teaching language minority students in the multicultural classroom.* Englewood Cliffs, N.J.: Prentice Hall.

Scarcella, R., and Higa, C. (1982). Input and age differences in second language acquisition. In S. Krashen, R. Scarcella, and M. Long, eds. *Child-adult differences in second language acquisition*, pp. 175–201. Rowley, Mass.: Newbury House.

Scarcella, R., and Krashen, S., eds. (1980). *Research in second language acquisition.* Rowley, Mass.: Newbury House.

Schachter, J. (1974). An error in error analysis. *Language Learning, 24,* 205–214.

Schachter, J. (1990). On the issue of completeness in second language acquisition. *Second Language Research, 6*(2), 93–124.

Schank, R., and Abelson, R. (1977). *Scripts, plans, goals, and understanding.* Hillsdale, N.J.: Lawrence Erlbaum.

Schmidt, R. (1984). The strengths and limitations of acquisition: A case study of an untutored language learner. *Language Learning and Communication, 3*(1), 1–16.

Schmidt, R. (1990). The role of consciousness raising in second language learning. *Applied Linguistics, 11*(2), 129–158.

Schoenberg, I. (1989). *Talk about values: Conversation skills for intermediate students.* White Plains, N.Y.: Longman.

Schouten, M. (1979). The missing data in second language learning research. *Interlanguage Studies Bulletin, 4,* 3–14.

Schultz, M., and Fisher, A. (1988). *Games for all reasons: Interacting in to language classroom.* Reading, Mass.: Addison-Wesley.

Schumann, J. (1976). Second language acquisition research: Getting a more global look at the learner. In H. D. Brown, ed. *Papers in second language acquisition. Language Learning Special Issue, 4.*

Schumann, J. (1978a). The acculturation model for second-language acquisition. In R. Gingras, ed. *Second language acquisition and foreign language teaching*, pp. 27–50. Arlington, Va.: Center for Applied Linguistics.

Schumann, J. (1978b). *The pidginization process: A model for second language learning.* Rowley, Mass.: Newbury House.

Schumann, J. (1978c). Second language acquisition: The pidginization hypothesis. In Hatch, *Second language acquisition: A book of readings*, pp. 256–276.

Schumann, J. (1979). Lecture presented at the First TESOL Institute, University of California, Los Angeles.

Schumann, J. (1980). Affective factors and the problem of age in second language acquisition. In K. Croft, ed. *Readings in ESL*, pp. 222–247. Cambridge, Mass.: Winthrop.

Schumann, J., Holroyd, J., Campbell, R., and Ward, F. (1978). Improvement of foreign language pronunciation under hypnosis: A preliminary study. *Language Learning, 28,* 143–148.

Scovel, T. (1981). The effects of neurological age on nonprimary language acquisition. In Andersen, pp. 58–61.

Segal, B. (1984). *Teaching English as a second language: Shortcuts to success.* Paso Robles, Calif.: Bureau of Education and Research.

Seliger, H. (1975). Inductive method and deductive method in language teaching: A reexamination. *IRAL, 13,* 1–8.

Seliger, H. (1977). Does practice make perfect? A study of interaction patterns and L2 competence. *Language Learning, 27*(2), 263–278.

Seliger, H. (1978). Implications of a multiple critical periods hypothesis for second language learning. In W. Ritchie, ed. *Second language acquisition research.* New York: Academic.

Seliger, H. (1982). On the possible role of the right hemisphere in second language acquisition. *TESOL Quarterly, 16,* 307–314.

Seliger, H. (1991). Strategy and tactics in second language acquisition. In L. Malave and G. Duquette, eds. *Language, culture, and cognition: A collection of studies in first, and second language acquisition.* Clevedon, England: Multilingual Matters Ltd.

Seliger, H., and Long, M. (1983). *Classroom oriented research in second language acquisition.* Rowley, Mass.: Newbury House.

Selinker, L. (1972). Interlanguage. *International Review of Applied Linguistics, 10,* 209–230.

Selinker, L., and Lamendella, J. (1978a). Fossilization in interlanguage. In C. Blatchford and J. Schachter, eds. *On TESOL '78: EFL policies, programs, practices.* Washington, D.C.: Teachers of English to Speakers of Other Languages.

Selinker, L., and Lamendella, J. (1978b). Two perspectives on fossilization in interlanguage learning. *Interlanguage Studies Bulletin, 3,* 143–191.

Selinker, L., Swain, M., and Dumas, G. (1975). The interlanguage hypothesis extended to children. *Language Learning, 25,* 139–152.

Semke, H. (1984). The effects of the red pen. *Foreign Language Annals, 17,* 195–202.

Shaftel, F., and Shaftel, G. (1967). *Role-playing for social values.* Englewood Cliffs, N.J.: Prentice Hall.

Sharwood-Smith, M. (1981). Consciousness-raising and the second language learner. *Applied Linguistics, 2,* 159–169.

Shih, M. (1986). Content-based approaches to teaching academic writing. *TESOL Quarterly, 20*(4), 617–648.

Shih, M. (1992). Beyond comprehension exercises in the ESL academic reading class. *TESOL Quarterly, 26*(2), 289–318.

Shoemaker, C., and Shoemaker, F. (1991). *Interactive techniques for the ESL classroom.* Boston, Mass.: Heinle and Heinle.

Shohamy, E. (1983). The stability of the oral proficiency trait on the oral interview speaking test. *Language Learning, 33,* 527–540.

Shuy, R. (1978). Problems in assessing language ability in bilingual education programs. In H. Lafontaine, H. Persky, and L. Golubchick, eds. *Bilingual education.* Wayne, N.J.: Avery Publishing Group.

Shuy, R. (1981). Conditions affecting language learning and maintenance among Hispanics in the United States. *NABE Journal, 6,* 1–18.

Silverstein, S. (1981). *A light in the attic.* New York: Harper and Row.

Simon, S., Howe, L., and Kirschenbaum, H. (1972). *Values clarification.* New York: Hart.

Sinclair, J., and Coulthard, M. (1975). *Towards an analysis of discourse.* London: Oxford University.

Skinner, B. F. (1957). *Verbal behavior.* New York: Appleton-Century-Crofts.

Skinner, D. (1981). Bimodal learning and teaching: Concepts and methods. Unpublished manuscript. Hispanic Training Institute.

Skutnabb-Kangas, T., and Toukomaa, P. (1976). *Teaching migrant children's mother tongue and learning the language of the host country in the context of the socio-cultural situation of the migrant family.* Helsinki: The Finnish National Commission for UNESCO.

Slavin, R. (1983). When does cooperative learning increase student achievement? *Psychological Bulletin, 94*(3), 429–445.

Slobin, D. (1971). *Psycholinguistics.* Glenview, Ill.: Scott Foresman.

Slobin, D. (1973). Cognitive prerequisites for the development of grammar. In C. Ferguson and D. Slobin, eds. *Studies of child language development.* New York: Holt, Rinehart and Winston.

Slobodkina, E. (1984). *Caps for sale.* New York: Blue Ribbon Books.

Smallwood, B. (1991). *The literature connection: A read-aloud guide for multicultural classrooms.* Reading, Mass.: Addison-Wesley.

Smith, D. (1972). Some implications for the social status of pidgin languages. In D. Smith and R. Shuy, eds. *Sociolinguistics in cross-cultural analysis.* Washington, D.C.: Georgetown University.

Smith, E. B., Goodman, K., and Meredith, R. (1970). *Language and thinking in school.* New York: Holt, Rinehart, and Winston.

Smith, F. (1982). *Understanding reading,* 3rd ed. New York: Holt, Rinehart, and Winston.

Smith, F. (1988). *Joining the literacy club: Further essays into education.* Portsmouth, N.H.: Heinemann.

Soh, B. L., and Soon, Y. P. (1991). English by e-mail: Creating a global classroom via the medium of computer technology. *English Language Teaching Journal, 45*(4), 287–292.

Sokolik, M. E. (1993). *Global views: Reading about world issues.* Boston, Mass.: Heinle and Heinle.

Sorenson, A. (1967). Multilingualism in the northwest Amazon. *American Anthropologist, 69,* 670–684.

Spolsky, B. (1969). Attitudinal aspects of second-language learning. *Language Learning, 19,* 271–283.

Srole, L. (1956). Social integration and certain corollaries: An exploration study. *American Sociological Review, 21,* 709–716.

Stafford, C., and Covitt, G. (1978). Monitor use in adult language production. *Review of Applied Linguistics, 39–40,* 103–125.

Stark, I., and Wallach, G. (1980). The path to a concept of language learning disabilities. *Topics in Languages Disorders, 1,* 1–14.

Stauble, A. (1980). Acculturation and second language acquisition. In Scarcella and Krashen, pp. 43–50.

Steinbeck, J. (1947). *The pearl.* New York: Viking.

Stempleski, S., and Tomlin, S. (1990). *Video in action: Recipes for using video in language teaching.* Englewood Cliffs, N.J.: Prentice Hall.

Stern, S. (1983). Why drama works: A psycholinguistic perspective. In Oller and Richard-Amato, pp. 207–225. Also in *Language Learning 30*(1) (1980), 77–100.

Stevick, E. (1976a). *Memory, meaning, and method.* Rowley, Mass.: Newbury House.

Stevick, E. (1976b). Teachers of English as an alien language. In J. Fanselow and R. Crymes, eds. *On TESOL '76,* pp. 225–228. Washington, D.C.: Teaching English to Speakers of Other Languages.

Stevick, E. (1980). *Teaching languages: A way and ways.* Rowley, Mass.: Newbury House.

Stevick, E. (1982). *Teaching and learning languages.* Cambridge, Mass.: Cambridge University.

Strevens, P. (1978). The nature of language teaching. In Richards, pp. 179–203.

Sullivan, N. (1993). Teaching writing on a computer network. *TESOL Journal, 2*(1), 34–35.

Sutherland, K. (1979). *Accuracy vs. fluency in the second language classroom. CATESOL occasional papers.* California Association of Teachers of English to Speakers of Other Languages, No. 5, pp. 25–29.

Sutherland, K. (1981). *English alfa,* teacher's ed. (p. 11). Boston Mass.: Houghton Mifflin.

Swaffer, J., and Woodruff, M. (1978). Language for comprehension: Focus on reading. *Modern Language Journal, 62,* 27–32.

Swain, M. (1975). Writing skills of grade 3 French immersion pupils. *Working Papers on Bilingualism, 7,* 1–38.

Swain, M. (1985). Communicative competence: Some roles of comprehensible input and comprehensible output in its development. In Gass and Madden, pp. 235–253.

Swain, M., Dumas, G., and Naiman, N. (1974). Alternatives to spontaneous speech: Elicited translation and imitation as indicators of second language competence. *Working Papers on Bilingualism: Special Issue on Language Acquisition Studies, 3,* 68–79.

Swain, M., Lapkin, S., and Barik, H. (1976). The doze test as a measure of second language proficiency for young children. *Working Papers on Bilingualism, 11,* 32–43.

Tarone, E. (1981). Some thoughts on the notion of communication strategy. *TESOL Quarterly, 15*(3), 285–295.

Tarone, E. (1982). Systematicity and attention interlanguage. *Language Learning, 32,* 69–82.

Tarone, E. (1983). On the variability of interlanguage systems. *Applied Linguistics, 4*(2), 143–163.

Tarone, E., and Yule, G. (1989). *Focus on the language learner.* New York: Oxford University Press.

Taylor, B. (1980). Adult language learning strategies and their pedagogical implications. In K. Croft, ed. *Readings in English as a second language,* pp. 144–152. Cambridge, Mass.: Winthrop.

Taylor, B. (1983). Teaching ESL: Incorporating a communicative, student-centered component. *TESOL Quarterly, 17*(1), 69–87.

Terrell, T. (1983). The Natural Approach to language teaching: An update. In Oller and Richard-Amato, pp. 267–283. Also in *Modern Language Journal, 66*(2) (1982), 121–132.

Terrell, T. (1987). Presentation in a colloquium entitled "Achieving Grammatical Accuracy: Advice for ESL/EFL Students" at the 21st Annual TESOL Convention, April 21–25, Miami Beach, Fla.

Terrell, T. (1991). The role of grammar instruction in a communicative approach. *The Modern Language Journal, 75*(1), 52–63.

Thonis, E. 1984. Reading instruction for language minority students. In *Schooling and language minority students: a theoretical framework.* Office of Bilingual Education, California State Department of Education, Sacramento, California. Los Angeles: Evaluation, Dissemination and Assessment Center, California State University, Los Angeles, pp. 147–181.

Thorndike, E.L. (1914). *The psychology of learning.* New York: Teachers College.

Tomaselli, A., and Schwartz, B. (1990). Analyzing the acquisition stages of negation in L2 German: Support for UG in adult SLA. *Second Language Research, 6*(1), 1–38.

Tucker, G., and d'Anglejan, A. (1971). Language learning process. In *The Britannica Review of Foreign Language Education* (3), 163–182. Chicago: Encyclopedia Britannica.

Tucker, G., and d'Anglejan, A. (1972). An approach to bilingual education: The St. Lambert Experiment. In M. Swain, ed. *Bilingual schooling: Some experiences in Canada and the United States*, pp. 15–21. Toronto: The Ontario Institute for Studies in Ontario.

Van Allen, R., and Allen, C. (1967). *Language expenence activities.* Boston, Mass.: Houghton Mifflin.

van Dijk, T. (1977). *Text and context: Explorations in the semantics and pragmatics of discourse.* London: Longman.

Van Lier, L. (1989). Reeling, writhing, drawling, stretching, and fainting in coils: Oral proficiency interviews as conversation. *TESOL Quarterly, 23*, 489–508.

Van Patten, B. (1986). Second language acquisition research and the learning/teaching of Spanish: Some research findings and their implications. *Hispania 69*, 202–216.

Vann, R., Meyer, D., and Lorenz, F. (1984) Error gravity: A study of faculty opinions of ESL errors. *TESOL Quarterly, 18*, 427–440.

Violand-Sánchez, E., Sutton, C., and Ware, H. (1991). Fostering home-school cooperation: Involving language minority families as partners in education. NCBE 6, Washington, D.C.: National Clearinghouse for Bilingual Education.

Voge, W. (1981). Testing the validity of Krashen's input hypothesis. Paper presented at the International Congress of Applied Linguistics, Lund, Sweden.

Vygotsky, L. (1962). *Thought and language.* Cambridge, Mass.: M.I.T.

Vygotsky, L. (1978). *Mind in society.* Cambridge, Mass.: Harvard University.

Wagner-Gough, J., and Hatch, E. (1975). The importance of input data in second-language acquisition studies. *Language Learning, 25*, 297–308.

Wallerstein, N. (1983). *Language and culture in conflict: Problem posing in the ESL classroom.* Reading, Mass.: Addison-Wesley.

Walsh, T., and Diller, K. (1981). Neurolinguistic considerations on the optimum age for second-language learning. In K. Diller, ed. *Universals in language learning aptitude.* Rowley, Mass.: Newbury House.

Wegrzecka-Monkiewicz, E. (1992). *High school English as a second language: A comparative study of content based and regular programs.* M.A. thesis, California State University, Los Angeles.

Wells, G. (1981). *Learning through interaction: The study of language development.* Cambridge: Cambridge University.

Wesche, M. (1987). Communicative testing in a second language. In Long and Richards, pp. 373–394.

Wesche, M., and Ready, D. (1985). Foreigner talk in the university classroom. In Gass and Madden, pp. 89–114.

White, L. (1989). *Universal grammar and second language acquisition.* Amsterdam/Philadelphia, Pa.: John Benjamins.

White, L., Spada, N., Lightbrown, P., and Ranta, L. (1991). Input enhancement and L2 question formation. *Applied Linguistics, 12*, 416–432.

Whitecloud, T. (1938). "Blue winds dancing." *Scribner's Magazine*, February. Also in *Variations: A contemporary literature program: In touch*, pp. 148–152. New York: Harcourt Brace Jovanovich, 1975.

Widdowson, H. (1978). *Teaching language as communication.* Oxford: Oxford University.

Widdowson, H. (1979a). *Explorations in applied linguistics.* Oxford: Oxford University.

Widdowson, H. (1979b). Rules and procedures in discourse analysis. In T. Myers, ed. *The development of conversation and discourse.* Edinburgh: Edinburgh University.

Widdowson, H. (1984). *Learning purpose and language use.* Oxford: Oxford University.

Wilkins, D. A. (1976). *Notional syllabuses.* London: Oxford University.

Wilkins, D. A. (1979a). Grammatical, situational, and notional syllabuses. In Brumfit and Johnson, pp. 82–90.

Wilkins, D. A. (1979b). Notional syllabuses and the concept of a minimum adequate grammar. In Brumfit and Johnson, pp. 91–98.

Winn-Bell Olsen, J. (1977). *Communication starters and other activities for the ESL classroom.* Englewood Cliffs, N.J.: Prentice Hall.

Winn-Bell Olsen, J. (1984). *Look again pictures.* Hayward, Calif: Alemany.

Wode, H. (1978). Developmental sequences in naturalistic L2 acquisition. In Hatch, *Second language acquisition: A book of readings,* pp. 101–117.

Wode, H. (1980). Operating principles and "universals" in L1, L2, and FLT. In D. Nehls, ed. *Studies in language acquisition.* Heidelberg: Julius Groos.

Wong-Fillmore, L. (1976). The second time around: Cognitive and social strategies in second language acquisition. Unpublished doctoral dissertation, Stanford University, Stanford, Calif.

Wong-Fillmore, L. (1985). When does teacher talk work as input? In Gass and Madden, pp. 17–50.

Wright, A., Betteridge, D., and Buckby, M. (1984). *Games for language learning.* Cambridge: Cambridge University.

Yorio, C. (1980). The teacher's attitude toward the students' output in the second language classroom. *CATESOL Occasional Papers.* California Association of Teachers of English to Speakers of Other Languages, No. 6, pp. 1–8.

Yoshihara, K. (1993). Keys to effective peer response. *CATESOL Journal, 1,* 17–37.

Zamel, V. (1985). Responding to student writing. *TESOL Quarterly, 19*(1): 79–101.

Zamel, V. (1992). Writing one's way into reading. *TESOL Quarterly, 26*(3), 463–485.

Zobl, H. (1985). Grammars in search of input and intake. In S. Gass and C. Madden, eds., pp. 329–344.

Index